Tools for Teaching Computer Networking and Hardware Concepts

Nurul I. Sarkar, Auckland University of Technology, New Zealand

 Information Science Publishing

Hershey • London • Melbourne • Singapore

NORTHWEST MISSOURI STATE
UNIVERSITY LIBRARY
MARYVILLE, MO 64468

Acquisitions Editor:	Michelle Potter
Development Editor:	Kristin Roth
Senior Managing Editor:	Amanda Appicello
Managing Editor:	Jennifer Neidig
Copy Editor:	Beth Arnesen
Typesetter:	Jennifer Neidig
Cover Design:	Lisa Tosheff
Printed at:	Yurchak Printing Inc.

Published in the United States of America by
Information Science Publishing (an imprint of Idea Group Inc.)
701 E. Chocolate Avenue
Hershey PA 17033
Tel: 717-533-8845
Fax: 717-533-8661
E-mail: cust@idea-group.com
Web site: http://www.idea-group.com

and in the United Kingdom by
Information Science Publishing (an imprint of Idea Group Inc.)
3 Henrietta Street
Covent Garden
London WC2E 8LU
Tel: 44 20 7240 0856
Fax: 44 20 7379 0609
Web site: http://www.eurospanonline.com

Library of Congress Cataloging-in-Publication Data

Tools for teaching computer networking and hardware concepts / Nurul Sarkar, editor.
    p. cm.
  Summary: "This book offers concepts of the teaching and learning of computer networking
and hardwar eby offering undamental theoretical concepts illustrated with the use of
interactive practical exercises"--Provided by publisher.
  Includes bibliographical references and index.
   ISBN 1-59140-735-4 (h/c) -- ISBN 1-59140-736-2 (s/c) -- ISBN 1-59140-737-0 (ebook)
  1. Computer networks--Study and teaching. 2. Computer input-output equipment--Study
and teaching. I. Sarkar, Nurul.
   TK5105.5.T66 2006
   004.6071--dc22
                          2005027411

British Cataloguing in Publication Data
A Cataloguing in Publication record for this book is available from the British Library.

Dedication

To my wife, Laila A. Sarkar

Tools for Teaching Computer Networking and Hardware Concepts

Table of Contents

Foreword viii

Preface ix

Section I: Introduction

Chapter I. Introduction to Computer Networking and Hardware Concepts 1
Nurul I. Sarkar, Auckland University of Technology, New Zealand

Section II: Teaching and Learning Computer Networking

Chapter II. WebLan-Designer: A Web-Based Tool to Enhance Teaching and Learning Wired and Wireless LAN Design 21
Nurul I. Sarkar, Auckland University of Technology, New Zealand
Krassie Petrova, Auckland University of Technology, New Zealand

Chapter III. INetwork: An Interactive Learning Tool for Communication Networks 39
K. Sandrasegaran, The University of Technology Sydney, Australia
M. Trieu, The University of Technology Sydney, Australia

Chapter IV. Effectively Using a Network Simulation Tool to Enhance Students' Understanding of Computer Networking Concepts 62

    Cecil Goldstein, Queensland University of Technology, Australia
    Karen Stark, Queensland University of Technology, Australia
    Susanna Leisten, Queensland University of Technology, Australia
    Alan Tickle, Queensland University of Technology, Australia

Chapter V. Teaching Protocols through Animation 86

    Kenneth J. Turner, University of Stirling, UK

Chapter VI. Enhancing Student Understanding of Packet-Forwarding Theories and Concepts with Low-Cost Laboratory Activities 101

    Anthony P. Kadi, The University of Technology Sydney, Australia

Chapter VII. Ethereal: A Tool for Making the Abstract Protocol a Concrete Reality 119

    David Bremer, Otago Polytechnic, New Zealand

Section III: Wireless Networking and Information Security

Chapter VIII. Enhancing Teaching and Learning Wireless Communication Networks Using Wireless Projects 135

    Trevor Craig, Wollongong College Auckland, New Zealand
    Nurul I. Sarkar, Auckland University of Technology, New Zealand

Chapter IX. Teaching and Learning Wi-Fi Networking Fundamentals Using Limited Resources 154

    Wilson Siringoringo, Auckland University of Technology,
        New Zealand
    Nurul I. Sarkar, Auckland University of Technology,
        New Zealand

Chapter X. Information Security Risk Analysis: A Pedagogic Model Based on a Teaching Hospital 179

    Sanjay Goel, University at Albany, SUNY, and NYS Center for
        Information Forensics and Assurance, USA
    Damira Pon, University at Albany, SUNY, and NYS Center for
        Information Forensics and Assurance, USA

Section IV: Teaching and Learning Computer Hardware

Chapter XI. A Practical Introduction to Input and Output Ports 201
David L. Tarnoff, East Tennessee State University, USA

**Chapter XII. Enhancing Teaching and Learning Computer
Hardware Fundamentals Using PIC-Based Projects** 229
*Nurul I. Sarkar, Auckland University of Technology,
    New Zealand*
Trevor Craig, Wollongong College Auckland, New Zealand

**Chapter XIII. Assistant Tool for Instructors Teaching Computer
Hardware with the PBL Theory** 249
*Maiga Chang, National Science and Technology Program for
    e-Learning, Taiwan*
Kun-Fa Cheng, Chih-Ping Senior High School, Taiwan
Alex Chang, Yuan-Ze University, Taiwan
Ming-Wei Chen, Chih-Ping Senior High School, Taiwan

Chapter XIV. A Simulator for High-Performance Processors 267
John Morris, University of Auckland, New Zealand

**Chapter XV. A Remotely Accessible Embedded Systems
Laboratory** 284
Steve Murray, The University of Technology Sydney, Australia
Vladimir Lasky, The University of Technology Sydney, Australia

**Chapter XVI. LOGIC-Minimiser: A Software Tool to Enhance
Teaching and Learning Minimization of Boolean Expressions** 303
*Nurul I. Sarkar, Auckland University of Technology,
    New Zealand*
Khaleel I. Petrus, University of Southern Queensland, Australia

Section V: Data Communication Protocols and Learning Tools

Chapter XVII. A Practical Introduction to Serial Protocols 319
David L. Tarnoff, East Tennessee State University, USA

Chapter XVIII. VMware as a Practical Learning Tool **338**
> *Eduardo Correia, Christchurch Polytechnic Institute of*
> *Technology, New Zealand*
> *Ricky Watson, Christchurch Polytechnic Institute of Technology,*
> *New Zealand*

Appendix Section **355**

Glossary **359**

About the Authors **375**

Index **383**

Foreword

Computer networking and hardware concepts have come alive! With *Tools for Teaching Computer Networking and Hardware Concepts*, the teaching and learning of computer networking and hardware are made more interesting and applied. Fundamental theoretical concepts are illustrated with the use of interactive practical exercises.

Each chapter presents learning objectives, figures and illustrations, real-world examples as well as review questions, all of which provides teachers and students with a resource to enhance learning.

This book is somewhat unique in that it brings together experiences from academics in countries such as Scotland, Taiwan, the United States of America, Australia, and New Zealand. In sharing their use of online tools and flexible learning practices, I hope that you will find this book a useful resource in the teaching and learning of computer networking and hardware essentials.

Dr. Felix B. Tan
Professor of Information Systems and Head
School of Computer and Information Sciences
Auckland University of Technology
New Zealand

Preface

Because of the high demand for networking and hardware skills in commerce and in industry worldwide, computer networking and hardware courses are becoming increasingly popular in universities, polytechnic institutions, postsecondary colleges, and private training institutions around the globe. Despite this, it is often difficult to motivate students to learn computer networking and hardware concepts because students appear to find the subject technical and rather dry and boring. We strongly believe, as do many others, that students learn computer networking and hardware fundamentals better and feel more engaged with their courses if they are given interactive practical exercises that illustrate theoretical concepts.

There are numerous textbooks on computer networking and hardware concepts as well as publications, including journals and conference proceedings, in computer education and Web-based learning. However, these publications have very limited discussion on software and hardware tools that enhance teaching and learning computer networking and hardware concepts. To address this need, we have written *Tools for Teaching Computer Networking and Hardware Concepts*, focusing on the development and use of innovative tools for teaching and learning various aspects of computer networking and hardware concepts.

We believe the proposed book is unique and is a useful resource to both students and teachers at university, polytechnic, postsecondary, and private training institutions. This book: (1) provides comprehensive coverage of tools and techniques for teaching and learning computer networking and hardware concepts at introductory and advanced levels; (2) can be used as a resource both by students and by teachers in different teaching and learning contexts; (3) offers both students and teachers an opportunity to benefit from the experience of teachers and researchers in other countries in the areas of teaching and learning computer networking and hardware; (4) represents a rich starting point for researchers interested in developing innovative tools for teaching and learning computer networking and hardware concepts; and (5) raises the awareness of the need to enhance face-to-face teaching through the use of online interactive learning and flexible mode of delivery of papers. Although various hardware and software tools, methods, and laboratory settings are discussed in the text, an emphasis has been placed on the development and use of tools and techniques in the classroom that enhance the teaching and learning of various aspects of computer networking and hardware concepts.

Organization and Outline

The book is organized into five sections.

Section I: Introduction. Section I (Chapter I) provides a rationale and introduction to the book. It provides an introduction to computer networking and hardware concepts and highlights the use of software and hardware tools as an aid to enhance teaching and learning computer networking and hardware fundamentals. It also outlines the remainder of this book.

Section II: Teaching and Learning Computer Networking. Section II consists of six chapters (II through VII) and provides detailed coverage of the software and hardware tools and lab activities designed to enhance teaching and learning various aspects of computer networking. Chapter II describes the development and use of an interactive software tool (named WebLan-Designer) as an aid to enhance teaching and learning both wired and wireless LAN design. Chapter III describes INetwork, an interactive learning tool for communication networks. Chapter IV emphasizes the use of a network simulation tool in large classes to enhance student understanding of computer networking concepts effectively. Chapter V highlights the use of simulation and animation tools in teaching communication protocols. Chapter VI describes a low-cost laboratory infrastructure for enhancing student understanding of packet-forwarding concepts and theories. Chapter VII examines the use of the tool Ethereal in the classroom for teaching TCP/IP protocols in a practical way.

Section III: Wireless Networking and Information Security. Section III consists of three chapters (VIII through X) and provides detailed coverage of the software and hardware tools, cases, and lab activities designed to enhance teaching and learning various aspects of wireless networking concepts and information security risk analysis. Chapter VIII describes a series of wireless projects for teaching and learning wireless communication networks. Chapter IX focuses on teaching and learning Wi-Fi networking and propagation measurements using limited resources. Chapter X highlights teaching and learning information security risk analysis using a teaching hospital model.

Section IV: Teaching and Learning Computer Hardware. Section IV consists of six chapters (XI through XVI) and provides software and hardware tools, including processor simulator and lab activities, to enhance teaching and learning various aspects of computer hardware concepts. Chapter XI provides a practical introduction to input and output ports. Chapter XII describes a set of PIC-based practical laboratory exercises for teaching and learning computer hardware concepts. Chapter XIII focuses on teaching computer hardware concepts using PBL theory. Chapter XIV discusses the use of a processor simulator in teaching computer architecture both at introductory and advanced levels. Chapter XV describes a remotely accessible embedded systems laboratory for teaching and learning computer hardware. Chapter XVI reports on the development and use of a software tool (named LOGIC-Minimiser) for teaching and learning minimization of Boolean expressions.

Section V: Data Communication Protocols and Learning Tools. Section V consists of two chapters (XVII and XVIII) and provides detailed coverage of learning tools and techniques designed to enhance teaching and learning various aspects of data communication protocols. Chapter XVII provides a practical introduction to serial protocols for data communications, and Chapter XVIII describes the use of VMware in teaching and learning contexts.

Target Audience for This Book

Teachers, tutors, and students in schools of business, information technology, engineering, computer and information sciences, and other related disciplines will benefit from the use of this book. Moreover, the book will provide insights and support for both instructors and students involved in training courses in networking and hardware fundamentals at various vocational training institutions.

How to Use This Book

The innovative open source software and hardware tools and new ideas presented in the book enable the book to be used by both teachers and students as a resource to enhance teaching and learning computer networking and hardware concepts in a variety of teaching and learning contexts. Students can also benefit from the learning aids, such as learning objectives, summary, key terms and definitions, figures and illustrations, examples and review questions, and references that are provided in each chapter.

Learning Aids

The book provides the following learning aids:

- **Learning Objectives:** Each chapter begins with a list of learning objectives that previews the chapter's key ideas and highlights the key concepts and skills that students can achieve by completing the chapter. Learning objectives also assist teachers in preparing a lesson plan for a particular topic.

- **Figures and Illustrations:** The key concepts in both computer networking and hardware are illustrated using diagrams and screenshots throughout the book. These illustrations help students to develop a better understanding of the key concepts in computer hardware and networking.

- **Examples:** Various real-world examples have been introduced in the chapters to explain the use of tools and techniques learned from the text.

- **Summary:** Each chapter provides a brief summary of the contents presented in the chapter. This helps students to preview key ideas in the chapter before moving on to the next chapter.

- **Key Terms and Definitions:** Each chapter provides a set of key terms and their definitions. Both students and teachers can benefit by using the listing of key terms and definitions to recall key networking and hardware concepts before and after reading the chapter.

- **Review Questions:** Each chapter provides a set of end-of-chapter review questions linked to the learning objectives, allowing the teachers to evaluate their teaching effectiveness. Answers to most of the review questions can be found in the relevant chapter(s), and hence students are encouraged to revisit the relevant sections of the chapter in order to find the answers. By answering the review questions, students can develop a deeper understanding of many key networking and hardware concepts and tools. Teachers and instructors can use the review questions to test their teaching effectiveness and to initiate class discussion.

Contributing Authors

This book contains contributions from many leading professors and researchers from around the world in the field of computer networking and hardware concepts. One of the most challenging tasks for the editor was to integrate the individual submissions from the 26 authors involved (including the editor) into a coherent book. Toward this end, to enhance the readability of the book and to make it a useful resource, the editor has introduced some additional material, including learning objectives, an end-of-chapter summary, and review questions. The editor maintained close liaison with the contributing authors throughout the manuscript preparation process. Each chapter was reviewed by two or more anonymous reviewers and then revised to address the concerns of the reviewers. While most individual chapter authors were contacted for the revisions, the editor revised some of the chapters. The list of authors who contributed full chapters to this book is as follows:

- *Nurul I. Sarkar*, Auckland University of Technology, New Zealand
- *Krassie Petrova*, Auckland University of Technology, New Zealand
- *K. Sandrasegaran*, University of Technology, Australia
- *Minh Trieu*, University of Technology, Australia
- *Cecil Goldstein*, Queensland University of Technology, Australia
- *Karen Stark*, Queensland University of Technology, Australia
- *Susanna Leisten*, Queensland University of Technology, Australia
- *Alan Barry Tickle*, Queensland University of Technology, Australia
- *Kenneth J. Turner*, University of Stirling, Scotland
- *Anthony P. Kadi*, University of Technology, Australia
- *David Bremer*, Otago Polytechnic, New Zealand
- *Trevor M. Craig*, Wollongong College, New Zealand
- *Wilson Siringoringo*, Auckland University of Technology, New Zealand

- *Sanjay Goel*, University at Albany, SUNY, and NYS Center for Information Forensics and Assurance
- *Damira Pon*, University at Albany, SUNY, and NYS Center for Information Forensics and Assurance
- *David L. Tarnoff*, East Tennessee State University, USA
- *Maiga Chang*, National Science and Technology Program for e-Learning, Taiwan
- *Kun-Fa Cheng*, Chih Ping Senior High School, Taiwan
- *Alex Chang*, Yuan-Ze University, Taiwan
- *Ming-Wei Chen*, Chih Ping Senior High School, Taiwan
- *John Morris*, The University of Auckland, New Zealand
- *Steve Murray*, University of Technology, Australia
- *Vladimir Lasky*, University of Technology, Australia
- *Khaleel I. Petrus*, University of Southern Queensland, Australia
- *João de Jesus Eduardo Correia*, Christchurch Polytechnic Institute of Technology, New Zealand
- *Ricky Watson*, Christchurch Polytechnic Institute of Technology, New Zealand

Acknowledgments

I would like to thank each of the chapter authors, without whose contributions this book would not have been possible. I am indebted also to the anonymous reviewers for their invaluable time and effort in reviewing the manuscripts. Their constructive comments and suggestions helped to improve the quality of the book significantly. My thanks go also to Mr. Michael Taler for providing feedback on Chapter II and to the entire production team at Idea Group Inc. for their ongoing support. Lastly, but most importantly, to my wife for her patience, love, and encouragement throughout this project.

Nurul I. Sarkar

Section I

Introduction

Chapter I

Introduction to Computer Networking and Hardware Concepts

Nurul I. Sarkar, Auckland University of Technology, New Zealand

Abstract

This chapter provides an introduction to computer networking and hardware concepts and highlights the use of software and hardware tools as an aid to enhance teaching and learning computer networking and hardware fundamentals. A basic knowledge of network topology, channel access protocol, network traffic, and networking devices is needed when designing and implementing a LAN. The term computer hardware refers to the physical components of a computer system — those that one can see and touch. The CPU, memory, and input and output devices are the main components of a computer. To understand the operation of a modern processor, it is important that the student grasp the basic concepts of computer hardware.

Learning Objectives

After completing this chapter, you will be able to:

- Give an overview of computer networking and hardware fundamentals.
- Draw a block diagram of a computer.
- Discuss the significance of interactive teaching in introductory computer networking and hardware courses.
- Appreciate the need for software/hardware tools for teaching and learning various aspects of computer networks and hardware.

Overview of Computer Networking

A computer network consists of two or more computers or other intelligent devices linked by communication media (e.g., cable or wireless media) to achieve successful communication. Computer networking is used in many aspects of our lives, and its applications are proliferating. For example, computer networks can be found in universities, secondary schools, and colleges, while in the corporate world, networks link geographically separated offices. Local and state government offices use computer networks, as do military organizations, medical facilities, and the Internet.

Computer networks can be categorized as: (1) local area networks (LANs), (2) metropolitan area networks (MANs), and (3) wide area networks (WANs). The fundamental differences among LANs, MANs, and WANs are distance coverage, transmission speed, media, and error rate. A LAN is a class of computer network that covers a relatively small geographic area, for example, a room, a building or a campus. A LAN is owned by a single organization and physically located within the organization's premises. IEEE 802.3 Ethernet CSMA/CD (Carrier Sense Multiple Access with Collision Detection) is an example of a LAN (IEEE 802.3, 1998). More details about LANs, in general, can be found in many textbooks (Forouzan, 2003; Keiser, 2002; Stamper, 2001), and LAN design is discussed in Fitzgerald and Dennis (2002) and Sarkar and Petrova (2005b). A MAN is a backbone network that links multiple LANs in a large city or a metropolitan region covering up to 40 km. The IEEE 802.6 Fibre Distributed Data Interface (FDDI) is an example of a MAN (Comer, 2001; Forouzan, 2004). A WAN is a class of network that covers a large geographical area (e.g., a country or a continent). Telephone networks and the Internet are examples of WANs.

How to Design a LAN

To implement a LAN, both hardware and software are required. A network operating system (NOS), such as Novell NetWare or MS Windows 2003, needs to be installed on a PC (called the server), and client software is installed on every PC (called a workstation or client) that is linked to the network. Each workstation and the server must have a network interface card (NIC). A cable then connects the NIC to the LAN's hub or switch.

Table 1 lists the LAN topologies, access protocols, and corresponding networking devices and cables for wired LAN design. In designing and implementing a LAN, it is important to have a plan for the: (1) network architecture and channel access protocol (e.g., Ethernet CSMA/CD or token passing), (2) network size (i.e., number of servers, workstations, printers, etc.), and (3) connecting devices (e.g., hub-based or switched network).

Figure 1 shows an Ethernet LAN with one file server, 10 workstations, and two printers using a star physical and logical topology.

Overview of Computer Hardware

A computer is an electronic machine that can process data/information extremely quickly and accurately. Computer hardware is the visible, physical component of the computer that we can touch. There are four main components of a computer system: (1) processor (also called central processing unit, or CPU), (2) memory, (3) input devices, and (4) output devices. Figure 2 shows a block diagram of a computer.

Table 1. LAN topologies, access protocols, and networking devices and associated cables

Topology/Architecture	Channel Access Method	Device	Cable
Physical Bus Logical Bus	Ethernet CSMA/CD	-------	Coaxial
Physical Star Logical Bus	Ethernet CSMA/CD	Ethernet Hub	UTP
Physical Star Logical Star	Ethernet CSMA/CD	Ethernet Switch	UTP
Physical Star Logical Ring	Token Passing	Token Ring Hub	UTP/Optical Fibre
Physical Ring Logical Ring	Token Passing	------	UTP/Optical Fibre

Figure 1. A server-based Ethernet LAN with 10 PCs and two printers (physical and logical star topology)

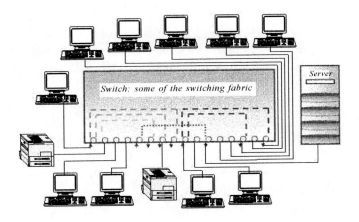

Figure 2. Block diagram of a computer

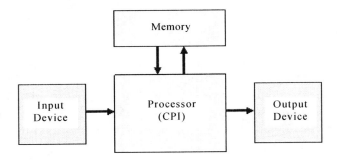

The CPU can be thought of as the heart of a computer. Examples of CPUs include Intel Pentium 4, Motorola M68000, and Zilog Z-80. The memory is used to store data and instruction. Random access memory (RAM) is an example of main memory. The input devices are used to enter data (or programs) into the computer, and output devices are used to display the results. The keyboard and mouse are common examples of input devices, while the monitor and printer are common output devices.

The CPU has two main components: (1) arithmetic and logic unit (ALU), and (2) control unit (CU). The ALU performs all arithmetic, comparison and logical operations, and the CU controls the processing of instructions and movement of

Figure 3. Components of a control unit

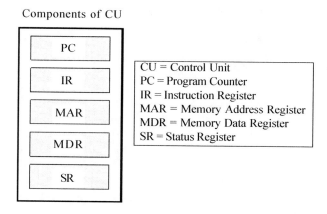

internal data from one part of the CPU to another. Arithmetic operations include addition, subtraction, multiplication, and division. Logical operations include AND, OR, NOT, and Compare. The ALU contains a set of general-purpose registers called the accumulator. An accumulator is a temporary storage used to hold data that is used for arithmetic and logical operations. It is also used to hold results of arithmetic and logical operations. More details about CPUs and memory can be found in many textbooks (Englander, 2000; Shelly, Cashman, & Vermaat, 2003).

The CU has several special-purpose registers and their functions are briefly described below:

- **Program counter (PC)**: The PC holds the address of the next instruction to be executed.

- **Instruction register (IR)**: The IR holds the actual instruction being executed currently by the computer.

- **Memory address register (MAR)**: The MAR holds the address of a memory location.

- **Memory data register (MDR)**: The MDR holds a data value that is being stored to or retrieved from the memory location currently addressed by the memory address register.

- **Status register (SR)**: The SR indicates the results of an arithmetic and logic unit operation. For example: carry, overflow, negative.

Figure 3 shows the main components of a control unit.

Figure 4. The CPU-memory interaction

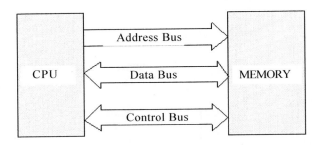

The CPU-Memory Interaction

A computer processes and stores data as a series of binary digits called bits. A bus is a collection of wires or lines used for transferring data and instructions between the CPU and the main memory; one line for each bit (data and address). There are three types of CPU buses: (1) address bus, (2) data bus, and (3) control bus. The address bus is used to select a memory address or location and can be 8-bit, 16-bit, or 32-bit. The data bus is used to carry data or the address of the data between the CPU and main memory and vice versa. The data bus can be 8-bit, 16-bit, 32-bit, or 64-bit. The control bus is used to carry control signals (e.g., READ, WRITE, HALT) to perform specific operations. For example, when the READ signal is activated (i.e., R/W line is high or 1), the memory performs the READ operation. Figure 4 illustrates the CPU-memory interaction.

The Fetch-Execute Cycle

Depending on the complexity of each operation (i.e., task), the computer may take two or more machine cycles in order to complete the task. A machine cycle consists of both fetch and execution cycles. In the fetch cycle, the CU brings the program instruction from the memory, decodes it (i.e., translates the instruction into commands), and then sends the data to the ALU for execution. In the execution cycle, the ALU performs an operation and then sends the result to the memory for temporary storage. Figure 5 illustrates the basic concept of the fetch-execution cycle.

Figure 5. Fetch and execution cycle

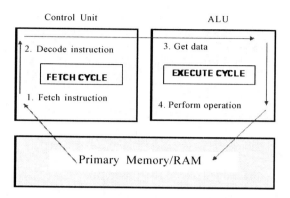

Tools for Teaching Computer Networking and Hardware Concepts

Computer networking and hardware courses are becoming increasingly popular in universities, polytechnical institutions, postsecondary colleges, and private training institutions worldwide because of the high demand for people with computer networking and hardware skills.

The learning-by-doing approach is an essential component in courses on computer networking and hardware fundamentals (Abe et al., 2004; Burch, 2002; Comer, 2002; Sarkar, 2005). The view is frequently supported in the educational literature (Anderson, Reder, & Simon, 1996; Young, 1993) that students learn computer networking and hardware concepts better if they are given hands-on practical exercises that illustrate theoretical concepts. Yet, despite the Chinese adage, attributed to Confucius (551-479 BC), "I hear, I know. I see, I remember. I do, I understand," only a limited amount of material designed to supplement the teaching of computer networking is publicly available, as searches of the Computer Science Teaching Center Web site (http://www.cstc.org/) and the SIGCSE Education Links page (http://sigcse.org/topics/) on the Special Interest Group on Computer Science Education Web site reveal.

To enable students to appreciate and understand computer networking and hardware fundamentals, a teaching and learning tool should be Web-based, portable, modular, configurable, and extensible. Some existing tools for teaching and learning computer networking and hardware concepts are described next.

Some Existing Tools for Teaching Computer-Networking Concepts

Both open source and commercial tools are available for building a variety of network models and visualization of network topologies. We briefly highlight some of the tools reported in the computer-networking literature that are suitable for classroom use.

- **ns-2 (Fall & Varadhan, 2003)**: The network simulator ns-2 is a powerful, text-based simulation software package suitable for performance analysis and evaluation of computer networks. It is a discrete event simulator originally developed at Lawrence Berkeley Laboratory at the University of California, Berkeley, as part of the Virtual InterNetwork Testbed (VINT) project. The Monarch project at Carnegie Mellon University (Monarch, 2004) has extended the ns-2 by adding support for IEEE 802.11 wireless LANs.

- **OPNET (2004)**: OPNET is a popular commercial software package commonly used by researchers and practitioners for modeling and simulation of computer networks. Unlike ns-2, OPNET is menu-driven with an easy-to-use graphical user interface for rapid model construction, data collection, and other simulation tasks. As working with the simulator involves setting up complex experiments, it might be suitable as a learning environment in advanced networking classes.

- **cnet (McDonald, 2004)**: The *cnet* network simulator enables experimentation with protocols at the data link, routing, and transport layers in networks consisting of any combination of WANs and LANs. Although *cnet* is being used worldwide in undergraduate networking courses, the need to prepare a network topology file as the basis of topology visualization might be a challenging task for beginners.

- **JASPER (Turner & Robin, 2001)**: JASPER (Java Simulation of Protocols for Education and Research) is a protocol simulator that can be used as an aid to enhance teaching and learning communication protocols. It is an extensible tool in which students can readily add new protocols.

- **WebLan-Designer (Sarkar & Petrova, 2005a)**: WebLan-Designer is a Web-based tool for interactive teaching and learning both wired and wireless LAN design. Using the "modeling" page, students can experiment with a variety of LAN topologies and channel access protocols. Students can also test their knowledge of various aspects of LAN design by using two interactive quizzes. Each quiz consists of a set of more than 25 multiple-choice questions, each with four possible answers. At the end of each quiz session, the system displays the total score, which allows students to assess their prior knowledge about LAN design. The system provides a friendly environment for interactive quiz management. This is particularly useful for the teacher to update quizzes on a regular basis.

- **DlpSim (King, 2004)**: DlpSim (data link protocol simulator) may be suitable for classroom use to enhance teaching protocols through simulation. However, its emphasis is exclusively on data link layer protocols.

- **WebTrafMon (Hong, Kwon, & Kim, 1999)**: The WebTrafMon is a Web-based system for network analysis and traffic monitoring. However, the system focuses exclusively on network analysis and traffic monitoring, and the system needs to be configured and set up for use in a teaching environment.

- **NetMod (Bachmann, Segal, Srinivasan, & Teorey, 1991)**: The NetMod is a network modeling tool which uses some simple analytical models, providing designers of large, interconnected local area networks with an in-depth analysis of the potential performance of such systems. The tool can be used in university, industrial, or governmental campus networking environments and might serve as a useful demonstration in the classroom.

- **iNetwork (see Chapter III)**: iNetwork is an interactive software tool for teaching and learning data communication networks. iNetwork allows students to assemble and build customised networks using networking devices such as workstations, switches, routers, DNS servers, and DHCP servers. Students can simulate data communication between networking devices and identify and troubleshoot problems in their custom-built networks. Through experimenting with key parameters, students gain insights into the key concepts of communication network design and analysis.

Some Existing Tools for Teaching Computer Hardware Concepts

A number of open source tools exist for modeling and simulation of computer hardware and processors. We briefly review some existing tools, suitable for classroom use, that have been reported in the literature.

- **Logisim (Burch, 2002)**: Logisim is a software tool for logic circuit design and simulation which is suitable for classroom use. It has a graphical user interface, which helps students to gain a better understanding of the design and simulation of logic circuits. Logisim is a Java application and can be run on both Windows and UNIX workstations.

- **DigitalWorks 3.0 (Anonymous, 2006)**: DigitalWorks is similar to Logisim in that it provides a graphical toolbox interface for composing and simulating logic circuits.

- **WinLogiLab (Hacker & Sitte, 2004)**: WinLogiLab is an interactive Microsoft-Windows-compatible computerized teaching suite suitable for classroom use as an aid to enhance teaching and learning digital logic design concepts. It provides a set of interactive teaching aids to approach the basics of combinatorial and sequential digital circuit design. WinLogiLab is targeted toward introductory digital design courses in electrical and computer engineering curricula.

- **Web-based processor simulator (see Chapter XIV)**: This is a Web-based modular and extensible processor simulator designed as an aid to teaching and leaning computer architecture and hardware concepts. Students in advanced classes are able to incorporate new modules by simply writing new Java classes and adding them to a configuration file, which specifies the new modules' connections to other modules. The modular structure means that it can be used for both introductory computer organization and more advanced processor architecture courses.

- **LOGIC-Minimiser (see Chapter XVI)**: LOGIC-Minimiser is an interactive software tool suitable for classroom use as an aid to enhance teaching and learning Boolean expression minimization. It serves as both student-centered, self-paced learning and a classroom demonstration tool. LOGIC-Minimiser is easy to use and can be run under MS-DOS/Windows machines.

- **Picocontroller simulator (Collier, 2003)**: This is an interactive applet in a Web page for PIC16F84 picocontroller simulation. It displays the source program, RAM locations, and the contents of special function registers. Users can step through programs observing the memory changes to facilitate an understanding of the operation of the picocontroller.

Outline of the Remainder of This Book

Chapter II. Motivating students to learn local area network (LAN) design can be difficult since students find the subject dry, technical, and boring. To overcome this problem, the authors have developed a Web-based software tool named WebLan-Designer for interactive teaching and learning both wired and wireless LAN design. Chapter II reports on the development and use of WebLan-Designer as an aid to enhance teaching and learning LAN design. It also highlights the educational benefits of using WebLan-Designer in classroom settings.

Chapter III. A country or a nation would be immobilized without its computer and data communication networks. Computer networking courses are being offered by not only universities and tertiary institutions but also many technical colleges and secondary schools worldwide. The cost associated with purchasing networking devices and equipment to enable students to gain practical experience in setting up a customised network can be significant. Therefore, networking fundamentals are taught by a combination of textbooks and lecture-only methods in many schools and publicly funded tertiary institutions. Chapter III describes the development and use of an interactive learning tool called iNetwork for teaching and learning computer communication networks. iNetwork provides an environment in which students can experiment with different network configurations and gain hands-on learning experience in computer and data communication networks without the need for expensive equipment.

Chapter IV. Teaching computer networking in large classes (e.g., 350-400 students) can be challenging compared to teaching in small classes of 15-20 students. This is partly because of the difficulty in motivating students to learn technical and rather dry subjects and also because of the lack of interaction among the students in large classroom settings. Network simulators allow students to build a network dynamically by placing network devices as icons on a screen and connecting them. The graphical display and animation brings more interactivity and liveliness in the classroom, and consequently it is easier for students to engage in learning computer networking more effectively. Chapter IV focuses on the use of a network simulator in large classroom settings to enhance teaching and learning computer-networking fundamentals.

Chapter V. Communication protocols are essential components of computer and data communication networks. Therefore, it is important that students grasp these concepts and become familiar with widely used protocols. Unfortunately, communication protocols can be complex and their behavior difficult to understand. In order to learn about protocols, a student therefore needs a more controlled and constrained environment. Chapter V describes the development and use of a protocol animator for teaching and learning communication protocols.

Chapter VI. Teaching packet-forwarding theories and concepts in a practical way to undergraduate students requires both a teaching and learning framework and a laboratory infrastructure. Creating a teaching and learning framework in which students can develop a deeper knowledge and understanding of abstract concepts is not a simple task. In addition to teaching materials, the teacher requires a clear idea about learning theories and issues: (1) What is learning? (2) What is knowledge? and (3) How do students go about learning? Chapter VI describes a low-cost laboratory infrastructure for teaching and learning packet-forwarding theories and concepts. The framework is learner-centred and is focused on learning *experiences* in both the classroom and the laboratory. The laboratory-based activities form a critical component of the overall framework.

Chapter VII. Students can learn data communication and networking protocols better if they are given hands-on practical exercises, in which the concept of abstract protocols can be linked to real-world communication concepts. For example, one can learn about address resolution protocol (ARP) by lectures and readings. However, by examining actual ARP traffic from a sample of packets, identifying their behavior, and performing troubleshooting, students gain first-hand experience that cannot be gained through theoretical study. One of the challenges that networking educators are facing is the problem of giving students an "up close and personal" interaction with protocols that are so heavily immersed in theory. Chapter VII emphasises that real experience with network protocols is crucial to effective student learning.

Chapter VIII. Due to the rapid developments in wireless communication and networking technologies and the high demand for wireless networking skills in the industry worldwide, wireless communication and networking courses are becoming increasingly popular in universities, polytechnics, and private training institutions around the globe. Unfortunately, wireless communication and networking is a challenging subject to teach in a meaningful way because many students appear to find the subject technical and rather boring. To overcome this problem, the authors introduce a set of new projects in order to provide students of wireless communication and networking with a hands-on learning experience. The projects are suitable for classroom use in introductory wireless networking courses.

Chapter IX. Wi-Fi networking has been becoming increasingly popular in recent years, both in terms of applications and as the subject of academic research papers and articles in the IT press. It is important that students grasp the basic concepts of both Wi-Fi networking and wireless propagation measurements. Unfortunately, the underlying concepts of wireless networking often intimidate students with their apparently overwhelming complexity, thereby discouraging the students from learning in-depth this otherwise exciting and rewarding subject. Chapter IX provides a tutorial on Wi-Fi networking and radio propagation measurements using wireless laptops and access points. Various hands-on learning activities are also discussed.

Chapter X. There is a strong need for information security education, which stems from the pervasiveness of information technology in business and society. Both government departments and private industries depend on information systems, as information systems are widespread across all business functions. Disruption of critical operational information systems can have serious financial impacts. According to the CSI/FBI report, losses from security breaches have risen rapidly in recent years and exceeded $200 million in 2003. The information security field is very diverse and combines disciplines such as computer science, business, information science, engineering, education, psychology, criminal justice, public administration, law, and accounting. The broad interdisciplinary nature of information security requires several specialists to collaboratively teach the curriculum and integrate different perspectives and teaching styles into a cohesive delivery. Chapter X presents a pedagogical model based on a "teaching hospital" concept that addresses the issues introduced above. By using a specific information risk analysis case, the chapter highlights the basic concept of the teaching hospital and its application in teaching and learning contexts.

Chapter XI. It is important that students grasp the basic concepts of communication between a processor and external devices, and become familiar with tools that are available to implement such systems. Chapter XI describes the operation of the processor bus and explains how I/O devices are connected to it. It also discusses advanced I/O techniques and how the operating systems use I/O to access a computer's resources.

Chapter XII. Computer hardware, number systems, CPU, memory, and I/O (input/output) ports are topics often included in computer science, electronics, and engineering courses as fundamental concepts involved in computer hardware. We believe that students learn computer hardware fundamentals better if they are given practical learning exercises that illustrate theoretical concepts. However, only a limited range of material designed specifically to supplement the teaching of computer hardware concepts is publicly available. Chapter XII describes a set of PIC-based projects that give students a hands-on introduction to computer hardware concepts and are suitable for classroom use in undergraduate computer hardware courses.

Chapter XIII. Students often get a good score in written exams but fail to apply their knowledge when trying to solve real-world problems. This applies particularly to computer hardware courses in which students are required to learn and memorize many key terms and definitions. Also, teachers often find it difficult to gauge students' progress when teaching computer hardware fundamentals courses. These problems are related to the learning process, so it is necessary to find an appropriate instructional model to overcome these problems. Chapter XIII describes a Web-based tool called an assistant tool based on problem-based learning (PBL) theory that not only assists instructors in teaching computer hardware fundamentals but also overcomes the above-mentioned problems.

Chapter XIV. Computer architecture educators are constantly looking for modular tools that allow processors to be configured in a transparent way; the visualization enables rapid verification that modules have been connected in the desired manner. Thus, simple experiments which demonstrate, for example, the effect of different cache organizations are readily configured by instructors or students. Advanced computer architecture students will also be able to add experimental capabilities (in the form of new modules or modifications to existing ones) and perform simple experiments to assess their effect on processor performance. Chapter XIV discusses the development and use of a processor simulator in teaching computer architecture at both introductory and advanced levels. It is written in Java, which allows it to be easily embedded in other Web-based course materials and run anywhere.

Chapter XV. To teach modern embedded systems, including operating systems, in a meaningful way, a moderately sophisticated processor is required to demonstrate many key concepts, such as multitasking, multithreading, structured and abstracted hardware management layer, communications utilising various protocols over network interfaces, and memory resident file systems. Unfortunately, high-end 32-bit embedded systems processors capable of supporting these facilities are expensive compared to conventional 8-bit and 16-bit targets, and it is not feasible to acquire a large number of them to house in a laboratory in an effort to enable practical exercises for over 100 students. Chapter XV describes the development and use of a remotely accessible embedded systems laboratory that uses a small number of 32-bit development systems and makes them available to students over the Internet.

Chapter XVI. Boolean algebra, minimization of Boolean expressions, and logic gates are often included as a subject in electronics, computer science, information technology, and engineering courses as computer hardware and digital systems are a fundamental component of IT systems today. We believe that students learn minimization of Boolean expressions better if they are given interactive practical learning activities that illustrate theoretical concepts. Chapter XVI describes the development and use of a software tool (named LOGIC-Minimiser) as an aid to enhance teaching and learning minimization of Boolean expressions.

Chapter XVII. Serial communication is used as a long-distance computer system interface due to its reliability and cost effectiveness. All information pertaining to the delivery of a message must be contained within a single stream of bits. In order to implement a serial data communication system, a well-defined set of rules called a protocol must exist to specify the placement and purpose of every bit sent across the link. Chapter XVII provides a practical introduction to serial protocols for data communications. It shows how a protocol analyser can be used in examining the frames of the data link layer and the packets of the network layer.

Chapter XVIII. Providing a dedicated lab to each group of students in order to gain hands-on learning experience is not always possible due to budget and space constraints. For example, in a class of 20 students, each student requires at least three computers with each computer capable of running three operating systems, such as UNIX, Linux, and Windows Server 2003. This requires a large computer laboratory with 60 computers in total. In addition, it is difficult to manage the laboratory to accommodate students from other classes. For example, once one class leaves the laboratory, another class of 20 students needs to start immediately, with each person configuring Windows Server 2003 Active Directory on four computers. This requires another large computer laboratory with eighty computers. Chapter XVIII presents VMware as a teaching and learning tool to overcome the problems mentioned above. Under the VMware system, students do not require administrative privileges on physical machines. Consequently, they have complete freedom to experiment within their own virtualised environments.

Conclusion

Because of the high demand for people with computer networking and hardware skills worldwide, computer networking and hardware courses are becoming increasingly popular in both tertiary and private training institutions. Unfortunately, motivating students to learn computer networking and hardware concepts is often difficult because students appear to find the subject technical and rather dry.

Interactive teaching and learning using software/hardware tools is an attractive solution to the problem of motivating students to learn computer networking and hardware fundamentals. This chapter describes the basic concepts of computer networking and hardware fundamentals and highlights various tools for interactive teaching and learning computer networking and hardware concepts. It also provides an outline of the remainder of the book.

Summary

Computer networks can be classified as local area networks, metropolitan area networks, and wide area networks. Each class of network has certain characteristics that make it suitable for certain networking applications. A basic knowledge of network topology, channel access protocol, network traffic, and networking devices is needed when designing and implementing a LAN.

The term *computer hardware* refers to the physical components of a computer system — those that one can see and touch. The CPU, memory, and input and output devices are the main components of a computer. To understand the operation of a modern processor, it is important that the student grasp the basic concepts of computer hardware. An overview of computer networking and hardware concepts is presented, and various tools for interactive teaching and learning computer networking and hardware essentials are highlighted.

Key Terms and Definitions

DHCP: DHCP stands for dynamic host configuration protocol. It is often used to dynamically assign IP addresses to hosts.

DNS: DNS stands for domain name system. It is a service used to map hostnames onto IP addresses and allow for resolution of hostnames to IP addresses.

Ethernet: A popular LAN technology that uses a shared channel and the CSMA/CD access method. Basic Ethernet operates at 10 Mbps, Fast Ethernet operates at 100 Mbps, and Gigabit Ethernet operates at 1,000 Mbps.

Hub: A networking device that interconnects two or more workstations in a star-wired local area network and broadcasts incoming data onto all outgoing connections. To avoid signal collision only one user can transmit data through the hub at a time.

LAN: LAN stands for local area network. A class of computer network suitable for a relatively small geographic area, for example, a room, a building, or a campus. A LAN is owned by a single organization and physically located within the organization's premises. Ethernet is the most popular LAN architecture.

Logical topology: This refers to the way the data is sent through the network from one computer (or device) to another.

MAN: MAN stands for metropolitan area network. A MAN is a backbone network that links multiple LANs in a large city or a metropolitan region.

NIC: NIC stands for network interface card. It is the hardware interface that provides the physical link between a computer and a network.

NOS: NOS stands for network operating system. It is a complex set of computer programs that manage the common resources of a local area network. In addition, NOS performs the standard operating system services. Examples are NetWare, Linux, and MS Windows 2003.

Optical fibre: A type of cable which consists of one or more glass or plastic fibre cores inside a protective cladding material, covered by an outer plastic PVC jacket. Signal transmission along the inside fibres is accomplished using light pulses. The optical fibre cable is characterised by an extremely large data-carrying capacity. Optical fibre is used for undersea cables and for countrywide telecommunications backbones.

Peer-to-peer network: A class of network in which a computer can communicate with any other networked computers on an equal or peer-like basis without going through an intermediary, such as a server or a dedicated host.

Physical topology: This refers to the way computers and other devices are connected within the network physically.

Protocol: A protocol is a collection of rules for formatting, ordering, and error-checking data sent across a network.

Switch: Unlike a hub, a switch allows multiple users to communicate simultaneously in order to achieve a higher throughput.

WAN: WAN stands for wide area network. A WAN covers a large geographical area (e.g., a country or a continent). Telephone networks and the Internet are examples of WANs.

Workstation: An end-user computer that has its own CPU and is used as a client to access another computer, such as a file server.

Review Questions

1. What is a network? Discuss the basic difference between a local area network and a wide area network.

2. List and describe three important components of a communication system.

3. Define the following networking terms: LAN, MAN, WAN, protocol, peer-to-peer network, and server-based network.

4. You are given the following components: one server, 10 PCs, and one printer. Draw a diagram to show how the above components can be connected to construct a LAN using: (a) bus topology, (b) ring topology, and (c) star topology. Use a hub/switch when appropriate.

5. Discuss the importance of interactive teaching in introductory computer networking and hardware courses.

6. List and describe four main components of a computer system.

7. List and describe two main components of a central processing unit.

8. Describe the function of address, data, and control buses.

9. Draw a diagram to illustrate the interaction between a CPU and the main memory.

10. Discuss the significance of software/hardware tools in teaching and learning computer networking and hardware concepts.

11. List and describe three software tools suitable for classroom use to enhance teaching and learning computer-networking concepts.

References

Abe, K., Tateoka, T., Suzuki, M., Maeda, Y., Kono, K., & Watanabe, T. (2004). An integrated laboratory for processor organization, compiler design, and computer networking. *IEEE Transactions on Education, 47*(3), 311-320.

Anderson, J. R., Reder, L. M., & Simon, H. A. (1996). Situated learning and education. *Educational Researcher, 25*(4), 5-11.

Anonymous. (2006). *Digital Works.* Retrieved January 5, 2006, from http://www.spsu.edu/cs/faculty/bbrown/circuits/howto.html

Bachmann, D. W., Segal, M. E., Srinivasan, M. M., & Teorey, T. J. (1991). NetMod: A design tool for large-scale heterogeneous campus networks. *IEEE Journal on Selected Areas in Communications, 9*(1), 15-24.

Burch, C. (2002). Logisim: A graphical system for logic circuit design and simulation. *Journal of Educational and Resources in Computing, 2*(1), 5-16.

Collier, M. (2003). A picocontroller training simulator in a Web page. *International Journal of Electrical Engineering Education, 40*(2), 158-168.

Comer, D. E. (2001). *Computer networks and Internets with Internet applications* (3rd ed.). Prentice Hall.

Comer, D. E. (2002). *Hands-on networking with Internet technologies.* Prentice Hall.

Englander, I. (2000). *The architecture of computer hardware and systems software: An information technology approach* (2nd ed.). Wiley.

Fall, K., & Varadhan, K. (2003). *The ns manual.* Retrieved January 5, 2006, from http://www.isi.edu/nsnam/ns/

Fitzgerald, J., & Dennis, A. (2002). *Business data communications and networking* (7th ed.). New York: Wiley.

Forouzan, B. A. (2003). *Local area networks* (1st ed.). McGraw-Hill.

Forouzan, B. A. (2004). *Data communications and networking* (3rd ed.). McGraw-Hill.

Hacker, C., & Sitte, R. (2004). Interactive teaching of elementary digital logic design with WinLogiLab. *IEEE Transactions on Education, 47*(2), 196-203.

Hong, J. W.-K., Kwon, S.-S., & Kim, J.-Y. (1999). WebTrafMon: Web-based Internet/intranet network traffic monitoring and analysis system. *Computer Communications, 22*(14), 1333-1342.

IEEE 802.3. (1998). *Information technology—Telecommunications and information exchange between systems—Local and metropolitan area networks specific requirements—Part 3: Carrier sense multiple access with collision detection (CSMA/CD) access method and physical layer specifications.* Unpublished manuscript.

Keiser, G. (2002). *Local area networks* (2nd ed.). McGraw-Hill.

King, P. J. B. (2004). *dlpjava. A data link protocol simulator.* Retrieved January 5, 2006, from www.cee.hw.ac.uk/~pjbk/dlpjava

McDonald, C. (2004). *The cnet network simulator (v2.0.9).* Retrieved January 5, 2006, from www.csse.uwa.edu.au/cnet/

Monarch. (2004). *CMU Monarch project.* Retrieved January 5, 2006, from http://www.monarch.cs.cmu.edu

OPNET. (2004). *OPNET Technologies—Commercial simulation software.* Retrieved June 20, 2004, from www.opnet.com

Sarkar, N. I. (2005). LAN-Designer: A software tool to enhance learning and teaching server-based LAN design. *International Journal of Information and Communication Technology Education, 1*(2), 74-86.

Sarkar, N. I., & Petrova, K. (2005a). *The WebLan-Designer.* Retrieved January 5, 2006, from http://elena.aut.ac.nz/homepages/weblandesigner/

Sarkar, N. I., & Petrova, K. (2005b, June 27-30). *WebLan-Designer: A Web-based system for interactive teaching and learning LAN design.* Paper presented at the 3rd IEEE International Conference on Information Technology Research and Education, Hsinchu, Taiwan (pp. 328-332).

Shelly, G. B., Cashman, T. J., & Vermaat, M. E. (2003). *Discovering computers 2004: Complete.* Course Technology.

Stamper, D. (2001). *Local area networks* (3rd ed.). Prentice Hall.

Turner, K. J., & Robin, I. A. (2001). An interactive visual protocol simulator. *Computer Standards & Interfaces, 23*, 279-310.

Young, M. F. (1993). Instructional design for situated learning. *Educational Technology, 41*(1), 43-58.

Section II

Teaching and Learning Computer Networking

Chapter II

WebLan-Designer:
A Web-Based Tool to Enhance Teaching and Learning Wired and Wireless LAN Design

Nurul I. Sarkar, Auckland University of Technology, New Zealand

Krassie Petrova, Auckland University of Technology, New Zealand

Abstract

It is somewhat difficult to motivate students to learn both wired and wireless local area network design because students find the subject technical, dry when delivered in class, and rather boring. This chapter introduces the case of a Web-based tool for class demonstration as well as modelling LAN design. The background of the case is presented and is followed by a review of some existing tools for network simulation and modelling. After introducing the learning theories and concepts (e.g., experiential learning and constructivism) relevant to the tools' pedagogical value, the chapter describes the architecture and components of WebLan-Designer. The main benefits of using WebLan-Designer are discussed in the light of educational theories, and their validation is supported by a summary of comments received. The chapter concludes with remarks on the strengths and weaknesses of WebLan-Designer and its future development.

Learning Objectives

After completing this chapter, you will be able to:

- Discuss the usefulness of WebLan-Designer in teaching and learning contexts.
- Use WebLan-Designer in both face-to-face and distance learning environments for teaching and learning LAN design.
- Verify the solutions to LAN design exercises using WebLan-Designer.
- Suggest further enhancements to WebLan-Designer.

Introduction

It is somewhat difficult to motivate students to learn both wired and wireless local area network design because students find the subject technical, dry when delivered in class, and rather boring. Educators have experimented with different approaches to alleviate this problem. Examples include computer-assisted learning packages (Diab & Tabbara, 1995), game-based simulation (Shifroni & Ginat, 1997), approaches based on the constructivist paradigm (Chen, 2003), experiential learning (R. K. C. Chang, 2004), and learning research techniques such as the phenomenographical approach (Berglund, 2003).

This chapter introduces the case of a Web-based tool for class demonstration as well as modelling LAN design. The motivational background of the case is presented in the next section and is followed by a review of some existing tools for network simulation and modelling. After introducing the learning theories and concepts (e.g., experiential learning and constructivism) relevant to the tools' pedagogical value, the chapter describes the architecture and components of WebLan-Designer. The main benefits of using WebLan-Designer are discussed in the light of educational theories, and their validation is supported by a summary of comments received. The chapter concludes with remarks on the strengths and weaknesses of WebLan-Designer and its future development.

Background and Motivation

LANs are often included as a topic in computer science, information technology, engineering, and business courses as LANs are a fundamental component of IT systems today. We believe that students learn LAN design better if they are given interactive practical exercises that illustrate theoretical concepts. There is still very little material publicly available to supplement the teaching of LAN design, as a searches of the Computer Science Teaching Center Web site (http://www.cstc.org/) and the SIGCSE Education Links page (http://sigcse.org/topics/) on the Special Interest Group on Computer Science Education Web site reveal. Even less course material is available on wireless networking and related topics. The need for learner support in the areas of computer networking is especially strong (Petrova, 2002).

We strongly believe, as do many others (Abe et al., 2004; Bhunia, Giri, Kar, Haldar, & Purkait, 2004; Garcia & Alesanco, 2004; Hacker & Sitte, 2004), that students learn more effectively from courses that involve them in interactive learning activities. The theoretical underpinnings of this approach come from two theories of learning: experiential learning and constructivism. First, the hands-on learning experience is derived from learning which involves observation and experimentation and aims to help students develop skills in testing out different approaches to completing a project (Kolb, Boyatzis, & Mainemelis, 2000). Secondly, as students make their way through the basic framework of pre-supplied content-related constructs, they are given the opportunity to develop and reorganize their own concepts and ideas. Learning occurs not by absorption but through the construction of students' own knowledge in authentic context (Chen, 2003).

Computer networking is a particularly challenging subject to learn and to teach in a meaningful way; students may find the subject technical and rather dry when presented. A team of *Auckland University of Technology*-based researchers developed a Web-based tool called WebLan-Designer, aiming to provide students with an interactive learning experience in LAN design. A teacher involved in an introductory networking course might be able to use WebLan-Designer in the classroom as a demonstration to enhance the lecture environment. Students, on the other hand, can use the system to complete networking assignments and verify (interactively and visually) the solutions to LAN design exercises and in-class tasks. WebLan-Designer can be accessed at any time either through an intranet or the Internet. In addition to enhancing classroom teaching by including an element of online learning, WebLan-Designer also provides online support for off-campus students and enhances learning by engaging them in a flexible, learner-centered manner.

LAN design concepts are described in many textbooks (Bing, 2002; Dornan, 2002; Palmer & Sinclair, 2003), and Web-based tools are discussed extensively in the computer networking literature (Kofke & Mihalick, 2002; Rokou, Rokos, & Rokou, 2003; Sitthiworachart & Joy, 2003). In the following section we briefly review various existing software tools related to the proposed system described in this chapter.

Some Existing Tools: A Review

Various tools and simulators (both open source and commercial) are available for building LAN models (X. Chang, 1999; Sanchez & Manzoni, 2001; Zheng & Ni, 2003). However, these often powerful systems can have a steep learning curve, and while excellent for doing an in-depth performance evaluation of LANs, the simulated networking environment created is typically far more detailed than is necessary for introduction to fundamental concepts. Some of the tools which are reported in the networking literature are described below.

- **NetMod (Bachmann, Segal, Srinivasan, & Teorey, 1991)**: NetMod is a network modelling tool which uses simple analytical models to provide designers of large, interconnected LANs with an in-depth analysis of the potential performance of these systems. The tool can be used in university, industrial, or governmental campus networking environments, comprising thousands of computer sites. NetMod is implemented in combination with the easy-to-use software (HyperCard, Excel).

- **The Layer-Module set (Diab & Tabbara, 1995)**: This teaching tool for computer network systems includes graphical animation and simulation of the functions of a network. The environment provides textual information on the seven OSI layers, supplemented with figures, examples and demonstrations, and multiple-choice questions. Protocol simulation is used; for example, the shortest path first and network flow using graph theory.

- **WebTrafMon (Hong, Kwon, & Kim, 1999)**: The WebTrafMon is a Web-based system for network analysis and traffic monitoring. It provides monitoring and analysis capabilities not only for traffic loads but also for traffic types, sources, and destinations. Using a Web browser, users can monitor traffic statistics and review traffic history.

- **ns-2 (Fall & Varadhan, 2003)**: Ns-2 (network simulator) is a powerful text-based simulation software package suitable for performance analysis of computer networks.

- **Network Intelligence (Nieuwelaar & Hunt, 2004)**: Network Intelligence (NI) provides an easy way to view complex traffic patterns in a wide area networking environment. NI can perform simulations of network topologies using actual gathered data as opposed to arbitrary data.

- **cnet (McDonald, 2004)**: The *cnet* network simulator enables experimentation with various data link, network, routing, and transport networking protocols in networks consisting of any combination of wide area networks (WANs) and LANs. As a learning tool, *cnet* has been used worldwide in undergraduate networking courses.

- **LAN-Designer (Sarkar & Lian, 2003)**: LAN-Designer is a prototype software tool for wired LAN modelling. The software is simple and easy to use and can be used either in the classroom or at home to enhance teaching and learning of some aspects of LAN design. However, the current version of LAN-Designer has very limited features and requires significant improvement.

- **WLAN-Designer (Sarkar, 2004)**: WLAN-Designer is a Web-based software tool for wireless LAN modelling (still a prototype). The software is easy to use and can be accessed either from an intranet or through the Internet to enhance learning and teaching of various aspects of wireless LAN design. As LAN-Designer, the current version of WLAN-Designer requires improvement.

WebLan-Designer, which we describe in the next section, has its own unique features, including the integration of wired and wireless LAN design, simplicity, ease-of-use, and a Web-based interactive system.

WebLan-Designer Architecture and Components

Figure 1 illustrates the three-tier client-server architecture approach used in implementing the system.

The components of WebLan-Designer are shown in Figure 2. The system consists of two parts: (1) wired LAN design and (2) wireless LAN design. Both parts of WebLan-Designer have the following main components:

Figure 1. Architecture of WebLan-Designer

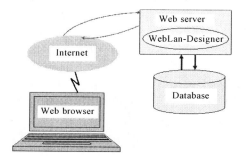

Figure 2. Components of WebLan-Designer

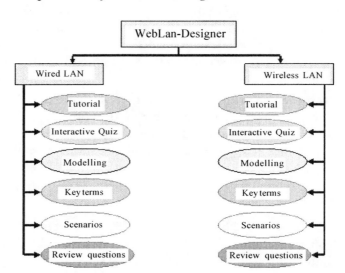

- **Tutorial**: A step-by-step guide designed to take the student through a set of tasks related to the type of network studied, aiming to enhance the student's knowledge and understanding of various aspects of LAN design. Each tutorial includes self-assessment both at commencement and after completion.

- **Quiz**: Students can test their knowledge on both wired and wireless LAN design at any time by using the two interactive quizzes. Each quiz consists of a set of 50 multiple-choice questions with four possible answers, and each question is designed to cover a key concept of LAN design. At the end of a quiz session, the system displays the total score, which allows the student to assess his or her knowledge about LAN design. This also allows the teacher to gauge students' prior knowledge; for example, how much students already knew about LAN design before starting the course. As students use WebLan-Designer's learning resources, such as LAN modelling and networking key terms and definitions, to learn about some aspects of LAN design, it might be useful to be able to see the impact of WebLan-Designer on students' learning about LAN design. This can be achieved by comparing the total scores obtained from two quiz sessions: (1) before and (2) after using the WebLan-Designer learning resources.

- **Modelling**: It provides an interactive and easy way to develop a variety of LAN models. Using the "modelling" page of WebLan-Designer, students

Table 1. Topologies and access protocols

	Topology/Architecture	**Channel access method**
Wired LAN	Physical Bus Logical Bus Physical Star Logical Bus Physical Star Logical Star Physical Ring Logical Ring Physical Star Logical Ring	Ethernet CSMA/CD Token Passing
Wireless LAN	Ad Hoc Network Infrastructure Network	CSMA/CA

can experiment with LAN topologies and channel access protocols to enhance their knowledge and understanding of LAN design. Table 1 lists the supported topologies and access methods.

Figure 3 shows a screenshot of a modelling page of WebLan-Designer. An infrastructure wireless LAN is modelled, including 10 workstations, eight personal digital assistants (PDAs), and two printers.

- **Key terms**: The key terms and definitions of various topics related to both wired and wireless networking are summarized in these pages. Examples of key terms related to LAN design include: bus, star, and ring physical topologies, logical topology, channel, channel access protocol, CSMA/CD,

Figure 3. A screenshot of a modelling page

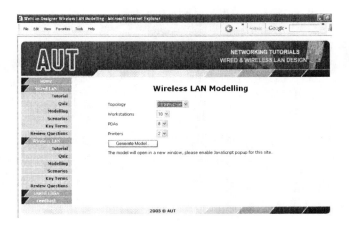

Table 2. Scenario examples

A wired network scenario	A wireless network scenario
Two of the university departments are about to be rehoused and jointly need to install a new computer laboratory. This laboratory will occupy two adjacent rooms, with each room containing 40 PCs. The requirements are: (1) Each laboratory must be capable of operating independently. It should be possible to disable the network in each room separately and at a single point. (2) The two laboratories should be capable of being combined for use with large classes. (3) Each laboratory needs to have its own Windows 2003 server. Both laboratories will need to have access to a Linux server, which they will share.	Pizza House wants to attract more customers to its pizza parlor in King Street and has decided to offer a Hotspot Internet Coupon (*Hroup*) with every pizza ordered on the spot. One *Hroup* gives a 30-minute free Internet access to any customer who has ordered a pizza and has a wireless-enabled PDA, a laptop, or a mobile phone that can access the Wi-Fi hotspot. The coupon expires if not used within 1 hour of the purchase. Pizza House has signed a deal with Broad Bush (a local ISP) to obtain from them cheap broadband (wireless) Internet access and use it to offer to *Hroup* holders.

token passing, workstation, file server, hub, switch, and UTP Cat 5e. Examples of key terms related to wireless LANs include: ad hoc network, infrastructure network, PCMCIA card, access point, wireless channel, CSMA/CA, OFDM, modulation, line of sight, direct sequence spread spectrum (DSSS), and frequency-hopping spread spectrum (FHSS).

- **Scenarios**: This feature allows students to examine example backbone networks based on small business and corporate case scenarios. By observing an integrated LAN which spans over multiple floors on two or more buildings (close or at a distance), students can enhance their knowledge and understanding about campus, small business, and corporate-wide LAN design. Two scenario examples are shown in Table 2.

- **Review questions**: The review questions in each part serve as an extension of the quiz and modelling tasks. Examples include: What layer of the OSI model is concerned with turning binary code into a physical signal? and What type of propagation is used by low-frequency radio waves traveling close to the Earth? The review questions broaden the scope of the system as they refer to knowledge gained through other activities, such as lectures or independent reading. We felt that adding a suggested answer would serve the purposes of learning better than leaving the questions unanswered.

WebLan-Designer is currently installed on a Web server at *Auckland University of Technology* (AUT) and is being tested for performance and robustness. The database-driven implementation is based on the use of PHP and MySQL and involves a combination of static and dynamic Web pages. Two examples of the models that the modelling engine creates are shown in Figure 4.

Figure 4. (a) A model of a wired LAN (Ethernet); (b) a model of a wireless LAN (ad hoc)

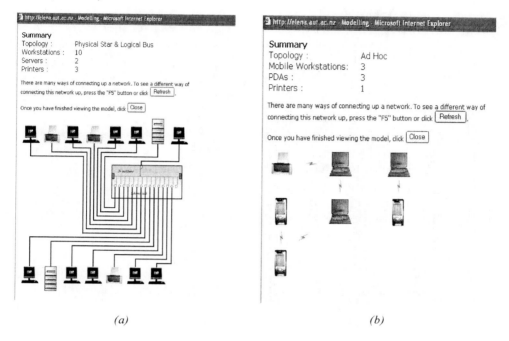

(a)   (b)

Teaching and Learning Aspects of Using WebLan-Designer

For simplicity and ease of use, WebLan-Designer has a graphical user interface (GUI). The GUI is not only user-friendly but self-explanatory.

Let us briefly highlight the value of WebLan-Designer and how we use it in teaching and learning contexts. At AUT, the authors teach various aspects of networking and LAN design, including wireless networks, across three different programmes: (1) bachelor of business, (2) bachelor of computer and information sciences, and (3) diploma in IT classes. In line with the observation made by other authors, for example, Berglund (2003), our experience shows that at times it is quite difficult to motivate students to learn about wired and wireless LAN design using the traditional lecture-only method. Students find the topic full of technical jargon, rather dry when delivered in lecture, and even boring.

To make the lessons more interesting and to encourage students' participation in class, we use WebLan-Designer as an integral part of two 2-hour sessions; for example, the first session might be based on wired LANs and the second session on wireless LANs. In the classroom, students are asked to design a server-based LAN on paper. After a prescribed period of time (e.g., 15 minutes), we introduce WebLan-Designer to the students and do a walk-through with them to verify (visually and interactively) their solutions and to learn more about server-based LAN design. The interactive quizzes, review questions, and key term definitions are also being used, complementing the modelling task.

In addition to classroom use, the students can access WebLan-Designer from home and work on exercises and tutorials in their own time and at their own pace. Thus the tool not only enhances lectures by including an element of online learning but also provides off-campus online support for students. This is especially important for students taking courses in a flexible mode, combining face-to-face classes with self-directed online learning. Figure 5 shows schematically two suggested study guidelines (wired LANs).

As discussed earlier, teaching networking concepts without the ability to engage students in some practical work makes networking classes dry and boring and does not motivate students. Consequently, the tool described here attempts to provide a space for experimentation and knowledge construction, building on findings in the literature on experiential learning (Kolb, Boyatzis, & Mainemelis, 2000; Kolb & Kolb, 2004) and the constructivist approach to teaching and

Figure 5. A suggested sequence of study

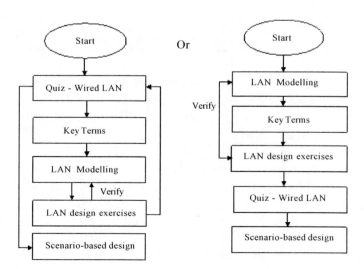

learning using computer-based tools (Chen, 2003; Resnick, 2002). Summarizing the findings of a large body of research in experiential learning, Kolb et al. point out that learners from a nontechnical background such as business and management tend to learn better when engaged in "concrete experimentation" and "active experimentation." With regard to teaching networking, Chen suggests that constructivism could provide a sound theoretical foundation for teaching given the complexity of the domain. We believe that the tool described in this chapter offers educational benefits aligned with the view that students today need to learn actively and independently, "with the teacher serving as consultant, not chief executive" (Resnick, 2002).

Firstly, the tool is easy to use and navigate and is accessible through the Internet. Therefore, it is suitable for a distance learning (off-campus) environment. The user access to the system can be restricted through a login/password to comply with additional requirements or constraints. Secondly, the learner is engaged in a broad and dynamic learning experience. For example, the modelling function provides a simple and easy way to develop a variety of network configurations, and students can experiment with LAN topologies and channel access protocols and thus gain a better understanding of LAN design. In addition to LAN modelling, eight business case scenarios and suggested solutions, which provide real-world examples to students about the organization and corporate networking requirements, are included in the system. The combining experimentation through modelling and observation using scenarios enable students to construct their own knowledge (Chen, 2003), which might be especially important for learners from a nontechnical background (Kolb et al., 2000).

WebLan-Designer was trilled for the first time during semester 1 of 2005 in three classes, and the informal feedback from students was positive. We asked the teaching community in New Zealand to send us comments, and we hoped to receive feedback from visitors to the Web site. At the time of writing, we have received comments from seven lecturers involved in teaching networking (three from AUT, three from other New Zealand institutions, and one from an overseas university). The responses are positive (see Table 3) and confirm the validity of the educational benefits stated above, as lecturers perceive the tool's components as valuable and express interest in using WebLan-Designer in class.

The critical comments are about improving the presentation (spelling and typos) and also about the need to use the tool with care as not to create an illusion of "easiness" while trying to make it easy to learn. We agree with these comments wholeheartedly. The suggested improvements include adding more functions and adding more internal links; we will consider these suggestions carefully in our future work.

Table 3. Evaluation by peers

Positive ... I like the network designer part especially (i.e., the physical star logical bus, etc.). ... Web-based questions and answers are useful for students. I have experienced that students like to use these for self-review. The different scenarios are useful for students to see and analyze different network configurations. ... Easy-to-use tutorial and good interface, helpful for learners especially to review and test their knowledge on wireless LAN, useful Links is a very good idea, especially for students who would like to explore and learn more. ... A very useful resource ... good for learning. (2) ... Interested to use WebLan-Designer ... in class. (2)
Critique ... A link from task 5: wireless Design Exercises to Scenarios/Exercises required. ... Some spelling mistakes in the quiz texts. ... A couple of [typographical] errors in your LAN test ... [suggested corrections]. ... The modeller part may help the visualization of the different network layouts but may also convey an oversimplified idea of network design.
Recommendations ... More navigation links might make the tutorial easier to navigate and use; for example, after completing the quiz, there is a link to reattempt the quiz. Similarly links to other parts of the Designer such as tutorial might make it more navigable. ... There can be more user-friendly feedback and interaction features added. ... It would be helpful to have some graphic-related questions too (i.e., a picture of a network and a multiple-choice question set about what it is called, etc.). It looks good for the students for revision especially. ... A usability testing may also be done.

Concluding Remarks

The design of a new networking tutorial suite (named WebLan-Designer) follows our previous efforts in both a flexible teaching and learning model (Petrova, 2002) and a tool to enhance teaching and learning (Sarkar, 2004; Sarkar & Lian, 2003). WebLan-Designer is a Web-based interactive tool for teaching and learning LAN design. The tool can be used either in the classroom to enhance the lecture environment or at home (i.e., off campus) as an aid to enhance learning various aspects of computer networking and LAN design (Reinig & The, 1998). Objectifying network topology concepts is one of the aspects of the constructivist approach towards teaching computer networking. As WebLan-Designer provides both visual and animated representations, it supports constructivist pedagogical approaches and can improve students' participation in flexible learning activities (Chen, 2003). The flexibility in modelling LAN design enhances learning as it introduces variation — an experience stimulating the understanding of the concept under investigation (Berglund, 2003). Both flexibility and variation provide opportunities for students to build and refine their own knowledge, which they can apply further to solve problems and develop deeper understanding of properties and relationships — a necessary component of self-learning (Shifroni & Ginat, 1997).

Compared to the traditional method of classroom teaching of computer networking, WebLan-Designer provides students a different way of learning more LAN design concepts (e.g., modelling component of the tool). The mixed (and often very minimal) level of prior student knowledge, recognised by R. K. C. Chang (2004) as one of the challenges in teaching computer networks, is addressed by the inbuilt flexibility. More experienced students can go through quizzes and scenario-based LAN design. Students exposed to networking for the first time can do a walk-through and learn about computer networks. Finally, learning is further enhanced by multi-coverage of the content (e.g., quiz, key terms, and review questions have many commonalities) and making the concepts interesting and engaging (e.g., when working with the scenarios). Students are given the opportunity to identify their misconceptions and reconstruct their knowledge, which helps them internalise, rather then absorb, the basic ideas and concepts (Chen, 2003).

The tool has some limitations. Currently, WebLan-Designer displays LAN diagrams with up to 20 workstations, four file servers, and four printers. The software can easily be upgraded to accommodate any number of components. The incorporation of wireless personal area networks (Bluetooth technology) is also suggested for future work. Other developments might include expanding the scope of the tool to include interactive content at the higher layers of the TCP/IP protocol stack, such as NAT translation and IP subnetwork modelling.

WebLan-Designer is available at no cost to faculty interested in using it to supplement their teaching. More information about WebLan-Designer can be obtained by contacting the first author or through the WebLan-Designer Web site at http://elena.aut.ac.nz/homepages/weblandesigner/.

Acknowledgments

This work was supported in part by AUT's RELT Contestable Grant (Grant No. CJ9987105000, 2004). An earlier version of this chapter appears as: Sarkar, N., & Petrova, K. (2005, June). WebLan-Designer: A Web-based system for interactive teaching and learning LAN design. *Proceedings of the 3rd International Conference on Information Technology: Research and Education (ITRE 2005).*

Summary

Interactive teaching and learning by using software tools is an attractive solution to motivate students to learn a rather technical and dry subject such as LAN design. This chapter described a Web-based tool called WebLan-Designer that gives students an interactive and flexible learning experience in both wired and wireless LAN design. Both teacher and students can benefit from the use of WebLan-Designer in different teaching and learning contexts. A teacher is able to use it in the classroom as a demonstration, to liven up the traditional lecture. Students, on the other hand, can use the system in achieving the following learning outcomes: (1) complete tutorials on both wired and wireless LAN design; (2) test prior knowledge on networking through interactive quizzes; (3) verify the solution to in-class tasks and exercises through LAN modelling; and (4) learn more about scenario-based LAN design. In addition to enhancing face-to-face teaching by including an element of online learning in the classroom, WebLan-Designer provides online support for off-campus students and facilitates learning through flexible course delivery. The effectiveness of WebLan-Designer as an aid to teaching and learning LAN design has been evaluated both by students and teaching team.

Key Terms and Definitions

Access point (AP): AP stands for access point. Typically, infrastructure-based wireless networks provide access to the wired backbone network via an AP. The AP may act as a repeater, bridge, router, or even gateway to regenerate, forward, filter, or translate messages. All communication between mobile devices has to take place via the AP.

Ad hoc network: A class of wireless network architecture in which there is no fixed infrastructure or wireless access points. In ad hoc networks, each mobile station acts as a router to communicate with other stations. Such a network can exist on a temporary basis to share some resources among the mobile stations.

Constructivism: A theory of learning which regards learning as a process of developing knowledge through the construction and reconstruction of concepts and ideas, providing learners with motivation, and supporting self-directed learning. It suggests that learners are particularly likely to make new ideas when they are actively engaged in making some type of external artifact, which they can reflect upon and share with others (http://mia.openworldlearning.org/constructivism.htm).

Experiential learning: A process through which a learner constructs knowledge, skill, and value based on direct experiences. Engage students in critical thinking, problem solving, and decision making in contexts that are personally relevant and connected to academic learning objectives by incorporating active learning. This approach requires the making of opportunities for debriefing and consolidation of ideas and skills through reflection, feedback, and application of the ideas and skills to new situations (http://www.stolaf.edu/services/cel/definition.html).

GUI: GUI stands for graphical user interface. Most of the modern operating systems provide a GUI, which enables a user to use a pointing device, such as a computer mouse, to provide the computer with information about the user's intentions.

IEEE 802.11b/a/g: Generally refers to wireless LAN standards. The IEEE 802.11b is the wireless LAN standard with a maximum bandwidth of 11 Mbps operating at 2.4 GHz. The IEEE 802.11a is the high-speed wireless LAN with a maximum bandwidth of 54 Mbps operating at 5 GHz. The IEEE 802.11g is backward compatible with the IEEE 802.11b, with a maximum bandwidth of 54 Mbps operating at 2.4 GHz.

Infrastructure network: A class of wireless network architecture in which mobile stations communicate with each other via access points, which are usually linked to a wired backbone. Such a network has a fixed infrastructure and a centralized control.

MySQL: An open source relational database tool which is used for Web development (often used in conjunction with PHP).

NAT: Stands for Network Address Translation; a process of converting internal IP addresses to external ones and vice versa, establishing a sort of a "firewall" between a LAN and the rest of the network.

PHP: "Hypertext Preprocessor"; a general-purpose scripting language which can be embedded in HTML, widely used for Web development. It is compatible with a variety of database management systems.

TCP/IP: The family of protocols used for Internet communication.

Wired LAN: This term refers to a LAN which uses cable media (e.g., UTP Cat 5e) for LAN connectivity and typically covers a limited area, such as a room, a building, or a campus.

Wireless LAN: This term refers to a LAN which uses infrared or radio frequencies rather than physical cable as the transmission medium.

Review Questions

1. List and describe the main features of WebLan-Designer.

2. Discuss the difference between an ad hoc and an infrastructure wireless LAN.

3. State two advantages and two disadvantages of wireless LAN over wired LAN.

4. State two advantages and two disadvantages of wired LAN over wireless LAN.

5. Define the following key terms: ad hoc network, access point, infrastructure network, and wireless LAN.

6. Explain how WebLan-Designer can be used in the classroom as an aid to enhance teaching and learning LAN design.

7. Explain how WebLan-Designer can be used for class demonstration.

8. Explain how WebLan-Designer can be used to verify the solutions to LAN design exercises.

9. List and describe possible enhancements to WebLan-Designer.

References

Abe, K., Tateoka, T., Suzuki, M., Maeda, Y., Kono, K., & Watanabe, T. (2004). An integrated laboratory for processor organization, compiler design, and computer networking. *IEEE Transactions on Education, 47*(3), 311-320.

Bachmann, D. W., Segal, M. E., Srinivasan, M. M., & Teorey, T. J. (1991). NetMod: A design tool for large-scale heterogeneous campus networks. *IEEE Journal on Selected Areas in Communications, 9*(1), 15-24.

Berglund, A. (2003, November). What is good teaching of computer networks? *Proceedings of the 33rd ASEE/IEEE Frontiers in Education Conference*, Boulder, CO (pp. S2D13-S2D19).

Bhunia, C., Giri, S., Kar, S., Haldar, S., & Purkait, P. (2004). A low-cost PC-based virtual oscilloscope. *IEEE Transactions on Education, 47*(2), 295-299.

Bing, B. (2002). *Wireless local area networks: The new wireless revolution*. New York: Wiley.

Chang, R. K. C. (2004, June). Teaching computer networking with the help of personal computer networks. *Proceedings of the 9th annual SIGCSE conference on Innovation and Technology in Computer Science Education (ITiCSE)*, Leeds, UK (pp. 208-212).

Chang, X. (1999). Network simulations with Opnet. *Proceedings of the 1999 Winter Simulation Conference: Simulation - A Bridge to the Future* (pp. 307-314).

Chen, C. (2003). A constructivist approach to teaching: Implications in teaching computer networking. Information. Technology. *Learning and Performance Journal, 21*(2), 17-27.

Diab, H. B., & Tabbara, H. S. (1995). An educational tool for computer networks. *Australasian Journal of Engineering Education, 6*(1).

Dornan, A. (2002). *The essential guide to wireless communications applications: From cellular systems to Wi-Fi* (2nd ed.). Prentice Hall.

Fall, K., & Varadhan, K. (2003). *The ns manual*. Retrieved January 5, 2006, from http://www.isi.edu/nsnam/ns/

Garcia, J., & Alesanco, A. (2004). Web-Based system for managing a telematics laboratory network. *IEEE Transactions on Education, 47*(2), 284-294.

Hacker, C., & Sitte, R. (2004). Interactive teaching of elementary digital logic design with WinLogiLab. *IEEE Transactions on Education, 47*(2), 196-203.

Hong, J. W.-K., Kwon, S.-S., & Kim, J.-Y. (1999). WebTrafMon: Web-based Internet/intranet network traffic monitoring and analysis system. *Computer Communications, 22*(14), 1333-1342.

Kofke, D. A., & Mihalick, B. C. (2002). Web-based technologies for teaching and using molecular simulation. *Fluid Phase Equilibria, 194-197*, 327-335.

Kolb, A., & Kolb, D. A. (2004). *Learning styles and learning spaces: Enhancing the experimental learning in higher education*. Retrieved April 23, 2005, from http://www.learningfromexperience.com/images/uploads/Learning-styles-and-learning-spaces.pdf

Kolb, D. A., Boyatzis, R., & Mainemelis, C. (2000). Experimental learning theory: Previous research and new directions. In R. J. Sternberg & L. F. Zhang (Eds.), *Perspectives on cognitive, learning, and thinking styles*. NJ: Lawrence Erlbaum.

McDonald, C. (2004). *The cnet network simulator (v2.0.9)*. Retrieved January 5, 2006, from http://www.csse.uwa.edu.au/cnet/

Nieuwelaar, M. van den, & Hunt, R. (2004). Real-time carrier network traffic measurement, visualisation and topology modelling. *Computer Communications, 27*, 128-140.

Palmer, M., & Sinclair, R. B. (2003). *Guide to designing and implementing local and wide area networks* (2nd ed.). Canada: Course Technology.

Petrova, K. (2002, December 3-6). The quest for the best mix: An ongoing project in e-learning. *Proceedings of the International Conference on Computers in Education (ICCE)* (pp. 227-228).

Reinig, B., & The, J. (1998). Supporting higher education with the World Wide Web. *Journal of Computer Information Systems, 39*(1), 76-83.

Resnick, M. (2002). Rethinking learning in the digital age. In G. Kirkman, J. D. Sacns, K. Schwab, & P. Cornelius (Eds.), *The global information technology report 2001-2002: Readiness for the networked world* (pp. 31-37). Center for International Development, Harvard University.

Rokou, F. P., Rokos, Y., & Rokou, E. (2003, July). InfoLab: A Web learning pedagogical based content repurposing approach. *Proceedings of the 3rd IEEE International Conference on Advanced Learning Technologies (ICALT'03)*, Athens, Greece (pp. 150-154).

Sanchez, M., & Manzoni, P. (2001). ANEJOS: A Java based simulator for ad hoc networks. *Future Generation Computer Systems, 17*, 573-583.

Sarkar, N. I. (2004, August/September). WLAN-Designer: A Web-based software tool to enhance learning and teaching wireless LAN design. *Proceedings of the 4th IEEE International Conference on Advanced Learning Technologies*, Joensuu, Finland (pp. 260-261).

Sarkar, N. I., & Lian, J. H. (2003, July). LAN-Designer: A software tool for teaching and learning LAN design. *Proceedings of the 3rd IEEE International Conference on Advanced Learning Technologies*, Athens, Greece (pp. 624-628).

Shifroni, E., & Ginat, D. (1997). Simulation game for teaching communications protocols. *ACM SIGCSE Bulletin. Proceedings of the 28th SIGCSE Technical Symposium on Computer Science Education, 29*(1), 184-188.

Sitthiworachart, J., & Joy, M. (2003, July). Web-based peer assessment in learning computer programming. *Proceedings of the 3rd IEEE International Conference on Advanced Learning Technologies (ICALT'03)*, Athens, Greece (pp. 180-184).

Zheng, P., & Ni, L. M. (2003). EMPOWER: A network emulator for wireline and wireless networks. *Proceedings of the 22nd annual Joint Conference of the IEEE Computer and Communication Societies (INFOCOM)* (pp. 1933-1942).

Chapter III

INetwork:
An Interactive Learning Tool for Communication Networks

K. Sandrasegaran, The University of Technology Sydney, Australia

M. Trieu, The University of Technology Sydney, Australia

Abstract

A country or a nation would be immobilized without computers and data communication networks. Computer networking courses are being offered by not only universities and tertiary institutions but also many technical colleges and secondary schools worldwide. The cost associated with purchasing networking devices and equipment to enable students to gain practical experience in setting up a customised network can be significant. Therefore, networking fundamentals are taught by combination of textbooks and lecture-only methods in many schools and publicly funded tertiary institutions. This chapter describes the development and use of an interactive learning tool called iNetwork for teaching and learning computer communication networks. iNetwork provides an environment in which students can experiment with different network configurations and gain hands-on learning experience in computer and data communication networks without the need for expensive equipment.

Learning Objectives

After completing this chapter, you will be able to:

- List and describe the main features of iNetwork.
- Discuss the usefulness of iNetwork in teaching and learning contexts.
- Explain how iNetwork can be used in the classroom to enhance teaching and learning various aspects of computer communication networks.
- Define the following key terms: ARP, DHCP, DNS, firewall, OSPF, RIP, TCP/IP, and VPN.
- Suggest further enhancements to iNetwork.

Introduction

Communication networks form an important part of business and society today. As the Internet has continued to expand, so has the demand for education in networking. Traditionally providers of networking subjects and courses were limited to universities and technical colleges. At present, IT and networking subjects are being introduced into most high schools. The cost involved with providing every student with the equipment necessary to set up a practical network is significant, particularly for schools and publicly funded tertiary institutions, and consequently most networking concepts are taught using a combination of standard textbook- and lecture-based approaches and limited laboratories on small networks.

In this chapter, we present a solution to the above-mentioned resource and cost problem which aims at improving the way networking is commonly taught. Our solution will allow users to gain authentic practice in experimenting with different network configurations without the cost of providing each student with their own networking equipment. The chapter reports on the requirements, development, and evaluation of an interactive learning tool called iNetwork, which allows users to assemble and simulate custom networks composed of commonly used networking devices. iNetwork lets students simulate the running of these custom-built networks, identify problems, and learn more about communication networks.

In the development of iNetwork, a packet-capturing software was used to monitor the behaviour of an experimental network. The data thus obtained was integrated into this tool so that it could simulate the real-life behaviour of a network. The iNetwork Software allows users to configure real-life networks as the software emulates configuration settings (e.g., IP addresses and routing tables) obtained from commercial network equipment. The iNetwork Software was evaluated by a number of undergraduate engineering students through a survey. The results of the survey are presented at the end of the chapter. This is followed by a conclusion and future work.

Background and Motivation

In general, the motivation for building an interactive learning tool is to improve the quality of education by supplementing the work done in the classroom with appropriate and realistic laboratory or practical work. The basis for the use of computers as an educational tool is well supported by evidence from researchers in the educational field. Bloom (1984) reports that conventional teaching, that is, teacher in front of 20 to 200 students, provides one of the least effective methods for educational delivery, and one-to-one tutoring is far superior to conventional teaching and is the most effective educational delivery method. Studies on human retention conclude that instructional environments that use several human senses result in better retention: On average people retain 25% of what they hear; 45% of what they hear and see; and 70% of what they hear, see, and do (Edwards, 1985). A computer equipped with the appropriate hardware and software provides an excellent medium to invoke visual, auditory, and tactile senses. Edwards reports that information is better retained if a student is an active participant rather than a passive absorber during the learning phase.

Interactive learning environments (ILEs) provide an opportunity for students to do tasks relevant to information gathered in the classroom. A student's attention is heightened by the interactivity of the system. The availability of the tool at all times of the day coupled with the fact that the tool can be used without constant human supervision is an added bonus to the student. Furthermore, the fact that the pace of learning is controlled by the student will assist learning. Interactive learning environments provide a protected environment where students can explore and perform actions without the fear of real-life consequences, such as damaging costly equipment, components, and so forth. Another possible use is for simulation of fault scenarios that are difficult to observe due to infrequent occurrence, thus preparing the student to handle such situations in real life. Training should be possible in remote areas where expertise or equipment may not be readily available, thus promoting distant learning.

A number of ILEs have been successfully trialled in the field. One example of this is the system known as Sherlock, which was developed to teach air-force trainees the skills of electronic troubleshooting. It has been reported that trainees using the Sherlock tutor for 20 to 25 hours gained proficiency equivalent to that of trainees with four years' on-the-job experience (Lesgold, Lajoie, Bunzo, & Eggan, 1992). Another ILE to be reportedly successfully trialled in the field is the LISP tutor (Anderson, 1990), which provided students with programming exercises and tutorial assistance. The times to complete identical exercises under various tutoring strategies were 11.4 hours (human one-to-one tutored), 15.0 hours (LISP tutored), and 26.5 hours (conventional teaching). These successes provide some of the motivation for this work on developing an interactive learning tool for communication networks.

A small number of proprietary tools that serve a similar purpose as the iNetwork Software currently exist. The main problem with these proprietary tools is that they heavily specialise in certain market products, protocols, and operating systems. For example, RouterSim (http://www.routersim.com) and Boson NetSim (http://www.boson.com/netsim) focus much on configuring Cisco routers and switches using Cisco's proprietary operating system. Due to these reasons, these tools have become inappropriate learning tools for students undertaking fundamental networking subjects.

Description of the System

The iNetwork Software is an interactive learning tool that focuses mainly on general data communication networks. It aims at teaching anyone the fundamentals of communication networks and internetworking and was built based on a number of features that have made RouterSim's Network Visualizer very popular. Such features include operating system emulation and user-friendly interface. The software was developed based on principles of network operation that were covered in a Communication Network Subject (Sandrasegaran, 2003) and other resources (Davis, n.d.; Lavigne, 2001; Network Sorcery, n.d.; Stallings, 2000).

iNetwork allows users to assemble or build custom networks using common networking devices, including workstations, switches, routers, domain name system (DNS) servers, and Dynamic Host Configuration Protocol (DHCP) servers. The tool allows users to simulate communication between devices, allowing users to identify and troubleshoot problems in their custom-built networks. Users can develop a better understanding of the workings of a communication network by simulating communication between networking devices.

Software Requirements

The iNetwork Software was designed to satisfy the following requirements:

Graphical User Interface Requirements

- The iNetwork Software interface shall be graphical and easy to use.
- It will allow for drag and drop functionality when assembling a network so to allow users the ability to build networks.
- The GUI should contain drop-down menus or icons containing fundamental networking devices, such as workstations, switches, routers, and so forth.
- It should allow the properties of network elements to be specified by left-clicking on the network objects on the GUI.
- It will allow users to save and load custom-built networks for future use.

Networking Requirements

- The networking devices will include workstations, switches, routers, servers, and cables. More sophisticated networking components, such as firewalls and coaxial cables, will be implemented in the future releases of iNetwork.
- The workstation device will act as a simple computer. For the first release of iNetwork, it was decided that the majority of emulation of networking elements will be performed using these workstations.
- The server device will be an extension of a workstation but with additional services such as DNS service and DHCP services.
- For iNetwork Release 1, the switch device will have up to four ports to allow a maximum of four network elements to be attached to it.
- The router device will have up to three network interfaces to allow for communication between three different networks in Release 1.
- The router device shall allow for static routing. Features such as adding routes, deleting routes, and modifying routes should be available.
- The router device shall allow dynamic routing. The software shall emulate dynamic routing protocols such as RIP, OSPF, or both.
- The functions of the networking devices should mimic real-life networking devices as closely as possible. For example, all networking interfaces should have a MAC address, switches should have a MAC-interface memory table, and so on.

- The workstations and servers should adopt common TCP/IP properties, similar to the ones found in Microsoft Windows. The routers shall also adopt a similar setting for each of its network interfaces.

- The DHCP server should allow for IP addresses, gateway addresses, and DNS addresses to be leased. Another important requirement is to display an address lease table showing leased addresses.

- The DNS server should allow for mapping of IP addresses to hostnames and vice versa. There should be options to add, change, and remove DNS entries.

- The software should emulate configuration settings obtained from real-life commercial network equipment, giving users exposure to the set of parameters that requires configuring in real-life networks; for example, subnet mask, gateway, and DNS servers.

- The interface to configuring the configuration setting the TCP/IP properties on the software should be similar to ones found on a Microsoft Windows operating system.

Simulation Requirements

- If required, it should provide users with an output to track events that occur during simulation when users invoke a command; for example, output showing important packet header information that is sent during DNS resolution.

- It should allow users to test their custom-built networks using DOS/UNIX utilities, such as ping, tracert, route, arp, and ipconfig.

- The ipconfig command shall display appropriate settings of components. The layout of output shall be similar to the ipconfig command under DOS.

- The route command shall display the routing tables of the workstation or server. The layout of output shall be similar to the route command under DOS.

- The ping simulation shall have similar output to DOS pings upon successful and unsuccessful pings.

- The tracert simulation shall display the list of intermediate network nodes required to reach the destination from the source. The layout of output shall be similar to the tracert command under DOS.

- The ARP simulation shall allow for adding of IP-MAC addresses, removal of IP-MAC mappings, flushing of ARP cache, and displaying of ARP cache. The layout of output shall be similar to the ARP command under DOS.

Software Architecture

The iNetwork tool is written in C# using Microsoft Visual Student .NET 2003. To run the software, a computer loaded with Windows 2000/XP, Microsoft .NET framework, and the iNetwork executable is required. The top-level architecture of the iNetwork Software is shown in Figure 1. There are four important components, namely, the graphical user interface (GUI), the device simulator, the network simulator, and the network calculator.

The iNetwork core components perform the following functions:

- The GUI component allows user interaction with iNetwork. It allows users to build their own networks by adding, removing, and configuring the properties of networking devices.

- The network simulator (or emulator) component emulates common networking utilities such as ipconfig, ping, tracert, and arp.

- The device simulator component emulates a variety of real-life networking devices such as switches, routers, workstations, servers, and so forth.

- The network calculator component performs mathematical and logical calculations. These include calculating network ID, determining if an address is within the correct subnet, calculating appropriate destination routes, checking ARP tables, and so on.

During the development phase of the software, a prototype was built. Feedback from the iNetwork Software prototype indicated that the user interface was of considerable importance as an interactive learning tool. As seen in Figure 2, the iNetwork GUI is tidy, consistent, informative, and appealing.

Figure 1. Core components of iNetwork

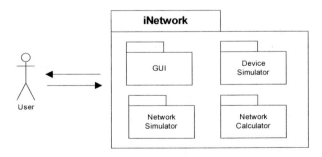

Figure 2. iNetwork Software interface

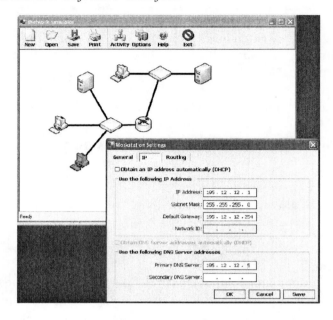

Usefulness and Benefits of the System

The iNetwork Software eliminates the cost associated with purchasing, setting up, and maintaining hardware and software required to provide users with practical experience in computer networking. It provides an environment that is available to students at all times. Students can explore networking without the fear of disturbing a live network. Another benefit is the ability to teach networking concepts more effectively because the students are engaging with the concepts on an interactive and explorative basis.

The software is capable of simulating many hardware devices, allowing users to build fairly complex networks all on a single computer. The software can be upgraded to cover other important aspects of communication networks such as network security. The upgrades could include adding additional networking components such as firewalls and wireless access points.

Lecturers and trainers can design laboratory exercises for students and allow them to work through the exercises either in class or from home without supervision. This provides students with the opportunity to learn at their own pace. Distance learning of networking should be possible in remote areas where expertise or equipment may not be readily available.

The iNetwork Software provides an environment in which students can practice or perform tasks relevant to information gathered in the lectures or laboratory.

Some of the features of this tool — for example, capturing and viewing the contents of packets, flushing the contents of memory — are beneficial for a detailed understanding of network operation.

Typical Laboratory Exercise

To demonstrate the usefulness of the software, a typical laboratory exercise performed by an iNetwork user is described below.

Step 1

Double Click on iNetSim.exe to start the interactive learning tool. Note that the application has a toolbar with buttons to save, open, and print your network schematics. The white surface underneath the toolbar is your workspace and will be used to build your network.

Step 2

If you right click anywhere within the white workspace, a menu will appear with a list of networking devices similar to the one shown in Figure 3.

Step 3

Add six workstations and two switches onto the workspace. To move the device, left click on a device and hold the mouse button down. Move the networking devices to a suitable location as shown in Figure 4.

Step 4

Right click on the top left workstation and a menu will appear as shown in Figure 5.

Figure 3. List of networking devices

| Add Workstation |
| Add DHCP Server |
| Add DNS Server |
| Add Switch |
| Add Router |

Figure 4. Device layout

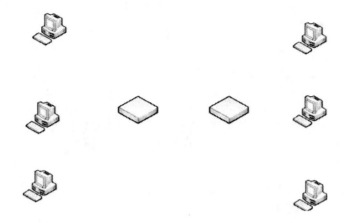

Figure 5. Workstation menu

Step 5

Select Connect with Cable, and draw a cable to the switch. When both the switch and workstation are highlighted in green, right click for the cable to be drawn as shown in Figure 6.

Step 6

Continue to draw all the remaining cables as shown in Figure 8.

Step 7

Right click on a workstation and select Configure IP. A window will pop up, allowing users to enter an IP address for the workstation. Provide the workstation with the addresses as shown in Figure 9, and then click on OK.

Figure 6. Connecting device with cable

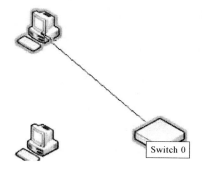

Figure 7. Connecting device with cable

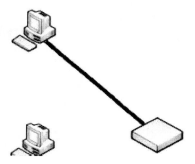

Figure 8. Connecting networks

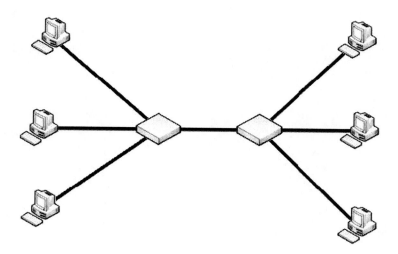

Figure 9. Connecting networks

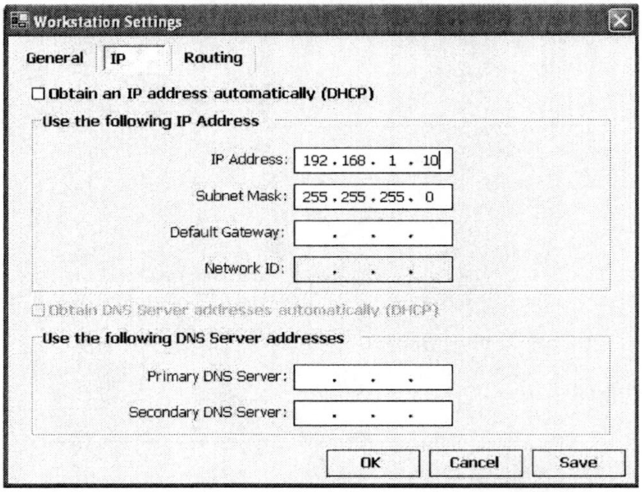

Step 8

Configure another workstation with an IP address of 192.168.1.20 and a subnet mask of 255.255.255.0.

Step 9

Right click on the workstation that was given the IP address of 192.168.1.10 and select Command Prompt. Type "ipconfig" and press Enter; the output should be as shown in Figure 10.

Step 10

Type "ping 192.168.1.20" and press Enter; if everything was set up correctly, the output should be as shown in Figure 11.

Note that the output of the ping command in the iNetwork Software is similar to the output found on Windows XP, if the same command were entered on a Windows XP workstation. This allows students to familiarise themselves with the outputs received from commercial operating systems.

Step 11

Close the Command Prompt by typing "exit."

Figure 10. Command Prompt

```
Command Prompt
Microsoft windows XP [version 5.1.2600]
(C) Copyright 1985-2001 Microsoft Corp

C:\WINDOWS>ipconfig

windows IP Configuration

Ethernet adapter Local Area Connection:

        Connection-specific DNS suffix  . : uts.edu.au
        IP Address. . . . . . . . . . . . : 192.168.1.10
        Subnet Mask . . . . . . . . . . . : 255.255.255.0
        Default Gateway . . . . . . . . . :

C:\WINDOWS>
```

Figure 11. Successful ping

```
Command Prompt
Microsoft windows XP [version 5.1.2600]
(C) Copyright 1985-2001 Microsoft Corp

C:\WINDOWS>ping 192.168.1.20

Pinging 192.168.1.20 with 32 bytes of data:

Reply from 192.168.1.20: bytes=32 time=1ms TTL=128
Reply from 192.168.1.20: bytes=32 time=1ms TTL=128
Reply from 192.168.1.20: bytes=32 time=1ms TTL=128
Reply from 192.168.1.20: bytes=32 time=1ms TTL=128

Ping statistics for 192.168.1.20:
        Packets: Sent = 4, Received = 4, Lost = 0 (0% loss),
Approximate round trip times in milli-seconds:
        Minimum = 1ms, Maximum = 1ms, Average = 1ms

C:\WINDOWS>
```

Step 12

Click on the Activity icon on the toolbar and an Activity Log window will appear as shown in Figure 12. The activity log provides detailed information on activities occurring during the simulation process. Step through the activities to trace exactly what was going on for the successful ping to occur.

Another possible use is simulation of network fault scenarios that rarely occur in real-life troubleshooting, thus preparing the student to handle such situations in real life. A typical example would be to provide students with the network shown in Figure 13. We can purposely introduce an error in the network by

Figure 12. Activity Log

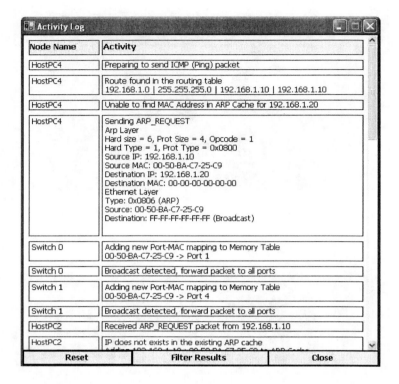

providing an incorrect DNS server address to pc2. We can then get students to determine why pc1 is able to ping the DNS server as shown in Figure 14, whereas pc2 is experiencing a problem as shown in Figure 15. Students can then perform a combination of tasks that includes running ipconfig to check the IP configurations, inspecting the DNS hostname mappings, pinging the DNS server using its IP address, or tracing through the activity logs to understand the DNS communication process. Students should then be able to isolate the problem and apply a suitable fix to resolve the problem.

Complex Scenario

A more complex scenario is shown in Figure 16. In this scenario, we might have a router with some missing routes in its routing table. Students may be asked to determine why pc1 can communicate with pc2 and pc3, whereas pc2 can only communicate with pc1. Students can then run a variety of tests on the network,

Figure 13. Simple network with a name resolution problem

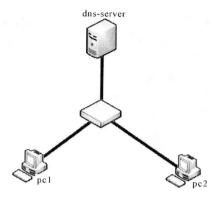

Figure 14. PC1 is able to ping DNS server

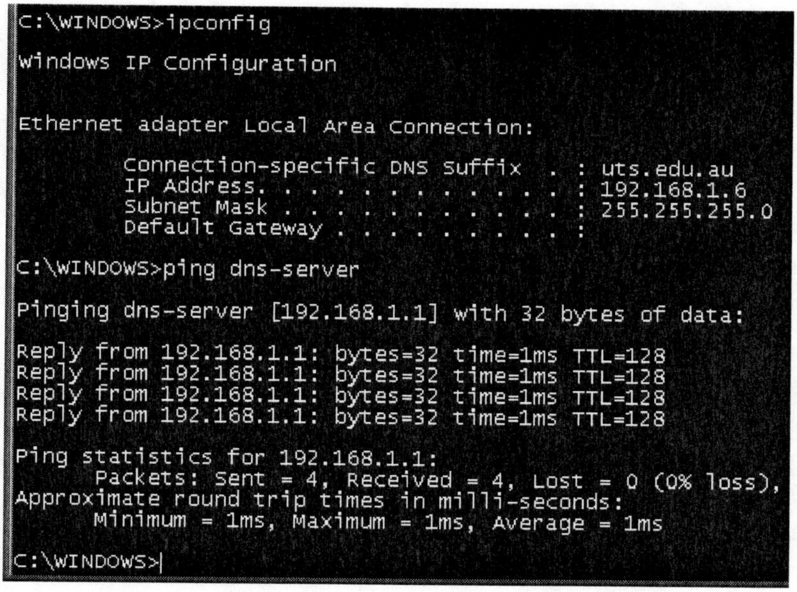

```
C:\WINDOWS>ipconfig

windows IP Configuration


Ethernet adapter Local Area Connection:

        Connection-specific DNS suffix  . : uts.edu.au
        IP Address. . . . . . . . . . . . : 192.168.1.6
        Subnet Mask . . . . . . . . . . . : 255.255.255.0
        Default Gateway . . . . . . . . . :

C:\WINDOWS>ping dns-server

Pinging dns-server [192.168.1.1] with 32 bytes of data:

Reply from 192.168.1.1: bytes=32 time=1ms TTL=128
Reply from 192.168.1.1: bytes=32 time=1ms TTL=128
Reply from 192.168.1.1: bytes=32 time=1ms TTL=128
Reply from 192.168.1.1: bytes=32 time=1ms TTL=128

Ping statistics for 192.168.1.1:
        Packets: Sent = 4, Received = 4, Lost = 0 (0% loss),
Approximate round trip times in milli-seconds:
        Minimum = 1ms, Maximum = 1ms, Average = 1ms

C:\WINDOWS>
```

Figure 15. PC2 is unable to ping DNS server

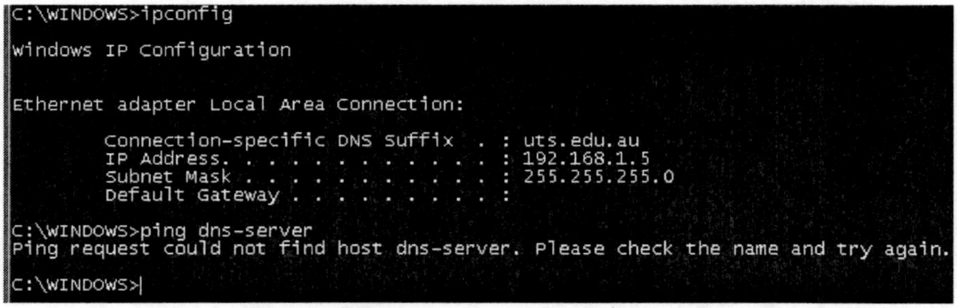

C:\WINDOWS>ipconfig
Windows IP Configuration
Ethernet adapter Local Area Connection:
Connection-specific DNS Suffix . : uts.edu.au
IP Address. . . . . : 192.168.1.5
Subnet Mask . . . . : 255.255.255.0
Default Gateway . . . . :
C:\WINDOWS>ping dns-server
Ping request could not find host dns-server. Please check the name and try again.
C:\WINDOWS>

Figure 16. A network with routing problems

pc2
router1
pc1
router2
router3
pc3

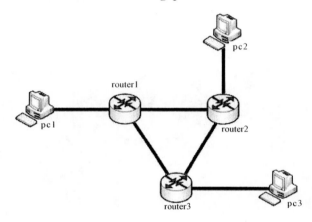

either using the ping or tracert utilities. As shown in Figure 17, students may then experiment with adding and removing routes in a router's routing table in an attempt to find a solution to the problem. Additional follow-up exercises where students are asked to fix the problem using dynamic routing (RIP) will only further strengthen their understanding of routing.

Experimental Investigation

To ensure that the iNetwork Software performs accurate simulation, a real (physical) experimental local area network was set up as shown in Figure 18. The experimental local area network consisted of a switch and three workstations,

Figure 17. Adding routes to a router's routing table

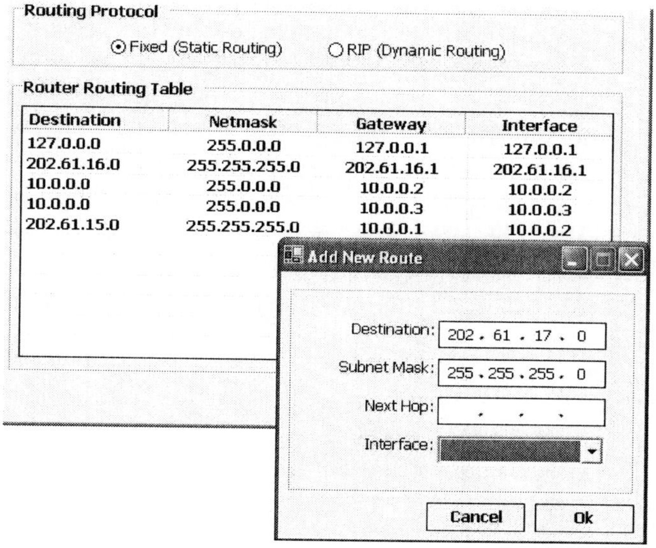

Routing Protocol
Fixed (Static Routing)
RIP (Dynamic Routing)
Router Routing Table
Destination
Netmask
Gateway
Interface
127.0.0.0
255.0.0.0
127.0.0.1
127.0.0.1
202.61.16.0
255.255.255.0
202.61.16.1
202.61.16.1
10.0.0.0
255.0.0.0
10.0.0.2
10.0.0.2
10.0.0.0
255.0.0.0
10.0.0.3
10.0.0.3
202.61.15.0
255.255.255.0
10.0.0.1
10.0.0.2
Add New Route
Destination: 202 . 61 . 17 . 0
Subnet Mask: 255 . 255 . 255 . 0
Next Hop:
Interface:
Cancel
Ok

Figure 18. Experimental laboratory configuration used to retrieve TCP/IP simulation data for the iNetwork Software

Internet
Windows XP
192.168.1.2
100 Mbps
100 Mbps
100 Mbps
8 Port
Dlink Switch
100 Mbps
Windows 2000 Server
192.168.1.1
10.0.0.1
138.130.188.235
10 Mbps
Motorola
Cable Modem
Windows XP
192.168.1.6

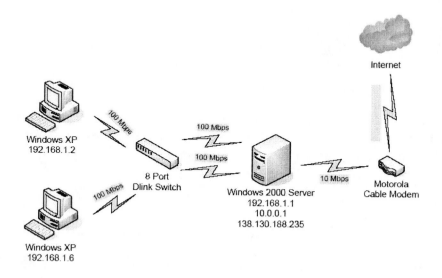

with one workstation also acting as a router. This configuration was sufficient to capture most TCP/IP data traffic that will flow in a real network.

Different types of network traffic were generated in this experimental network, including ARP request, ARP Reply, ICMP Request (Ping), ICMP Reply (Ping), ICMP Request (Tracert), ICMP Reply (Tracert), DNS Query, DNS Response, DHCP Discover Message, DHCP Offer, DHCP Request, DHCP ACK, and RIP v1 Response traffic. Network behaviour data was captured through the use of Ethereal, which is a freely available packet capturing software. The results from Ethereal were documented and analysed carefully. The results of the analysis have been used to design the simulation components of the iNetwork Software. This ensures that simulation output from the GUI is accurate and detailed.

Evaluation and Interpretation

The iNetwork Software was evaluated in June 2004 by 37 undergraduate engineering students (20 male and 17 female) from the University of Technology Sydney (UTS) who were undergoing the 48740 Communication Networks subject. The evaluation survey consisted of several laboratory exercises which the students were asked to complete. Upon completing the exercises, students were asked to assess the iNetwork Software based on factors revolving around functionality and usability. The results of the survey have been statistically compiled and presented in Figure 19. The survey provides an indication of the strengths and weaknesses of the iNetwork Software.

Only one student reported that the iNetwork would not be useful as a laboratory tool for 48740 Communication Networks with the reason being that the student could not run the iNetwork Software from home using the Linux operating system. Since a large number of users run Microsoft operating systems, the results from the surveys proved to be very positive.

Conclusion

In this chapter, a description of the motivation, requirements, design, benefits, usage, and evaluation of the iNetwork Release1 Software has been presented. The software requirements analysis, design, and implementation have been successful. Evaluation of the software by students at UTS was very positive.

Figure 19. Students' response to survey

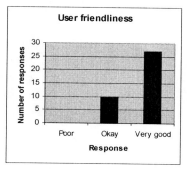

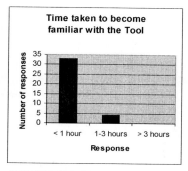

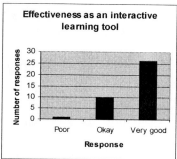

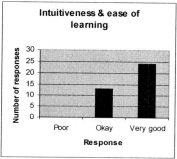

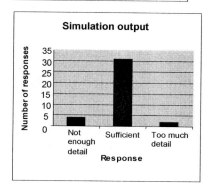

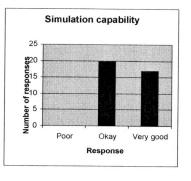

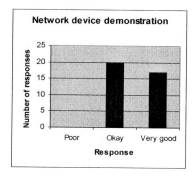

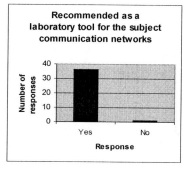

Evaluation by other groups of students at high schools is also envisaged for the near future. A number of options are available to further improve the iNetwork Software and enhance its use as a learning tool. These options include adding additional networking devices such as firewalls, Web servers, mail servers, virtual private networks (VPNs), and wireless networks and devices such as access points and wireless LAN cards. Students who have completed the evaluation survey have suggested adding animation, improving the simulation interface, and reducing the occurrences of bugs when running the iNetwork Software. More complex problem-solving scenarios are planned for the future.

For students to obtain the most educational benefit from the iNetwork Software, prior knowledge of communication networks is required. The tool is best used as a supplementary tool to further reinforce and extend students' understanding of certain network topics. One of the major problems with the iNetwork Software is its ability to be upgraded. Due to the existing design adopted, external developers will find it difficult adding additional network devices to the iNetwork Software. This problem can be addressed by spending more time redesigning critical modules in the software.

In light of the survey responses, the iNetwork Software proves to have much potential. With educational institutions facing economical constraints and budgetary cutbacks, the iNetwork Software serves as an ideal solution for not only preventing the loss or degradation of learning outcomes but also possibly enhancing students' learning and understanding of communication networks.

Acknowledgments

Acknowledgments to Anthony Kadi and Keiko Yasukawa for reviewing this manuscript and the students of 48740 Communication Networks (Autumn 2004) for taking the survey.

Summary

The computer communication network is an important topic for many computer networking courses around the globe. Unfortunately, it is difficult to motivate students to learn computer communication networks because many students appear to find the topic technical and rather dry and boring. This chapter described the development and use of a software tool (called iNetwork) for teaching and learning communication networks.

Both the teacher and students can benefit for the use of iNetwork in different teaching and learning contexts. A teacher is able to use it in the classroom as a demonstration, to liven up the lecture environment. Students, on the other hand, can use the system in developing a better understanding of the communication networks. Through experimenting with key parameters, the students gain insights into the key concepts of communication network design and analysis. The software has been tested and found to be robust. Student responses to the survey were mostly favourable. The students indicated that they had found iNetwork easy to use and helpful in gaining an understanding of communication networks concepts.

Key Terms and Definitions

ARP: Address Resolution Protocol is used to translate between IP addresses and hardware addresses. There is an arp utility found on both Microsoft and UNIX operating systems which can be used to view and modify the ARP cache.

DHCP: Dynamic Host Control Protocol is a service used to provide dynamic IP addresses for client workstations.

DNS: The domain name system is a service used to map between hostnames and IP addresses and allow for resolution of hostnames to IP addresses.

Firewall: A software application running on a device that is responsible for filtering incoming and outgoing traffic.

GUI: A graphical user interface is a computer application which interacts with its users via graphical interface rather than command line instructions.

iNetwork Software: An interactive learning tool that teaches students about data communication and networking.

OSPF: Open Shortest Path First is a dynamic routing protocol used to update routing tables in routers using a more sophisticated routing algorithm.

Ping: A network diagnostic tool found on both Microsoft and UNIX operating systems that is used to show communication successes or failures between nodes.

RIP: Routing Information Protocol is a dynamic routing protocol used to update the routing tables in routers.

TCP/IP: Transmission Control Protocol/Internet Protocol is a protocol used to facilitate communication between computers.

Tracert: A network diagnostic tool found on both Microsoft and UNIX operating systems. The diagnostic tool is used to track the path of network communication.

VPN: A virtual private network Is a networking technology that involves network tunnels being created between nodes within a public network.

Web server: A software application running on a computer that is responsible for serving Web pages on a network.

Wireless network: A network that is not constrained by cable and relies on high-frequency radio waves for communication.

Review Questions

1. List and describe three important features of iNetwork.

2. Explain how iNetwork can be used in the laboratory to enhance teaching and learning computer communication networks.

3. Explain how you would add and remove routes in the router's routing tables.

4. Explain how iNetwork can be configured to capture data traffic from a LAN.

5. Define the following key terms: ARP, DHCP, DNS, firewall, OSPF, RIP, TCP/IP, and VPN.

6. List and describe possible enhancements to iNetwork.

References

Anderson, J. (1990). Diagnostic monitoring of skill and knowledge acquisition. In N. Fredericksen et al. (Eds.), *Analysis of student performance with LISP Tutor*. Hillsdale, NJ: Lawrence Earlbaum.

Bloom, B. S. (1984). The 2 sigma problem: The search for methods of group instruction as effective as one-to-one tutoring. *Educational Researcher*, *13*, 3-16.

Davis, D. (n.d.). *Select the right routing protocol for your network*. Retrieved May 14, 2004, from http://techrepublic.com.com/5100-6265-1040261.html

Edwards, M. (1985). The Mercedes Benz of interactive video. *Hardcopy, 14,* 74-80.

Lavigne, D. (2001). *Examining ICMP packets.* Retrieved December 20, 2003, from http://www.onlamp.com/pub/a/bsd/2001/04/04/FreeBSD_Basics.html

Lesgold, A., Lajoie, S., Bunzo, M., & Eggan, C. (1992). SHERLOCK: A coached practice environment for an electronics troubleshooting job. In R. W. Chabay & J. H. Larkin (Eds.), *Computer assisted instruction and intelligent tutoring systems: Establishing communication and collaboration.* Hillsdale, NJ: Lawrence Erlbaum.

Network Sorcery. (n.d.). *RFC sourcebook.* Retrieved February 23, 2004, from http://www.networksorcery.com/enp/default0602.htm

Sandrasegaran, K. (2003). *Supplementary Communication Networks lecture notes.* Sydney, Australia: University of Technology Sydney.

Stallings, W. (2000). *Data & computer communications* (6th ed.) NJ: Prentice Hall.

Chapter IV

Effectively Using a Network Simulation Tool to Enhance Students' Understanding of Computer Networking Concepts

Cecil Goldstein, Queensland University of Technology, Australia

Karen Stark, Queensland University of Technology, Australia

Susanna Leisten, Queensland University of Technology, Australia

Alan Tickle, Queensland University of Technology, Australia

Abstract

This chapter discusses the effective use of a simulation tool in the teaching of data communication concepts. Because such concepts can be abstract and therefore difficult to visualise and understand, simulation can help facilitate learning. In looking to develop a structured approach to optimally utilising a network simulator in teaching networking concepts, a series of targeted exercises were developed. These applied the principles of active learning to the use of the simulator in practical exercises to encourage independent and analytical processes and facilitate deeper learning. The background to this, as well as the design and implementation of the exercises, is presented. Similarly, the features of an appropriate network simulator that can be effectively used in this context are discussed, and a brief overview of the simulation tool used, Packet Tracer, is given. To illustrate the methodology, examples are provided from the actual exercises given to students. The system was also evaluated through an experiment that measured the improvement in understanding of a particular topic, switched networks, after students participated in a practical on this topic using the exercises discussed. A clear increase in understanding was shown. The incorporation of the simulator in developing case studies to progressively integrate concepts learned as an ongoing, practical exercise is also presented. In addition, the use of simulation to learn troubleshooting skills and strategies by employing a simulated network containing deliberately created errors that need to be resolved is discussed.

Learning Objectives

After completing this chapter, you will be able to:

*   Develop exercises using a network simulator to enhance the teaching and learning of data communications concepts in large classes.
*   Apply the principles of active learning in a practical teaching environment.
*   Utilise the methods detailed to encourage independent learning of such concepts as collisions, Internetworking, IP addressing, ping, protocols, and routing.
*   Use the ideas outlined as a basis for innovation in the application of a simulator in teaching networking.
*   Suggest further enhancements to the laboratory activities described in this chapter.

Introduction

The challenge of teaching data communications in depth to a large cohort of students is compounded by the fact that the subject material is inherently intangible, is difficult to visualise, and is conceptually different than what students are usually familiar with. Data moving across a network and network processes such as routing cannot readily be "seen." Similarly, a concept like protocol layering, which refers to peer protocols when talking of communication but to a protocol hierarchy when talking of data transfer, can often appear contradictory until really understood. Unlike, for instance, the study of programming, where many concepts (e.g., conditional loops) are directly paralleled in an actual language construct and then used in real coding exercises, network behaviour and ideas cannot be so readily shown. Indeed, because of the considerable resources required, it is difficult, if not impossible, to expose a large class of students studying networking even to basic tools such as "sandpit" networks or some real network devices.

In teaching a second-year subject in Internetworking at the Queensland University of Technology in Brisbane, we have, like others in this area, sought to overcome these limitations and to enhance the learning experience for our students by utilising various tools and techniques. These have included simulation, visualisation, animation, demonstration, and use of analogy. While such methods generally seem to have a positive effect on the teaching environment and are received favourably by students, two issues have concerned us: whether there were ways in which we could improve our use of these tools, and whether such tools actually aided the learning process and led to a deeper understanding.

Since one of the main tools we use in supporting our teaching is a network simulator, we determined to focus our efforts on developing and evaluating an approach to using simulation in a structured manner, so as to provide a framework to facilitate active independent learning. This does not detract from the use of simulation to demonstrate activities and for stepped, recipe-type exercises, such as router configuration, but represents a specific effort to use the simulator to provide a directed, flexible, and engaging environment for the student to learn independently even when removed from immediate teacher support.

This chapter will outline the way we designed, structured, and implemented a set of practical exercises to achieve this purpose, the nature of the simulation tool we used, and how we evaluated the effectiveness of this approach. We will further comment on the use of the simulation tool in developing a framework for an ongoing practical exercise linking material together from week to week and using the simulator to teach troubleshooting skills. It should also be emphasized that our approach was geared to working with a large teaching class of 350 to 400 students and that the needs and dynamics are therefore different from working with a small (10 to 15) group in a workshop or lab environment with accessibility to actual network equipment.

Background and Motivation

Understanding networks and how networks operate requires an understanding of concepts and processes that are both complex and abstruse. The tools that can be used to demonstrate, simulate, or visualise networks and network behaviours lend themselves very readily to teaching in this area. Some tools, such as network or packet analysers, are utilities employed professionally in the industry, and their very use is in itself is an important skill. Others, such as simulators, are expressly for the purposes of teaching and learning and are generally used to create a specific environment which enables the student or trainee to interact as if in the real situation. In this respect, simulators can mimic reality very closely. A flight simulator can create an environment so authentic that even sensory stimuli such as motion, sound, and visuals are evident. Others simply provide a representation of the reality in a different format, allowing actions to be observed and demonstrated. For example, a queuing simulator might simply show the behaviour of a queue as a graph of numbers in a queue against time waited in that queue. Simulators become more effective when parameters can be changed, randomly or specifically, to create different scenarios requiring different responses or reactions from the student. Furthermore, by recording the student's interaction their performance can be later analysed and lessons learned.

Network simulators usually enable a network to be designed and built dynamically as a computer-based graphic by placing network devices as icons on a screen and connecting these devices. This visualisation in itself immediately makes the material more tangible. A network is then more realistic, even though it is actually a graphic! It makes it easier to understand the components and nature of a genuine network, which we can often see parts of (devices, computers, cabling) but cannot generally observe in its entirety or at its lower level of operation. The simulated network can be configured by opening simulated interfaces to the different devices and setting the various parameters required, such as, for example, network interface addresses and gateway addresses. The level of configuration and authenticity of the device interfaces will depend on the sophistication of the simulator. In the simulator we used, it was possible to configure devices using a simple graphical interface or a console window that very effectively replicated a subset of IOS (Internetwork Operating System) commands. This will be discussed in greater detail later in the chapter.

When we initially introduced the simulator into practical sessions, the exercises used were mainly "recipe" based, stepping the students through a series of configuration exercises to build a network and then testing this by using simulated "pings." While students appeared to enjoy doing this, the learning outcomes were in many cases largely limited to the rote learning of commands. Indeed, the work of learning theorists such as Biggs (1999), Salomon (2000), and Ehrmann (1995) indicates that without engaging in sound pedagogical practice, the use of simulation tools can be limited in their effectiveness. Educators such as Ramsden (1992), Entwistle (1981), and Biggs distinguish between deep and surface approaches to learning. Biggs, for example, describes the *surface approach* to learning as "an intention to complete a task with the minimum effort." In contrast, the *deep approach* to learning "arises from a felt need to engage the task appropriately and meaningfully" (Biggs, p. 16). Deep learning approaches have been "consistently associated with the types of quality outcomes appropriate for higher education" (Cope, 2003, p. 135).

Just performing tasks in a simulation exercise, while appearing to impart a good understanding, is surface learning and generally does not provide the student with a deep understanding of the issue. Indeed, student performance over a number of semesters showed no marked difference in understanding between the semesters when the simulator was used and earlier semesters when it was not. The use of the simulator did however appear to add to students' enjoyment of the classes and did improve their skills in actually interacting and configuring devices such as routers and switches. The question then asked was, could surface learning be reduced and deep learning increased, particularly when students are working independently, and could we develop a framework, using the simulation tool to effectively implement this?

"It's not just the tool, but the educational rationale that counts" (Salomon, 2000). Salomon believes that the assumption that a tool alone can achieve optimum learning outcomes is misdirected. He states: "Whether information is turned into meaningful knowledge or stays as a collection of scattered bits and pieces, like an assortment of screws and nails in a shoe box, greatly depends on numerous factors, and technology plays but a minor role among them." It is essential to consider the specific learning objective when deciding how a tool should be used. Perkins and Salomon (1992) distinguish between near transfer (to closely related contexts and performances) and far transfer (to rather different contexts and performances). If the objective is to train a student in the operation of a device, this is near transfer and the approach might be to include a series of repetitive tasks. However, if the objective is far transfer, as it is in our case, then we need to involve the student in "deliberate effortful abstraction and a search for connections" (Perkins & Salomon, p. 2). In considering the pedagogical approach to address this, we felt that the methods suggested in the application of active learning could be incorporated to achieve our objective.

Active learning can be seen as "instructional activities involving students in doing things and thinking about what they are doing" (Bonwell & Eison, 1991). Bonwell and Eison explain that a framework that promotes active learning should include higher-order thinking tasks such as problem solving, analysis, synthesis, and evaluation. Such a framework challenges the student and encourages deeper understanding. Our objective was to design practical exercises that used the simulation tool for active learning and so facilitated a deeper understanding of network concepts.

There appears to be very little literature that specifically seeks to evaluate the effectiveness of using simulation tools. In the teaching of ICT (information and communication technology), it seems that formal evaluation of the effectiveness of teaching tools is often neglected. A literature survey of methods used to evaluate innovations in computer science teaching showed that "the teacher's own impression of the teaching and the students' comments is the most common way of evaluating novelties in teaching" (Carbone & Kaasbøll, 1998). In our literature survey of the area of data networking, only two papers, Cameron (2003) and Yaverbaum and Nadarajan (1996), were found which formally evaluated the teaching innovation they described. We determined that formal evaluation of the effectiveness of the simulation tool was integral to its use and that we would attempt to actually measure whether any improvement in understanding occurred.

Description of the System

The main emphasis of this system is to use the simulation tool as a framework to facilitate and engage the student in active learning. The practical session is therefore structured to promote active learning by progressively leading the student through the concepts incrementally while challenging them to synthesise, interpolate, and apply their evolving knowledge. As part of this process, students need to be able to assess their answers, receive feedback, and correct any misconceptions before progressing further. For this, the simulator must have functionality that not only allows the student to create, visualise, configure, and manipulate their networks but must also provide a framework for the student to be able to assess their progress through self-evaluation and feedback mechanisms.

While any simulator with suitable features could be used, the simulation tool that provided the basis for the implementation in this discussion is Packet Tracer, a network simulator developed by Cisco Systems. Although Packet Tracer is not a generally available tool, we were able to use it with permission of QUT's Cisco Networking Academy program. Our choice of this product was based on both its powerful and appropriate features and its availability to us. The suitability of Packet Tracer for use as an interactive learning system was confirmed by mapping it against the 14 pedagogical dimensions described by Reeves (2003).

While we found Packet Tracer appropriate for our needs, it is not the intention of this chapter to evaluate Packet Tracer as a software simulation package or to compare it to other simulators. Rather, we hope to demonstrate how such a tool can be used to promote active learning. Any network simulation program that can provide similar features could be used.

A key feature of the simulation tool used is that it should be easy to work with and, if possible, fun to use since students should not be distracted from the learning objectives by having to contend with a complex system. In other words, the means should not transcend the ends. Furthermore, the simulator should accurately and adequately mimic the reality. While, understandably, a simulator might not be able to include every possible feature available in the actual device, the subset provided must be sufficient so as to make the interaction meaningful. In other words, it would be pointless to provide a simulation of IOS without including commands to configure an interface! Similarly, the operation of the simulator must be accurate. Again, for example, if a packet is incorrectly routed to its destination, it would mislead and confuse the students.

Packet Tracer is a powerful, highly visual, but simple-to-use network simulation application. It enables a simulated network to be built in a topography view (see Figure 1) by connecting a range of network devices (routers, switches, bridges, hubs, servers, and PCs) together using a variety of connection media. These devices can then be appropriately configured. Interfaces can be set and routing tables can be built. The network created can be extensive or simple, and the specific functionality of individual devices is also available. For example, switches can be used to implement virtual local area networks (VLANs).

In simulation mode, Packet Tracer enables data packets to be created and sent from device to device. The behaviour of the packet and the path it follows are

Figure 1. Topography view of a simulated network

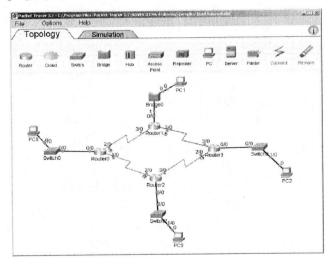

Figure 2. Simulation view (showing failure of data transmission)

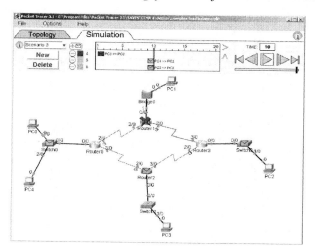

Figure 3. Simulation showing packet information and routing table

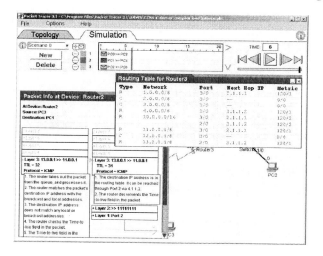

animated and simulate the way a packet will act in an actual network. Errors in the network configuration, for example, incorrect routes, will therefore cause a data transmission to fail, and this is shown in the visualisation (see Figure 2).

Furthermore, at each hop in a transmission, the state of the transmission as well as the message headers in a packet can be examined. Device information can also be viewed (see Figure 3). Devices such as routers can even be configured using IOS commands through a console window (see Figure 4).

Figure 4. Console window allowing router configuration using IOS

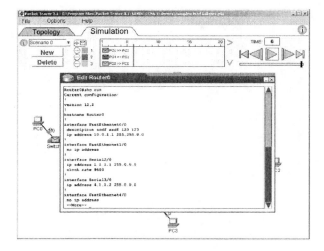

This makes it a powerful tool not only for practicing network configuration but also for investigating network behaviour. By observing the network activity and then analysing the network and packet status, the cause and effect of a particular configuration or setting can be identified, confirmed, and understood. This capability lends itself strongly to the use of Packet Tracer to facilitate active learning. Laurillard (2002) believes that the ability to offer intrinsic feedback "forms the core of any understanding of the contribution that ICT can make in education" (p. 126). We believe that the ability of Packet Tracer to give students meaningful intrinsic feedback is one of the keys to why this tool effectively supports independent learning.

Packet Tracer networks, including their configurations, can be saved and stored as files. Multiple networks can therefore be used. For example, two versions of the same network can be built and then compared. Similarly, a network can be modified and extended over a period of time as more and more concepts are learned. This feature is used to build an integrated, ongoing exercise and will be elaborated on further in this chapter.

In addition, Packet Tracer allows scenarios to be built and saved. A scenario is essentially a stored animation within a simulated network that can be run anytime and be observed. Together with the analytical features within Packet Tracer already referred to, this feature plays a crucial role in facilitating active learning since specific actions can be modelled and then analysed.

The concepts or material to be covered in the exercises should be material either already introduced to the students in another mode, for example, in a lecture, or ideas that can be extrapolated or evolved from previous knowledge, for example, troubleshooting. An example of this will be given further in this chapter. If possible, the topics should be structured so that the fundamental concepts are initially presented and then used as the basis to incrementally and logically move to more complex topics. A simulated network is then built that includes components illustrating the concepts being targeted. Questions that test the students' knowledge about these concepts are then designed by referring to the concept in the context of the simulated network. For example, if considering routing, the question might ask what path a packet might follow as it is routed across the network from a particular source to a particular destination.

For each question, a scenario is included which in essence provides an animation of the activity referred to in the question. In the example above, this animation would show a packet actually being sent through the path referred to. That is, the scenario contains the "answer" to the question. So, if the question asked how a packet would be routed from node A to node B, the corresponding scenario would actually show this as a simulated packet sent from A to B. While not directly presenting a solution, the animation would enable the student to determine what actually happens by observing the action. This would either confirm their understanding or encourage them to ascertain why their assessment was not correct. To do this they would be able to analyse the action and infer what should be happening by examining headers, consulting notes, rerunning the action in steps, changing the action and observing differences, and generally interacting with the resources available. The main thing is that they are actively seeking the solutions.

Where predefined scenarios are not suitable, students can be asked to modify their network (this provides practice in network configuration) and then asked about the effect that these changes will bring. The student can also create a scenario in the changed network to enable them to test and investigate these effects. So if, for example, subnets were added to the network, the students would be able to build a scenario sending a packet to the subnet and examining how this impacts on the network.

The sequence of the exercises is quite simple but important. Students are asked to open the simulated network in the simulator, examine the network in its visualised form first, and then answer the questions about the specific topic. They are then able to switch to the simulation mode and run the animated scenarios that relate to each question to confirm and evaluate their responses. If their assessment is not correct, then, by analysing the scenario and looking at the device or packet configuration at each step of the process, they are able to learn what went wrong and why. In this way the simulation provides them with the framework for analysis, feedback, synthesis, and evaluation. On completion of the topic, a broader question is presented which leads them to the next topic. Topics are structured in such a manner that they increase incrementally in complexity so that questions in later topics require understanding gained in earlier ones, and this provides a continuous and contextually meaningful environment. To illustrate this we will look at two exercises taken from a practical given as part of the normal course work of the unit.

The topic presented in the practical is "switched networks and VLANs (virtual local area networks)." This topic and the theory behind it were presented in an earlier lecture. The practical exercises were then based on five concepts taken from this topic area. The five concepts were: collision domains, broadcast domains, switching, VLANs, and inter-VLAN communication. For each of the concepts, a separate Packet Tracer network and configuration were built. Similarly, for each concept, a series of questions was designed to test under-standing of that concept (remembering that this had already been introduced in the lecture). For each question on a concept, a simulated scenario was included that implemented and demonstrated the situation referred to in the question. Furthermore the structure of these practical exercises was fairly uniform in order to encourage students to be methodical in their approach.

Below are the two actual exercises. Images of the visualised networks are also shown although these would have been viewed by the students directly in Packet Tracer.

The introduction to the exercises briefly presents the objectives and explains the processes and rationale involved. It should be remembered that the exercises were part of the normal program for this unit, so the material had already been presented in a lecture and the students were familiar with the general conduct of the practicals and with using Packet Tracer.

The first exercise is straightforward and clearly illustrates the methodology and use of predefined scenarios. The second exercise is somewhat more complex and requires that the students modify their networks and then create their own scenarios to analyse network processes, in this case, inter-VLAN routing. Students were given detailed information on how to modify their networks. This was because the objective was to achieve an understanding of the concepts involved rather than focusing on configuration changes that needed to be made.

Example

Two exercises from the practical on switched networks and VLANs

The objective of this prac is to illustrate the concepts of:

- collision domains
- broadcast domains
- switching
- VLANs
- inter-VLAN communication

For each exercise you will be given a Packet Tracer network and be asked to examine this network and answer questions about it. You will then be able to run a number of predefined scenarios for the network, observing and analysing the resultant actions. This will further help you understand your answers and, where necessary, correct these. In some cases you will be required to modify the network topography and configuration and then observe the effects of these changes. The networks are all related to each other, and so you will be able to see how progressive changes in the network topography and architecture impact on network behaviour.

In order to derive the most benefit from these exercises, you should do these in sequence and not jump ahead since subsequent exercises and situations relate to previous ones.

Setup

Download the following files from the Unit OLT site (Prac Index page) into a temporary folder on your PC:

PT_exercise1.pkt

PT_exercise2.pkt

PT_exercise3.pkt

Start Packet Tracer

Exercise 1

Open the file PT_exercise1.pkt (see Figure 5) and examine the network shown.

Answer the following questions:

1. If a packet is sent from PC1 to PC4, what path will the packet travel and why?

2. If a packet is broadcast from PC2, what path will that packet travel and why?

Figure 5. Exercise 1, initial network

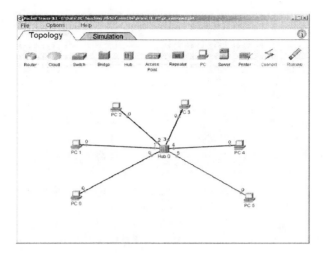

Figure 6. Scenario for Question 4 showing a collision

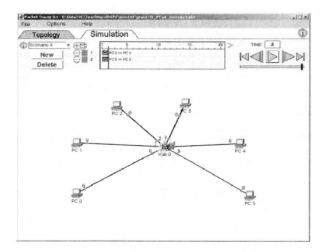

3.   What is the difference between the two actions in 1 and 2 above and why? What happens to the packet sent?

4.   If one packet is sent from PC3 and another from PC5 at the same time, what will occur and why? (see Figure 6)

Now, go to the simulation screen and run Scenarios 1, 2, and 4 in turn. Each scenario corresponds to the situation outlined in the previous questions, for example, Scenario 1 relates to Question 1, but for Question 3, consider both Scenarios 1 and 2. At the end of each scenario, consider whether the action you observed agrees with the action you thought would occur. If not, try to determine what is occurring and where your assessment was wrong. To help, run the scenarios in step mode and click on the packet at each stage to see what is happening at each protocol layer at that stage and what the state of the transmission is. (Remember, clicking on the + next to a layer will expand that layer and show a detailed explanation of the state for that layer.)

Answer the following question based on your observations from the scenarios shown:

Question

The above network demonstrates a **collision domain.** Why is this? In this instance is there any difference between a collision domain and broadcast domain?

Exercise 2

Like any other network based on TCP/IP, for communication to occur between VLANs a router must be introduced to connect the VLANs (networks) together. Each VLAN must be considered as a separate network (or subnet) with an appropriate network id, and routing must be implemented to send data from one VLAN to another.

Refer again to the network in Packet Tracer.

In **topology mode** now add a router. For clarity, position it at the bottom of the layout between PC0 and PC5 (see Figure 7).

For the router to connect the VLANs together, each VLAN must be connected to a separate interface. This can be done by simply connecting two ports on the switch to two separate interfaces on the router and configuring these ports to be in VLAN1 and VLAN2. Each VLAN is then configured as a separate network (or subnet) with its own IP network address, and each interface is given an IP address appropriate to the VLAN it is on.

Connect the router to the switch. The connection should be between Interface 0 on the router and Port 6 on the switch. **Note:** Now make **another** connection. This connection should be between Interface 1 on the router and Port 7 on the switch.

Figure 7. Modified network for Exercise 2 with the added router, in simulation mode

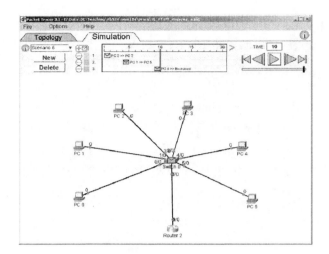

Now configure Port 6 on the switch to be in VLAN1 (it should be by default) and Port 7 to be in VLAN2.

On the router now configure Interface 0 with the IP address 212.1.1.1 and network mask 255.255.255.0.

Configure Interface 1 with the IP address 212.1.2.1 and network mask 255.255.255.0.

Because VLAN2 now has a different IP network address, the PCs in VLAN2 (PCs 3, 4, 5) must have their IP addresses reconfigured. The easiest way to do this is to click on each of these PCs in turn and then click on "use DHCP." Note that the IP address changes to an address in network 212.1.2.0. Also, the PCs in VLAN1 must have a default gateway configured as well. Again the easiest way to do this is to click on these in turn and then click on "use DHCP." The IP addresses will change, but these will still be in network 212.1.1.0 and the default gateway will be configured.

Note: Usually a router will be configured on a single trunk and the interface for each VLAN configured as a subinterface. Traffic for each VLAN is then identified through frame tagging. The net result, however, is the same as the configuration we have implemented.

Consider the following questions:

1.   What will happen when a packet is sent from PC0 to PC2?

Now create a packet to do this and confirm your answer.

2.   What path does a packet sent from PC1 to PC5 take to reach its destination? Explain each stage.

Now create a packet to do this and analyse the path by stepping through this action and examining the packet state at each stage. If your own conclusions are different, try to understand what is occurring here by sending and examining packets sent between PCs on the same VLAN and PCs on different VLANs.

3.   What path would a packet broadcast on VLAN2 follow and why?

Now create a broadcast packet (from PC4) to do this and observe what happens to confirm your answer. Remember to use "expert mode" to create a broadcast packet.

End Practical Exercises

Continuing Practice

To further utilise the simulation and to enhance deeper learning, an ongoing exercise was developed as a case study to progressively build an expanding network. This network was changed and enhanced to reflect the topics, concepts, and processes that were discussed from week to week. In this way, new ideas were incorporated into the network in a logical and contextual manner. There was continuity, and students were led to an understanding of how new concepts and processes fitted into the network as it grew in complexity. Rather than focusing on the concepts and processes in isolation, the objective was to focus on how they were integrated in a network and the function they fulfilled in that network.

In week 1 the idea of a simple, single segment network was introduced and then simulated in Packet Tracer. This was used to illustrate the concepts of network connectivity, direct delivery, and simple addressing. Later, when routing was covered, the simulated network was changed to include routers and to examine both static and dynamic routing. Later again, the network changed and grew to reflect the inclusion of features such as subnetting, switching, and Network Address Translation (NAT). To provide a context for this expanding network, a story line was maintained which followed the growth of a fictitious company as it developed and required changes and more sophisticated functionality from its network. So, for example, the introduction of subnets was required to enable the company to build additional networks for new sections and branches, and new servers had to be added and configured as the company's range of services expanded. NAT was introduced when the company required external Internet access. To the student this made the material more relevant, provided a meaningful context as well as a sense of achievement as they saw their work grow.

The features available in Packet Tracer also enable the simulator to be used to develop troubleshooting skills in students. Students are given simulated networks with errors in them. They use scenarios to test the network and then, when problems are found, identify these by analysing the details available from Packet Tracer about packet headers, state information, IP addresses, and routing tables. The errors can be corrected within Packet Tracer and immediately checked. Students can therefore learn how to check their networks, identify which errors can occur, how these are manifested, and how they can be corrected. For example, a network can be provided to the students with a number of scenarios (animations), each of which fail. These scenarios could include: invalid or missing gateway on a PC, invalid TTL (time-to-live) in a packet, invalid IP address, route missing, no default route, invalid subnet address or incorrect subnet mask used, trunking not configured in a switch, VLANs not correctly assigned, incorrect cabling used, or invalid NAT configuration. Faulty hardware can even be simulated by leaving a device in the simulation in an off state. Using these scenarios the students can develop troubleshooting strategies and an understanding of the errors involved. Later in an assessment exercise, students can be provided with a network with similar errors and be asked to locate, identify, and correct these using the troubleshooting strategies they had developed.

Usefulness and Benefits

The benefit in using this approach is that students are involved in active learning. They are required to think deeply about what they are doing and what is occurring, and as they work through the exercises they get rapid feedback from the simulator. This enhances the students' learning experience by providing a framework for active, independent study. The simulation tool provides a hands-on, practical environment which engages the student and is more exciting and real because of the use of relevant visuals and animations. Material can be placed in a context, continuity can be achieved, and analytical and troubleshooting skills can be developed. Students seek understanding and explanation through analysing, synthesising, and extrapolating information and knowledge through dynamic interaction with the system rather than just being told. Students can therefore work more effectively and independently. Finally, in terms of data communication, the system enables concepts and process that are otherwise esoteric to be made more tangible and accessible and, ultimately, more understandable.

Evaluation and Interpretation

Educational technology "if applied without deliberative study of its use in context and without the evaluation of the technology's impact on this use ... remains a toy" (Almstrum et al., 1996, p. 201). While it was clear that students enjoyed using Packet Tracer and found the exercises engaging, we also wanted to determine whether the use of simulation in such an active learning framework did indeed improve their understanding of the concepts presented.

Our evaluation strategy was based on the framework developed by Naps et al. (2002) that considered the relationship between a learner's form of engagement with a visualisation and the types of understanding that are affected by that engagement. The evaluation included a pretest, a posttest, a student background questionnaire, and learner feedback questions. The pre- and posttests were isomorphic. The same questions were used in each test but in a different order.

Students attended normal practical sessions, but at the start of the session that was used to assess the exercises, they were tested to determine their current understanding of the material by completing a pretest multiple-choice questionnaire. Since Packet Tracer was used as an integral part of all the practical classes in the subject and students were familiar with its functionality and operation, there was no need to focus on its operation. After the students completed the practical exercises as discussed in this chapter, they were given a posttest similar to the initial pretest. We found that student understanding appeared to improve considerably following completion of the practical.

Table 1. Paired-samples statistics

		Mean	N	Std. Deviation	Std. Error Mean
Pair 1	POSTOTAL	6.67	60	1.56	.20
	PRETOTAL	5.55	60	1.54	.19

Table 2. Paired-samples test

Pair 1	t-value	df	Sig
Postotal-Pretotal	4.89	59	<0.01

Results

Sixty-six students participated in the practical and responded to the pre- and posttests. Of these, six were excluded from the analysis because of missing data. The pre- and posttests were marked out of 10. In the pretest the average was 55%. In the posttest this improved to 67%, an average increase of 12% (see Table 1).

The difference between pre- and posttests was shown to be statistically significant (see Table 2). We calculated the standardised effect size to be d= 0.63 suggesting that participation in the practical session was a significant factor in improving the understanding of the concepts presented.

In terms of individual results, 63.3% of the students improved their results in the posttest, 18.3% showed no change, but 18.3% actually showed deterioration. The average improvement in marks for those who did improve was 23% while those did worse went down by an average 15%. There was no clear reason why some students did not improve their results since this was not confined to any single identifiable group. Factors such as becoming confused, not being as familiar with the analytical functionality of Packet Tracer, or simply guessing might have played a role, and this will require further investigation.

On a question by question basis, overall there was an improvement in the responses for 8 out of the 10 questions. For one question there was no change, and for one the results in the posttest were actually worse. This could have been related to a difficulty in understanding the question. The average improvement for individual question scores was 12% (see Table 3).

Table 3. Individual question response

	Q1	Q2	Q3	Q4	Q5	Q6	Q7	Q8	Q9	Q10	Ave
Pre	45	52	36	22	11	47	27	40	30	23	33.3
Post	59	54	33	41	17	52	27	44	53	27	40.7
Diff	14	2	-3	19	6	5	0	4	23	4	7.4
%	23	3	-5	31	10	8	0	6	38	6	12

We collected demographic data from students related to their previous experience in data communication and IT studies and found that this did not have any evident impact on how they performed. We did note however that students who perceived themselves as coping well with studies in the unit as a whole showed a greater improvement in understanding after doing the exercise.

Conclusion

This chapter focuses on the use of a network simulator to provide a dynamic framework to facilitate active learning in the study of data communication concepts. By taking advantage of the visualisation, animation, and feedback features of the simulator, a set of practical exercises were designed to enable students to independently examine a series of networking concepts by:

- Reviewing a given network
- Explaining activity on the network
- Confirming their assessment through evaluation, analysis, the synthesis of previous knowledge and feedback provided by the simulator

The key to success lies in the structured use of the simulation tool based on a defined pedagogical approach. We do not suggest that simulation cannot effectively be used in other ways but offer some ideas on how the tool can be used to enhance the student experience. A marked improvement in student understanding over the course of the practical session was shown by pre- and posttesting.

Student response to doing the exercises was very positive. Students remained engaged during the practical and demonstrated a high level of concentration and interest. No student left the practical session early. Student feedback questions in the posttest confirmed this positive response. (The majority of students indicated that they felt that the approach had been effective.) Anecdotally as well, good feedback was received about the practical and about the use of Packet Tracer.

Not every topic would lend itself to being presented in exactly the same manner. However applying sound pedagogical practice to the innovative use of simulation tools can produce good outcomes and can extend the benefits of these tools. Furthermore, we have demonstrated how simulation tools can be used to address the practical needs of large classes or in situations where there are restrictions in the availability of real equipment.

In future work we will investigate why in some cases student understanding of the topic seemed to be impeded by participation in the practical session. We would also like to compare the effectiveness of using simulations to other teaching methods.

Summary

It is often difficult for students to understand data communications concepts when in a large class because, without firsthand experiences, students can find the subject technical and rather dry and boring. This chapter describes the use of a network simulator in large classroom settings to enhance the teaching and learning of various aspects of data communication at both the introductory and advanced levels. By using the visualisation, animation, feedback, and analytical features of the simulator in an active learning framework, a set of practical exercises was designed for students to examine and independently explore a number of key networking concepts. Results were positive and students indicated that they had found the simulation tool very effective and helpful in gaining an understanding of these concepts.

Key Terms and Definitions

Broadcast domain: Devices networked together and which will receive a broadcast packet sent from any of these devices are said to be in a broadcast domain.

Collision: When two or more packets are simultaneously sent on a common network medium that only can transmit a single packet at a time. The packets collide and are corrupted and need to be resent.

Collision domain: A single physical or logical network segment using Ethernet technology through which collisions will be propagated. Devices in a collision domain communicate directly with each other and share the network medium.

Gateway address: Usually the address of the default route to be used to reach a network that is not specifically known.

Internetwork (or Internet): A network of networks made up of separate networks connected by devices such as routers. The global Internet is the definitive example of this.

IP address (Internet address): A network address expressed as a 32-bit number and usually represented in dotted decimal as four decimal numbers separated by full stops. Every device connected to an internet, including the global Internet, has a unique IP address. The IP address identifies the device and the network that device is on. This form is currently the standard, but later Internet protocols define addresses in a different format.

Network simulator: A computer program that simulates the layout and behaviour of a network and enables network activity to be initiated and observed.

Packet: A generic term used to define a unit of data including routing and other information that is sent through an internet.

Ping: The name of a utility program used to test availability of a device on an IP network. It works by sending a small packet to the target device and then waiting for a response. The term is also now used as a verb meaning to check if a device is accessible.

Protocols: A set of rules defining the standards for network communication usually implemented as a suite of programs running on computers connected to the network.

Router: The network device that connects networks together and implements routing.

Routing: It is a process that occurs on a network when a packet is shunted from router to router along the path to the target destination. Routing is based on identifying the destination network from the IP address of the target machine.

Switch: A network device that connects communication links together, enabling networks to be built that are on the same network but do not have to share the same link. This reduces collisions and improves network efficiency.

TTL (time-to-live): A parameter set in a data packet that defines how long that packet can remain active on the network.

VLAN (virtual local area network): A logical shared network created by connecting devices to configurable switches so that the network is not constrained by any physical boundary.

Review Questions

1.   List and describe the desirable features of a network simulator.

2.   Explain how a network simulator can be used in large classes to enhance teaching and learning data communications concepts.

3.   Consider the effectiveness of a simulation tool in the teaching and learning contexts.

4.   Explain how a simulator can be used in conjunction with active learning methodologies.

5.   What is Packet Tracer? Explain how Packet Tracer can be used as an aid to enhance teaching and learning data communications.

6.   Understand the functions and facilities of a teaching-orientated network simulator program.

7.   List and describe possible enhancements to the proposed practical activities described in this chapter.

References

Almstrum, V. L., Dale, N., Berglund, A., Granger, M., Currie Little, J., Miller, D. M., et al. (1996). Evaluation: Turning technology from toy to tool: Report of the Working Group on Evaluation. In *Proceedings of the 1st Conference on Integrating Technology into Computer Science Education* (pp. 201-217).

Biggs, J. B. (1999). *Teaching for quality learning at university: What the student does.* Buckingham, UK: Open University Press.

Bonwell, C., & Eison, J. (1991). *Active learning: Creating excitement in the classroom* (ASHE-ERIC Higher Education Rep. No. 1). Washington, DC: George Washington University.

Cameron, B. (2003). Effectiveness of simulation in a hybrid online networking course. *Quarterly Review of Distance Education, 4*(1), 51-55.

Carbone, A., & Kaasbøll, J. J. (1998). A survey of methods used to evaluate computer science teaching. *Proceedings of the Annual Joint Conference Integrating Technology into Computer Science Education* (pp. 41-45).

Cope, C. (2003). A framework for using learning technologies in higher education to enhance the quality of students' learning outcomes. *Proceedings of the 20th Annual Conference of the Australian Society for Computers in Learning in Tertiary Education (ASCILITE)* (pp. 134-141).

Ehrmann, S. C. (1995). Asking the right question: What does research tell us about technology and higher learning? *Change, 27*(2), 20-27.

Entwistle, N. J. (1981). *Styles of learning and teaching: An integrated outline of educational psychology for students, teachers and lecturers.* Chichester, UK: Wiley.

Laurillard, D. (2002). *Rethinking university teaching: A conversational framework for the effective use of learning technologies* (2nd ed.). London: Routledge/Falmer.

Naps, T., Rößling, G., Almstrum, V., Dann, W., Fleischer, R., Hundhausen, C., et al. (2002). Exploring the role of visualization and engagement in computer science education: ITiCSE 2002 working group report. *ACM SIGCSE Bulletin, 35*(2), 131-152.

Perkins, D., & Salomon, G. (1992). Transfer of learning. In *International encyclopedia of education* (2nd ed.). Oxford, UK: Pergamon Press. Retrieved February 6, 2004, from http://learnweb.harvard.edu/alps/thinking/docs/traencyn.pdf

Ramsden, P. (1992). *Learning to teach in higher education.* London: Routledge.

Reeves, T. C. (2003). *Interactive learning systems evaluation.* Englewood Cliffs, NJ: Educational Technology.

Salomon, G. (2000). *It's not just the tool, but the educational rationale that counts.* Retrieved July 24, 2004, from http://construct.haifa.ac.il/~gsalomon/edMedia2000.html

Yaverbaum, G., & Nadarajan, U. (1996). Learning basic concepts of telecommunications: An experiment in multimedia and learning. *Computers & Education, 26*(4), 215-224.

Chapter V

Teaching Protocols through Animation

Kenneth J. Turner, University of Stirling, UK

Abstract

Communication protocols are essential components of computer and data communication networks. Therefore, it is important that students grasp these concepts and become familiar with widely used protocols. Unfortunately, communication protocols can be complex and their behavior difficult to understand. In order to learn about protocols, a student therefore needs a more controlled and constrained environment. This chapter describes the development and use of a protocol animator for teaching and learning communication protocols.

Learning Objectives

After completing this chapter, you will be able to:

- List and describe the desirable features of a protocol animation tool.
- Describe the main features of the JASPER protocol animator.

- Explain how an animation tool can be used in the classroom to enhance teaching and learning communication protocols.
- Define the following key terms: animation, simulation, message, time-sequence diagram, medium, protocol, and protocol entity.
- Consider further enhancements to JASPER and the protocols it simulates.

Introduction

Communications protocols are a vital ingredient of all networks. It is essential for students to grasp their fundamental principles and to become familiar with widely used protocols. Unfortunately, communications protocols can be complex and difficult to understand. Even the simple Alternating Bit Protocol displays surprising depths of complexity. It is easy to understand static aspects of a protocol such as message formats. Where protocols become difficult is in their dynamic behavior.

The main behavior of a protocol is often straightforward. However that may account for only 20% of its functionality. Protocols may be used in different configurations such as client-server or peer-to-peer. They have to operate reliably over a communications link that may exhibit a variety of faults. The complications in protocol design usually arise in error recovery: dealing with message loss, misordering, duplication, or misdelivery. Protocols operate in real time, so tracing their behavior in practice can be difficult.

In order to learn about protocols, a student therefore needs a more controlled and constrained environment. This chapter explains how a protocol animator has been developed to meet these needs. The animator is platform-independent, being written in Java, and is available in source code form, precompiled, and on the Web.

Background and Motivation

Existing Work

The term *protocol animation* is used in this chapter in the sense of giving life to a protocol definition (from Latin *anima* meaning soul). Protocol animation has received surprisingly little attention. An overview of work on the topic can be found in Turner (2002).

Formal modeling of protocols is commonly used as a basis for protocol simulation. However the goal is to discover flaws in the design of a protocol rather than to explain how it works. MSCs (Message Sequence Charts; ITU, 2000a) and SDL (Specification and Description Language; ITU, 2000b) are popular specification techniques used with communications protocols. Both SDL and MSCs have graphical syntaxes and can be simulated visually to investigate a specification. As examples of protocol simulation to gain understanding, Stepien and Logrippo (2002) and Yasumoto, Umedu, Yamaguchi, Nakata, and Higashino (2002) graphically animate specifications written in LOTOS (Language of Temporal Ordering Specification; ISO, 1987).

There are many network simulators to support modeling and performance analysis of networks and protocols. Two major examples are the *ns/nam* network simulator/network animator (Network Simulator Team, 2005; Yu & Salehi, 2000) and the *cnet* computer network simulator (McDonald, 1991, 2005). A variety of network simulations have been developed under the auspices of the VINT (Virtual Internet) project. The basis of these simulations is normally some form of queuing network model. Such simulators are aimed at analyzing performance issues rather than conveying an understanding of protocols.

The *dlpjava* data link protocol simulator (King, 1992, 2004) has the aim of teaching protocols through simulation. However, it focuses exclusively on the data-link layer. The Pascal-based tool of Lindsay (1992) uses a scripting language to animate protocol interaction diagrams. A number of one-off protocol simulators have also been developed. Hudek (2005) presents a Java applet that graphically simulates the ATM UNI (asynchronous transfer mode user-network interface). The operation of a simple data transfer protocol has been illustrated using JavaScript with SDL (Bayfront Technologies, 2003).

Yet other types of simulators deal with distributed algorithms. Here, the emphasis is on algorithm design rather than protocol design. However Krumm (1997) shows how the approach can be used to animate the Alternating Bit Protocol with sequence diagrams.

The JASPER Protocol Animator

The author teaches data communications to undergraduate and graduate students. Although a variety of techniques have been used in this (such as message sequence diagrams), it was found that students grasped only the bare essentials of protocols. It was felt that a visual, dynamic animation would allow students to understand protocols more thoroughly. In addition, the advantage of a tool is that students can learn in their own time and at their own pace.

As explained earlier, no existing tool meets the specific requirements for teaching protocols. The ideal protocol animation tool should have the following characteristics:

- It should demonstrate protocol behavior graphically. A visual animation captures the student's interest much more than a tool that just produces traces of protocol messages.

- It should focus on the dynamics of a protocol. Syntactic clutter such as detailed message formats should be kept to a minimum.

- It should run stand-alone (e.g., on a student's PC) and also in a Web environment (e.g., in a computing laboratory). The tool should be written in a modern, platform-independent language. These features increase the possibilities for deployment.

- It should support a library of well-known protocols, including standard pedagogical examples like Alternating Bit as well as realistic protocols used on the Internet. The tool should have a well-defined API (application programming interface) that allows new protocol animations to be developed.

These goals have been realised in the protocol animator called JASPER (Java Simulation of Protocols for Education and Research). JASPER is intended for a number of uses:

- It animates well-known protocols as a teaching aid in networking courses. An instructor can readily deploy protocol animations to Java-enabled Web browsers.

- It is an extensible tool to which students can readily add new protocols. Creating a new animation for JASPER is a valuable learning exercise in its own right. The tool respects object-oriented design principles; for example, its architecture is that of MVC (model-view-controller). Development for JASPER therefore reinforces good software design practice.

- Although its main aim is to support teaching, JASPER can also be used in research and development of protocols. The extensibility and visual animation offered by the tool are valuable adjuncts to more formal kinds of modeling and simulation.

Turner and Robin (2001) discuss the design of JASPER in some detail. The same reference also gives a worked example of how to extend the tool for new protocols. JASPER can immediately be used by anyone over the Internet: http:/

/www.cs.stir.ac.uk/~kjt/software/comms/jasper. The code is open source and can be downloaded in precompiled form from the same location. JASPER has been extensively used in the author's own institution and is also employed by several other universities.

Description of the System

Animation Examples

Figure 1 shows a screenshot of the animator executing the Alternating Bit Protocol. This figure is taken from a Web browser window running the animator as an applet. It illustrates a three-column display with two protocol entities (sender, receiver) and the communications medium (i.e., communications link or network). DATA and ACK messages flow between the sender and the receiver. In this simulation, messages are simply numbered since the content of data messages is unimportant.

The control panel at the bottom left allows the user to select protocol actions. The Clear button restarts an animation. The Undo and Redo buttons move backwards and forwards in the animated behavior. Run is used to animate the protocol automatically; while this is happening, the button is labeled as Stop. When the animator is executed as an application (as opposed to an applet), it allows scenarios to be loaded and saved. This is useful to place a protocol into a known state (e.g., connected) and to demonstrate finer points of its behavior. An application can also print out an entire animation.

To the right of the control panel is a menu of user choices determined by the protocol rules. Only one choice is currently possible in Figure 1, namely, to send a DATA message numbered 1. Other choices in this simulation include transferring messages through the medium, losing them in the medium, and timing out at the sender.

Figure 2 shows a much more complex animation: TCP (Transmission Control Protocol) working in peer-to-peer mode. This is a five-column display showing two service users, two protocol entities, and the medium. The animator interface allows the main protocol parameters to be defined: user message sizes, protocol window sizes, and maximum packet size in the medium. Data in transit can be flushed by either user setting the push flag.

TCP users (most likely, applications) make use of a service interface to set up a connection, exchange data, and close the connection. In Figure 2 each user has initiated an active open, leading to a connection being established. User A has

Figure 1. Alternating Bit Protocol animation

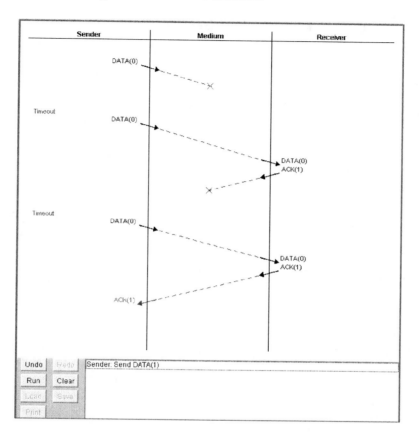

then sent 100 octets (i.e., bytes) to User B, asking that the data be flushed. The protocol messages to achieve this are shown. Each carries a sequence number (Seq) and a receive window size (Win). Connection setup messages carry the synchronization (SYN) flag, while flushed data carries the push (PSH) flag. The menu in Figure 2 shows that the two users may continue to send data or to close the connection. By varying the protocol parameters, the tool user can experiment with fragmentation and the effects of packet loss on parts of a message.

Currently JASPER supports the following protocols, though its design makes extension straightforward:

Figure 2. Transmission Control Protocol animation

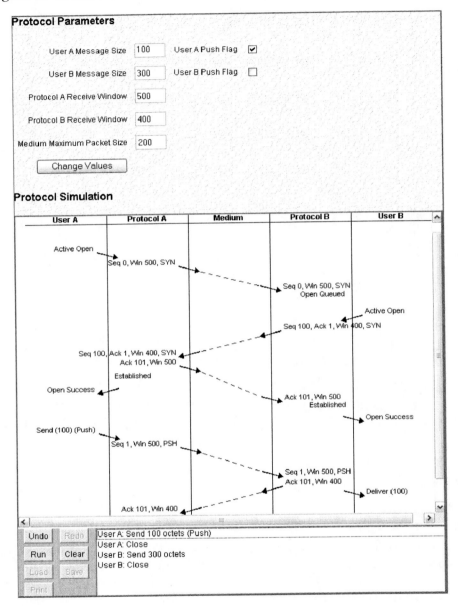

- ABP (Alternating Bit Protocol)
- ABRA (Abracadabra Protocol)
- BOOTP (Boot Protocol)
- HTTP (Hypertext Transfer Protocol)
- IP (Internet Protocol)
- SMTP (Simple Mail Transfer Protocol)
- SWP (Sliding Window Protocol, three- and five-column variants)
- TCP (Transmission Control Protocol, peer-to-peer and client-server variants)
- TFTP (Trivial File Transfer Protocol)
- UDP (User Datagram Protocol)

Tool Architecture

The animator follows the familiar MVC paradigm.

- **Model**: The model of a protocol is its behavior defined by Java classes. No particular implementation style is mandated by JASPER. However, many protocols are already defined by (extended) finite state machines. These are readily represented in Java using a table-driven approach. The major state describes whether the protocol is disconnected, processing an incoming connection, and so forth. The state variables contain extra protocol information such as the current sequence number and the window size. The model contains one object for each communicating party, for example, the two users, the two protocol entities, and the underlying medium. Although these have individual classes, they extend generic definitions that apply to any protocol.
- **View**: The view of a protocol is the graphical display of its behavior as a time-sequence diagram. This is a common way of displaying protocol message exchanges. It would have been possible to make strict use of MSCs (Message Sequence Charts) for this purpose. However, for instructional purposes it was felt that a simplified notation was preferable. In fact, the time-sequence diagrams are based on the standard for service conventions (ISO, 1992). The columns represent the communicating parties, such as the two protocol entities and the medium. Time runs down the page, with message exchanges shown as arrows between the parties. The diagrams are also annotated by JASPER to show situations such as message loss or the receiver becoming blocked.

- **Controller**: The main JASPER class acts as overall controller of the animation. It coordinates the objects for the communicating parties. The protocol rules determine which actions are permitted at each step in the animation (e.g., send or receive a message, lose a message in the medium, time-out, and retry). The tool user selects an action at each stage. The controller can also be placed in automatic mode, when it will randomly select permitted actions at regular intervals. This often highlights unusual error cases that could be missed during manual simulation.

Animator Interfaces

The animator defines abstract classes and interfaces that are specialized for each protocol. The *Protocol* class is the basic framework for any protocol; it is subclassed for each particular protocol. Protocol entities and the medium are coordinated by exchange of *ProtocolEvent* messages. Apart from transmission and reception, events also include time-outs and comments that allow the protocol to explain what it is doing.

The *ProtocolEntity* interface defines the framework for entities that support a protocol. This is subclassed to create conventional protocol entities as well as users of communications services. The *ProtocolEntity* interface requires generic methods to be implemented, such as initializing the protocol and sending/receiving messages.

The *Timeouts* class handles message timers. Since the aim of animation is educational, the tool does not run in real time. Rather, the tool user decides on time-out through a menu choice. This gives more control when investigating error recovery in the protocol. The protocol definition determines whether it supports time-outs. These are normal in lower-level protocols but not in higher-level ones.

The *Medium* base class defines the generic properties of a communications medium. These include the ability to transfer a message successfully or to lose a message (e.g., due to noise or congestion). This class may be subclassed for particular protocols. For example, some protocols are expected to operate over a medium that may duplicate or reorder messages.

Evaluation and Interpretation

JASPER has been class-tested over a period of 4 years at the author's institution (a total of about 250 students). It has been used in the following ways:

- Networking courses cover the basic principles of protocol design as well as major Internet protocols. These are introduced through textual descriptions and graphical snapshots of a protocol in action. However, JASPER allows live walk-throughs to be given of protocol behavior. This is easily the most effective way of conveying how a protocol works.

- Students use Web pages containing the protocol animations. This allows them to experiment with the protocols at their own pace. Students are encouraged to investigate *corner behavior*, whereby a protocol gets into an unusual state and then recovers from it. There are often so many situations like this that they cannot be presented formally by the instructor. It is preferable for students to discover these for themselves. The automatic run feature is particularly useful for this, allowing an animation to evolve by itself. If the student sees unusual behavior develop, automatic animation can be suspended so the situation can be analyzed in depth.

- Students may also download the animator code. It is instructive for them to see how a protocol is defined (typically, by its state machine). As an application, the animator can also be used to load, save, and print animation scenarios.

- Protocol animations have been used in class assignments. Animations also provide insight into protocol development. For example, an assignment to implement SMTP is greatly helped by studying the protocol first through animation.

- New protocol animations have also been set as student projects. In fact a number of the protocols supported by JASPER have been developed in this way.

The effectiveness of JASPER has not been evaluated formally. However each course is assessed by a questionnaire that includes the provision of Web-based facilities. On a 5-point scale, these are regularly rated 4 (very good).

JASPER has a number of intentional limitations, imposed due to its primary goal of protocol education:

- The animation does not have any concept of real time, partly because the animation would then be too fast to follow and partly because the tool user is required to have full control over how protocol behavior evolves. Certain protocols are, of course, required to respect real-time constraints. The animation of such protocols must abstract away from time.

- Protocol messages are shown only in outline since detailed formats would confuse and complicate the graphical presentation. As a result, students must learn separately about how protocol messages are actually formatted.

- Currently, only three-column and five-column diagrams can be shown. This is a limitation of the graphical presentation, not of the core animation approach. Most protocols can be adequately represented in this way. However some protocols are not strictly peer-to-peer or client-server. For example, distributed transaction processing and certain bus protocols involve multiple entities. These can be represented only as pairs of communicating protocol entities.

- The protocols currently supported are based on the author's understanding of their defining standards. The animation may not completely reflect what a conforming implementation should do. Certain aspects have also been simplified in the interests of effective training rather than absolute completeness. For example, TCP has sophisticated traffic management procedures that are missing from the current animation.

Impact on Students' Performance

The impact of JASPER on students' performance has been assessed only qualitatively. However the author's experience (substantiated by course questionnaires and student grades) is that the animation tool has been valuable. Since the introduction of JASPER, an understanding of protocols has been demonstrated in greater depth during tutorials, and protocol development assignments have been completed more effectively.

From the instructor's point of view, the availability of protocol animation means that more realistic assignments can be set (and not just trivial protocols). The instructor can also set more in-depth questions in formal examinations. For example, these can address tricky issues such as error recovery and protocol performance over lossy mediums.

From the student's point of view, it is easier and quicker to learn about protocols. This has been evident in the students' grasp of subtler issues during tutorial discussions. Students have also been able to tackle more complex protocols in assignments than could previously have been set.

Conclusion

A thorough understanding of communications protocols is vital to any networking course. However the dynamic and complex nature of many protocols makes it difficult for students to gain any real insight into them. It has been argued that a graphical protocol animator is an important tool in allowing students to study protocols — especially their behavior under error conditions.

Although a number of network simulation tools exist, their focus is quite different from that required of an instructional aid. The JASPER protocol animator has therefore been developed as an adjunct to other network teaching techniques. The animator is graphical and can be Web-based or stand-alone. It exploits Java as an object-oriented, platform-independent implementation language. The animator can be driven manually by the tool user or can be set to run automatically. Through experimenting with key protocol parameters and unusual behaviors, the student can gain new insights into general principles of protocol design, as well as into the operation of well-known protocols.

Acknowledgments

The bulk of the design and implementation work for JASPER was undertaken by I. A. Robin while a master's student under the author's supervision. Further protocol animations were added by P. K. Johnson and K. J. A. Whyte as student projects.

Summary

Communications protocols are an essential part of many computer networking courses around the globe. Unfortunately, it is difficult to motivate students to learn communication protocols because the topic appears to be rather technical and complex. This chapter describes the design and use of a graphical protocol animator called JASPER that enhances the teaching and learning of protocols.

Both instructors and students can benefit from the use of JASPER in different teaching and learning contexts. An instructor is able to use it in the classroom for practical demonstrations that liven up lectures and also to use it in support of assessments. Students can use the system to develop a better understanding of communication protocols, especially their behavior under error conditions. Through experimenting with key protocol parameters, students can gain an insight into the basic principles of protocol design and analysis, as well as into the operation of well-known protocols.

Key Terms and Definitions

Animation, simulation: The abstract execution of a system model. The two terms are barely distinguished, though animation has the sense of symbolic execution while simulation has a more general sense and may deal with performance.

Formal language, formal method: A mathematically based technique for precisely specifying and analyzing systems through abstract models. Major classes of formal methods include those based on process algebras (e.g., the LOTOS language) or on state machines (e.g., the SDL language).

Medium: The communications link or network that carries protocol messages.

Message: The structured data communicated by a protocol. Parameters of a message typically include the message type, sequence number, control flags, and user data.

Protocol: The formats and rules governing exchange of messages among communicating systems.

Protocol entity: The component of a system that implements a protocol.

Service: The abstract interface to a protocol. Details of how the protocol works are hidden from the service user. For example, protocol error recovery mechanisms such as retransmission on time-out are not visible in the service.

State machine: An abstract model that characterizes the behavior of a system through the transitions it makes between states. Practical models have a finite number of states. An extended finite state machine has a major state that controls its main behavior and also state variables that have a smaller impact on the general operation of the system.

Three/five-column diagram: A form of time-sequence diagram that shows the two protocol entities and the medium (three-column) or also the two service users (five-column).

Time-sequence diagram: A graphical presentation of message exchange among communicating systems. Time flows down the page. Arrows show messages between carried from one system element to another.

User: The system element that employs a service. This may be a human end-user or, more typically, a communications application that provides further services to the end user.

Review Questions

1.   Describe three important features of a protocol animator.

2.   Discuss how JASPER might be used to enhance teaching and learning of protocols.

3.   Illustrate the behavior of the Alternating Bit Protocol and the Transmission Control Protocol by drawing the kinds of time-sequence diagrams that JASPER supports.

4.   Define the following key terms: animation, time-sequence diagram, and protocol.

5.   Describe enhancements that might make JASPER more user-friendly.

6.   List some additional protocols that might be supported by JASPER using the current style of animation. What kinds of protocols would be unsuitable for this approach?

References

Bayfront Technologies. (2003). *DataXfer protocol simulation in JavaScript.* Retrieved April 2005, from http://www.bayfronttechnologies.com/101fun.htm

Hudek, D. (2005). *UNI 3.1 signaling package simulator.* Retrieved April 2005, from http://www.ultranet.com/~dhudek/junidemo1.shtml

International Organization for Standardization/International Electrotechnical Commision. (1987). *Information processing systems – Open systems interconnection – LOTOS – A formal description technique based on the temporal ordering of observational behaviour* (ISO/IEC 8807). Geneva, Switzerland: International Organization for Standardization.

International Organization for Standardization /International Electrotechnical Commision. (1992). *Information processing systems – Open systems interconnection – Conventions for the definition of OSI services* (ISO/IEC TR 10731). Geneva, Switzerland: International Organization for Standardization.

International Telecommunications Union. (2000a). *Message Sequence Chart (MSC)* (ITU-T Z.120). Geneva, Switzerland: International Telecommunications Union.

International Telecommunications Union. (2000b). *Specification and Description Language* (ITU-T Z.100). Geneva, Switzerland: International Telecommunications Union.

King, P. J. B. (1992). Data link simulation. *IEEE Transactions on Education, 40*(3), 172-178.

King, P. J. B. (2004). *Data link protocol simulator.* Retrieved April 2005, from http://www.cee.hw.ac.uk/~pjbk/dlpjava

Krumm, H. (1997). *Verteilte Algorithmen.* Retrieved April 2005, from http://ls4-www.cs.uni-dortmund.de/RVS/MA/hk/OrdnerVertAlgo/AltBit.html

Lindsay, D. (1992). Visualising computer communications. In D. C. Bateman & T. Hopkins (Eds.), *Developments in the teaching of computer science* (pp. 72-79). Canterbury, UK: University of Kent.

McDonald, C. S. (1991). A network specification language and execution environment for undergraduate teaching. In *Proceedings ACM Computer Science Education Symposium* (pp. 25-34). New York: ACM Press.

McDonald, C. S. (2005). *The cnet network simulator.* Retrieved April 2005, from http://www.cs.uwa.edu.au/pls/cnet

Network Simulator Team. (2005). *Network simulator version 2.* Retrieved April 2005, from http://www.isi.edu/nsnam/ns

Stepien, B., & Logrippo, L. (2002). Graphic visualization and animation of LOTOS execution traces. *Computer Networks, 40*(5), 665-681.

Turner, K. J. (Ed.). (2002). Protocol animation [Special issue]. *Computer Networks, 40*(5).

Turner, K. J., & Robin, I. A. (2001). An interactive visual protocol simulator. *Computer Standards and Interfaces, 23*, 279-310.

Yasumoto, K., Umedu, T., Yamaguchi, H., Nakata, A., & Higashino, T. (2002). Protocol animation based on event-driven visualization scenarios in real-time LOTOS. *Computer Networks, 40*(5), 639-663.

Yu, H., & Salehi, N. (2000). The network simulator ns-2. In *Proceedings Network Simulator Workshop.* Cooperative Association for Internet Data Analysis.

Chapter VI

Enhancing Student Understanding of Packet-Forwarding Theories and Concepts with Low-Cost Laboratory Activities

Anthony P. Kadi, The University of Technology Sydney, Australia

Abstract

Teaching packet-forwarding theories and concepts in a practical way to undergraduate students requires both a teaching and learning framework and a laboratory infrastructure. Creating a teaching and learning framework in which students can develop a deeper knowledge and understanding of abstract concepts is not a simple task. In addition to teaching materials, the teacher requires a clear idea about learning theories and issues: (1) what is learning; (2) what is knowledge; and (3) how do students go about learning. This chapter describes a low-cost laboratory infrastructure for teaching and learning packet-forwarding theories and concepts. The framework is learner-centred and is focused on learning experiences in both classroom and laboratory. The laboratory-based activities form a critical component of the overall framework.

Learning Objectives

After completing this chapter, you will be able to:

- Explain how packet-forwarding theories can be taught in a practical way.
- Discuss the effectiveness of hands-on laboratory activities in teaching and learning contexts.
- Define the following key terms: experiential learning, packet forwarding, and static and dynamic routing.
- Suggest further improvements to the laboratory activities described in the chapter.

Introduction

This chapter presents a teaching and learning framework for packet-forwarding concepts which aims to give students a deep understanding of these concepts. The framework is learner-centred and focuses on learning *experiences* in the classroom and the laboratory. The laboratory-based activities form a critical component of the overall framework; however, the other elements of the framework are equally important in achieving the intended aim. The chapter begins with a philosophical basis for the teaching and learning framework and then describes the elements of the framework and how these are put into practice, illustrated by several examples. The chapter concludes with a discussion on some initial indicators of the efficacy of the framework and directions for future work.

Enhancing Student Understanding

Creating a teaching and learning framework in which students can come to deeply understand abstract concepts is not necessarily a simple task. Among other things, the teacher needs to have a clear idea of such fundamental, yet often glossed-over issues such as:

- What is learning?
- What is knowledge?
- How do students go about learning?

An individual teacher's answers to the above questions will have a profound impact on precisely what activities take place in the classroom and how these activities are conducted. This, in turn, has a major impact on what students learn (the subject *content*), but also how they go about learning (the *process*) and the resulting level of understanding that they are able to demonstrate (the *depth* of understanding). Although seemingly simple questions, there is significant debate within the global education community on the answers to these questions. This chapter presents a set of answers to these questions which forms the philosophical basis for the teaching and learning framework described. The answers are drawn from one of the more widely accepted viewpoints on learning from the scholarly education literature.

Kolb (1984) provides a "working definition" of learning: "Learning is the process whereby knowledge is created through the transformation of experience." He then goes on to say that "to understand learning, we must understand the nature of knowledge, and vice versa." Kolb is one of many who reject the absolutist view of knowledge, which says that knowledge is an independent entity that exists in the world, waiting to be discovered or acquired. Such a view would imply that teaching is simply a process of transmitting knowledge from a source into the mind of a student. Kolb's alternative theory is that knowledge is something that exists only within individual minds, and that it has to be created by a process of learning involving transformations and negotiations between existing knowledge and experiences. Whether or not a teacher makes a deliberate choice about which learning theory they accept, their understanding of what learning is and how it occurs will largely influence the type of activities that students in their classes are asked to do.

Kolb's theory of experiential learning has numerous synergies with the notion of constructivism, in which, as Duffy and Jonassen (1992) explain, "meaning is imposed on the world by us, rather than existing in the world independently of us."

There are many ways to structure the world, and there are many meanings or perspectives for any event or concept. Thus there is not a correct meaning that we are striving for." The focus, in this instance, is on meaning. However, it can be argued that meaning is actually a facet of knowledge itself. Gorman (2002) describes three classes of knowledge and four facets of the more commonly understood type of knowledge:

- **Tacit knowledge**: Knowledge that is learned without conscious understanding of underlying theory.
- **Explicit knowledge**: There are four types:

  > **Information**: sometimes also called propositional knowledge.
  > **Skills**: knowing *how* to use information, also referred to as procedural knowledge.
  > **Judgment**: knowing *when* it is appropriate to use skills and information in a given context.
  > **Wisdom**: knowing *why* it is appropriate to use certain judgments, skills, and/or information in the right combination for a given set of circumstances; wisdom and judgment are sometimes referred to collectively as dispositional knowledge.

- **Distributed knowledge**: collectively owned knowledge that is owned as a result of teamwork.

In comparison, it would seem that Duffy and Jonassen's notion of meaning could be considered as a combination of Gorman's judgment and wisdom.

A critical aspect of all of these theories is that knowledge is not simply information or facts that can be presented to a student for regurgitation. Deep understanding of a concept involves knowing about it, how to apply it, when to apply it, and also why to apply it.

Successful teaching which results in deep understanding of a given set of concepts also requires an understanding of how students go about learning. Entwistle (1997) describes three different approaches that students take to learning. Table 1 summarizes the three approaches of learning.

If a teacher wants his or her students to take a deep approach to learning, what conditions need to be in place to enable and/or encourage this? Biggs (1987) addressed this question in his research. He found that there are a number of factors that will contribute to the choice of learning approach taken by a given

Table 1. Entwistle's three different student approaches to learning

Deep Approach (transforming)	Surface Approach (reproducing)	Strategic Approach (organising)
Intention: to understand ideas for yourself by: • Relating ideas to previous knowledge and experience • Looking for patterns and underlying principles • Checking evidence and relating it to conclusions • Examining logic and argument cautiously and critically • Becoming actively interested in the learning materials and processes	Intention: to cope with learning requirements by: • Studying without reflecting on either purpose or strategy • Treating learning as unrelated bits of knowledge acquisition • Memorising facts and procedures routinely • Finding difficulty in making sense of new ideas presented • Feeling undue pressure and worry about work and/or learning	Intention: to please oneself and significant others with high marks, grades etc. by: • Putting consistent effort into studying • Finding the right conditions and materials for study • Managing time and effort effectively • Being alert to assessment requirements and criteria • Gearing work to the perceived preferences of assessors
Focus is on learning process and meaning	Focus is on facts and procedures	Focus is on assessment of learning

student in a give instance, and these include personal attributes such as ability, experiences, and *locus of control* (extent to which the learner can control their learning experience to suit them); and situational attributes such as the nature of the task, situational stipulations (e.g., student must pass this subject in order to progress towards graduation), instructional set (things that students actually have to do), and formal teaching. Biggs concluded "Whether or not a deep approach is used will depend more on the way the task is presented in context, than on the individual student doing it."

In the application of these teaching and learning theories to the aim of having students coming to a deep understanding of packet-forwarding concepts, there is very little in the literature on this specific topic. There are examples of writings that describe laboratory equipment and configuration or software (e.g., Bokhari et al., 2004; Casado, Vijayaraghavan, Appenzeller, & McKeown, 2002), but these do not link the laboratory activities to the teaching and learning approach used within a given context and, hence, do not describe how the lab activities contribute, if at all, to student understanding. Other works do attempt to link teaching and learning theories with the broad area of computer networking (see, e.g., Chang, 2004); however, these are often nonspecific regarding packet-forwarding concepts. They may incorporate some aspects of this specific area but rarely focus on it. There are many courses and training programs that do deal with this specific topic (e.g., Cisco courses such as Cisco Certified Network Associate); however, these are rarely reported in the literature, if at all (e.g., Liang, 2000), and rarely link education theory with specific learning outcomes.

The Teaching and Learning Framework

Using the learning and teaching theory briefly outlined above, a framework has been developed and successfully applied in a relatively large class (approximately 60 students) at the postgraduate level in the Faculty of Engineering, University of Technology, Sydney. The class is known as 49202 Communication Protocols and is taken by students enrolled in the master of engineering or master of engineering studies program with a major in telecommunications. The only difference between these two programs is that students in the master of engineering also need to complete a graduate project (which is like a half-thesis). The focus of the class is on generic concepts that are critical to an understanding of communication protocols, and these concepts are illustrated predominantly with examples from the TCP/IP protocol suite. The textbook used for the class is Forouzan (2003).

The framework is focused on and best described by the set of learning experiences that students are asked to undertake as part of the class. These are:

- Reading specific chapters/sections from the textbook. This experience introduces the student to a specific topic area and begins to situate this topic within the course as a whole.

- Participating in a "lecture" session. During this experience, the student is introduced to abstractions of specific examples and begins to construct a basic understanding of the underlying concepts. The teacher-centred lecturing is regularly interrupted, and the student is asked to solve basic problems. This keeps the student active and is a critical component of building understanding as it tests the students' current knowledge with what they have just been exposed to. The result is either reinforcement of current knowledge or realignment.

- Completing a set of prework questions for a laboratory session that is held at least one week after the lecture session. These questions relate specifically to the concepts developed in the lecture session, and some of the problems solved during the lecture session by the students are related to or form part of the laboratory prework.

- Sitting for a short (e.g., 15-minute) online quiz of concepts developed in the lecture session. This quiz is held in the week following the lecture class to give students time to further develop their understanding through self and group study. The quiz contributes 15% of the final grade. The main reason for this is to provide an incentive to keep up-to-date each week and spread the learning out over the entire semester. Some of the questions in the quizzes are specifically related to the laboratory prework.

- Undertaking a series of laboratory activities that are linked to the concepts developed during the lecture sessions. The basic aim of each lab session is to confirm (or deny) the work that was done in the lecture and the lab prework. Observations made during the lab are discussed in groups, and students help each other to gain a better understanding of the concepts and theory. The laboratory activities are not entirely prescriptive but do allow for some individual experimentation and observation (Biggs' locus of control).

- Writing a laboratory report for documenting prework and results obtained in the lab and explaining the results with regard to the theory from the textbook, lectures, and prework. The report also includes answers to higher-level conceptual questions that probe deeper understanding of key concepts. The report is assessed, and overall, lab reports contribute 30% of the total assessment. The successful completion of laboratory reports is thus one of Biggs' institutional stipulations.

- Reflecting on the assessment of their laboratory report and quiz to determine whether their understanding of key concepts and theories is aligned with the teacher's. This alignment of the student's understanding with the teacher's understanding is a critical element of the teaching and learning process, which Laurillard (2002) models using what she calls a "conversational framework." Detailed feedback on laboratory reports, as well as the posting of the best report on the Web, allows students to validate their knowledge — if there is substantial alignment, then the knowledge is reinforced; if there is misalignment, the student can realign and eliminate misconceptions by comparing their report with the one posted on the Web or by individual discussions with the teaching staff during consultation times.

- Completing a final examination at the end of semester which has some questions from lectures, quizzes, and labs, as well as questions that the students have not previously seen. The exam contributes 55% of the final grade. The questions in the final exam are designed to test understanding and application of the key concepts, not regurgitation of information or facts.

The semester consists of six modules of 2 weeks each. The first week in each module consists of pre-lecture readings, attending and participating in the lecture, and then doing the lab prework. The second week in each module consists of sitting for the short quiz, doing the lab activities, and then writing and submitting the report. A detailed report assessment is returned 2 weeks after submission and is discussed during a subsequent lecture. Quiz questions are also briefly discussed in lectures to clarify any ambiguities.

The learning and teaching framework, therefore, is based on *learning experiences* and specifically links theory with reality. A carefully constructed series of learning experiences, of which the laboratory activities are the nexus, allows the student to construct knowledge over time and enables misconceptions to be revealed and dealt with, if present. These learning experiences also enable deepening of understanding by reinforcing theory with real observations and the need to demonstrate knowledge in various assessment tasks over the course of the semester.

Laboratory Activities and Infrastructure

A number of important practical considerations in the implementation of the learning and teaching framework are:

- What is the cost associated with the laboratory infrastructure required to deliver the various learning outcomes?
- Can the laboratory infrastructure be used for other purposes to help justify its acquisition and operation?

In the Faculty of Engineering at the University of Technology, Sydney (UTS), we have a networking teaching laboratory which can be used by a number of different classes and courses. Normally, this is a nontrivial matter because both software and hardware may need to be significantly altered for different activities and different classes. We have implemented a system using removable hard-disk drives and easily accessible networking hardware which allows rapid reconfiguration of both the hardware and software. We use this laboratory infrastructure for many different subjects and lab activities, but the one that is detailed in this chapter is on layer-3 packet-forwarding concepts known as *routing*.

A laboratory session consists of a number of learning activities. Each activity in the routing lab session is designed to demonstrate the behaviour of the network in a particular state and link this to the theory. Questions in the lab notes which need to be answered as part of a lab report are designed to link these activities together and to assist students in constructing knowledge of packet-forwarding concepts in general.

The 2-and-a-half-hour laboratory session that focuses on routing consists of the following seven specific activities:

1. Static routing using default routes around a logical ring topology;
2. Static routing using fixed routes in a mesh topology;
3. Static routing incorporating a deliberate routing loop;
4. Dynamic routing using Routing Information Protocol (RIP);
5. Simulated failure and subsequent recovery of a router using RIP;
6. Dynamic routing using Open Shortest Path First (OSPF); and
7. Simulated failure and subsequent recovery of a router using OSPF.

The lab infrastructure is described next.

The Laboratory Infrastructure

For the routing lab activities, the following equipment is used and is interconnected as shown in Figure 1:

*   50 personal computers (PCs) spread amongst 10 benches

    ➢   10 of these PCs (one PC on each bench, shown in green in Figure 1) configured with RedHat Linux version 9.0 (http://www.redhat.com) on a removable hard-disk drive to act as a router. These PCs are equipped with:

        *   One four-port Ethernet network interface card (NIC; D-Link DFE-580TX; D-Link Australia, 2003).
        *   Two single-port Ethernet NICs (D-Link DFE-538TX; D-Link Systems, 2005). One of these acts as the "management interface" to the router.

    ➢   The remaining 40 PCs to act as "client" computers. These have a CD drive (but not a hard disk) and can boot and run a version of Linux called Knoppix (http://www.knoppix.net). Each of these PCs has a single-port Ethernet NIC (D-Link DFE-538TX). Students are assigned to these client computers in pairs. Thus, the lab can accommodate up to 80 students in a session.

- Ten eight-port unmanaged Ethernet switches (one on each bench) to connect each of the client PCs on that bench to one port of the router.

- One 16-port unmanaged Ethernet switch to connect all management interfaces of all the routers together to form a management subnetwork (shown in dotted lines in Figure 1).

- A number of Ethernet cables:

  > Standard Cat-5e patch cables for connecting the PCs to the Ethernet switches (shown in blue in Figure 1).

  > Cat-5e crossover cables for connecting the routers to each other (shown in red in Figure 1). These cables are "strung up" to the ceiling and labelled on each end, so that staff and students can clearly identify where each of the cables originates and terminates and they are easily accessible for simple and rapid reconfiguration.

All of this hardware (apart from the four-port NICs) can be purchased from most retail computer outlets. The infrastructure can be scaled up or down to suit local needs. If computers with more than three PCI expansion slots are used, an equivalent result can be achieved with using only the more commonly available and inexpensive single-port NICs. The software, RedHat Linux, Knoppix Linux, and other software mentioned in this chapter are all freely available on the Web.

One of the routers (or an additional PC connected to the management subnet) acts as a management station. From here, the logical topology and forwarding

Figure 1. UTS laboratory configuration

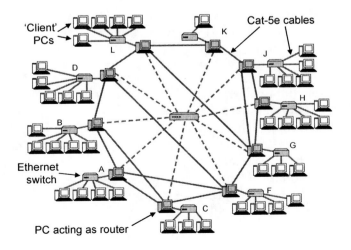

behaviour of the network can be changed by issuing a single command. For example, to transition the routers from activity 3 (static routing) to activity 4 (dynamic routing with RIP), a single command is entered at the management station console. This command is generally a script that makes secure shell command calls to each of the routers via the management interfaces to change routing tables manually, start/stop routing daemons, or configure routing software. For dynamic routing activities, a software package known as GNU Zebra (http://www.zebra.org) is used for the implementation of the routing protocols and associated behaviours. This freely available software has a command line interface that emulates Cisco routers.

In each activity, students can use the ping program, usually with the route recording option enabled, to determine the following information:

- if there is connectivity in both the forward and reverse paths to a particular destination from their location;
- the details of the forward and reverse paths (i.e., the router interfaces traversed);
- the end-to-end delay statistics of multiple pings (minimum, maximum, and average) as well as the first ping (generally delayed due to address resolution process taking place).

The IP addressing structure used for the routing laboratory enables a simple translation between physical location and IP address. This allows students to ping particular destinations and examine the routes taken with relative ease. Details of this can be obtained from the author, if desired.

Students are also able to use a packet sniffer, in this case, the freely available Ethereal (http://www.ethereal.com), on both client and router interfaces to gain more details about forwarding behaviour. Ethereal is one of the packages available in Knoppix Linux, and it can also be installed from the RedHat 9.0 distribution.

Unfortunately, due to space limitations, it is not possible to share the details of each of the activities with the reader; however, a couple of examples will illustrate the design and implementation philosophies described earlier.

Example Activity 1: Static Routing With Logical Mesh Topology

The students are given copies of the routing tables for each router, which are manually configured for optimal mesh routing. An example routing table is shown in Table 2. For prework, students are asked to:

Table 2. Example routing table

ROUTING TABLE FOR ROUTER A (Activity 2)			
Destination	Next Hop	Genmask	Iface
10.1.6.0	Direct	255.255.255.252	eth0
10.1.2.0	Direct	255.255.255.252	eth1
10.1.3.0	Direct	255.255.255.252	eth2
10.1.1.0	Direct	255.255.255.0	eth3
10.2.2.0	10.1.2.2	255.255.255.0	eth1
10.3.3.0	10.1.3.2	255.255.255.0	eth2
10.4.4.0	10.1.2.2	255.255.255.0	eth1
10.6.6.0	10.1.6.2	255.255.255.0	eth0
10.7.7.0	10.1.6.2	255.255.255.0	eth0
10.8.8.0	10.1.6.2	255.255.255.0	eth0
10.10.10.0	10.1.6.2	255.255.255.0	eth0
10.11.11.0	10.1.2.2	255.255.255.0	eth1
10.12.12.0	10.1.2.2	255.255.255.0	eth1
10.2.3.0	10.1.2.2	255.255.255.252	eth1
10.2.4.0	10.1.2.2	255.255.255.252	eth1
10.3.6.0	10.1.3.2	255.255.255.252	eth2
10.4.6.0	10.1.6.2	255.255.255.252	eth0
10.4.12.0	10.1.2.1	255.255.255.252	eth1
10.6.7.0	10.1.6.2	255.255.255.252	eth0
10.7.8.0	10.1.6.2	255.255.255.252	eth0
10.7.10.0	10.1.6.2	255.255.255.252	eth0
10.7.12.0	10.1.6.2	255.255.255.252	eth0
10.8.10.0	10.1.6.2	255.255.255.252	eth0
10.10.11.0	10.1.6.2	255.255.255.252	eth0
10.11.12.0	10.1.2.2	255.255.255.252	eth1

- Determine the forward and reverse routes for particular source and destination pairs.
- Compare the total number of hops between various destinations for a particular source with those if a logical ring topology were used.
- Predict what would happen if particular links fail and compare to the case of a logical ring topology.

During the lab activity, they actually ping various destinations from the source that they have been assigned and verify that their predictions are consistent with reality and the theory. They also do this for the logical ring topology in a previous activity.

This activity allows students to learn and understand:

- Routing in networks at layer 3 can be done manually through the use of routing tables stored at each router.

- The logical topology of the network need not necessarily follow the physical topology of the network, and this can be changed by modifying the routing tables.

- A ring topology provides a more consistent routing delay but is prone to catastrophic failure by the failure of a single link.

- An optimal mesh topology provides a lower, but more variable routing delay (for different destinations in the network, not for different packets!) and is more resilient to link or node failures.

Example Activity 2: Dynamic Routing Using OSPF

In this activity, there is no prework, as it follows on from previous activities. The students determine a destination that requires a path through a particular router. They begin to ping that destination with the route recording option and with a ping frequency of 5 seconds. The tutor then announces that the particular router has failed and simulates this by disconnecting all of the network cables to that router. The ping packets stop getting responses until the OSPF protocol rearranges the topology and provides alternate paths. At this point, the pings begin to work again, and by counting the number of ping packets lost, students can estimate the recovery time of the network. The "failed" router is then re-enabled by plugging the cables back in, and after a brief delay, the routes are updated to the original, more optimal routes. Again, the time required for reconfiguration can be estimated. These times can then be compared to those obtained from the same activity but using RIP. The students are asked to answer the following questions:

- Why does the ping continue after some delay following the failure of a router?

- Why does the route change when the failed router is re-enabled?

- Why are the recovery times different for the different routing protocols?

- From this activity, students develop a better understanding of:

- A dynamic routing protocol can allow the network to adapt to link and/or router failures and provide alternate forwarding paths, if they are available.

- A routing protocol will always result in the most "optimal" route being chosen, and this can vary over time as routers and/or link states change.

- The performance of routing protocols varies depending on their design and implementation. (In the previous activity, students investigate the size, frequency, and format of routing messages exchanged between routers for both RIP and OSPF.)

Student Results and Feedback

Initial results from the implementation of the teaching and learning framework described in this chapter have been very encouraging. At the time of writing, a formal study and analysis of the efficacy of this framework have not been carried out. This section describes some initial indicators of its effectiveness and acceptance by the students.

In the autumn semester of 2004, a class of 55 postgraduate coursework students undertook the laboratory activities described above. In the final exam (3 hours duration, five questions, 20 marks each), the average score in the final exam question specifically related to routing was 13.9/20 (»70%), which was the highest of all the questions asked that semester. This was quite different to previous semesters in which a more traditional teaching and learning approach was used, and the scores for questions on routing were much worse.

Students also responded very favourably to the experiential teaching and learning approach in the end-of-semester survey. Here is a selection of the comments that students made in open-ended questions such as "What did you like best about this subject and why?":

- "[The lecturer] made the learning process a fun activity to do, and this is quite [a] difficult thing to do. I really enjoyed it and also can appreciate the amazing preparation for one of the labs, particularly the one relating to routing. ... Having done five Cisco courses, I believe the coordination put together in the routing is just outstanding. Appreciating the differences of OSPF and RIP functionalities, for example, and static and dynamic routing in a single session ... well, [it] is just fantastic."

- "I liked the lab activities the most, because it was helpful to understand what we learnt from the class time. Especially, most of lab activities were deeply related to the practical ideas."

- "I particularly enjoyed the fortnightly rotation of theory and practical work. It gives students enough time to prepare and absorb materials and to test those ideas and theories out during the quiz and laboratories. The first week provides the background, and the second week grounds and cements that information into knowledge. Having this duality helps keep the subject 'alive' and 'fresh'; pure book reading tends to reduce student interests and 'zest' for learning materials. The rotation helps keep a healthy interest in study."

- "The labs strongly bought home the theoretical concepts. They made us see what was happening right before our eyes. There is nothing worse than not understanding how theory has meaning."

Conclusion and Directions for Future Work

Although it is too early to conclusively say that the approach described in this chapter to helping students learn and understand packet-forwarding concepts is better than traditional approaches, the results to date are very encouraging. With a focus on *learning experiences* rather than on *content* and with the low-cost laboratory infrastructure described briefly in this chapter (which can also be used for many other purposes), the teacher can ensure that appropriate knowledge is constructed by the learners in an effective and efficient manner.

Further work is required to gauge the effectiveness of this teaching and learning approach and to determine whether the approach used in this particular context can be applied to other contexts. More information about the laboratory infrastructure and course materials can be found by contacting the author.

Summary

It is often difficult to motivate students to learn packet-forwarding theories and concepts because many students appear to find the topic technical and rather dry and boring. This chapter described a framework for enhancing teaching and learning various aspects of packet-forwarding theories and concepts at both introductory and advanced levels. The framework is based on a set of learning activities: readings, class participation, laboratory session, problem solving, quizzes, practical laboratory activities, report writing, and summative assessments.

Both teacher and students can benefit from the use of laboratory infrastructure in different teaching and learning contexts. A teacher is able to use the system both in the classroom and laboratory as a demonstration to liven-up the lecture environment. Students, on the other hand, gain a practical hands-on learning experience by setting up and configuring routing protocols. Through experimenting with key parameters, the students can gain insights into the key concepts of packet-forwarding theories. Student responses to the end-of-semester survey were mostly favourable. The students indicated that they had found the laboratory activities easy to use and helpful in gaining an understanding of packet-forwarding theories and concepts.

Key Terms and Definitions

Constructivism: A theory of learning and knowing that holds that learning is an active process of knowledge construction in which learners build on prior knowledge and experience to shape meaning and construct new knowledge.

Deep learning: The process by which a person comes to achieve a critical awareness of a particular item of information or an idea as well as how this information can be used in the real world, why it should be used, in what ways and what situations it is applicable, and its relationship to other matters.

Dynamic routing: A form of routing in which the routes that packets take in a network are able to change as a function of time. The routes can change as a result of node or link failures or as a result of node or link characteristics (speed, cost, etc.), including the volume of traffic that is currently being serviced.

Experiential learning: A theory about the process of learning that involves a four-stage cycle consisting of concrete experience, reflective observation, abstract conceptualisation, and active experimentation.

Packet forwarding: The process by which protocol data units in a packet-based network are sent from their source to their destination.

Routing: The process of packet forwarding that is done at layer 3, usually called the "networking" layer in a protocol architecture. The most common protocol used at layer 3 in the world is the Internet Protocol (IP).

Static routing: A form of routing in which the routes that packets take in a network do not change as a function of time once they are configured.

Review Questions

1. Describe the low-cost laboratory infrastructure for enhancing teaching and learning packet-forwarding concepts.

2. Explain how learning theories are linked to teaching and learning packet-forwarding theories and concepts.

3. Explain how the teaching and learning framework for packet-forwarding concepts is put into practice.

4. Compare and contrast deep, surface, and strategic approaches to learning.

5. Explain how removable hard-disk drives can be used in the laboratory for experimenting with static and dynamic routings.

6. Discuss the difference between static and dynamic routing.

7. List and describe possible enhancements to the practical laboratory activities described in the chapter.

References

Biggs, J. B. (1987). *Student approaches to learning and studying*. Melbourne, Australia: Australian Council for Education Research.

Bokhari, S. H., Ahmed, M., bin Sohail, S., Khan, R. H., Mirza, J. A., & Ali, M. (2004). A networking laboratory for the developing world. *IEEE Communications, 42*(2), 106-113.

Casado, M., Vijayaraghavan, V., Appenzeller, G., & McKeown, N. (2002). The Stanford Virtual Router: A teaching tool and network simulator. *ACM SIGCOMM Computer Communication Review, 32*(3), 26.

Chang, R. K. C. (2004). Teaching computer networking with the help of personal computer networks. In *Proceedings of the 9th annual SIGCSE Conference on Innovation and Technology in Computer Science Education* (pp. 208-212). Leeds, UK: ACM Press.

D-Link Australia. (2003). *DFE-580TX: 4-port PCI fast Ethernet server adapter*. Retrieved January 21, 2005, from http://www.dlink.com.au/products/adapters/dfe580tx/

D-Link Systems. (2005). *DFE-538TX*. Retrieved January 21, 2005, from http://support.dlink.com/products/view.asp?productid=DFE%2D538TX

Duffy, T. M., & Jonassen, D. H. (1992). Constructivism: New implications for instructional technology. In T. M. Duffy & D. H. Jonassen (Eds.), *Constructivism and the technology of instruction: A conversation*. Lawrence Erlbaum.

Entwistle, N. (1997). Contrasting perspectives on learning. In F. Marton, D. Hounsell, & N. Entwistle (Eds.), *The experience of learning* (2nd ed, p. 19). Edinburgh, UK: Scottish Academic Press.

Forouzan, B. (2003). *TCP/IP protocol suite* (2nd ed.). New York: McGraw-Hill.

Gorman, M. E. (2002). Turning students into professionals: Types of knowledge and ABET engineering criteria. *Journal of Engineering Education, 91*(3), 327-332.

Kolb, D. A. (1984). *Experiential learning: Experience as the source of learning and development.* Prentice Hall.

Laurillard, D. (2002). *Rethinking university teaching: A conversational framework for the effective use of learning technologies* (2nd ed.). Routledge.

Liang, C. (2000). A course on TCP/IP networking with Linux. In *Proceedings of the 5th annual CCSC Northeastern Conference on The Journal of Computing in Small Colleges* (pp. 256-264). Consortium for Computing Sciences in Colleges.

Redhat | The Open Source Leader. Viewed January 21, 2005, at http://www.redhat.com/

Chapter VII

Ethereal:
A Tool for Making the Abstract Protocol a Concrete Reality

David Bremer, Otago Polytechnic, New Zealand

Abstract

Learning the nature of data communication and networks requires understanding of how a theoretical protocol is implemented as actual communication. Taking ARP as a simple example, it is one thing to be able to understand its purpose and operation from readings and lectures. It is another thing entirely to be able to identify the actual ARP traffic from a sample of packets, identify any unusual behavior, and perform troubleshooting activities based on previous practical experience. A theoretical understanding may be enough to describe a particular aspect of networking, perhaps even enough to pass an exam. Practical knowledge, however, shows a deeper understanding that comes from actual experience with the protocol, beyond that of reading and discussion. One issue for educators in the field of networking is the problem of giving the students an "up close and personal" interaction with protocols that are so heavily immersed in theory. How do we make the theoretical protocol a more concrete reality for the students?

Learning Objectives

After completing this chapter, you will be able to:

- Recognise the difficulty that students face in becoming familiar with networking protocols when approached from a purely theoretical perspective.

- Explain how a packet sniffer tool such as Ethereal can be used to make the protocols more accessible to students and ease the learning process.

- Critically consider one example for designing a series of related lessons.

- Suggest further enhancements to laboratory activities that make use of packet analysis.

Introduction

Learning the nature of data communication and networks requires understanding of how a theoretical protocol is implemented as actual communication. Taking ARP as a simple example, it is one thing to be able to understand its purpose and operation from readings and lectures. It is another thing entirely to be able to identify the actual ARP traffic from a sample of packets, identify any unusual behavior, and perform troubleshooting activities based on previous practical experience.

A theoretical understanding may be enough to describe a particular aspect of networking, perhaps even enough to pass an exam. Practical knowledge, however, shows a deeper understanding that comes from actual experience with the protocol, beyond that of reading and discussion. One issue for educators in the field of networking is the problem of giving the students an "up close and personal" interaction with protocols that are so heavily immersed in theory. How do we make the theoretical protocol a more concrete reality for the students?

Background and Motivation

Within the field of general education, it is fairly well established that it is desirable to have students work with a "real" system in order to learn the theoretical foundations of that system. Proponents of making the theoretical concrete include Dewey (1987), Kolb and Fry (1975), and Papert (1980). These educationalists advocated the avoidance, or perhaps the postponement, of actually teaching the theory in favor of allowing the students to discover the underlying principles for themselves. Kolb and Fry (1975) describes learning as a continuous spiral of concrete experience, observation and reflection, development of abstract concepts, and testing in new situations.

As Sarkar (2005) points out, even Skinner, the archetype behaviorist, favored an experiential approach to learning (Skinner, 1964). Dewey (1987) suggested that the language and concepts formed when children were asked to create a chair were much deeper than when chairs were simply discussed. Papert (1980) created a child-centered environment (the programming environment LOGO) that would allow students to engage with geometry on a personal and concrete level through which they discovered geometric rules for themselves. The common element is that the learner is working directly with the thing that is being studied. Unfortunately, while experiential and discovery learning can be very powerful, most students do not have the time available to independently reinvent 30 years of research into networking, at least not in the 17 weeks that we have available for teaching a one-semester paper. However, the core principles proposed by these educationalists are important.

Many networking educators are searching for tools that will allow their students to experience the abstract theory of networking in a practical way (Cigas, 2003; Francia & Chao, 2004). This entire book is directed towards this aim. Various tools and techniques are used to enhance the learner's understanding of networks, including simulation and modeling (Cameron & Wijekumar, 2003; Perez-Hardy, 2003) and the expression of the concept as a graphical animation (Holliday, 2003). The most concrete approach is having the student interact with a real network. A number of educators are moving in this direction (McDonald, Rickman, McDonald, Heeler, & Hawley, 2001).

Comer (2004) quite forcibly argues that "the best way to learn is by doing — there is no good substitute for hands-on experience with a real network. Interconnecting the hardware, configuring network systems, measuring performance, observing protocols in action, and creating client-server programs that communicate over a network all help sharpen one's understanding and appreciation" (p. 15).

We should remember that networking is *not* about abstract theory. Sometimes instructors and lecturers get so immersed in the theory that we forget the reality that *is* networking. Even the dry RFCs are in fact describing actual, real, concrete things that are able to be implemented and are directly observable with the right tool. We have found that a very powerful educational tool in network education is one that allows students to capture traffic that they themselves have created and then to analyze that traffic.

This tool is variously known as a packet analyzer or packet sniffer and will be known to most networking professionals and educators. We use the open source product Ethereal in this role within our courses. Many other products, such as

Network Associates Sniffer, Etherpeek, and Microsoft Server Network Monitor, exist. Network educators have reported that these tools are very useful for "enhancing the sense of concreteness by giving the student a firsthand look at TCP/IP transport and protocols" (Mechtly & Decker, 2003). Most sniffers perform adequately for educational purposes. Ethereal has the advantages that it is free and cross-platform and performs almost all of the network analysis tasks that we wish to undertake. The only exception to this that we have encountered is the monitoring of the PPP connection process. Because of certain interface restrictions it is not possible to capture the LCP and IPCP traffic in Linux or any NT-based system. We have however captured such traffic under Windows 98.

Use a Tool or Program a Sniffer?

Our courses have taken the approach that students will analyze real traffic that occurs within a typical network using an existing tool rather than have the students develop their own sniffer as a way of learning about network protocols. There are numerous tutorials available that guide students through the process of making their own packet analyzer (for those who are interested, refer to Insolvibile, 2001; Renfro, 1999). Our decision follows the reasoning of Jipping, Bugaj, Mihalkova, and Porter (2003), who suggest that "If students program network sniffing themselves, it is very easy to get mired in the data structures and system interfaces needed to properly fetch a network packet and extract data that can be analyzed. Students should focus on the analysis itself, not the mechanics of traffic sniffing."

In some courses (especially computer science), the data structures may indeed be the focus of the study. Our course, similar to Adams and Erickson's (2001), is targeted more towards a network and system administration model rather than towards either computer science or business systems. In our situation we wish to develop an understanding of the network protocols rather than focus on the data structures involved in programming a network application.

Description of the System

Ethereal

Ethereal is available as open source software (Open Source Initiative, 2004) distributed under the GNU General Public License (Free Software Foundation, 1991) and is freely available at http://www.ethereal.com. It is a graphical tool that captures and displays an interpretation of packets that become available to the network card. Providing the network card can be placed in promiscuous mode, all packets seen by the network card can be displayed, even if they were not destined for the device on which Ethereal is installed.

One of the criticisms of Ethereal has been the lack of documentation. This has changed recently with the publication of the online "Ethereal User's Guide" (Sharpe, 2004) and the printed "Ethereal Packet Sniffing" (Orebaugh & Ramirez, 2004).

Overview of Ethereal Operation

Ethereal's display interface is broken into three sections as shown in Figure 1. The top section shows a separate packet in each row. This provides a useful summary of the traffic that has been captured. The middle section contains an interpretation of the packet contents with the data arranged in layers resembling the OSI model. The bottom section displays, in both hexadecimal and ASCII, the raw data that was captured.

In Figure 1, a line is selected in the top section. This selection is a summary showing that we have selected a packet traveling from 10.1.0.50 to 10.100.0.145 and that it is an HTTP version 1.1 OK response. The middle section displays an interpretation of the data within the packet, arranged according to the various protocols. In this example we would normally see:

- Ethernet II (data link layer),

- Internet Protocol (network layer),

- Transmission Control Protocol (transport layer), and

- HTTP (application layers). To see this you would scroll up in the middle section.

Figure 1. Ethereal display interface

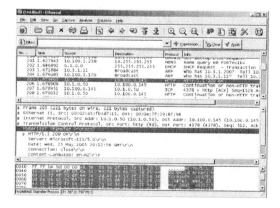

Each protocol heading contains a summary of the data within that protocol. The user may drill down and obtain the detailed protocol data by clicking on the triangle icon next to the protocol data, as has been done for Hypertext Transfer Protocol in Figure 1.

The bottom section shows the raw data that was captured. It is worth noting that the CRC or Frame Check Sequence is not captured. This is removed by the network card before Ethereal manages to capture any data.

Classroom Use

The procedure used within the class is very simple. We normally follow a routine of:

- Start Ethereal,
- Begin the data capture,
- Create the traffic that we wish to analyze,
- Stop the capture,
- Analyze the traffic.

The capture interface is shown in Figure 2. Introducing this interface to students allows us to readdress the various delivery aspects of the data link layer and to reinforce the fact that traffic may be received by a device that is not actually intended for that device. This is especially important in a logical bus network that uses hubs rather than switches. The network card's promiscuous mode is usually introduced at this point.

We normally do not introduce the capture filter until well into the course. The capture filter only records packets matching specified conditions and uses a rather difficult syntax. Instead we rely on the display filter, which restricts the display of packets after they have been captured.

Usefulness and Benefits of the System

We began this discussion of Ethereal by identifying the desirability of turning abstract theory into a concrete reality for the learner. It is perhaps useful to look at a particular example of using Ethereal to support the learning of a specific topic.

Figure 2. Capture Options dialog box

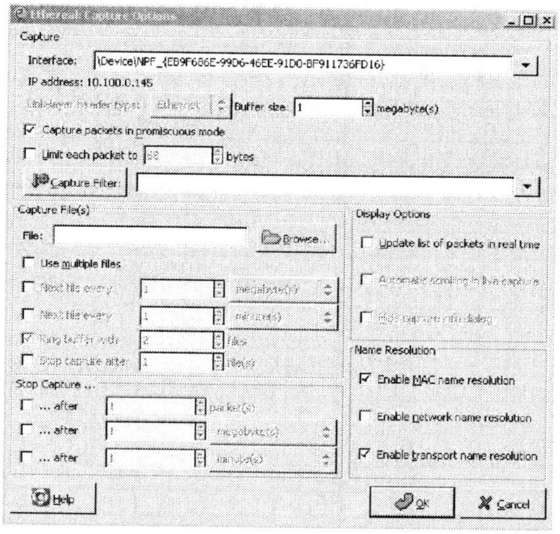

We have developed a structured or "scaffolded" approach for many of our topics. While generally favoring the open discovery model of educationalists such as Kolb, we prefer to include an initial structure that directs students, while allowing for more open-ended experimentation. The aim is to bring the student from a stage of reasonable ignorance of a topic through to being able to problem-solve new or novel aspects of the topic. We try to provide a sequence of related activities that will provide a scaffolded and staged progression between these two extremes. Our approach involves the following series of five activities:

1. **Instruction**: An introductory lesson where the topic is explained to the student.

    The student is a passive participant.

2. **Directed task**: Modeling and sometimes extreme hand-holding, often with worksheets.

    The student is a very constrained but active participant.

3. **Independent activity**: The student reproduces their own version of activities modeled previously.

    The student is an active participant demonstrating that they can reproduce a previously modeled activity.

4. **Novel situation, troubleshooting, and diagnostic problem-solving**: Introduce novel situations in which the learner has to investigate, diagnose, troubleshoot, and problem solve.

The student begins to show mastery of the topic by demonstrating an understanding of an activity that is related but not previously modeled.

5. **Reinforcement**: The student applies the skills and knowledge from one topic to activities that are being used to learn subsequent topics.

Example Use of Ethereal in Lessons and Labs

It may be useful to describe the use of this structure by presenting our approach to teaching the three-way handshake used by TCP to establish a connection.

Stage 1: Instruction — Old-Fashioned Teaching

We begin a sequence of lessons with a lecture that includes an explanation of the three-way handshake as one stage within TCP (Postel, 1981). The lesson is typical of any lecture; the instructor is in charge and in full control. Student activity is reduced to asking occasional questions from the floor, answering questions posed by the instructor, and note-taking.

Stage 2: Directed Task — Modeling an Investigation of the Topic

The first activity is a very directed worksheet, which directs students to open a file containing the data already captured from a connection to a Web site. The students are then asked to answer a number of questions, each designed to point out aspects of the three-way handshake that were introduced during the lecture.

In many ways the worksheet tells the students what it is they are seeing. One example taken from the worksheet is shown in Figure 3.

The worksheet is merely an introduction. Such directed learning is not ideal on its own, but we believe that it has a place in the overall development of the learner's understanding. Ethereal captures a large amount of information. The worksheet is designed to highlight certain aspects of the traffic to the student. A useful reference for the students in these labs is an article by Chappell (2000) which discusses this topic using packet analysis.

Stage 3: Independent Activity — Analyze and Discuss a New Connection

The student is then asked to start a capture session of a connection to a Web site of their own choosing. They are to stop the capture once the page has loaded.

Figure 3. Student exercise

Packet 3 is the first part of the three way handshake. Within this packet identify the following:

Packet 3, IP Packet (Layer 3)

Source IP Address: _____

Destination IP Address: _____

Packet 3, TCP Segment (Layer 4)

Field	Value
Source Port	
Destination Port	
SYN Flag	
ACK Flag	
Sequence Number	
Acknowledgement Number	N/A

The students must identify the three-way handshake that opened the connection, noting the packet place in the capture sequence, TCP flags, sequence numbers, and acknowledgment numbers.

By this stage, students are sometimes beginning to associate the three-way handshake with an HTTP connection, which is fine when considering that HTTP uses TCP but a harmful misunderstanding if they begin to assume that TCP implies HTTP. A number of small tasks are usually performed during which students capture an FTP, Telnet, and SMTP session of their own making.

Stage 4: Novel Situation, Troubleshooting and Diagnostic Problem-Solving

Finally, the students are given a capture file of a denial-of-service SYN Flood attack along with a scenario:

Clients were reporting that the network seemed slow when opening files. You performed a packet capture from the file server, which is supplied. Does this capture help explain the problem? What is happening? What solution may be appropriate?

We then discuss the traffic and the effect that this would have on the network. The capture shows that the FIN, URG, and SYN bits are all set, which is almost saying, "We are finishing a connection and beginning a connection while also needing to pass some urgent data." Students are asked to research the effect of a flood of SYN flags. This allows a discussion of the resource limitation of transmission control blocks (a device only has a limited number; one is used for each packet received with a SYN flag set). A class discussion is encouraged to reflect on the result of this strange combination. The detail of the conversation is less important than the participation of students in actively engaging in thinking about the repercussions of this type of traffic.

Stage 5: Reinforcement at a Later Stage

We return to this topic at a later stage when we discuss FTP in detail. During those labs the students look into the way that FTP opens separate connections for the data transfer. By the time the students are looking at the detail of the FTP protocol, they can readily identify the new handshake occurring within the FTP session.

Evaluation and Interpretation

Security and Political Issues: Our Experience

The use of a packet analyzer within a class is not without a number of risks, both perceived and actual. The approach taken must vary between institutions and will depend entirely on the institutional policies and relationship between the academic department and the department that is charged with maintaining the network. In some cases the network labs are separated from the institutional network, either logically via a router or physically separated. Other labs are fully integrated with the campus network.

In our situation we are able to install our own software within the computer suites used in the networking classes; this is not the case for other computer suites. However, we felt that it would be unethical and irresponsible to begin using Ethereal in our classes without first discussing this with the department that maintains our institution's network. Initially the CIO (chief information officer) was hesitant and referred us to the network engineer. He was very encouraging and saw value in teaching students the use of what he viewed as an important tool within his profession. From his perspective there was no issue with using

Ethereal as our network is fully switched; any workstation will only be able to capture packets destined for or sourced from itself and broadcast packets.

It was decided that any information gained by students would be of minor importance, resulting in a low probability of subsequent harm. At a later stage our networking lab was placed behind a router and firewall so that we could teach DHCP without upsetting our network neighbors. The separation provided by the router, primarily to block DHCP broadcasts, also reduces the risk that students may capture sensitive data originating outside of the lab.

It is recommended that all teaching staff consult with their IT support department before proceeding with using a packet-capturing tool on the main institutional network. The risk of harm on any reasonably well designed network (i.e., without hubs) is exceptionally low. But it is always better to work alongside departments that are responsible for maintaining an area rather than risk causing disputes due to lack of consultation.

Student Evaluation

Students in all courses have the opportunity to complete a course evaluation form. Following the introduction of Ethereal into the classes, we observed a reduction in the negative comments stating that the course was too theoretical. A number of students have commented that they value the experience of using tools commonly used by network professionals.

Student Grades

We believe that there has been a minor improvement in the detail of the answers in the written exam questions relating to topics in which Ethereal has been used. However we have observed an increased enthusiasm in studying the protocols via Ethereal and an increased richness in the classroom discussions during these topics. The tool may not have dramatically improved the final understanding, at least as measured by the final exam, but it appears to have made the topic more pleasant to study. We have also observed students using Ethereal in other courses to solve problems occurring when using networked-based applications. Examples include students in subsequent courses using Ethereal to help in their implementation of a DNS server, troubleshooting a client-server setup, and troubleshooting an online booking package. This voluntary transference of skills between courses was not expected but is pleasing.

Conclusion

Packet sniffing with Ethereal gives students the ability to view the abstract protocols as real artifacts that can be captured and examined. We have found it to be a very useful tool that increases student engagement in the study of various aspects of networking. The fact that students return to this tool to help solve problems encountered within tasks in other courses is a strong recommendation. Ethereal not only assists the learning of networking aspects but enhances the students' problem-solving tool set for use in other related topics. I now could not imagine teaching protocols such as ARP, IP, TCP, and DHCP without using a packet sniffer at some stage.

Summary

It is important that students grasp the basic concepts behind the operation of commonly used protocols such as ARP, IP, TCP, and DHCP. Unfortunately, it is difficult to motivate students to learn these protocols because many students appear to find the topics technical and rather dry.

To overcome this problem many networking educators use software tools to enhance teaching and learning network protocols in a practical way. This chapter emphasizes the importance of hands-on learning activities in teaching and learning various aspects of network protocols. By using Ethereal, students can view the abstract protocols as real artifacts that can be captured and examined. The tool not only assists students in developing a better understanding of network protocols but also enhances the students' problem-solving skills. The students indicated that they had found Ethereal easy to use and helpful in gaining an understanding of networking theories and concepts. In summary, this chapter answers the question: How do we make the theoretical protocol a more concrete reality for the students?

Key Terms and Definitions

Concrete: Something that involves the immediate experience rather than an abstraction. A "concrete learner" is someone who prefers learning primarily through hands-on activities rather than by studying a theoretical model.

Ethereal: An open source implementation of a *packet sniffer*. Available freely at http://www.ethereal.com.

Experiential learning: Learning as a continuous spiral of *concrete* experience, observation and reflection, development of abstract concepts, and testing in new situations.

GNU: Technically means "Gnu's Not Unix" (a weak recursive pun). GNU is a project run by the Free Software Foundation, established to produce a free Unix-style operating system (not to be confused with Linux, even though it often comes with some GNU tools). Ethereal uses the copyright license (sometimes called "copyleft") developed by this project (Free Software Foundation, 1991).

Open source: A software distribution model in which the source must be available to the user, and in addition anyone distributing the software must do so for free and without any restriction being placed on anyone receiving the code (apart from that defining *open source*). Refer to Open Source Initiative (2004) for a more complete definition.

Packet sniffer: Also known as *packet analyzer* or just *sniffer*. Software that captures network traffic and displays the data for analysis. The data is normally interpreted in some way so that the user does not need to manually identify the individual fields within a packet.

RFC: Request for comment. A set of documents that identifies issues, describes best common practice, and defines standards for the Internet. Published by the Internet Engineering Task Force (IETF).

SYN flood: A form of denial-of-service attack. The attacker sends a victim an excessive number of packets that initiate the three-way handshake and then does not follow up with further responses. This leaves the target unable to deal with legitimate connection requests.

Three-way handshake: The initial exchange of messages that occurs when two devices are establishing a connection using TCP. Understanding this is essential to understanding the TCP connection and things that can potentially go wrong with the connection.

Review Questions

1. List and describe three main features of a packet sniffer.
2. Explain how Ethereal can be used in the classroom to enhance teaching and learning networking protocols.

3. Define the following networking terms: ARP, IP, Ethereal, packet sniffer, and DNS server.

4. Explain how Ethereal can be used in the classroom to teach ARP, IP, TCP, and DHCP protocols in a practical way.

5. Explain how you would capture data traffic using Ethereal.

6. Describe further enhancements to the laboratory activities for packet-forwarding concepts presented in this chapter.

References

Cameron, B. H., & Wijekumar, K. (2003). The effectiveness of simulation in a hybrid and on-line networking course. In *Proceedings of the 34th Special Interest Group in Computer Science Education Technical Symposium on Computer Science Education* (pp. 117-119). New York: ACM Press.

Chappell, L. (2000, March). Inside the TCP handshake. *NetWare Connection*. Retrieved April 27, 2005, from http://www.novell.com/connectionmagazine/2000/03/hand30.pdf

Cigas, J. (2003). An introductory course in network administration. *Proceedings of the 34th Special Interest Group in Computer Science Education Technical Symposium on Computer Science Education* (pp. 113-116). New York: ACM Press.

Comer, D. E. (2004). *Hands-on networking with Internet technologies* (2nd ed.). Upper Saddle River, NJ: Prentice Hall.

Dewey, J. (1987). *Experience and education*. New York: Free Press. (Original work published 1938.)

Francia, G. A., & Chao, C. (2004). Computer networking laboratory projects. *Journal of Computing Sciences in Colleges, 19*(3), 226-237.

Free Software Foundation. (1991, June). *GNU General Public License* (Version 2). Retrieved April 27, 2005, from http://www.gnu.org/licenses/gpl.html

Holliday, M. A. (2003). Animation of computer networking concepts. *Journal of Educational Resources in Computing, 3*(2), 1-26.

Insolvibile, G. (2001, June). The Linux Socket Filter: Sniffing bytes over the network. *The Linux Journal*.

Jipping, M. J., Bugaj, A., Mihalkova, L., & Porter D. E. (2003). Using Java to teach networking concepts with a programmable network sniffer. In

Proceedings of the 34th Special Interest Group in Computer Science Education Technical Symposium on Computer Science Education (pp. 120-124). New York: ACM Press.

Kolb, D. A., & Fry, R. (1975). Toward an applied theory of experiential learning. In C. Cooper (Ed.), *Theories of group process*. London: Wiley.

McDonald, M., Rickman, J., McDonald, G., Heeler, P., & Hawley D. (2001). Practical experiences for undergraduate computer networking students. *Journal of Computing Sciences in Colleges, 16*(3), 226-237.

Mechtly, B., & Decker, J. (2003). Using Ethereal and TCPportconnect in undergraduate networking labs. *Journal of Computing Sciences in Colleges, 19*(1), 289-298.

Open Source Initiative. (2004). *The open source definition* (Version 1.9). Retrieved April 27, 2005, from http://www.opensource.org/docs/definition.php

Orebaugh, A. D., & Ramirez, G. (2004). *Ethereal packet sniffing*. Syngress.

Papert, S. (1980). *Mindstorms: Children, computers and powerful ideas*. New York: Harper Colophon Books.

Perez-Hardy, S. (2003). The use of network simulation to enhance network curriculum. In *Proceedings of the 4th Conference on Information Technology Education* (pp. 93-95).

Postel, J. (1981, September). *Transmission Control Protocol* (RFC 793). Retrieved April 27, 2005, from ftp://ftp.rfc-editor.org/in-notes/rfc793.txt

Renfro, C. (1999). *Basic packet-sniffer construction from the ground up: Part 1*. Retrieved April 27, 2005, from http://packetstormsecurity.org/sniffers/Sniffer_construction.txt

Sarkar, N. I. (2005). LAN-Designer: A software tool to enhance learning and teaching server-based LAN design. *International Journal of Information and Communication Technology Education, 1*(2), 74-86.

Sharpre, R. (2004). *Ethereal user's guide: V2.00 for Ethereal 0.10.5*. Retrieved April 27, 2005, from http://www.ethereal.com/docs/user-guide/

Skinner, B. F. (1964). *Technology of teaching*. New York: Appleton-Century-Crofts.

Section III

Wireless Networking and Information Security

Chapter VIII

Enhancing Teaching and Learning Wireless Communication Networks Using Wireless Projects

Trevor Craig, Wollongong College Auckland, New Zealand

Nurul I. Sarkar, Auckland University of Technology, New Zealand

Abstract

Due to the rapid developments in wireless communication and networking technologies and the high demand for wireless networking skills in the industry worldwide, wireless communication and networking courses are becoming increasingly popular in universities, polytechnics, and private training institutions around the globe. Unfortunately, wireless communication and networking is a challenging subject to teach in a meaningful way because many students appear to find the subject technical, dry, and rather boring. To overcome this problem, the authors introduce a set of new projects in order to provide the students of wireless communication and networking with a hands-on learning experience. The projects are suitable for classroom use in introductory wireless networking courses.

Learning Objectives

After completing this chapter, you will be able to:

- Discuss the usefulness of the wireless projects in teaching and learning contexts.

- Explain how wireless projects can be set up for class demonstrations.

- Define the following key terms: ad hoc network, access point, infrastructure network, modulation, and wireless link.

Introduction

Wireless communication and networking is a challenging subject to teach in a meaningful way because many students appear to find the subject rather dry and technical and so quite boring. To overcome this problem, the authors have prepared a set of projects in order to provide the students of wireless communication and networking with a hands-on learning experience. These projects are designed around low-cost wireless modules and PC cards that are available from local electronics shops. The projects are suitable for classroom use in introductory-level wireless networking courses. The effectiveness of these projects has been evaluated by both students and a teaching team. The implementation of the wireless projects was successful not only because of the positive student feedback but also in that students scored better in the final exam. This chapter describes these projects completed to date, their overall effectiveness, and our plans for further projects. It also discusses the impact of wireless projects on student learning and comprehension.

Background and Motivation

Wireless communication and networking courses are becoming increasingly popular in universities, polytechnics, postsecondary colleges, and private training institutions around the globe. This is partly because of rapid developments in wireless communication and networking technology and the high demand for wireless communication networks skills in the industry worldwide. Unfortunately, it is difficult to motivate students to learn wireless communication and networking fundamentals because many students appear to find the subject rather dry, full of technical jargon, and boring. However, the view is frequently supported in the educational literature (Anderson, Reder, & Simon, 1996; Young, 1993) that incorporating practical demonstrations into these courses, thereby illustrating theoretical concepts and providing the opportunity for hands-on learning experiences, significantly enhances student learning about wireless communication and networking. Yet, despite the Chinese adage, attributed to Confucius (551-479 BC), "I hear, I know. I see, I remember. I do, I understand," only a limited amount of material designed to supplement the teaching of wireless communication and networking fundamentals is publicly available, as searches of the Computer Science Teaching Center Web site (http://www.cstc.org/) and the SIGCSE Education Links page (http://sigcse.org/topics/) on the Special Interest Group on Computer Science Education Web site reveal.

We strongly believe, as do many others (Hacker & Sitte, 2004; Klassen & Willoughby, 2003; Lopez-Martin, 2004; Moallem, 2004), that students learn more effectively from courses that provide for active involvement in hands-on learning experiences. To that end, we have prepared some interesting projects that facilitate an interactive approach to learning wireless communication and networking concepts. The first of these projects used the PIC sound generator project described in Sarkar and Craig (2004) and the infrared (IR) signals produced by a pair of TV remote controls. The second project involved setting up a wireless link between two computers. This project used a pair of commercially available receiver and transmitter modules which operate in the 2.4 GHz band and have audio and video inputs and outputs, respectively. The third project involved the students in experimenting with a Wi-Fi antenna. The fourth project involved the students setting up a peer-to-peer wireless link using a pair of computers fitted with commercially available Wi-Fi PC cards. Finally, several such links were formed into a wireless network. These projects can be used either in the classroom as a demonstration to enhance the lecture environment or in the laboratory to provide a practical hands-on learning experience in wireless communication and networking fundamentals.

Wireless communication and networking is described in many textbooks (e.g., Holloway, 2003; Rappaport, 2002; Sikora, 2003). A number of sophisticated network simulators exist for building a variety of network models (Commsimm, 2001; Fall & Varadhan, 2003; Jipping, Bugaj, Mihalkova, & Porter, 2003; McDonald, 2005). Nevertheless, by setting up and configuring actual wireless communication networks, the students gain firsthand experience that cannot be gained through computer simulation and modelling.

This hands-on learning approach to teaching and learning wireless communication and networking was first trialled during semester 2 of 2004 in the E-business IT Infrastructure undergraduate course at Auckland University of Technology

(AUT). This course covers various aspects of wireless communication and networking.

The focus of the projects discussed in this chapter has been on preparing demonstration projects to support teaching wireless communication and networking fundamentals. These projects are described in the next section, while the effectiveness and the main benefits of wireless projects as a means of enhancing the teaching and learning of wireless networking fundamentals are discussed in the remainder of the chapter. A brief conclusion section ends the chapter.

Project Description

Table 1 lists the six projects that have been developed and trialled during a period of one semester in the E-business IT Infrastructure undergraduate course at AUT.

Project 1: Infrared Remote Controls

Attention is drawn in Wesel (1998) to the similarities between communication links that utilize IR and wireless links that utilize radio transmission in the 2.4 GHz band. The first project exploits these similarities as a means of introducing Wi-Fi to students via a technology with which they are already familiar — IR remote control units. Project 1 uses an IR-detector module from a dismantled computer to detect the IR pulse-modulated signals produced by a pair of TV remote controls. The IR detector and power supply were assembled on a breadboard as

Table 1. Wireless projects and related wireless networking concepts

Projects	Wireless networking concepts
1. Infrared (IR)	IR transmission link; signal interference; modulation / demodulation
2. 2.4 GHz wireless link	FM transmission; encoding and decoding; microwave radiation, wireless link throughput
3. Wi-Fi Antenna	External Wi-Fi antenna; signal strength; response time and throughput
4. Ad hoc network	Peer-to-peer networking; file sharing; security
5. Infrastructure network	Infrastructure-based network; centralised network control; wireless access point , basic service set, Extended service set
6. Network security	Access control; Firewalls; encryption; SSID

Figure 1. Testing the infrared detector

Figure 2. Two IR remote controls and a display of their signals

shown in Figure 1. The IR detector is the black unit on the right-hand side of the PCB. When the detector unit receives an IR signal, it turns on a transistor, which, in turn, drives the LEDs seen on the left side of the PCB. The switch in the centre of the PCB enables the transistor to be turned on in the absence of an IR signal, as seen in Figure 1. The output from the IR detector was captured on a Tektronix 2230 storage oscilloscope, which is seen together with the remote control units in Figure 2.

The same signals were also fed to the PIC sound generator project described in Sarkar and Craig (2004), where they were filtered and then passed to the audio amplifier built into that project. As a result, students could both see and hear representations of the IR signals being produced by the two remote control units. Figure 3 shows the signal train produced by a single remote control. In Figure 4, the overlapping of the IR signals produced by a pair of TV remote controls when one controller is operated slightly later than the other can be seen. The importance of the receiver being able to distinguish between overlapping signals

Figure 3. The signal produced by a single remote control unit

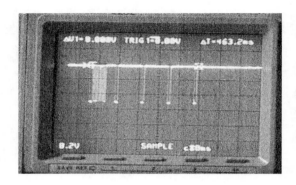

Figure 4. The overlapping signal trains from the two remote control units

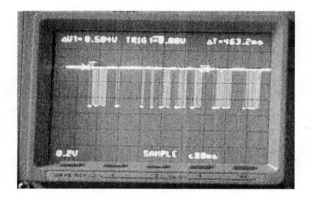

can be well demonstrated by the refusal of devices (such as a TV set) to react as expected when both remote control units are used simultaneously. The storage oscilloscope can be used to capture also a display of the serial signal used to control the LCD display described in Sarkar and Craig, as well as the RS232C signals produced by the project described in Corcoran and Lusted (2004). Many students have indicated that they found being able to experience in new ways something as familiar to them as a TV remote control unit was both enlightening and intriguing, and they were thus better able to appreciate the behaviour of a wireless communication link.

In completing this project, students develop a better understanding of IR transmission link, signal interference, and modulation techniques.

Project 2: A 2.4 GHz Wireless Link

Leading on from the first project, this project endeavors to provide students with an appreciation of the characteristics of another part of the electromagnetic spectrum, namely, microwave radiation as an information carrier. The project is based around two commercially available kits (from Oatley Electronics, www.oatleye.com), which comprise an FM transmitter and a matched receiver. These modules are pre-tuned to one of four frequencies within the 2.4 GHz band. Again, students will be familiar with the some aspects of the technology involved through their experience with FM broadcasting and TV broadcasts, although these services operate at lower frequencies than Wi-Fi. The kits were installed in plastic project boxes, and the transmitter was fitted with a socket so that it could be fitted with an external antenna, as seen in Figures 5 and 6.

The transmitter module has inputs for both audio and video. In this project, only the audio inputs were utilized, these being connected to the speaker jack on the sound card of a PC (computer A). Similarly, the receiver has audio and video outputs, but only the audio outputs were utilized, these being connected to the line-in socket on the sound card of a second PC (computer B). Students could then arrange to play a music CD on computer A and listen to the contents of the CD on computer B via the radio link. The influence of the distance between the transmitter and the receiver, the polarization of the respective antennas, the presence of obstacles between the transmitter and the receiver, as well as interference by out-of-phase reflected signals and the polarization of the signal were all easily observable via the changing quality of the music produced by

Figure 5. Linking a laptop computer (foreground) with a benchtop computer (background) via a wireless link

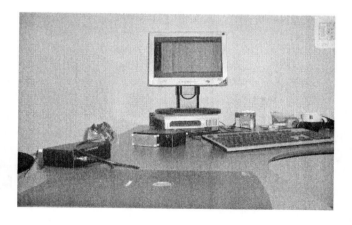

Figure 6. Close-up view of the transmitter and receiver modules

computer B. The ability to switch between the four different channels within the 2.4 GHz band that are built into the modules would enable channel-hopping to be explored as a future project using a PIC microcontroller. The currently active channel is indicated by one of the LEDs seen in Figure 6.

In completing this project, students develop a better understanding of FM transmission, the effect of transmitter-receiver separation, polarization of the antennas, obstacles between the transmitter and the receiver, as well as interference by out-of-phase reflected signals on wireless link throughput.

Project 3: Wi-Fi Antenna

The transmitter module in Project 2 was fitted with a BNC socket so that an external antenna could be attached. Numerous antenna designs have been published (Clark, 2003; Gardelli, La Cono, & Albani, 2004), and students were encouraged to consult these sources and to build an antenna of their own design. One such endeavour, consisting of the bow-tie PCB antenna supplied by the module manufacturer (from Oatley Electronics, www.oatleye.com) coupled with a CD disc used as a reflector, can be seen in Figure 6. The student's work does not need to be an elaborate design for it to be an effective means of engendering student interest and confidence. In fact, the wireless can be established with a 50-ohm terminator (as used in Ethernet networks) connected to the transmitter antenna socket, provided the receiver and transmitter modules are located within a few meters of each other. This link however is easily broken if the separation between the modules is increased to around 5 meters. The influence of objects in or near the signal path is more apparent when the signal strength is restricted in this way, one indicator of the link quality being the quality of the sound produced by the receiving computer (B). A second way of determining the strength of the signal being received by the receiving computer is to use either a proprietary software program, such as NetStumbler (2004), or the program that is provided within Windows XP (by double-clicking on the Network Connection icon on the status bar). Projects 1 and 2 appear to provide students with a qualitative grasp of the behaviour of IR and radio links, thereby preparing them to set up a peer-to-peer link between two computers using commercially available Wi-Fi computer cards, as described next.

Project 4: Ad Hoc Network

The basic concept of wireless ad hoc networks and their potential application areas are discussed during lectures. This project showed students how to set up a wireless ad hoc network. In addition, students were able to investigate the effect of transmitter-receiver separation, floors, and line-of-sight blockage on the file transmission time as well as link throughput of a typical IEEE 802.11b wireless local area network (WLAN) in peer-to-peer mode. The project involved the installation of two IEEE 802.11b Wi-Fi PC computer cards, purchased from an electronics store, in a pair of PCs. This procedure is well documented in textbooks such as Carter and Whitehead (2004), and most of the students found little difficulty in completing this step. Of greater interest to them was the question of how to achieve the transmission of the same music that they had become acquainted with through the 2.4 GHz FM wireless link. Should the file on the CD be sent as a compact disc audio track file (cda file) or should it be sent as a bit stream? In completing this project, students gain a better understanding of the operation of wireless ad hoc networks.

Project 5: Infrastructure Network

When more than two computers are to be connected, it is necessary to have a means of controlling the communication between each computer. In an infrastructure network, this task is allocated to a wireless access point (AP). The APs are more expensive than computer Wi-Fi cards, but only one is needed for a small network. The basic concepts of wireless access points, infrastructure-based wireless LANs, basic service set (BSS), and extended service set (ESS) are introduced during lectures. This project shows students how to set up an infrastructure-based network. As in Project 4, the procedure for setting up an infrastructure network is well documented, as in Carter and Whitehead (2004), and most students are able to complete this extension of their network with little supervision. In completing this project, students gain hands-on experience in setting up a wireless infrastructure network and develop a better understanding of its uses, benefits, and limitations.

Project 6: Network Security

This project demonstrates to students the basic concept of wireless network security (Khan & Khwaja, 2003; Lin, Sathu, & Joyce, 2004). In lectures, the basic concept of wireless LAN security and related issues and challenges were introduced. These concepts were reinforced when the students were setting up Project 4 and Project 5, in accordance with the procedures described in Carter and Whitehead (2004), because the information required when setting up the network software requires a good knowledge of both network operation and terminology, for example, terms such as service set identifier (SSID), access control, and Media Access Control (MAC) address.

Additional Projects

The following projects are being considered:

- **Integrating Wi-Fi with PIC projects**: The hands-on learning activities include using a Wi-Fi radio link to control a PIC microcontroller.
- **IEEE 802.11a/g**: The learning activities include experimenting with OFDM (orthogonal frequency-division multiplexing) technology and the 5 GHz radio spectrum.
- **Open**: A category for student-suggested projects.

Usefulness and Benefits of Wireless Projects

The wireless projects described in this chapter provide the following benefits:

- **Hands-on**: Wireless projects facilitate an interactive learning experience in wireless communication and networking.

- **Easy to use**: Wireless projects are easy to use and set up for demonstrations.

- **Low cost**: Wireless projects can be built with limited resources and budget (e.g., within a few hundred dollars).

- **Reusability**: Some hardware components of Wi-Fi projects can be reused in developing a variety of other projects.

- **Usefulness**: The wireless projects can be used either in the classroom or in the laboratory to provide hands-on learning experiences in wireless communication and networking.

- **Challenging**: Wireless projects provide a challenging, yet friendly environment in which students can test their knowledge of wireless communication and networking.

Classroom Experiences with Wireless Projects

Our experiences with the wireless projects have been favorable overall. The wireless projects were easy to use and set up for demonstrations, and it was observed that by participating in the wireless projects and demonstration activities, students became increasingly motivated to learn more about wireless communication networks and enjoyed this course more than previous courses that consisted of lectures only. The authors seek feedback regularly both from students and staff for further improvement of the demonstration materials.

The wireless projects were offered as a capstone project to two undergraduate diploma students, who carried out the project in the final semester towards the diploma in information technology (DipIT) qualification. The students had completed most of the courses required for a DipIT qualification, including data communications and computer networking, before taking up the wireless projects. The students achieved the following learning outcomes: (1) set up a wireless link using IR technology; (2) set up both ad hoc and infrastructure-based wireless LANs; (3) design a Wi-Fi booster antenna; (4) set up Wi-Fi projects for class demonstration and evaluate the effectiveness of the projects through student feedback; (5) write a report containing requirements analysis, a project plan, minutes of meetings, summary of findings, and reflective statements; and (6) give an oral presentation to an audience of staff and students.

The wireless projects were completed successfully, and the students indicated that they had learnt quite a lot about wireless communication and networking through the hands-on experience that the wireless projects provided. This is evident in the students' reflective statements, which follow:

"I learnt quite a lot about Wi-Fi technology and networking by doing hands-on projects."

"Even though we had passed the 'Data communication and networking' courses before taking up the Wi-Fi projects, we did not learn much about the practical aspects of wireless communication and networking until we carried out the Wi-Fi projects."

"Wireless communication and networking should be taught using hands-on learning activities as we did with the Wi-Fi projects."

Impact of Wireless Projects on Students' Performance

The wireless projects were trialled as a class demonstration in the E-business IT Infrastructure (EBITI) undergraduate course in semester 2 of 2004. The EBITI (Petrova, 2000) course is at level 6, or 1st-year degree level, and constitutes 15 credit points (52 contact hours) at AUT. Until this trial, the wireless communication and networking course was taught through of a series of lectures and tutorials only.

To estimate (quantitatively) the impact of the wireless projects and demonstrations on student learning and comprehension, the class was given an assessment test (multiple-choice questions) on wireless communication networks before the projects were introduced. Then, after the entire class had an opportunity to gain hands-on experience with the wireless projects, the same test was given again to measure any change in student learning and comprehension.

The class consisted of 11 students, five female and six male. While not a particularly large group, it was at least a diverse mix. The examination consisted of 19 multiple-choice questions covering various aspects of wireless and mobile networking technology, including ad hoc and infrastructure wireless LANs, Bluetooth, and wireless security (see Table 3 for assessment test questions).

Table 2 shows results of these tests. The question numbers of the 19 multiple-choice questions are indicated in the first column. The fraction of the students in the class who answered correctly (expressed as a percentage) in each of the 19 questions in the class test before and after they had experience with the wireless projects is shown in columns 2 and 3, respectively. As seen in Table 2,

Table 2. Impact of wireless projects on student learning and comprehension

Question	Percentage of class answering correctly		Improvement (%)
	Before	After	
1	33	100	67
2	67	91	24
3	11	73	62
4	56	91	35
5	44	100	56
6	33	64	30
7	0	100	100
8	67	91	24
9	56	64	8
10	22	36	14
11	22	82	60
12	22	36	14
13	56	64	8
14	44	91	46
15	56	64	8
16	22	55	32
17	56	64	8
18	22	45	23
19	33	45	12
Overall	38	71	33

on each of the 19 questions, the class as a whole showed an improvement ranging from 8% to 100%, and the overall improvement for the test is 33%. Because the tests (before and after) were conducted among students having the same background and who had been exposed to the same theoretical material, it is considered that much of this improvement can be accounted for by the effect of the practical experience that the students gained from the wireless projects.

Table 3. Assessment test (maximum time allowed to complete is 20 minutes)

1	What is the maximum distance an IEEE 802.11b network can cover?
	   a) 100 meters
	   b) 10 meters
	   c) 1000 meters
	   d) 20 meters

2	What is the maximum theoretical speed of IEEE 802.11b and IEEE 802.11g?
	       IEEE 802.11b IEEE 802.11g
	   a) 12 Mbps a) 12 Mbps
	   b) 54 Mbps b) 54 Mbps
	   c) 22 Mbps c) 22 Mbps
	   d) 11 Mbps d) 11 Mbps

3	What security protocols are commonly used in Wi-Fi?
	   a) MAC address restrictions
	   b) WEP Key 64/128 bit
	   c) BLT on rye
	   d) USB access key

4	What does SSID stand for?
	   a) Super Security Implementation Device
	   b) Seismic Standard Identification Deployment
	   c) Service Set IDentifier
	   d) Slow Service IDentifier

5	What is the difference between WEP and MAC filtering?
	   a) One's hardware and one's software
	   b) They're the same thing
	   c) One is a pie protocol
	   d) WEP has a greater maximum distance

6	What is a MAC address?
	   a) Location of the closet Mac Donald's
	   b) Management Address Character for Wi-Fi
	   c) The Numeral ID of your network card
	   d) Closet reseller of Mac Trucks

7	What is the difference between an Ad-hoc and an Infrastructure network?

8	What are hotspots?
	   a) Something you should avoid standing on
	   b) Areas that you can get open assess to a Wi-Fi Network
	   c) Areas on the Sun that are brighter

9	Which of the following characteristics differ between Bluetooth and Wi-Fi?
	   a) Speed
	   b) Frequency
	   c) Distance
	   d) Cost

10	List three advantages of wireless LANs over wired networks
11	List three disadvantages of wireless LANs over wired networks

12	What is DHCP?
	   a) A protocol that assign your computer an IP address?
	   b) A devise that lets Wi-Fi dial up ADSL
	   c) Decipher Help Character Protocol
	   d) Transdimensional Gateway to Pluto

13	What other common household items use the same frequency as Wi-Fi?
	   a) Cell Phone
	   b) Microwave
	   c) Cordless Phone
	   d) Sky Box

Table 3. cont.

14	What does Wi-Fi stand for? a) Wired-Fiction b) Wireless-Fitting c) Wireless-Fidelity d) Wired-Fix
15	Can a Wi-Fi network replace a wired network in every case? a) No b) Yes c) No clue what so ever
16	Is all Wi-Fi equipment compatible? a) No b) Yes
17	Is each Wi-Fi a secure network? a) Yes, better than wired networks b) No, Worse than wired networks c) Yes, Equal to wired networks
18	Does it cost more to set a Wi-Fi network than a wired network? a) Yes, a lot more than a wired network b) Yes, but not much more than a wired network c) No, The same d) No, a lot cheaper than a wired network
19	An access point is required to set up a wireless LAN. a) False b) True

Conclusion and Future Work

A series of interesting projects has been developed, which can be used either in the classroom for class demonstrations to enhance the traditional lecture environment or in the computer laboratory for hands-on practical work at an introductory level. The wireless projects described in this chapter are easy to use and set up for class demonstrations. The projects consist of inexpensive and widely available modules and kits and are thus likely to be within reach of even already extended budgets. Student responses to the project demonstrations were mostly favorable. The students indicated that they had found the wireless projects easy to use and helpful in gaining an understanding of wireless communication and networking fundamentals. The wireless projects demonstration has had a positive impact on student learning and comprehension.

More projects such as IEEE 802.11a, IEEE 802.11g, and integrating Wi-Fi and PIC are being prepared. These materials are available to faculty interested in using the wireless projects to supplement their wireless communication and networking courses or as the basis for more complex projects. More information about the wireless projects and demonstration materials can be obtained by contacting the first author.

Summary

This chapter describes a set of hands-on wireless projects that can be used either in the classroom to enhance traditional lecture environment or in the laboratory to provide hands-on learning experience in wireless communication networks. The wireless projects are designed around low-cost modules and PC cards that are available from local electronics shops. The effectiveness of these projects has been evaluated by both students and a teaching team. The students indicated that they had found the wireless projects easy to use and helpful in gaining an understanding of wireless communication and networking fundamentals. The wireless projects demonstration has had a positive impact on student learning and comprehension.

Key Terms and Definitions

Ad hoc network: A class of wireless networking architecture in which there is no fixed infrastructure or wireless access points. In ad hoc networks, each mobile station acts as a router to communicate with other stations. Such a network can exist on a temporary basis to share some resources among the mobile stations.

IEEE 802.11: Generally refers to wireless LAN standards. The IEEE 802.11 is the wireless LAN standard operating at 2.4GHz.

Infrared: Electromagnetic waves whose frequency range is above that of microwave but below the visible spectrum. The applications of infrared technology include TV remote control and wireless LAN systems.

Infrastructure network: A class of wireless networking architecture in which mobile stations communicate with each other via access points, which are usually linked to a wired backbone. Such a network has a fixed infrastructure and centralized control.

PIC microcontroller: PIC stands for programmable interface controller. A PIC microcontroller is an on-chip computer containing CPU, memory, programmable ROM, and input/output ports.

Wi-Fi antenna: This term generally refers to an antenna used with Wi-Fi equipment to enhance the transmission and reception of the wireless signals used in the transfer of data between the sending equipment and the intended receiving equipment.

Wireless link: Generally refers to a pathway for the transmission of information via a modulated unconstrained electromagnetic wave.

Review Questions

1. List and describe three main benefits of using the wireless projects.

2. Discuss the usefulness of the wireless projects in teaching and learning contexts.

3. Discuss the difference between an ad hoc wireless LAN and an infrastructure LAN.

4. Define the following wireless key terms: modulation, wireless link, Wi-Fi antenna, ad hoc network, and infrastructure network.

5. Describe how an infrastructure wireless LAN can be set up for demonstration.

6. Explain how the basic concept of wireless network security can be reinforced using Project 6 described in this chapter.

7. Describe further enhancements to the wireless projects.

References

Anderson, J. R., Reder, L. M., & Simon, H. A. (1996). Situated learning and education. *Educational Researcher, 25*(4), 5-11.

Carter, P., & Whitehead, T. (2004). *Teach yourself visually wireless networking*. Wiley.

Clark, R. (2003, August). Home-brew weatherproof 2.4GHz WiFi antennas. *Silicon Chip, 16*, 42-48.

Commsim 2001: Network & Communications Simulation [Computer software]. (2001). Toronto, Ontario, Canada: Electronics Workbench.

Corcoran, P., & Lusted, K. (2004). *Teaching programming techniques for embedded microcontrolllers:Back to basics with 8-bit RISC microcontrollers*. Retrieved December 12, 2004, from www.ulst.ac.uk/cticomp/corcoran.html

Fall, K., & Varadhan, K. (2003). *The ns manual*. Retrieved January 5, 2006, from http://www.isi.edu/nsnam/ns/

Gardelli, R., La Cono, G., & Albani, M. (2004). A low-cost suspended patch antenna for WLAN access points and point-to-point links. *Antennas and Wireless Propagation Letters, 3*(6), 90-93.

Hacker, C., & Sitte, R. (2004). Interactive teaching of elementary digital logic design with WinLogiLab. *IEEE Transactions on Education, 47*(2), 196-203.

Holloway, D. (2003). *Wireless networking: A guide to wireless networking and deployment.* Retrieved September 25, 2003, from http://www.hill.com/archive/pub/papers/2003/01/paper.pdf

Jipping, M. J., Bugaj, A., Mihalkova, L., & Porter, D. E. (2003). *Using Java to teach networking concepts with a programmable network sniffer.* Paper presented at the Proceedings of the 34th Technical Symposium on Computer Science Education (SIGCSE'03), Reno, NV (pp. 120-124).

Khan, J., & Khwaja, A. (2003). *Building secure wireless networks with 802.11.* Wiley.

Klassen, K. J., & Willoughby, K. A. (2003). In-class simulation games: Assessing student learning. *Journal of Information Technology Education, 2,* 1-13.

Lin, C.-T., Sathu, H., & Joyce, D. (2004, July). *Wireless network security.* Paper presented at the 17th annual conference of the National Advisory Committee on Computing Qualifications (NACCQ), Christchurch, New Zealand (pp. 337-340).

Lopez-Martin, A. J. (2004). Teaching random signals and noise: An experimental approach. *IEEE Transactions on Education, 47*(2), 174-179.

McDonald, C. (2005). The cnet network simulator (Version 2.0.9). Retrieved January 10, 2005, from www.csse.uwa.edu.au/cnet/

Moallem, M. (2004). A laboratory testbed for embedded computer control. *IEEE Transactions on Education, 47*(3), 340-347.

NetStumbler [Computer software]. (2004). Retrieved January 15, 2004, from www.netstumbler.com

Petrova, K. (2000). Teaching electronic commerce: An information technology infrastructure design & management approach. *New Zealand Journal of Applied Computing & Information Technology, 4*(1), 70-77.

Rappaport, T. S. (2002). *Wireless communications—Principles and practice* (2nd ed.). NJ: Prentice Hall.

Sarkar, N. I., & Craig, T. M. (2004, March 3-7). *Illustrating computer hardware concepts using PIC-based projects.* Paper presented at the 35th SIGCSE Technical Symposium on Computer Science Education, Norfolk, VA (pp. 270-274).

Sikora, A. (2003). *Wireless personal and local area networks*. Wiley.

Wesel, E. K. (1998). *Wireless multimedia communications—Networking video, voice and data.* Addison-Wesley.

Young, M. F. (1993). Instructional design for situated learning. *Educational Technology, 41*(1), 43-58.

Chapter IX

Teaching and Learning Wi-Fi Networking Fundamentals Using Limited Resources

Wilson Siringoringo, Auckland University of Technology, New Zealand

Nurul I. Sarkar, Auckland University of Technology, New Zealand

Abstract

Wi-Fi networking has been becoming increasingly popular in recent years, both in terms of applications and as the subject of academic research papers and articles in the IT press. It is important that students grasp the basic concepts of both Wi-Fi networking and wireless propagation measurements. Unfortunately, the underlying concepts of wireless networking often intimidate students with their apparently overwhelming complexity, thereby discouraging the students from learning in-depth this otherwise exciting and rewarding subject. This chapter provides a tutorial on Wi-Fi networking and radio propagation measurements using wireless laptops and access points. Various hands-on learning activities are also discussed.

Learning Objectives

After completing this chapter, you will be able to:

- Describe the architecture of Wi-Fi networks.
- Discuss the evolution of IEEE 802.11 standards.
- Set up Wi-Fi networks for class demonstration.
- Suggest future enhancements to the practical activities described in the chapter.

Introduction

In recent years, Wi-Fi networks (also called IEEE 802.11b) have been gaining in popularity, both in business and in home networking applications. With the growing proliferation of mobile equipment, this trend is likely to continue in the future. It is therefore important for students of information and telecommunication technologies to cover the fundamentals of wireless networking technologies as part of their curriculum.

Many people find that networking technology in general is somewhat arcane and difficult to understand. Similarly, the apparently overwhelming complexity of the underlying concepts of wireless networking often intimidates students. This perception can easily discourage the students from learning in-depth this otherwise exciting and rewarding subject.

This chapter attempts to overcome these problems by providing a hands-on introduction to Wi-Fi networking. A tutorial is also included to guide learners on how to set up Wi-Fi networks using relatively few computing resources. Although a host of problems are to be expected, given the technical limitations of commercially available hardware, students are encouraged to gain a hands-on learning experience in setting up Wi-Fi networks. The chapter also discusses the effectiveness, measured by student feedback, of Wi-Fi projects.

Background and Motivation

Background

Nowadays business organizations rely heavily on computer networks for their operation. The trend towards mobile communication and computing drives the networking industry further towards wireless technology — particularly Wi-Fi technology. As explained later in this chapter, the term Wi-Fi refers to the IEEE 802.11 standard for wireless LAN (WLAN). Therefore the terms Wi-Fi, IEEE 802.11, and WLAN are used interchangeably in this chapter.

Kaczman (2002) reports that an estimated 1 to 1.5 million Wi-Fi communication cards and Wi-Fi-enabled laptops were sold every month during 2002. Vaxevanakis et al. (2003) offer similar sales projections in their reports.

Wireless networks, especially the ones employing Wi-Fi technology, are gaining popularity not only in the business domain but also with home users (Vaxevanakis et al., 2003). The reasons for the popularity of wireless networks over the wired ones are highlighted below (Proxim, 1998):

- **Mobility**: Wireless LANs can provide users with real-time information within their organization without the restrictions inherent with physical cable connections.

- **Installation speed and simplicity**: The installation of wireless LANs does not involve the tedious work of pulling cables through walls and ceilings.

- **Installation flexibility**: Wireless LANs allow access from places un-reachable by network cables.

- **Cost of ownership**: Overall installation expenses and life-cycle costs of wireless LANs are significantly lower than wired LAN. The discrepancy is even higher in dynamic environments requiring frequent moves and changes.

- **Scalability**: Wireless LANs can be configured relatively easily since no physical arranging of network cables is required.

Although wireless networks may never completely replace wired networks, they will gain in importance as business assets in the future. Howard (2002) reports that the use of wireless networks for mobile Internet access is also becoming big business, as is indicated by the rising number of wireless Internet service providers in the United States. The increasing number of public hotspots also opens the possibility of providing continuous connection to a roaming business traveller (Vaughan-Nichols, 2003).

Motivation

Wireless technology is likely to continue evolving at rapid a pace in the near future.

Further developments will mainly involve bandwidth increase and optimization, which enable performance improvement in terms of throughput and reliability. In anticipation of the availability of increased bandwidth, various network-based business and multimedia applications are also being developed. Prasad and Prasad (2002) discuss some applications such as teleconferencing, telesurveillance, and video-on-demand operating on wireless network backbones.

Given the importance of research and implementation of Wi-Fi networking in the future, students need to prepare themselves by gaining a thorough understanding about the technology. An overview is presented to introduce the students to the significance of wireless networking technology from a technical standpoint. To facilitate a hands-on learning experience, a tutorial for setting up a Wi-Fi network is also provided.

IEEE 802.11 Wireless LAN

A wireless network is a data communications system which uses electromagnetic media such as radio or infrared waves instead of cables. Wireless networks are implemented either to complement or as an alternative to a wired network.

The most prominent feature of wireless networks is mobility, which provides users with freedom of movement while maintaining connectivity. Flexibility is another great advantage of wireless networks since they allow connectivity to places physically inaccessible to network cables.

The application of wireless networks is not confined only to substituting for wired networks. It also enables communication schemes not available in wired networks. With the proliferation of mobile computers and handheld devices such as PDAs and cellular phones, the role of wireless networks is becoming more important as a means of data exchange.

In more general terms, there are currently three primary applications for wireless network technology:

1. **Wireless local area network (WLAN)**: A class of wireless LAN which provides wireless connectivity within an organization. WLAN enables access to a corporate network by individual users without hindering their mobility. Access to WLAN is provided within a defined physical region, such as within an office building.

2. **Wireless personal area network (WPAN)**: The main role of WPAN is to simplify the communication process by eliminating the need for physical connection through cables at home. For example, linking all electronics devices at home using radio technology operating at 2.4 GHz.

3. **Wireless wide area network (WWAN)**: This provides wireless access to users outside the boundaries of WLAN. Currently, cellular technologies play the main role in making WWAN feasible. Typical example of WWAN use is when a user gets access to e-mail or Web sources through a mobile phone.

Several standards have emerged to implement the wireless network technology in the three areas above. The Bluetooth standard (IEEE 802.15) is now dominating the WPAN implementation, whereas the IEEE 802.11 family of specifications is now standard for WLAN implementations. In the WWAN domain, several mobile communication technologies such as GSM, GPRS, and CDMA 2000 are still competing with each other to become the ultimate standard.

Overview

The Institute of Electrical and Electronics Engineers (IEEE) 802.11 standards define the protocols at the physical (PHY) and MAC layers. The MAC layer makes the lower part of the data link layer in the OSI model as shown in Figure 1.

At the physical layer, three different transmission techniques are used by 802.11: frequency hopping spread spectrum (FHSS), direct sequence spread spectrum (DSSS), and infrared (IR). For the 802.11b specification, only the direct sequence spread spectrum is used. Other popular standards, such as Bluetooth, use frequency hopping spread spectrum instead, although it shares the 2.4 GHz band used by 802.11b.

The original 802.11 standard uses an 11-bit chipping code called the Barker sequence to send data via radio waves. Each 11-bit sequence represents one single bit of data. A transmission technique called binary phase shift keying (BPSK) is used to transmit the sequences at the rate of 1 million per second, which corresponds to the basic 1 Mbps data transfer rate of the 802.11. A more sophisticated technique referred to as quadrature phase shift keying (QPSK) is used to achieve a 2 Mbps data transfer rate.

Figure 1. IEEE 802.11 in the OSI layer

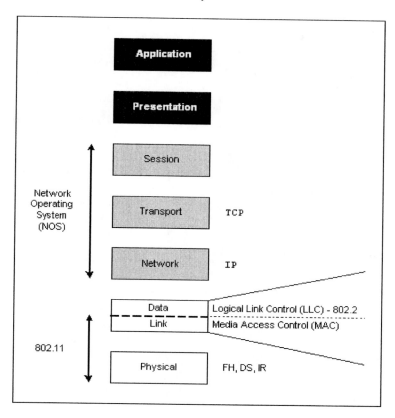

Instead of Barker sequences, the 802.11b uses Complementary Code Keying (CCK). When CCK is used, a 16-bit sequence transmitted over the radio channel contains either 4 or 8 information bits and can achieve data transfer rates of 5.5 Mbps and 11 Mbps, respectively.

At the MAC layer, the fundamental protocol component specified by the 802.11 is the distributed coordination function (DCF). The DCF utilizes a Carrier Sense Multiple Access with Collision Avoidance (CSMA/CA) channel access method. When a station realizes that no other has transmitted within a predetermined time called the interframe space (IFS), it transmits its own frame. In unicast transmission, the receiving station is expected to reply with an acknowledgment (ACK), in a similar fashion to the standard automatic repeat request (ARQ) control mechanism. A mechanism called backoff procedure is used by DCF to prevent frame collision, which results from stations transmitting simultaneously (Golmie et al., 2003).

To complement the DCF, an optional component at the MAC layer, referred to as point coordination function (PCF), provides a centralized, polling-based access mechanism. To utilize PCF, an AP is required to perform the point coordination function. The PCF is an optional feature of the IEEE 802.11 MAC layer and is not supported by all Wi-Fi devices.

In PCF, the AP acts as the central access coordinator. It applies the round robin algorithm to poll the stations within the service set. Unlike DCF, stations wishing to transmit data must first obtain permission from the AP using the request-to-send and clear-to-send (RTS/CTS) scheme. When a polled station does not have data to transmit, it sends a null frame. Otherwise the station is allowed to transmit its data frame (Youssef et al., 2002).

Wi-Fi Transmission Issues

The use of the unlicensed 2.4 GHz radio band for Wi-Fi transmission medium leads to interference problems. In most countries the 2.4 GHz spectrum is crowded with other radio devices such as cordless phones, microwaves, and Bluetooth WPAN devices. Due to the effect of radio interference, Wi-Fi performance degrades. With the ever increasing popularity of Bluetooth WPAN, the potential problem of interference becomes sufficiently serious to compel researchers to find mechanisms that allow Wi-Fi and Bluetooth to coexist (Ophir et al., 2004).

Wi-Fi networks have limited range, typically covering up to 46m indoors and 100m outdoors from the nearest access point (Ferro & Potorti, 2005). While significantly wider than Bluetooth coverage, which is 10m, performance degradation can be an issue when a station is located near the limit of Wi-Fi range from the other station or the access point.

The use of radio broadcast also raises security concerns. Unlike wired network where access is limited by physical cable connections, any device within range of Wi-Fi network can intercept the packets and potentially intrude into the network. This potential threat necessitates the use of data encryption in order to minimize the risk of intrusion.

Wi-Fi Network Design Issues

The basic building block of a wireless network is the basic service set (BSS). A BSS consists of a set of fixed or mobile Wi-Fi stations. The simplest network

Figure 2. A typical Wi-Fi network with ESS structure

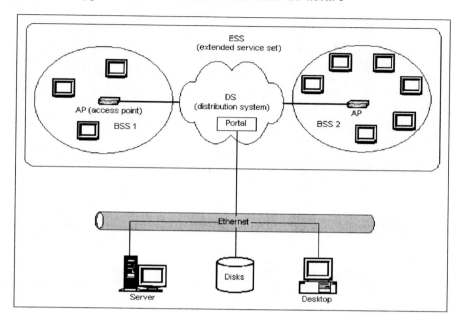

configuration is the independent BSS (IBSS), which is an ad hoc network consisting of two or more stations without any structure other than peer-to-peer cooperation.

When a set of BSSs are connected by a fixed network infrastructure, the resulting structure is called an extended service set (ESS). An ESS is a set of one or more BSSs connected by a distribution system (DS), which is not specified by the IEEE 802.11 standard. The DS can take the form of wired networks or some other form of wireless network. A Wi-Fi network with all the typical components is illustrated in Figure 2.

The stations connected to the DS are called access points (APs). An AP offers distribution system services, which allow data exchange between stations of different BSSs. An AP normally performs a function called point coordination (PC), which employs a round robin policy to poll each station for data transmission.

802.11 Standard Family

The IEEE released the 802.11 standard for wireless LAN (WLAN) in 1997. The specification requires a data transfer rate of from 1 Mbps up to 2 Mbps while

Table 1. IEEE 802.11 standards family (Ferro & Potorti, 2005)

Standard	Description	Status
IEEE 802.11	WLAN; up to 2 Mb/s; 2.4 GHz	Approved 1997
IEEE 802.11a	WLAN; up to 54 Mb/s; 5 GHz	Approved 1999
IEEE 802.11b	WLAN; up to 11 Mb/s; 2.4 GHz	Approved 1999
IEEE 802.11g	WLAN; up to 54 Mb/s; 2.4 GHz	Approved 2003
IEEE 802.11e	New coordination functions for QoS	Task group development
IEEE 802.11f	IAPP (Inter-AP Protocol)	Approved 2003
IEEE 802.11h	Use of the 5 GHz band in Europe	Approved 2003
IEEE 802.11i	New encryption standards	Approved 2004
IEEE 802.11n	MIMO physical layer	Task group development

retaining compatibility with existing LAN hardware and software infrastructure. The standard defines protocols for MAC layer and physical transmission in the unlicensed 2.4 GHz radio band. After successful implementation by commercial companies such as Lucent Technologies, amendment was made for a better performance in the same year. The resulting standard was IEEE 802.11b, which specifies higher data transfer rates of 5.5 and 11 Mbps.

The IEEE 802.11b differs from the 802.11 in the MAC layer even though it retains compatibility with its predecessor. The physical layer is left unchanged. The 802.11b standard was approved in 1999, and during that year the term wireless fidelity or Wi-Fi was introduced. The IEEE 802.11b has proven to be very successful in the commercial domain. The majority of Wi-Fi devices nowadays are made to the 802.11b standard.

In parallel with the IEEE 802.11b, another variant of the original 802.11 was also made. This variant is referred to as IEEE 802.11a, which differs from both IEEE 802.11 and IEEE 802.11b by using the 5 GHz band rather than the 2.4 GHz band. The 5 GHz radio band is unlicensed in the United States but not in many other countries, especially in Europe. The IEEE 802.11a provides up to 54 Mbps, which is much faster than both 802.11 and 802.11b. However the use of different radio frequencies denies compatibility between 802.11a and 802.11/802.11b. Nevertheless the 802.11a was found satisfactory and approved in 1999.

To resolve the incompatibility problem between the standards, an amendment to IEEE 802.11a was approved in 2003. The new standard is referred to as IEEE 802.11g, which operates at 2.4 GHz radio band while retaining the 54 Mbps data transfer rate of the 802.11a. There are other standards in the 802.11 family, as summarized in Table 1.

Experiment Details

In this section we describe the implementation aspect of an IEEE 802.11 wireless LAN using available wireless equipment. We first describe Wi-Fi networks set up both in ad hoc (IBSS) and infrastructure (ESS) modes. We then focus on the experiments and Wi-Fi performance measurement.

Hardware and Software Requirements

A number of hardware and software applications are used in the experiment. The requirement for IBSS, BSS, and ESS differs mainly in the presence of the AP. The following is the more detailed description of the resources used in the experiment.

Hardware

For the basic service set, at least two Wi-Fi capable computers are required. This is a fairly loose requirement, which can be satisfied by most commercial computer hardware. However, the configuration for wireless laptops and APs that we used in the experiment is shown in Tables 2 and 3.

A different configuration is used for the extended service set (ESS). In an ESS network, an AP is used in addition to two Wi-Fi stations. A third computer is also required to simulate the wired network the AP is attached to (see Table 3).

Table 2. Basic service set hardware specification

System	Specification	
Host 1 (H1)	Make:	Toshiba
	CPU:	Mobile Intel® Celeron® 2.4GHz
	RAM:	496MB
	OS:	Windows XP Professional 2002 SP 1
	Wi-Fi:	WLAN adapter D-Link 650+ 802.11b
Host 2 (H2)	Make:	Toshiba
	CPU:	Mobile Intel® Celeron® 2.4GHz
	RAM:	496MB
	OS:	Windows XP Professional 2002 SP 1
	Wi-Fi:	WLAN adapter Cisco 350 802.11b

Table 3. Extended service set hardware specification

System	Specification	
Host 1 (H1)	Make:	Toshiba
	CPU:	Mobile Intel® Celeron® 2.4GHz
	RAM:	496MB
	OS:	Windows XP Professional 2002 SP 1
	Wi-Fi:	WLAN adapter D-Link 650+ 802.11b
Host 2 (H2)	Make:	Dell
	CPU:	Intel® Pentium® M 1.4GHz
	RAM:	512MB
	OS:	Windows XP Professional 2002 SP 1
	Wi-Fi:	Intel® PRO/Wireless LAN 2100 3A Mini Adapter
AP Controller	Make:	Toshiba
	CPU:	Mobile Intel® Celeron® 2.4GHz
	RAM:	496MB
	OS:	Windows XP Professional 2002 SP 1
	Wi-Fi:	D-Link DWL-900AP+ connected through crossover Ethernet cable

Software

The IEEE 802.11b protocol automatically establishes data-link-level connection whenever the Wi-Fi-enabled hosts are active and within range to each other. To measure the actual throughput, however, connection at the application layer is also required. Special software applications are used to enable such connection to take place.

Colligo WE software from Colligo Networks Inc. enables users of Wi-Fi-capable devices to exchange information. The communication can take place either in ad hoc mode or infrastructure mode. It is necessary that every participant of a Colligo network session has a copy of the software installed on the computer. More complete information regarding the software can be obtained from the company's Web site at http://www.colligo.com/products/workgroupedition/. Evaluation copy of the software is also available to download from the Web site.

The software has many useful features, such as interactive chat, unidirectional message delivery, virtual whiteboard, and file transfer. The file transfer feature is crucial for this experiment, as it provides the means of measuring the link throughput (Colligo, 2005).

Colligo has been designed for nontechnical users. The implication is that Colligo is relatively easy to set up in a typical setting, such as in a wireless ad hoc network. On the other hand, very little control is provided for technical users to customize the settings. This restriction makes it especially difficult for setting up a wireless network in infrastructure mode.

To set up an infrastructure network, appropriate application is required to configure and control the AP. In this particular example, the AP hardware comes with AirPlus Access Point Manager configuration software. The AirPlus Access Point Manager is a Window-based program which allows setting up the access point parameters from a computer through a wired connection. The AP manager therefore is needed only in setting up the network in infrastructure mode. As an alternative, the AP can also be managed using an Internet browser such as Microsoft Internet Explorer.

IBSS Practical Setup

The following setup procedure creates a Colligo basic service set consisting of two Wi-Fi stations, as shown in Figure 3. Setting up such a Colligo ad hoc network session is relatively simple and straightforward.

To initiate a session, all participating stations must activate their Wi-Fi adapter and run the Colligo software. When Colligo is used for the first time, it is also necessary to enter a user name and other personal details for identification purposes.

Figure 4a shows the Colligo main screen for user *benny* after the program starts. Clicking the Create Instant Network button in the upper-right corner, as shown in Figure 4b, will either create a new BSS or join an existing ad hoc network. The same procedure is repeated by other users wishing to join the network.

Following a successful ad hoc network connection, the user names of other stations will be listed in the main window. The time it takes for hosts to detect each other varies from a few seconds to several minutes. Figure 5a shows that a remote user named *wilson* has been detected. The name of the remote user is written in italics to indicate that the user has not yet been authenticated and therefore is unable to communicate or gain access to the network resources.

Right-clicking on the remote user name will activate the authentication menu. The ensuing interactive authentication sequence ensures that the remote user is

Figure 3. Simple two-station BSS

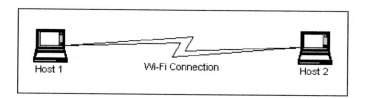

Figure 4. Colligo start-up main window

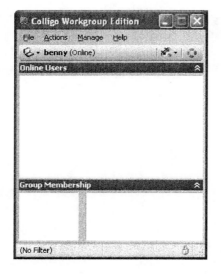 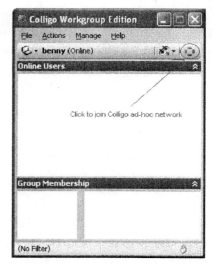

a. Initial window   *b. Starting an ad hoc network*

Figure 5. Authenticating a remote user

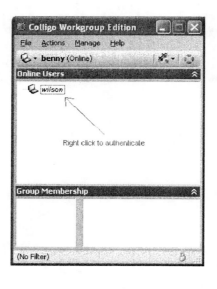

a. Remote user has no network access   *b. Access to network has been granted*

Figure 6. Initiating file transfer

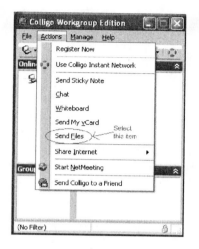 

a. Action menu   b. File transfer window

a legitimate member of the BSS. When the authentication is successful, the remote user name is no longer written in italics, indicating that access to network has been granted to the user, as shown in Figure 5b.

After the remote user is authenticated, all communication features of Colligo can be used. The next step is to set up a file transfer session in which the link throughput can be measured. Figure 6a shows the Colligo main menu to invoke the file transfer feature. Selecting the Send Files item brings a file transfer window similar to that shown in Figure 6b.

Colligo allows us to transfer a batch of files to a number of users. The empty lists in Figure 6b must be correctly populated before the file transfer can begin. Clicking on the Add Users button brings another window where all remote users are listed (see Figure 7a). In this example, only one remote user called *wilson* is selected. Now select the file(s) from the local drive for transmission (see Figure 7b). Clicking on the Send button will initiate a confirmation sequence, which is immediately followed by the actual file transfer.

BSS and ESS setup

In the infrastructure mode, the wireless network operates under the coordination of an AP. The AP itself is connected to a wired network such as a LAN. In a

Figure 7. Completing file transfer setup

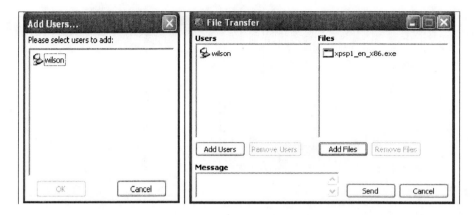

a. Selecting recipient   b. Completed file transfer setup

simple home network, the AP can be directly connected to a router, which provides access to the Internet (see Figure 8). Two stations such as Host 1 and Host 2 communicate through an AP to access the Internet.

The AP is connected to a wired network even when access to the Internet is not required. In our case, no access to the Internet is required. The wired network is simulated by a third host called AP controller. The AP controller is connected to the AP with a crossover Ethernet cable, as shown in Figure 9.

Figure 8. ESS for home use

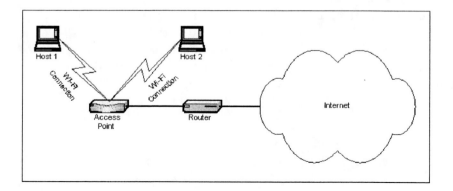

Figure 9. Simplified ESS

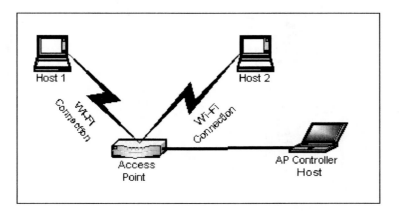

The AP must be configured in such a way that allows a Colligo network to be established. Configuring the AP can only be completed from the AP controller host using either the AP manager or the Web browser as discussed. When the AP is active and connected to the controller host, launching the AP manager will show the summary tab (see Figure 10). The screen capture shows the parameters set to run a Colligo wireless network in infrastructure mode.

Some of the parameters shown in the summary tab are static; whereas, others are variables that need to be set with correct values.

- **AP name** is the name assigned to the particular AP. In larger networks several APs may be used, which makes it necessary to assign unique names to each to avoid naming conflict.
- **SSID** stands for service set ID, which is a unique name for the service set. The Colligo software works correctly if the SSID is set to *COLLIGO*, as shown Figure 11. Setting the AP's SSID to anything other than COLLIGO will prevent the Colligo wireless network from establishing.
- **IP address** in this context is the address of the AP for the wired connection to the controller host. The default factory value is 192.168.0.50, which indicates that the AP is designed for the use in small networks only. The controller host must use a compatible IP address to communicate with the AP through the Ethernet cable.
- **MAC address** displayed in the summary tab is the one used in the wireless connection. This value is permanently assigned to the AP and cannot be changed.

Figure 10. AP manager summary tab

- **Channel** needs to be set to a number that does not conflict with another nearby AP. Since there is no other AP within range, an arbitrary channel number can be used.

- **WEP security** refers to the Wired Equivalent Privacy security scheme. When turned on, all devices in the network must use the same encryption key. For simplicity, this feature is turned off.

The most important settings are configured in the AP Setting tab. Figure 11 shows the configuration already set for a Colligo network in infrastructure mode.

The Mode Setting selector defines what role the AP device will assume in its operation. The device cannot perform on more that one mode at a time.

1.   **Access point**: The default operation mode of the device, which creates a wireless LAN on infrastructure mode.

Figure 11. AP setting tab

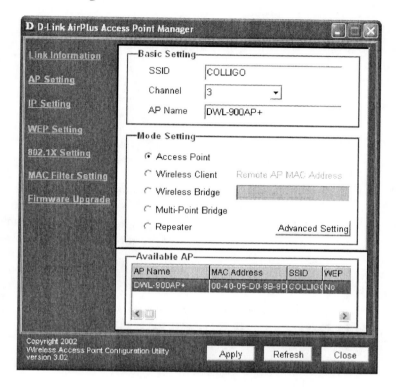

2. **Wireless client**: The AP acts as an adapter, which transforms an 802.3 Ethernet device into a 802.11b wireless client.

3. **Wireless bridge**: Used to utilize two APs to connect two wired LANs with wireless medium.

4. **Multi-point bridge**: An extension of the wireless bridge, where multiple APs are used to connect more LANs.

5. **Repeater**: The device is used to extend the range of the network when the wireless hosts are out of range of the actual LAN-connected AP.

In our experiment we set up the mode as Access Point. In practice, setting the mode to other than Access Point always results in the network failure. Once the AP is configured, the wireless infrastructure network is ready to operate, and the wireless hosts can join the network. The Colligo software automatically sets the SSID for each host to COLLIGO every time it is started. To join the ESS, a host only needs to launch Colligo and wait for the connection to establish automatically. In contrast to the procedure with the BSS, the Create Instant Network button should not be clicked. The user name of other hosts will appear on the main Colligo window list a few minutes after a host enters the ESS coverage. The routine for authenticating other users, sending files, and other actions is identical to that in ad hoc mode.

Experiment Results

A text file of size 137 MB was transferred from Host 1 to Host 2 using the Send Files feature of the Colligo Workgroup Edition 3.2, which allowed us to obtain the file transmission time (Colligo, 2005). Different host formations were used to examine the effects of distance on the throughput performance. Tables 4 and 5 summarize the experiment results.

Analysis and Interpretation

As seen in Table 4, a 4.5 Mbps throughput rate was achieved in ad hoc mode although the bandwidth was 11 Mbps. The poor performance was due to the

Table 4. File transfer time in ad hoc mode

Distance (m)	Obstacle	Transmission time	Throughput (Mbps)
1	0	3m50s	4.66
1	1	4m00s	4.46
16	0	3m57s	4.52

Table 5. File transfer time in infrastructure mode

Distance (m) H1-H2	Distance (m) H1-AP	Distance (m) H2-AP	Transmission time	Throughput (Mbps)
1	1	2	10m45s	1.66
1	2	2	9m50s	1.82
1	1	1	10m20s	1.73
2	1	1	15m10s	1.18
32	12	20	9m33s	1.87
17[1]	12	12	10m30s	1.70

retransmission of a large number of data packets that had been lost. Conducting the experiment within a room may also have contributed to the low throughput. At 2.4 GHz, the radio wavelength is only 12.5cm. At such a short length, signals echoed by various surfaces within the room will reach the receiver in various phases. The result is that at any given time, signals with varying phases and amplitudes will either reinforce or cancel each other as they reach the receiver's antenna. The original signal is therefore received in a distorted form. This problem is called multipath interference and is common in mobile communication (Stallings, 2002).

Increased distance and the presence of obstacles also degrade network performance noticeably. This effect is indeed unavoidable since the radio signals used have very low power. Overcoming obstacle and distance problems by increasing the power is not really an option since it will also increase the chance of interfering with other wireless networks nearby.

A drastic performance drop is observed when the network operates in infrastructure mode. On average the throughput in infrastructure mode is only around 40% that of ad hoc mode. Since the network uses PCF to synchronize the communications, the network is more efficient in using the available bandwidth by the use of fewer control packets. The poor throughput can therefore be explained by the mechanism by which data packets are transmitted from sender to the AP and then from the AP to the receiver. It is very likely that the AP uses a store-and-forward scheme, which results in the channel being occupied for twice as long.

On the other hand, the infrastructure mode makes it possible for wireless hosts to communicate when they are out of range from each other as long as both are within the AP's range. This implies that more flexibility and mobility are achieved at the expense of lower throughput.

Evaluation by Student Feedback

The Wi-Fi projects were offered to two graduate students as part of their summative assessment towards Net-centric Computing, a postgraduate course. The project learning outcomes include: (1) setting up and testing Wi-Fi projects; (2) demonstration of working prototype to project supervisors; (3) development of teaching resources for classroom use; (4) written report containing summary of findings and reflective statements; and (5) oral presentation to the staff and students.

The Wi-Fi projects were completed successfully, and students indicated that they had learned a great deal about Wi-Fi fundamentals in completing hands-on learning activities included in the Wi-Fi projects. This is evident from the students' reflective statements, as follows:

Student 1

The Wi-Fi project has helped me immensely to develop a sound knowledge of Wi-Fi technology. During the practical project, I discovered that there are various issues with regard to the deployment of Wi-Fi technology. The level of exposure and knowledge that I gained from the hands-on experiment, I would have never achieved from just a theoretical mode of learning.

There are many positives that can be drawn from a hands-on project like the Wi-Fi propagation measurement. A project such as this helps you to understand and appreciate technology better, which may not (be) possible from a mere theoretical form of learning. I would strongly recommend hands-on projects to others who are interested to gain in-depth knowledge and experience of the technology.

Student 2

By taking up the hands-on project, I realised that with a correct approach, the subject of networking in general and Wi-Fi in particular is no more difficult than other subjects in computing science. By understanding the basic issues of the technology, one can make sense on why the designers built the devices the way they did. Further, it challenges us to think about how various aspects of the technology can be improved.

With an engineering background, I never believe in any new technology unless I see it actually working. The project convinced me that the Wi-Fi technology does work, and any person willing to invest time studying and experimenting can learn to set up his or her own Wi-Fi network. Also the experience enriches us with another skill that may be important in our career later.

I would recommend similar projects to anyone interested in practical experiments and is not shy of technical challenges. They are also suitable for veterans of theoretical investigations who want to enrich their skill and experience with practical ones.

Conclusion and Future Work

Through a series of experiments and measurements made at various locations of the AUT's WY office building, we gained an insight into the performance of Wi-Fi links in an office environment. This project involves both literature review and practical investigation regarding the IEEE 802.11b protocol known as Wi-Fi. A number of conclusions can be drawn from the findings of this study.

The use of electromagnetic waves as the medium instead of cables presents many technical challenges. To begin with, the available radio band is limited, and most ranges are licensed by governments across the world. This restriction forces various wireless devices to crowd into the same unlicensed bands. Also problems inherent in radio communication, such as noise, interference, and security issues, also affect wireless networks. The implication is that, despite its growing importance in recent years, the wireless network is not going to replace the wired network. It is most likely that both wired and wireless networks will coexist in the future.

The experiments reveal that data transfer rate through the wireless medium is much lower than the wired network. The wireless connection is also fragile, which necessitates that the whole transmission process be repeated whenever the connection drops during file transfer session. Because of these limitations, wireless networks at present serve mainly as a connectivity solution rather than as a performance solution. This may change in the future, however, as new wireless technologies supporting quality of service (QoS) are also being developed.

For Wi-Fi networks, it is found that the ad hoc mode provides better throughput in a low-populated network. The same network operating in infrastructure mode provides only about half the throughput of the ad hoc network. It is very likely that the AP uses a store-and-forward algorithm in delivering the data packets, which results in the drastic performance drop. The AP, however, is indispensable when the stations are out of range of each other. The technical difficulties encountered during the experiment suggest that Wi-Fi technology is not yet mature. This is indicated by the complexity of the setting-up procedure and the incompatibility that is common between Wi-Fi devices.

As it grows, wireless technology will provide research opportunities in several areas. Future research relevant to the scope of this project will mainly involve bandwidth increase and optimization, which are aimed at throughput improvement. At present the IEEE 802.11b system has many limitations since it provides services on "best effort" basis. The development of new wireless standards providing QoS is the most effective way of achieving satisfactory network performance (Prasad & Prasad, 2002).

In anticipation of the increased available bandwidth, various network-based business and multimedia applications are also being developed. Prasad and Prasad discuss applications such as teleconferencing, telesurveillance, and video-on-demand operating on wireless network backbones. The required bandwidths for delivering the data in various presentation formats are also provided in their discussion.

Summary

The IEEE 802.11 wireless LAN standard has been gaining popularity worldwide in recent years. The IEEE 802.11b, commonly referred to as wireless fidelity (Wi-Fi), is by far the most successful commercially. There are other standards in the IEEE 802.11 family being developed to overcome the limitations of IEEE 802.11b.

This chapter focused on the teaching and learning aspects of Wi-Fi networking using limited hardware resources. A number of hands-on learning activities were reported, including setting up both ad hoc and infrastructure networks. We found that the throughput performance of Wi-Fi network under ad hoc mode is slightly better than the infrastructure mode. This is mainly due to the store-and-forward mechanism used by the access point.

Key Terms and Definitions

Ad hoc network: A class of wireless LAN where nodes communicate without wireless access points. A wireless network operating in ad hoc mode is also called an independent basic service set (IBSS).

AP: Or access point. A device which acts as a bridge between wireless LANs and a wired backbone network. An AP coordinates communication among the mobile stations.

BSS: Or basic service set. A wireless network consisting of mobile stations connected through an access point and any number of fixed stations.

Colligo software: A commercial software package that allows users to run collaborative applications such as interactive chat, unidirectional message delivery, virtual whiteboard, and file transfer.

DCF: Or distributed coordination function. DCF is the main channel access method used in the IEEE 802.11 protocol, which uses the Carrier Sense Multiple access with Collision Avoidance (CSMA/CA) protocol.

ESS: Or extended service set. A set of BSSs connected to a wired network infrastructure.

IBSS: Or independent basic service set. A wireless LAN configuration without access points. An IBSS is also referred to as an ad hoc mode wireless network.

IEEE 802.11: A family of wireless LAN standards.

Infrastructure network: A class of wireless network in which mobile stations are connected to the wired backbone network through wireless access points.

PCF: Or point coordination function. An optional component of the MAC layer protocol which provides a centralized mechanism for packet collision avoidance during transmission via radio waves.

SSID: Or service set ID. A unique name that must be assigned to a service set before the wireless network can operate.

Wi-Fi: Or wireless fidelity. A trade or commercial name for wireless networking equipment using IEEE 802.11b standard.

Review Questions

1. Discuss the main differences between wireless PAN and wireless LAN.
2. Describe the main limitations of current Wi-Fi technologies.
3. Explain why Wi-Fi equipment operates at 2.4GHz in most countries.
4. What are the main challenges in increasing bandwidth in wireless networking?
5. Describe the architecture of a typical Wi-Fi network.
6. Discuss the key characteristics of IEEE 802.11b standard.
7. Explain the significance of SSID in setting up a Wi-Fi network.
8. Can a Wi-Fi network simultaneously operate on both ad hoc and infrastructure modes? Provide sufficient argument or evidence to support your answer.

References

Anonymous. (2005). *Introduction to wireless LAN and IEEE 802.11.*

Colligo. (2005). Colligo Networks, Inc. — Workgroup Edition, Colligo Inc. 2005 [online]. Retrieved from http://www.colligo.com

Ferro, E., & Potorti, F. (2005). Bluetooth and Wi-Fi wireless protocols: A survey and a comparison. *IEEE Wireless Communications, 12*(1), 12-26.

Golmie, N., Van Dyck, R., et al. (2003). Interference evaluation of Bluetooth and IEEE 802.11 systems. *Wireless Networks, 9*(3), 201-211.

Howard, D. (2002). It's a Wi-Fi world. *netWorker, 6*(3), 26-30.

Kaczman, J. (2002). Wi-Fi hotspot networks sprout like mushrooms. *IEEE Spectrum, 39*(9), 18-20.

Ophir, L., Bitran, Y., et al. (2004). Wi-Fi (IEEE 802.11) and Bluetooth coexistence: Issues and solutions. In *15th IEEE International Symposium on Personal, Indoor and Mobile Radio Communications, PIMRC 2004.*

Prasad, N., & Prasad, A. (2002). *WLAN systems and wireless IP for next generation communications.* Boston: Artech House.

Proxim. (1998, March). *What is a wireless LAN?* (White Paper No. 7680). Mountain View, CA.

Stallings, W. (2002). *Wireless communications and networks.* NJ: Prentice Hall.

Vaughan-Nichols, S. (2003). The challenge of Wi-Fi roaming. *Computer, 36*(7), 17-19.

Vaxevanakis, K., Zahariadis, T., et al. (2003). A review on wireless home network technologies. *ACM SIGMOBILE Mobile Computing and Communications Review, 7*(2), 59-68.

Youssef, M. A., Vasan, A., et al. (2002). Specification and analysis of the DCF and PCF protocols in the 802.11 standard using systems of communicating machines. In *Proceedings of the 10th IEEE International Conference on Network Protocols.*

Endnote

[1]   There is no line of sight between H1 and H2.

Chapter X

Information Security Risk Analysis:
A Pedagogic Model Based on a Teaching Hospital

Sanjay Goel, University at Albany, SUNY, and
NYS Center for Information Forensics and Assurance, USA

Damira Pon, University at Albany, SUNY, and
NYS Center for Information Forensics and Assurance, USA

Abstract

There is a strong need for information security education, which stems from the pervasiveness of information technology in business and society. Both government departments and private industries depend on information systems, as information systems are widespread across all business functions. Disruption of critical operational information systems can have serious financial impacts. According to a CSI/FBI report (2004), losses from security breaches have risen rapidly in recent years and exceeded $200 million in 2003. The information security field is very diverse and combines disciplines such as computer science, business, information science, engineering, education, psychology, criminal justice, public administration, law, and accounting. The broad interdisciplinary nature of information security requires several specialists to collaboratively teach the curriculum and integrate different perspectives and teaching styles into a cohesive *delivery. This chapter presents a pedagogical model based on a "teaching hospital" concept that addresses the issues introduced above. By using a specific information-risk-analysis case, the chapter highlights the basic concept of the teaching hospital and its application in teaching and learning contexts.*

Learning Objectives

After completing this chapter, you will be able to:

- Discuss the issues associated with information assurance education.
- Describe the basic concept of teaching hospital approach in information security risk analysis.
- Understand the case development methodology used to support the teaching hospital.
- Suggest possible improvements to the cases described in the chapter.

Introduction

Information assurance (IA) is a complex field, especially due to the dynamically changing security environment and constant evolution of practices and procedures. It is difficult to provide training in such an area since material developed becomes obsolete very quickly. To develop a better understanding of IA, concepts should be assimilated from several disciplines (i.e., computer and information science, law, business, etc.) and blended into the context of real problems. In this chapter, a teaching hospital model that has been developed for IA training in the context of information security risk analysis is described. The teaching hospital approach involves incorporating real cases to supplement existing curriculum, which keeps teaching material relevant over time through infusion of current research problems in the curriculum and creates a rich learning environment that is both stimulating and dynamic. The New York State Center for Information Forensics and Assurance (CIFA) at the University at Albany has developed a teaching hospital for IA education (Goel & Pon, 2005). Within this teaching hospital, a research program that solves current industry problems is combined with a teaching program responsible for dissemination of curriculum. Problems from public and private sector organizations are introduced in the research lab, which are solved and abstracted into living cases that are then used to supplement the training material. Bridges and Hallinger (1999) have shown case-based learning to be a powerful pedagogical tool for dissemination of instruction. The teaching hospital model provides a constant stream of cases that keeps the curriculum current. Though effective, such an approach is still labor-intensive and contingent upon smooth functioning of research and educational case development programs. The field of security is so vast that a considerable time will elapse before most of the information security domain is covered through cases. Over time, it is envisaged that a library of cases will emerge, requiring less effort in new case development.

The general philosophy behind use of cases in curriculum and in context of the teaching hospital proposed is detailed in the chapter. The rest of the chapter is organized as follows: We first introduce the case-based learning techniques and the concept of a teaching hospital. We then present a case on risk analysis that demonstrates the use of the teaching hospital in information assurance curriculum. Finally, we conclude the chapter, followed by a brief summary

Teaching Hospitals and Case-Based Teaching

Teaching hospitals have been used extensively for medical training since the 20th century (Barzansky, Jonas, & Etzel, 1998). They enabled control on medical student production and medical education quality monitoring. Training is provided to medical students and doctors-in-training through direct clinical experience of treating actual patients under the supervision and guidance of attending physicians in medical wards. Medical teaching hospitals are important because their students need hands-on experience; otherwise, it is very difficult to translate the abstract knowledge from the literature into a diagnosis. This practice enables residents to crystallize theoretical knowledge into field knowledge, which they can utilize when practicing medicine. In IA education, it is also essential to find a balance between theory and practice. The field not only requires students to be able to conceptualize but also to practically apply what is learned within the classroom in the outside world. Teaching hospitals tend to offer "a comprehensive array of facilities" as well as possess sufficiently high volumes of patients from whom students can gain experience. Teaching hospitals have also traditionally "conducted a wide variety of clinical research" (MGT of America, 1999). Although derived from medical education, the teaching hospital model has been implemented with great effect within the pedagogical practices of other disciplines that require eventual application of theory into practice.

We propose a teaching hospital for training students in the IA field where students receive hands-on experience by working on real problems under the supervision of researchers and practitioners in the field. Our model attempts to emulate a teaching hospital by structuring an integrated program in IA research and education through collaboration with other organizations (problem-rich in the area of information security). Since the IA potential student population is large and few researchers in the area are available, it is not feasible to send students to directly apprentice with researchers in the field. As an alternative, cases from state and law enforcement agencies are utilized. Real problems are abstracted into living cases, which are used for classroom instruction; a constant stream of cases can thus be generated. This approach allows the context of real problems to be introduced into education and maintains the currency of the curriculum as newer cases replace (or supplement) older cases. An active research program and a mechanism for abstraction of projects into teaching cases are required for the constant infusion of new material.

The fundamental underpinning of the teaching hospital is incorporation of a case-based learning (Naumes & Naumes, 1999) approach. Cases assist in bringing real-life context to abstract concepts. Case-based learning is believed to provide more motivation for learning as well as a concrete framework from which complex concepts can be more easily understood. It reduces the potential for "inert knowledge," where the learned information is difficult or impossible to apply to realistic situations, and is critical to avoid learning inert knowledge since it uses significant mental resources without commensurate returns. When learning risk analysis, for example, simply learning the terms and definitions will leave students with inert knowledge, which is not sufficient when they have to perform a formal risk analysis in the field. Isolated facts are more difficult to integrate within memories than facts taught in a realistic context. Generic concepts should be applied and reiterated over multiple cases so students can begin to understand the diversity of uses for that information.

While such a teaching hospital approach is very powerful, it is also very resource-intensive (at least in the beginning). However, once streamlined, it can reduce the teaching and preparation effort significantly. Especially when a large case library is built, the time to collect data and build cases reduces significantly. In addition, if properly coupled with an educational research program, pedagogical research and domain research can synergistically operate, reducing the burden and amortizing efforts over multiple streams. Cases can be of several types, including detailed cases, narrative cases, mini cases, and bullet cases. They vary in size and scope, with narrative cases being the largest (10 to 100 pages) and bullet cases being the smallest (a few sentences). The use of cases depends on the impact that the instructional designer is trying to achieve, and often several different types of cases are used in various situations. As professed in this chapter, we will use a specific information-risk-analysis case to illustrate the concept of the teaching hospital. We chose the domain of risk analysis because it forms a classic example of where the teaching hospital can be beneficial. It is an abstract field where the terms and definitions are "inert knowledge" and application of that knowledge is difficult.

Risk Analysis

Risk can be defined as the inherent uncertainty and unpredictability in the outcomes of events or hazards that are faced while taking actions. Risk analysis is the assessment of what could go wrong (risks), determination of which risks warrant preventive or contingency actions, and development of strategies to deal with those risks. Operationally, risk analysis can be defined as a method of identifying the organizational assets, the threats to those assets, and the vulnerability of the system to those threats in order to determine the exposure of an organization and to determine suitable controls to reduce the exposure to manageable levels (Goel & Chen, 2005). Assets are the valuables of an organization which need to be protected, and vulnerabilities are weak character-istics of assets. Threats are potential causes of harm to assets through exploi-tation of vulnerabilities, and controls are implementations that reduce risk and vulnerability (Office of Information and Communications Technology, 2003). Risk analysis thus involves aggregating these parameters to determine the exposure of the organization to the threats, and management is the process of determination of controls that are necessary to reduce the impact of the risks to manageable levels. Accomplishing a risk analysis can be an enormously intimi-dating task since there are few management analysis topics that are as abstract and complex as risk analysis. While risk analysis has been practiced for a long time in various disciplines (Covello & Mumpower, 1985), its application to information security is relatively new. Information security risk analysis, though conceptually simple, is difficult in application. Managers and information security officers often struggle with understanding the information security risks and their relative importance.

The main issue in such analysis is the ambiguity in identifying the assets, vulnerabilities, threats, and controls, especially since the same parameter can be an asset, a vulnerability, and a control at the same time. Such problems provide fertile ground for use of cases, and a case was developed for the purpose of assisting students in articulating the assets, vulnerabilities, and threats; facilitat-ing their understanding in rating these values based on their relative importance; and assisting them in gaining experience in using a qualitative risk methodology. To understand risk analysis the students need to develop the concepts of risk and uncertainty to conceptualize the basic premise of risk analysis. Once conceptually grounded in theory, students need to gain a practical understanding by applying risk analysis to real problems. Finally, they need to gain familiarity with risk analysis tools and apply them to an actual risk analysis project.

In the pedagogic work presented here, students were provided basic skills in risk analysis and provided a historical perspective of risk analysis as well as its application in other fields. Once students were familiar with the concepts in risk, they were introduced to formal definitions of risk analysis and introduced to a risk analysis methodology. In most existing risk analysis tools, the tool and methodology are so complex that the students get defocused from the fundamental learning of risk analysis. To direct their focus on the subtle nuances of the risk analysis process, the students were given a set of simple matrices, which they used to collect the data on assets, threats, vulnerabilities, and controls. The students were presented with a working example in the class, and then a larger case was introduced to apply the knowledge learned. The students were expected to identify the organizational assets, threats, vulnerabilities, and controls; value the assets; and determine the relationships between assets, threats, vulnerabilities, and controls. A scale of 0 (none), 1 (low), 3 (medium), and 9 (high) was used to rate the impact of vulnerabilities on assets, threats on vulnerabilities, and controls on threats. A tool was provided to enter the data and compute the results. The students had knowledge of the basics of information security that they were expected to use in their work.

A narrative case was developed with some ambiguity built into the analysis so that the students were able to experience making subjective judgments about the relative importance of information gathered. The goals of the case were to reinforce the risk analysis concepts taught in class by assisting the students in applying these concepts to a real situation. The case presented in the next section was based on a business engaged in making and delivering natural soap products to customers, which was selected because the product could be easily understood and the business model was relatively transparent.

Natural Soap Company Case

Natural Soap Products, LLC, is a small (but rapidly growing!) family business located in upstate New York in Schoharie County. This small family-run business is engaged in making natural soap using recipes that have been in their family for several generations. Roughly, two-thirds of their business is through wholesale distribution of soaps and other products to specialty stores and commercial lodging facilities. The remaining third of their business is through online sales from their Web site. The business is managed and operated by a mother and her daughter; the mother is around 40 years of age and the daughter is around 20 years of age. The mother and daughter are responsible for the wholesale distribution of the products and the online sale of the products, respectively. The wholesale distribution catalog is mailed to potential customers, and those orders are collected via phone.

All orders are prepaid, and all major credit cards are accepted, including Visa, MasterCard, American Express, and Discover. U.S. bank checks and money orders are also accepted. All orders being paid with check or money order are not shipped until payments are received and have cleared the bank. A New York state tax of 8.25% (effective June 1, 2004) is added to both wholesale and retail orders. Their orders are shipped within 3 to 5 business days, depending on the shipping option selected by the customer. Shipping and handling charges are extra and are based on weight and method of shipment.

The mother and the daughter do all the manufacturing in house. The mother is responsible for making soaps, and the daughter is responsible for making lotions and other products. Each batch of soap is handcrafted, incorporating the natural ingredients supplied either through local vendors or through online orders. Soap making involves two steps. In the first step, all the ingredients are processed together. In the second step, the soaps are placed on large racks and cured until they are ready for delivery. They are constantly preparing new products to keep their product line vibrant. They advertise mainly through word of mouth from satisfied customers, and their business is growing very briskly.

A Web site has been developed that provides a catalog of their products and allows users to place orders online. Their Web site is hosted by Yahoo, which manages the content and ordering system, as well as the order data. Yahoo is privy to order information that is submitted via the Web site; however, it can only use aggregate data for its analysis and maintains user anonymity. Yahoo also automatically collects data on shopper experience if the Web site is accessed through Yahoo. The Yahoo Privacy Policy, located at http://privacy.yahoo.com, discusses how this information is used.

The privacy policy for Natural Soap is stated as follows:

At naturalsoapproducts.com we value our customers and respect their privacy. We assure you that we will maintain use of customer information responsibly. We will never sell or rent the information you provide to us online to third parties. We may wish to contact you via mail or e-mail to inform you of any promotions or specials taking place at Natural Soap Products. If you do not wish to receive such information, please let us know in the 'special instructions' box at checkout. If you have any questions about our privacy policy, please feel free to contact us at naturalsoapproducts@yahoo.com.

For legal protection, the company also posts a disclaimer:

Our products are not created to treat or cure any diseases or health problems. All descriptions and sizes are approximate. Actual colors, sizes, and styles may vary slightly from photos and descriptions and are subject to change. Prices and policies of this website are effective April 2004 and are subject to change without notice.

All orders are insured in value up to $100. If an item is damaged during shipping customers are expected to contact the company immediately and to save all packing materials and paperwork. If the damage to the package is noticed at the time of the delivery, the recipient is expected to inform the delivery person and have them verify the damage in writing. Damage caused to the order may then be claimed through UPS or USPS.

Returns are accepted, and refunds or credits are honored as long as all of the conditions listed below are met.

1. Item is unused and in its original condition.
2. The company is notified of the return within 7 days of customer's receipt of the item.
3. Customer assumes the responsibility of all shipping charges (original and return) and returns the item within 7 days of notifying the company of the return.

Two desktop computers are used for storing and processing the orders and invoices. The computers also contain all of their client and vendor information as well as inventory status. The daughter has some background in Web development but has very little knowledge of computer security. The mother has functional knowledge on how to use computers but has no knowledge of how to configure, alter, or secure her computer and network. They have a broadband network connection into the computer that the computers are constantly connected to. They do not use a firewall or an intrusion detection system.

The company has about $1 million in annual revenue, of which 20% goes towards raw material, 10% towards maintenance of equipment and temporary labor, and 30% towards the salaries of the two principals. In addition, they have fixed expenses for maintaining the office and utilities.

Instructions to the Student

You want to analyze the information security risks for the organization and determine the exposure of the organization due to security breaches. You will need to identify assets, vulnerabilities, threats, and controls for the organization and determine the most important controls that the organization will need to install. You will perform a qualitative analysis initially to determine the relative importance of the controls and then you will perform a quantitative analysis.

Results of the Analysis

The students were divided into groups of 4 to 5 who worked together in teams to determine the threats, assets, vulnerabilities, and controls. The students had a fair understanding of finance, economics, information technology, and security upon entering the class. The discussed the different elements of the case and built consensus in determining the values. Different teams did not communicate with each other, and at the end of the session, each team reported its results. As expected, the students had difficulty in identifying the risks, threats, controls, and vulnerabilities. Another area that they struggled with was valuing the assets, and they had vastly different concepts of the losses that could be incurred by exposure of specific assets. The case was then discussed in the class, and the numbers were rationalized during the discussion so that in the end a consensus analysis was computed. Sometimes there can be alternate answers to the same question based on the judgment of the analyst. Students tend to find it difficult to grasp the ambiguity in the analysis and always seek definitive answers. A sample solution is provided below. The solution also contains the rationalization that evolved in its development.

Valuation of Assets

Valuating the information assets of a company is a very difficult process when data is difficult to find and can be inaccurate, and some assets are intangible and cannot be easily quantified. In addition, the value of the assets is not simply their total values but should be considered as their estimated maximum loss. Estimated maximum loss, an insurance term, can be defined as the largest probable loss that could occur from a single event. This value could be well below the value of the total asset. The company's proprietary information is very important. If someone obtained their recipes, customer base, supplier base, and so forth, it would be possible to duplicate their product(s) and compete. In addition, the company

Table 1. Asset valuations

Assets	Description or Examples	Valuation
Proprietary Information	Recipes, Customer base, Supplier base, Orders	$25,000.00
Client Confidential Information	Identity, Credit Card #'s, Privacy of Transactions	$200,000.00
Personnel	Mother and Daughter	$60,000.00
Equipment	e.g. Soap Making Equipment, Computers, etc.	$30,000.00
Website/Web Database	Availability, Data Integrity, Data Confidentiality	$110,000.00
Reputation	Image of the Company	$100,000.00
Inventory	Processed Products (e.g. Soaps)	$3,000.00
Credit Line	Credit Score of the Company	$30,000.00
Premises	Home Office	$20,000.00
Documentation	Important Documents (e.g. Process Information)	$110,000.00
Raw Materials	e.g. Goat Milk, Lye, Essential Oils	$1,000.00
Revenue	Total Revenue of the Company	$150,000.00

would have to spend time in obtaining information on the customers or suppliers. However, the potential for all of their proprietary information to be stolen is relatively low and due to their customer loyalty would not be too affected, even though some time and effort would be needed for data collection and potentially a small loss in revenue. Therefore, the valuation would be about $25,000. If client confidential information is stolen through loss of credit card numbers and identity theft through either hacking or theft, then the company would probably have to report the incident to the customers involved and potential lawsuits are possible. This may result in loss of reputation and revenue as well as court fees. The valuation for this asset would be $200,000. Personnel are essential to this business. If something happened to the mother or daughter, it may be difficult to operate as normal, and additional staff may need to be hired. Death is not very probable because of the ages of the personnel; however, it is probable that the daughter could decide to get a separate job. Time would be needed in training and interviewing additional staff. The valuation would be $60,000 due to loss in revenue, staff training, and hiring. While the equipment is extensive, the potential of much of the equipment being affected is low. The computers or soap equipment may need to be replaced over time. However, in the case of theft, the cost may be up to $30,000, to include likely stolen or broken items as well as impact on operations and revenue. The Web site is hosted by Yahoo; however, the company is liable for any damage to its data and is expected to have business continuity measures and comply with the Cardholder Information Security Program. The data is currently also stored in house computers, but the Web site is not saved. Time and effort would need to be spent in reconstructing the Web site, and any loss of information would incur some damage to client confidential information located on the Web server. The estimated loss would be $110,000. The reputation is the basis of this company. Most of its customers come through word of mouth. Loss of reputation would likely occur through loss of data or loss of personnel (e.g., the mother, depending on how contact is made). It is more likely that loss of information will occur, and the resulting loss of reputation would be estimated at $100,000. Inventory can be stolen, degrade, or be damaged. It is a high probability that a batch of soap will be damaged or that some inventory items might be stolen. This is estimated at $3,000. The credit line can be damaged if overdrawn or someone takes a false credit card under the company's name. If a corporation loses its credit line, about $30,000 could be lost. The premises of the company is most likely to be damaged through a break-in or environmental damage such as rain, flood, lightning, or fire. The whole premises is not likely to be damaged at any one point in time; however, probable damage will be approximately $20,000. Documents may contain company proprietary informa-tion and client confidential information and result in loss of reputation, revenue, and time and effort of personnel. Maximum loss associated with theft or damage is approximately $110,000. The raw materials can degrade over time or be stolen. It is more probable that some raw materials will degrade, resulting in a loss of $1,000. Revenue can be lost through loss of reputation, competition, and slowdown of operations. It is estimated that loss occurring within one event would be $150,000.

Correlating Assets and Vulnerabilities

There is a subtle difference between vulnerabilities and threats that needs to be clear for accurately identifying vulnerabilities. Threats are the perpetrators of losses while vulnerabilities are facilitators that help the threats manifest and cause damage. The same vulnerability may affect different assets differently. The matrix shown in Table 2 aggregates the impacts of different vulnerabilities on the assets of the organization. The next paragraph provides the rationale that was used to determine the valuation. This is the most critical part in understand-ing the analysis.

Company proprietary information can be slightly impacted by Yahoo Web hosting since some customer information may be located on the Web site and database (1). Through the home network, there is a low probability of impact to company proprietary information since information will usually not be exchanged so often (1). The premises can be exploited through break-ins to gain access to some company proprietary information (1). Employees would not likely give out proprietary information and would not likely be persuaded to do so. However, due to negligence or mistakes, they could prove to be vulnerabilities (1). Suppliers may be able to give their own information but would not really have access to the company's information (0). Some of the client confidential information would be located on the Web servers, and there would be a medium impact (3). Getting

Table 2. Asset/Vulnerability matrix

Asset Values/ Vulnerabilities	Company Proprietary Information $25,000.00	Client Confidential Information $200,000.00	Personnel $60,000.00	Equipment $30,000.00	Website including Web Database $110,000.00	Reputation $100,000.00	Inventory $3,000.00	Credit Line $30,000.00	Premises $20,000.00	Documentation $110,000.00	Raw Materials $1,000.00	Revenue $150,000.00	Aggregates (Impact) Σ (asset value x vulnerability)
Yahoo Web Hosting	1	3	0	0	9	3	0	3	0	1	0	3	2565000
Home Network	1	1	0	3	1	1	0	3	0	1	0	3	1175000
Home Computers	3	9	0	3	3	9	0	3	0	3	0	3	4065000
Premises	1	1	1	3	0	1	1	1	9	1	1	1	949000
Employees	1	1	9	3	3	3	3	3	3	3	3	9	3327000
Suppliers	0	0	0	0	0	1	0	1	0	1	3	3	693000
Raw Materials	0	0	0	0	0	1	1	0	0	0	9	3	562000
Manufacturing Process	0	0	0	1	0	1	1	0	0	0	3	3	586000
Shipment	0	0	0	0	0	1	3	0	0	1	3	3	672000

client confidential information through transmission on the home network is not likely; however, it is still possible (1). Home computers would be a better source of getting information in terms of client confidential information (9). The premises is also similarly low impact of being exploited to gain client confidential information (1). While employees would have access to the information, they would be unlikely to give up client confidential information. However, just as said earlier with the company proprietary information, a mistake on the part of the employees could lead to vulnerability (1). Personnel would likely be affected through insecurity in the premises (1) and themselves (9). Equipment within the organization would not really be affected by a vulnerability within Web hosting at Yahoo (0). There is the chance of a medium impact of equipment through the home network since it affects computers and the network (3). Home computers will also have a medium impact on equipment since they are not all inclusive of the equipment available (3). A vulnerability in the premises would lead to a medium impact on equipment (3). Employees can have a medium impact on equipment due to negligence in security implementation, user errors, or mistakes causing damage (3). The manufacturing process can put wear on the equipment but not enough to damage it greatly. However, over time the manufacturing process will degrade the equipment. Shipment is not likely to damage the equipment since it will be located in the house and already exists (0). The Yahoo Web hosting is most likely to be affected through the Website (9). There is a possibility of gaining access permissions through vulnerabilities in the home network. However, the chance that this would occur is low (1). It is possible that through the home computers non-expired cookies or keyloggers could provide access to the Web site and database information (3). Suppliers are not dealing with the Web site so this is not likely (0). The company's reputation can be impacted through the Web hosting. For example, if credit card numbers are stolen through the Web database (3). The home network may lead to loss of reputation if it is exploited to gain access to something, but the chance of this is very small (1). The home computers have a higher impact on reputation loss since it is most associated with client confidential information (9). There is a low impact on the reputation from vulnerability in the premises (1). Employees have a medium impact on the reputation since the reputation of the company is dependent primarily on the mother (3). Reputation may suffer if the suppliers go away or the materials lose quality. In addition, if the process changes or the shipping is affected, then the reputation can also be affected slightly (1). The Web hosting, network, or computers will not affect inventory. However, inventory may be affected by a vulnerability in the premises. For example, leaving the door unlocked could allow someone to steal some inventory (1). Employees could damage inventory through physical accidents and through leaving security vulnerabilities (3). Suppliers take care of the raw material delivery so they would not impact the inventory (0). Inadequate raw materials and problems in the manufacturing could result in lower quality or lower amounts of inventory (1). Shipment is a likely cause of inventory damage (3). The credit score can be affected through overdrawing (probably through mistake of employees) or someone stealing the company's credit information. This can be done through the Yahoo Web hosting, the home network, or the home computers (3). The network and computers are vulnerable to negligence in security measures by employees (3). It is also possible for vulnerabilities in the supplier systems or weakness in the infrastructure to affect the credit. The premises is mostly impacted by itself (9) and can also be affected by the employees who work within there (3). Both suppliers and shippers would tend to have some documentation (1). In addition, exploitation of Yahoo Web hosting, the home network, and the premises could lead to impacts on some documents (1). Home computers and employees would most likely impact documents in terms of where they would be contained and the security and safety of them (3). Raw materials could be stolen due to weak physical security of the premises (1). Employees could handle the raw materials badly and cause other vulnerabilities due to weak security management (3). Suppliers and shipment providers would be responsible for the safe travel of the materials, where some could be damaged or degraded (3). In addition, the manufacturing process can result in destruction of raw materials (3). Raw materials are mostly impacted through natural elements such as degradation over time so they are self-degrading (9). Revenue is impacted through all vulnerabilities. The Web hosting is responsible for about half of the revenue generated (3). The network is used to communicate to the Web database where customers can place orders (3). In addition, the home computers store all the important information (3). The site does contain all the equipment, inventory, and employees (1). Employees may most affect revenue since the customers choose the company based on word of mouth and the personnel (3). Supplier availability and quality of raw materials all affect the potential revenue (3). In addition, the integrity of the manufacturing process and the shipment of the materials could affect revenue (3).

Vulnerabilities and Threats

Threats are probably easier to determine compared to vulnerabilities and assets. However, determining how important a given vulnerability is for a threat can be difficult and often requires domain knowledge. The students in the class had a detailed knowledge of the information security threats and technology from previous lectures, which were instrumental for them in developing this matrix. Since information security is a multidisciplinary field, it is often essential for the experts to have familiarity with other disciplines, such as psychology and law. The correlation between the threats and their interaction with vulnerabilities are presented in Table 3, and the corresponding rationale for selecting these values is provided in the next paragraph.

Accidental computer failure can result through weaknesses in the home computers themselves (9) and somewhat through employee actions with a machine (1). Malicious code could exploit Yahoo Web hosting; however, this is not so likely since Yahoo can afford more controls. This is still possible with new exploits where no definition has been made (3). Malicious code could also affect an asset through the network of the home and within home computers (3). Employees could let in malicious code through clicking on an e-mail, going to a Web site, or simply not securing the systems appropriately (3). A network intrusion on home computers would exploit vulnerabilities in the home network with no firewall or an improperly configured firewall (3) and the home computers (9). In addition, the employees can be exploited to give out information or because they improperly configure the firewall (1). A network intrusion or DOS attack on Yahoo is through Yahoo Web hosting (9). A DOS attack on the home computers would occur because of the network security (9) and employee misconfiguration (3). The password to the Web account or data theft could occur through Yahoo

Table 3. Vulnerability/Threat matrix

Impact Values/ Threats	Yahoo Web Hosting 2565000	Home Network 1175000	Home Computers 4065000	Premises 949000	Employees 3327000	Suppliers 693000	Raw Materials 562000	Manufacturing Process 586000	Shipment 672000	Aggregates (Threat Impact) Σ (impact value x threat value)
Accidental Computer Failure	0	0	9	0	1	0	0	0	0	39912000
Malicious Code	3	3	3	0	3	0	0	0	0	33396000
Network Intrusion on H.C.	0	3	9	0	1	0	0	0	0	43437000
Network Intrusion on Yahoo!	9	0	0	0	0	0	0	0	0	23085000
DOS Attack on H.C.	0	9	0	0	3	0	0	0	0	20556000
DOS Attack on Yahoo!	9	0	0	0	0	0	0	0	0	23085000
Password Theft by Spyware/Keyloggers	1	0	3	0	3	0	0	0	0	24741000
Data Theft by Spyware/Keyloggers	1	0	3	0	3	0	0	0	0	24741000
Accidental Data Alteration	1	0	0	0	3	0	0	0	0	12546000
Physical Theft of Equipment	0	0	0	9	0	0	0	0	0	8541000
Physical Theft of Data	3	1	3	0	1	0	0	0	0	24392000
Physical Theft of Inventory/Raw Materials	0	0	0	3	0	0	0	0	3	4863000
Poor Inventory Quality	0	0	0	0	3	0	3	3	1	14097000
Poor Raw Material Quality	0	0	0	0	0	1	1	0	0	1255000
Daughter/Mother Unable to Work	0	0	0	0	9	0	0	0	0	29943000
Damage to Inventory	0	0	0	0	3	0	0	0	3	11997000
Disruption of Supply Chain	0	0	0	0	0	3	0	0	1	2751000
Environmental Damage	0	0	0	3	0	0	0	0	0	2847000

Web hosting (1) and through the home computers (3). Spyware and keyloggers are likely to come into a system through negligence of an employee (3). Accidental data alteration may be impacted by Yahoo Web hosting (1) but will mostly be affected by user error (3). Physical theft of equipment is likely to occur through vulnerabilities in the premises (9). Data theft is likely through the Yahoo Web hosting and the home computers (3). It is also perpetuated through the home network, employees, and the premises if present in paper documents (1). Physical theft of inventory or raw materials could occur through the premises or when shipping (3). Poor inventory quality is mostly due to the quality of the raw materials, mistakes done by employees, and effects of the manufacturing process (3). However, the inventory can also be affected during shipment (1). Raw materials can be affected by degradation of themselves and the suppliers (1). The mother or daughter not being able to work occurs mostly within the employees themselves (9). Damage to inventory is most likely to occur through the shipment (3) but can also occur due to accidents of employees (3). Disruption of the supply chain is likely to occur due to problems with suppliers (3) or shippers (1). Environmental damage is likely to occur due to weaknesses in the premises (3).

Table 4. Threat/Control matrix

Impact Values/ Controls	Accidental Computer Failure	Malicious Code	Network Intrusion on H.C.	Network Intrusion on Yahoo!	DOS Attack on H.C.	DOS Attack on Yahoo!	Password Theft by Spyware/Keyloggers	Data Theft by Spyware/Keyloggers	Accidental Data Alteration	Physical Theft of Equipment	Physical Theft of Data	Physical Theft of Inventory/Raw Materials	Poor Inventory Quality	Poor Raw Material Quality	Daughter/Mother Unable to Work	Damage to Inventory	Disruption of Supply Chain	Environmental Damage	Aggregates (Control Impact) Σ (threat importance x impact of controls)
	39912000	33396000	43437000	23085000	20556000	23085000	24741000	24741000	12546000	8541000	24392000	4863000	14097000	1255000	29943000	11997000	2751000	2847000	
Network Security (Firewall/IDS)	0	3	3	0	9	0	1	1	0	0	0	0	0	0	0	0	0	0	464985000
Anti-Virus	0	9	3	0	0	0	0	0	0	0	0	0	0	0	0	0	0	0	430875000
Physical Security	0	0	0	0	0	0	0	0	0	9	3	3	0	0	0	1	0	3	185172000
Warranties	9	0	0	0	0	0	0	0	0	0	0	0	0	0	0	0	0	0	359208000
Business Insurance	0	0	0	0	0	0	0	0	0	9	0	3	0	0	0	3	0	9	153072000
Org. Policies	0	3	3	3	0	0	1	3	3	0	0	0	3	0	3	1	0	0	580473000
Encryption	0	0	3	0	0	0	0	0	0	0	9	0	0	0	0	0	0	0	349839000
Source Diversification	0	0	0	0	0	0	0	0	0	0	0	0	0	0	3	0	9	0	28524000
Secure Packaging	0	0	0	0	0	0	0	0	0	0	0	0	0	0	0	3	0	0	35991000
Anti-Spyware	0	0	0	0	0	0	9	9	0	0	0	0	0	0	0	0	0	0	445338000
Back-up of Data	3	3	0	0	3	0	0	0	0	0	1	3	0	0	0	0	0	0	363309000

Threats and Controls

Domain knowledge is also critical for selection of controls, as analysts need to understand the mechanisms behind the controls and the manifestation of threats to accurately determine their impact on threats. Field experience is often necessary for accurate characterization of the associations between threats and controls that novice learners often lack. This matrix results in computation of the relative utility of different controls for ensuring security. Based on this ranking, controls can be selected. One should be cautious, however, since some controls may be more expensive than others. A cost-benefit analysis must be performed to determine the most effective control strategy. In addition, dropping some controls altogether may not be feasible, even if their impact is low. It is perhaps better to implement the control at a lower potency rather than eliminating it. Table 4 presents the threat/control matrix.

The rationalization of the different values as perceived by the students is presented in this paragraph. This is perhaps not the most comprehensive list of controls or the most accurate of correlations; however, it demonstrates the thinking behind the analysis. Network security should have a medium impact on malicious code and network intrusion on the home computers (3). It will have a low impact on password and data theft by spyware and keyloggers (1) but a high impact on DOS attacks on the home computers (9). Anti-virus would be very helpful in preventing the spread of malicious code (9) and would help somewhat in network intrusions on the home computers (3). Physical security would greatly assist in the physical theft of equipment (9). It would also impact the theft of data in the form of documents (3). In addition, it would assist somewhat in the theft of inventory and raw materials (3). In addition, physical security such as a locked room would keep damage to inventory lower (1) and protect against environmental damage by having a good roof which keeps water out (3). Warranties would affect the accidental computer failure the most and allow free maintenance of the computers (9). Business insurance would be likely to cover most of the physical theft of equipment and environmental damage since the losses associated with these are high (9). It would also cover some of the losses due to theft of inventory or raw materials and damage to inventory (3). Organizational policies could help in the performance of employees and revenue by incorporating rewards for work or quality assurance standards increasing inventory quality and impacting poor inventory quality (3), inability of the daughter and mother working (3), and damage to inventory (1). This can affect accidental data alteration in that the employee is required to have data entries checked by another employee (3). Also, incorporation of liability waivers and an improved privacy policy could manage effects of data theft, for example, malicious code, network intrusion on home computers and Yahoo, or data theft by spyware and keyloggers (3). It will also affect the password theft by spyware and keyloggers for the home but not Yahoo (1). Encryption of stored and transmitted data will help with network intrusions on the home computers as well as physical theft of data (9). Having multiple sources of raw material should help with ensuring the quality of the raw material (3) as well as having alternate sources to prevent supply chain disruption in case one of the suppliers goes out of business or temporarily closes (9). Secure packing of the inventory, such as using the bubble wrap or Styrofoam packing peanuts, will help with prevention of damage to the inventory when shipping (3). Anti-spyware (if updated with latest signatures) should be able to identify most spyware and keylogging software that can lead to data and password theft (9). Data backups will help in terms of time when there is accidental computer failure (3), a DOS attack occurs on a computer (3), data is stolen (3), or computer equipment that contains the data is stolen (3).

The matrices can evolve over time as new assets are acquired, more vulnerabilities and threats are determined, and new controls are devised. This lightweight approach is dependent on the rationalization of the data by the analysts. Field experience is often essential to accurately perform risk analysis. Given the lack of experience of the students, cases can substitute for fieldwork experience and prepare the students for employment in the area.

Conclusion

Dissemination of abstract material in a classroom is usually a challenge that can be overcome by using thoughtful examples to illustrate a case. Although such examples may be effective in assisting students in conceptualizing the problem, they are not adequate for clarifying the concepts enough to extend their conceptualization in new domains. According to Bloom's taxonomy, there are six stages of learning: (1) knowledge (definition), (2) comprehension (conceptual understanding), (3) application (usage), (4) analysis (understanding of mechanics), (5) synthesis (adaptation of knowledge for problems), and (6) evaluation (knowing when to apply knowledge). Without a case-based approach, students remain in the application and analysis stages. Use of cases allows students to learn in the synthesis and analysis stages. To develop practitioners who effectively use their knowledge to business problems, it is imperative that their learning allows them to understand the mechanics of a solution as well as to adapt the knowledge gained to other similar problems.

The students acquired a basic understanding of risk analysis concepts and terminology through the classroom lecture. However, the knowledge gained was shallow, and they were unable to apply that to all but the simplest problems through initial questions. Once the case was investigated in the classroom, the students eagerly participated, but the concepts were abstract and conceptualization of the learning was not consolidated. The feedback received from the students makes it clear that the real learning came when they were provided with a partially structured case and had to ask questions regarding the different elements of the case as well as the methodology. Some of the students misapplied the concepts; however, through class discussions they were all able to get a correct understanding of the material. Casework alone is not sufficient for the learning; group learning through active discussions is equally important.

Summary

The teaching hospital model presented here is a very effective learning tool for abstract subject matter. The students gain a deeper knowledge of the material and are able to better retain it in memory. While implementation of this model requires a significant organizational effort, when operational it can be self-sustaining, wherein an educational program dovetails a research program, creating a constant flow of fresh cases into the curriculum. This is however contingent upon an active research program in the area of interest. Such an approach would be useful for most curriculums, but the impact is greatest when there is abstract material that is hard to conceptualize through theory or has practical applications in multiple domains. The model proposed here has been adapted from the classic medical teaching hospital in that not all students work directly on the research problems and cases are abstracted from research to support learning. Risk analysis is a complex area, where the subtleties of its application are often missed in understanding of terminology and definitions. The teaching hospital approach was very pertinent and effective in this case and certainly led to improved understanding and learning. Some issues that resulted within its initial implementation were mainly related to logistics and case development effort. If a sustainable research program already exists, it would be worthwhile for instructors to try to incorporate case development work into the curriculum.

Acknowledgments

We would like to thank Kendall McGillycuddy from McGillycuddy's Natural Soap for providing the material to develop the case. We would also like to thank the New York State Center for Information Forensics and Assurance for its support. This work is done with partial assistance of National Science Foundation NSF 01-67 Grant 020657151 and U.S, Department of Education FIPSE Grant P116B020477.

Key Terms and Definitions

Assets: Valuables of an organization which need to be protected.

Cases: Abstraction of real problems that are used for training purposes.

Controls: Implementations for reduction of risk and vulnerability.

Inert knowledge: Knowledge that is theoretical but difficult to apply in other areas.

Information assurance: Conducting operations that protect and defend information and information systems by ensuring availability, integrity, authentication, confidentiality, and non-repudiation. This includes providing for restoration of information systems by incorporating protection, detection, and reaction capabilities.

Risk analysis: An assessment of what could go wrong (risks), determination of which risks warrant preventive or contingency actions, and development of strategies to deal with those risks.

Teaching hospital: A hospital that is affiliated with a medical school and provides the means for medical education to students, interns, and residents. It also functions as a formal center of learning for the training of physicians, nurses, and allied health personnel.

Threats: Potential causes of harm to assets through exploitation of vulnerabilities.

Vulnerabilities: Weak characteristics of assets in an organization.

Review Questions

1. Why is information assurance a unique problem?

2. Where did the concept of the teaching hospital emerge? Describe the concept of the teaching hospital in the context of information assurance.

3. Define case-based learning. What are the advantages of using cases in curriculum?

4. What different types of cases exist? Describe them and explain their role in the teaching hospital.

5. Define risk analysis and explain the meaning of assets, threats, vulnerabilities, and controls.

6. Why is asset valuation hard?

7. What is the relation between vulnerabilities and assets?

8. Are employees of an organization assets, vulnerabilities, threats, or controls? Explain why or why not.

9. What are the different stages of learning according to Bloom's taxonomy?

10. Take your own life as an example and find out the assets, threats, vulnerabilities, and controls in it. Then, perform a risk analysis and figure out how you should change your life to minimize your risk exposure. Consider things like your habits, career plans, and options that you have in life.

References

Barzansky, B., Jonas, H. S., & Etzel, S. I. (1998). Educational programs in US medical schools, 1997-1998. *Journal of the American Medical Association, 280*, 803-808.

Bridges, E. M., & Hallinger, P. (1999). The use of cases in problem based learning. *Journal of Cases in Educational Leadership, 2*(2), 1-6.

Covello, V. T., & Mumpower, J. (1985). Risk analysis and risk management: An historical perspective. *Risk Analysis, 5*, 103-120.

CSI/FBI. (2004). CSI/FBI computer crime and security survey. *Computer Security Institute Publications,* 1-18.

Goel, S., & Chen, V. (2005). Information security risk analysis—A matrix-based approach. In *Proceedings of the Information Resource Management Association (IRMA) International Conference.*

Goel, S., & Pon, D. (2005). An innovative model for information assurance curriculum: A teaching hospital. In *Proceedings of the Information Resource Management Association (IRMA) International Conference.*

MGT of America. (1999, November). *Accredited models for clinical training of physicians in medical schools that operate without a teaching hospital under the control of the university.* Tallahassee, FL: Author. Retrieved September 24, 2004, from Florida State University, College of Medicine Web site: http://med.fsu.edu/pdf/03_clin_training_of_phys.pdf

Naumes, W., & Naumes, M. J. (1999). *The art and craft of case writing.* Thousand Oaks, CA: Sage.

Office of Information and Communications Technology. (2003, June). *Information security guideline for NSW government—Part 1 Information security risk nanagement* (Issue No. 3.2). Retrieved on June 28, 2005, from http://www.oit.nsw.gov.au/pdf/4.4.16.IS1.pdf

Section IV

Teaching and Learning
Computer Hardware

Chapter XI

A Practical Introduction to Input and Output Ports

David L. Tarnoff, East Tennessee State University, USA

Abstract

This chapter discusses how microprocessors interact with devices. It takes the student from the basics of input and output, through the design of the interface between a processor and an external device, and concludes with a discussion of how to improve the performance of the I/O interface using interrupts. The PC parallel port is examined to give the student a chance to apply these concepts in hardware and software. Once the student has studied the material of this chapter and completed the hands-on experiments, they will be prepared to begin a study of how device drivers work within the context of an operating system.

Learning Objectives

After completing this chapter, you will be able to:

*   Describe the interaction between a processor, bus, and I/O devices.
*   Explain how operating systems use I/O to access a computer's resources.
*   Define the following key terms: device interface, digital logic probe, IC, and I/O ports.
*   Suggest further enhancements to the materials presented in the chapter.

Introduction

Although the typical desktop computer has evolved into a stand-alone device, isolated from its environment except for a keyboard, a monitor, and a connection to a network, many computer applications still exist where the processor is used to control devices or read data from external processes or events. Outputs are needed for actions as simple as starting or stopping a process or as complex as positioning a robotic arm. Inputs are needed to monitor sensors ranging in capability from a simple switch to high-frequency analog input sampling circuitry. The discipline of sampling signals from the physical world so that the data can be analyzed or processed by a computer is called *data acquisition* (DAQ).

There are two types of input and output (I/O) signals associated with computer systems: analog and digital. Digital signals are usually associated with binary control, levels that can be either on or off. In some cases, however, they can be associated with scaleable input or output values. A stepper motor, for example, is a digitally controlled motor, the position of which can be controlled with binary outputs from a processor. There are also digital position encoders that can provide a processor with the position of a rotating shaft using digital patterns of ones and zeros.

An analog signal is a value read from the physical world such as temperature or pressure. A device called an analog-to-digital converter (ADC) measures the analog signal and sends a numeric representation of the measurement to the processor. The process of reading an analog signal has a number of issues regarding accuracy and timing. These issues are beyond the scope of this chapter though.

Even the basic desktop machine depends on I/O for its operation. The processor must be able to transfer data to and from devices such as a hard drive or a flash

RAM, receive data from inputs such as the keyboard and mouse, and send data to outputs such as the video system.

The purpose of this chapter is to examine the issues surrounding the communication between a processor and its external devices and to introduce the reader to some of the tools that are available to implement such systems. It begins with a description of the operation of the processor bus and how I/O devices are connected to it. One of the most basic I/O devices, the parallel or printer port, is then presented along with the details needed to create a simple interface to it. Finally, some advanced I/O techniques are presented to give the reader an idea of how operating systems use I/O to access a computer's resources. Throughout the chapter, the circuitry behind some basic controls and sensors is presented along with some of the tools used for testing them.

Basic Structure of a DAQ and Control System

As Moore (1965) observed, every year brings higher and higher densities of digital circuitry. This allows integrated circuit (IC) designers to pack greater functionality into each successive generation of processors and to do it without increasing the cost. One of the effects of Moore's law is to allow device I/O circuitry to be incorporated into the processor silicon. When this is done, I/O can be accomplished merely by reading from or writing to one of the processor's registers.

Either due to the unusual type of I/O, the complexity of the I/O, or special needs of the application, many I/O devices are still external to the processor. This chapter assumes this configuration. In this case, the I/O must be connected through a generic interface, specifically the processor's bus.

Figure 1 presents the basic structure of the interface between a processor and the external I/O devices with which it is meant to communicate. At the far end of this organization are the sensors and controls that come in direct contact with the physical world. The purpose of the sensors is to convert a physical phenomenon, such as temperature, pressure, or sound, into electrical signals. These electrical signals are captured by the *device interface* and converted into binary data readable by the computer. Controls, on the other hand, are outputs to the physical world. In this case, the purpose of the device interface is to take digital commands from the processor and convert them into signals that drive the controls. Examples of this include digital signals to turn on or off lights, protocols sent to a display to print text or graphics, or data streams to control a printer's

Figure 1. Basic organization of an external I/O device

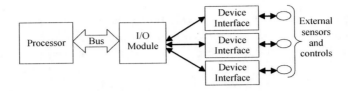

output. Finally, the I/O module acts as a liaison between the processor and the I/O device interface. It is this generic interface that allows the processor to use a common method to communicate with all devices regardless of their special communication needs.

Using the Bus to Communicate with I/O Devices

Up to this point, the discussion has concentrated on the device end of I/O. In order to show how the programmer can access these devices, it must be shown how the bus is used to connect the devices to the processor.

The primary external interface to a processor is its memory bus. A bus is a collection of parallel wires or conductors that connect the processor and all of the devices with which it is to communicate. There are three types of wires in a bus: data, address, and control. The data lines are used to pass information between the processor and the other devices on the bus; the address lines are used to identify which device is being addressed and which memory location or subsystem within the device is of interest to the processor; and the control lines are used to define the characteristics of the transfer, such as the timing and direction of the data flow. Although any device on the bus may place data on the data lines in order to send information, only the processor controls the address and control lines of the bus.

The wires of the bus, usually referred to as conductors, are each capable of delivering one binary digit or bit, that is, they are either transmitting a one or a zero. The data lines are labeled using a capital letter D with a subscript identifying the bit that conductor represents. For example, the least significant digit of the data bus is labeled D_0, the next D_1, and so on. The address lines are labeled using a capital letter A along with the same subscripting method that is used for the data lines. The highest address line is labeled A_{n-1}, where n represents the total number of address lines. This information can be used to identify the amount of memory that the processor can access, specifically, the processor can access 2^n memory locations on its bus.

The devices of the bus, including the processor, are all connected in parallel to the conductors of the bus, each bit of each connection type having its own conductor. For example, all of the devices have a connection for address line A_0, and all of these connections are tied together using the same conductor. This method of connecting devices to a bus is referred to as *daisy-chaining*. An example of daisy-chaining is shown in Figure 2, where address line A_{19} of the processor is connected to A_{19} of Memory Device 1, which is in turn connected to A_{19} of Memory Device 2. This is true for each of the address, data, and control connections.

Two of the most important control lines are the *read* control line and the *write* control line. The processor uses these binary lines to control the direction of the data transaction. Table 1 presents the operation of the bus for the different settings of the read and write control lines.

The configuration of the address lines is also important. They are a vital part of the system that identifies which device on the bus is being addressed by the processor. Without the address lines, the processor would require a separate bus to each device. The problem is that with multiple devices on the same bus, only one device can be enabled at a time. If two devices tried to drive the data lines simultaneously, data would be lost. It would be like two people trying to talk at the same time. This condition is called *bus contention*.

Figure 3 presents a situation where data is being read from Memory Device 1 while Memory Device 2 remains "disconnected" from the bus. Disconnected is in quotes because the physical connection is still present; it just does not have an electrical connection across which data can pass.

Notice that Figure 3 shows that the only lines disconnected from the bus are the data lines. This is because bus contention only occurs when multiple devices are

Figure 2. Daisy-chained configuration of the processor bus

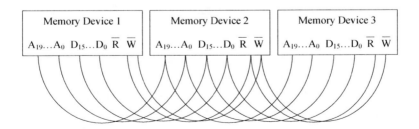

Table 1. Summary of read and write control line settings

Read Line	Write Line	Bus Operation
0	0	This is an illegal setting and should never happen.
0	1	Setting the read line low indicates that the processor wishes to receive data (read) from memory.
1	0	Setting the write line low indicates that the processor wishes to store data (write) to memory.
1	1	The memory bus is idle. There is no transmission of data.

trying to output to the same conductors at the same time. Since only the processor outputs to the address and control lines, they can remain connected.

In order for this scheme to work, an additional control signal must be sent to each of the memory devices telling them when to be connected to the bus and when to be disconnected. This control signal is called a *chip select*, and it is derived from the address lines.

Note that a memory device will always have a smaller capacity than that addressable by the processor. Because of this, some of the higher address lines from the bus do not have corresponding connections at the memory device. These leftover address lines are used to create the chip select that uniquely identifies the device. If a different binary pattern is selected for each set of high-order address lines going to each device, then only one device can be enabled at a time. Table 2 shows how four chip selects might be used to enable only one of the four devices or leave all of them disabled.

Figure 3. Block diagram of two memory devices sharing a bus

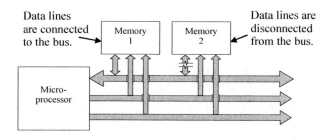

Table 2. The allowable settings of four chip selects

	CS$_0$	CS$_1$	CS$_2$	CS$_3$
High-order address bits set to enable device 0	enabled	disabled	disabled	disabled
High-order address bits set to enable device 1	disabled	enabled	disabled	disabled
High-order address bits set to enable device 2	disabled	disabled	enabled	disabled
High-order address bits set to enable device 3	disabled	disabled	disabled	enabled
High-order address bits match no device	disabled	disabled	disabled	disabled

Using the address lines, data lines, and the read and write control lines, the basic interface to a collection of memory devices can be created. Figure 4 presents the basic interface to a memory device. A NAND gate is used to represent the chip select circuitry.

The Intel 80x86[1] processors use the names ^MRDC and ^MWTC for the read and write control lines, respectively.

So why bother going into such detail regarding the memory bus? The reason is that most I/O devices are connected to the processor using the same bus. Although I/O devices may have little or no memory, sending data to them is equivalent to storing data in a memory device while receiving data from an I/O device is like reading a memory device.

Figure 4. Typical bus connections for a memory device

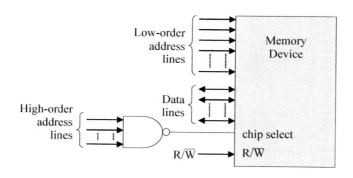

Memory Mapped I/O vs. Port Addressed I/O

The Intel 80x86 family of processors, the ones on which the IBM PC-clone architecture is based, treats I/O devices slightly different than it does memory devices. The Intel 80x86-based systems access external devices through reads and writes to *I/O ports*. An I/O port allows a processor to access an external device using an addressing scheme identical to that of the memory bus addressing scheme. In fact, the 80x86 I/O devices are wired to the same bus as processor's memory. There are two minor differences that distinguish I/O port communication from transactions with main memory.

First, the I/O ports use different read and write control lines. For the Intel 80x86 processors, the read and write lines for I/O ports are named ^IORC and ^IOWC, respectively. Table 3 summarizes how the processor uses the signals ^MRDC, ^MWTC, ^IORC, and ^IOWC to distinguish between I/O port and memory operations.

In some cases, I/O devices are connected to the memory bus so that they act just like a memory device. This practice, called memory mapping, is quite common, and for processors that do not have separate read and write control lines for their I/O ports, it is necessary. In the case of the Intel processors though, the majority of I/O devices use these alternative read and write control lines.

The second difference between memory and I/O port communication on the Intel 80x86 processor bus is that only the lower 16 address lines are used when communicating with an I/O port. This means that only $2^{16} = 65,536$ addresses are available to any processor in the 80x86 family. This generally is not a problem. The typical I/O device only requires a few memory locations to perform all of its transactions with the processor as opposed to the large amount of storage associated with a memory device. Therefore, all but a few of the address lines can be connected to the chip select circuitry, meaning fewer address lines are needed from the processor for I/O ports.

Table 3. Control signal differences between I/O and memory transactions

	^MRDC	^MWTC	^IORC	^IOWC
Reading data from memory	low	high	high	high
Writing data to memory	high	low	high	high
Inputting data from an I/O port	high	high	low	high
Outputting data to an I/O port	high	high	high	low

These issues have a direct effect on the software that accesses I/O ports. To store data to memory, all that the software needs is an address. By assigning an address to a pointer, software can store or retrieve the data in either a memory location or a memory-mapped I/O device using the same methods it would to modify a program variable. For I/O ports, however, a different set of instructions is needed so that the second set of read and write control lines are used and not the memory read and write control lines. At the Intel 80x86 assembly language level, these instructions are IN and OUT. A different set of instructions for accessing I/O ports using a high-level programming language will be presented in the next section.

As would be expected, I/O devices function differently than memory. When a processor reads a memory location, the value retrieved should be the same as the last value written to it. In most cases, reading from an I/O device accesses an entirely different service than writing to it does. For example, assume that one of the processor's I/O ports is a serial communication device. Writing data to one of the port's addresses may send data out the serial port while reading from the same address may retrieve the last piece of data received by the port. Writing to another address may enable the transmitter and receiver while reading from the same address may return the status of the receive and transmit buffers. For programmers unfamiliar with I/O ports, it may seem odd to write to a port and then receive completely different data when the port is read.

Operating systems benefit greatly from having separate mechanisms for accessing memory and I/O ports. If an I/O device is memory mapped instead of connected to an I/O port, any communication to it would be subject to the operating system's memory management. This would prohibit direct access to the device and make the sharing of devices very difficult.

Structure of the Parallel Port

Although the original purpose of the parallel port of a PC was to provide a connection to a printer, this digital port provides a quick, simple method for implementing digital I/O. Typically, this port is free on most computers since printer manufacturers have begun taking advantage of the versatility of the USB interface.

The parallel port is a 25-pin port on the back of almost every PC. It has sockets where the pins from a printer cable connector are inserted. These sockets, however, can also be accessed using a section of 24 AWG solid-core telephone wire with about one quarter of an inch of insulation stripped from each end. By looping the wire from one socket to another, a test circuit can be created where output connections can drive input connections.

Figure 5 presents the pin definitions of the parallel port. Signal names preceded by a "^" are active low signals. To indicate the direction of the data flow, arrows going away from the pin represent outputs (from the PC to the printer or other external device) and arrows going into the pin represent inputs (from the printer or external device into the PC). The figure's perspective is from the outside of the female connector coming off the back of the PC.

This port offers numerous opportunities for performing digital I/O using a PC. Possible projects include motor control for robotics, digital sensor input for data acquisition, and LCD display control for user interfaces (Tarnoff, 2004).

Each parallel port uses three separate addresses that point to registers used to control the port or retrieve its status. The first register, the *data output register*, is used to send data to the data lines (pins 2 through 9). This register is a one-to-one mapping of the bits from an 8-bit data value to the eight individual outputs. The least significant bit of the data value corresponds to pin 2 while the most significant bit corresponds to pin 9.

The second register is used to receive data from the status inputs (pins 10, 11, 12, 13, and 15). This register is called the *status register*, and it also uses an 8-bit data value. Since there are only five status inputs, three of the bits are left unused. The most significant bit of the 8-bit status register represents the value present at the busy input (pin 11). The next bit contains the value from the ACK input (pin 10). After that comes the paper empty signal (pin 12), then the printer selected input (pin 13), and finally the error input (pin 15).

Figure 5. Pinout of a DB25 parallel port

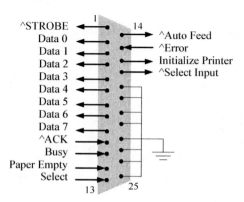

Figure 6. Organization of the three parallel port addressable registers

Data Output Register

D_7	D_6	D_5	D_4	D_3	D_2	D_1	D_0
pin 9 output	pin 8 output	pin 7 output	pin 6 output	pin 5 output	pin 4 output	pin 3 output	pin 2 output

Status Register

S_7	S_6	S_5	S_4	S_3	unused		
busy input	ACK input	paper end input	select input	error input			

Control Register

unused			C_4	C_3	C_2	C_1	C_0
			IRQ ctrl	select output	init output	auto fd output	strobe output

The *control register* is the third register, and it functions on two levels. Four of its bits are used to send control signals out of the 25-pin port to control the operation of a printer. These include the strobe (pin 1), a paper feed signal called auto feed (pin 14), a signal to initialize a printer (pin 16), and a printer select signal (pin 17) that is used to enable the printer connected to that port. The remaining used bit of the control register is used to enable and monitor the parallel port's interrupt operation through pin 10 of the interface. Interrupts will be discussed later in this chapter.

Figure 6 presents the organization of these three registers.

Each register has its own I/O port address that is used in conjunction with the IN and OUT commands. Regardless of the specific address where the parallel port is located within the address range of the I/O ports, these three addresses are located next to each other. The address of the data register is often considered the *base address* since it has the numerically lowest address of the three. Its address is equivalent to the address assigned to the parallel port by the system. The next address is the one that points to the status register. The address for this register is the base address plus 1. The control register is located at the next address, the base address plus 2.

The typical Intel-based PC uses one of the following three addresses for the base address of the parallel port: 378 (hex), 278 (hex), or 3BC (hex). There are two methods available to the user to determine this base address. First, since the address is usually set in the BIOS rather than the operating system, the user can access this value through the system setup. By referring to the system documentation, the user can go into system setup when the machine is booted. Within the setup menu, there should be an option to set or view the parameters of the computer's integrated devices. From this menu, the user may record the I/O address of the parallel port.

The parallel port's base address can also be found using an operating system such as Microsoft Windows. In Windows, go to Control Panel and select System. From the System window, select the Hardware tab, and then click on the button that provides information on the devices. In Windows XP, this button is labeled Device Manager. From the Device Manager, there should be an entry labeled Ports (COM and LPT). LPT refers to the parallel port hardware. When the plus sign next to the ports entry is clicked, a list of the available ports should drop down below it. By right-clicking on the LPT port, a context-specific menu should allow the user to select Properties. It is from this Properties window that the resource settings can be examined. This is where the address for the parallel port can be found. Make a note of this address so that it can be referenced in the application software presented later in this chapter.

Simple Digital I/O Circuits

Before developing the software behind a device driver for digital I/O, the basics of some simple test circuitry must be explained. The simplest output from a digital circuit is a light-emitting diode (LED). An LED is a solid-state device that glows brightly when a small current passes through it from one input to the other. No light will appear if there is no current or if the current tries to flow in the opposite direction. This means that one of the first things to check when debugging an LED circuit is to verify the orientation of the LED.

Figure 7 presents the schematic symbol of an LED. For the LED to turn on, current must flow from the A terminal to the B terminal.

There are two things to note here. First, the current must be very small. The solid-state circuitry possesses no mechanism to limit the amount of current flowing through it, and if too much current flows, the LED will be destroyed. An external device called a resistor must be added in order to keep the current small enough to protect the LED. By placing a resistor in series with the LED, the current is choked enough to protect the LED. Without the resistor, the LED will emit a soft popping sound followed by a strong, acrid odor. Figure 8 shows a typical LED circuit.

The second item of importance is that the LED circuit of Figure 8 will turn on only when the output from the IC is a binary zero. The LED is turned off by sending a binary 1 to the circuit. This is the optimum way to drive an LED. If an IC is expected to provide the current to an external circuit, it must draw extra current

Figure 7. Schematic symbol of a light-emitting diode (LED)

Figure 8. Typical LED circuit

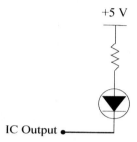

from its own power source. This increased power consumption will generate heat and reduce the reliability of the IC. It is much better for an IC to act as a connection to dissipate (sink) current rather than provide (source) it.

The simplest input to a digital circuit is a switch. It seems that the logical way to connect a switch to a digital circuit would be to connect it so that it toggles between a direct connection to a binary 1 and a direct connection to a binary 0. Switching back and forth between these connections should produce binary 1s and 0s, right?

Due to the internal electronics of an IC, this is not the case. Instead, connections to positive voltages are made through resistors called *pull-up resistors*. This protects the IC by limiting the current flowing into it while still providing a positive voltage that can be read as a binary 1.

Figure 9 presents a generic switch design for a single input to a digital circuit. It uses a pull-up resistor connected to 5 volts, which represents the circuit's power source. When the switch is open, the pull-up resistor creates a binary 1 at the IC's input. When the switch is closed, the IC's input is connected to ground, which acts as a binary 0.

By using these circuits for switches and LEDs, simple test circuitry for digital I/O can be built.

Figure 9. Generic switch circuit to an IC's input

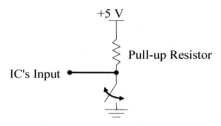

Measuring Digital Voltage Levels

There is an alternative method to using an LED to test the output of a digital circuit. Each digital output of a PC uses two voltage levels to represent ones and zeros. Traditionally, a voltage of 5 volts represents a binary 1 while a ground or 0 volts represents a binary 0. If this is the case, there is a ubiquitous circuit testing device that can be used to detect whether a 1 or a 0 is present on a digital output. This simple device, a sample of which is pictured in Figure 10, is called a *digital logic probe*.

The digital logic probe has a metallic tip that the user places on the portion of the circuit to be analyzed. The opposite end of the probe has a pair of wires to be connected to a power supply. Typically, the red clip of the power supply connections is connected to 5 volts, and the black clip is connected to ground.

Figure 10. An example of a digital logic probe

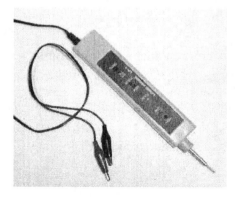

These voltages are available from the power supply of the computer.

As for the controls and indicators on the probe body, the typical logic probe combines some or all of the following:

- An LED indicating when the tip of the probe is touching a low or binary 0.
- An LED indicating when the tip of the probe is touching a high or binary 1.
- An LED indicating when the tip of the probe is touching a signal that is pulsing. (Typically this LED is used in conjunction with the low and high LEDs, the brighter of the two indicating whether the signal is more often high or more often low.)
- A CMOS/TTL switch which is used to switch between different types of digital circuits. (CMOS is most common in today's circuitry.)
- A memory switch used simply to let the probe keep the LEDs lit to whatever the last setting was even after the probe is removed from the circuit.

As far as gaining access to voltages within the computer, all standard computer power supplies provide enough power to run not only the motherboard and its supporting peripherals but also enough power to support a few external devices. For example, the +5V and ground signals that are referred to in the LED circuit, the switch circuit, and the logic probe connections are available from the same connector that is used to power the hard drives and CD-ROMs. The four-pin connecter shown in Figure 11 has four wires, one yellow, two black, and one red. The yellow wire supplies +12 volts, the black wires provide ground connections, and the red wire is a +5 volt supply.

Figure 11. Basic four-pin Molex connector from a PC power supply

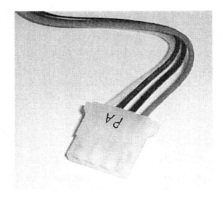

I/O Port Software

As stated earlier in this chapter, I/O ports can be accessed directly using the assembly language commands IN and OUT. IN retrieves data from an I/O device. It uses as its operands (data arguments) the address of the I/O port and the register in the processor where the retrieved value is to be stored. OUT sends data to an I/O device. It uses as its operands the address of the I/O port and the data to send to the I/O device.

Access to I/O ports is not limited to assembly language programmers however. Similar commands are available to the high-level programming languages of both Linux and Microsoft Windows. The problem is that modern operating systems have isolated the programmer from the hardware to a great extent. In many cases, the programmer must add special libraries of functions or run the programs as administrators in order to access the I/O ports.

In Microsoft Windows, a number of third-party vendors have created dynamic link libraries (DLLs) that provide additional functionality to the programmer in the form of high-level language functions that replace the assembly language routines IN and OUT. It is important to note that by offering these functions as part of a DLL, these vendors have provided port functionality to almost any Windows programming language. The following is a short list of some of these DLLs and the vendors that supply them.

- Inpout32.dll (Axelson, 2003) from Logix4u
- Win95io.dll (1997) and Vbasm.dll (1997) from SoftCircuits Programming
- NTPort Library (2002) from Zeal SoftStudio

Typically, all that is needed to install a DLL is to copy it to the appropriate folder under the Windows directory. In the case of the libraries shown above, the DLL needs to be copied into the folder \windows\system\.

Accessing the routines within the DLL depends on the programming environment being used. The following discussion shows how the functions from Logix4u's Inpout32.dll can be used with Microsoft Visual Basic 6 to create an interface to the parallel port. (It is assumed that the reader is at least somewhat familiar with the programming environment. Development in Linux will be discussed later in the chapter.)

In order to send and receive data from an I/O port, a number of controls will be needed. To begin with, since an I/O port is referred to with a memory address, the user must have a method to set the address for the I/O port. As discussed earlier, the parallel port on the PC uses one of the three base addresses: 378

(hex), 278 (hex), and 3BC (hex). Therefore, a combo box will be added to the interface to select from one of the three standard parallel port addresses.

Next, a text box is needed to allow a user to enter data to be sent to the parallel port's output. Since the data bus for the parallel port is 8 bits wide, the values sent to it must be limited to positive integers from 0 to 255. In addition to the text box for output data, a button is needed to cause the data to be sent to the port. Another text box is needed to display data retrieved from the parallel port along with a second button to cause the application to retrieve the data from the port. Lastly, some labels are needed to identify the components of the interface.

After opening the Visual Basic development environment, create a new project by selecting New Project from the File menu. A standard executable is sufficient since all that is needed is to create a small window with a few text inputs, a combo box, two buttons, and some labels. Figure 12 presents a sample configuration of the inputs needed for a simple window to send and receive data to and from an I/O port.

To make the application function more appropriately, the window is titled, forced to remain a fixed size, and given a start-up position of the screen's center. The inputs are also labeled and given initial values. Figure 13 presents the modified window.

Figure 12. Sample I/O control window

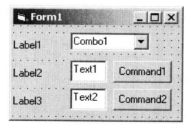

Figure 13. Sample I/O control window with components identified

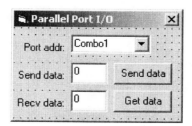

To aid in the programming of this application, the combo box has been renamed *Port_addr*, the text box containing data to be sent is renamed *out_data*, the text box used to display incoming data is renamed *in_data*, the button used to initiate a send is renamed *Send_data*, and the button used to initiate a read from the port is renamed *Get_data*. It is also helpful to set the DataFormat properties of both the *out_data* and *in_data* text boxes to Number with no digits allowed after the decimal point. This will avoid any errors due to improperly formatted inputs.

Since the combo box is used to limit the I/O port addresses to the ones available for the parallel port, it needs to be initialized to the three standard values for the parallel port I/O addresses. In Visual Basic 6, adding values to the list of items for a combo box is done with code, specifically, the *AddItem* method. This needs to be done as soon as the application is first loaded. To gain access to the code that is executed upon loading an application, right-click on the form and select View Code from the context-specific menu that appears.

The code window that appears should have two list boxes at the top, one from which to select the object (it probably says (General) in it) and one from which to select the event. In the object list box, select the form's name, and from the event list box select Load. A block of code similar to that shown in Figure 14 should appear in the code window.

Three items need to be added to the combo box. Figure 15 shows these three items added with the *AddItem* event. The last line of the added code selects the default value as index 0, that is, 378 (hex).

Now that the interface is fully defined, the functions from the DLL need to be made visible to the code of this application. From the Project menu, select Add

Figure 14. Template for code to be executed upon loading a VB form

```
Private Sub Form_Load()

End Sub
```

Figure 15. Template for code to be executed upon loading a VB form

```
Private Sub Form_Load()
    Port_addr.AddItem "378 (hex)"
    Port_addr.AddItem "278 (hex)"
    Port_addr.AddItem "3bc (hex)"
    Port_addr.Text = Port_addr.List(0)
End Sub
```

Figure 16. VB function declarations for Inpout32.dll

```
Public Declare Function Inp Lib "inpout32.dll" Alias
    "Inp32" (ByVal PortAddress As Integer) As Integer

Public Declare Sub Out Lib "inpout32.dll" Alias "Out32"
    (ByVal PortAddress As Integer, ByVal Value As Integer)
```

Module. A window will appear allowing a module to be inserted into the project. Click on the Open button to insert this new module.

Open this module, and from the general declarations area, add the declarations shown in Figure 16 to point to the functions of the DLL. By doing this, the code now has access to the I/O port controls *Inp* and *Out* of the Inpout32 DLL. All that needs to be done now is to associate these functions with the controls of the application.

The first function, *Inp*, is used to retrieve data from an I/O port. Just like the assembly language instruction IN, it requires the address of the I/O port. This is declared as the integer variable *PortAddress*. The function returns an integer representing the value read from the I/O port's inputs.

The second function, *Out*, is used to send data to the I/O port. It is equivalent to the assembly language instruction OUT, and just like OUT it requires two pieces of data: the address of the I/O port (*PortAddress*) and the data to send to it (*Value*).

From the design view, double-click on the *Send_data* button. This should open the code window with a function inserted called *Send_data_Click()*. This function is called when the button *Send_data* is clicked by the user. Two things need to be done within this function. First, the address represented by the combo box *Port_addr* must be retrieved. This can be done with a simple Select-Case block. Second, the Inpout32 function *Out* must be called to send the data to the I/O port. Figure 17 presents the code that performs this function.

In the line of code that assigns the value read from *out_data* to the integer *out_value*, a logical AND is performed on the data in order to limit the output value to integers from 0 to 255.

Now to receive data from the five status input pins on the parallel port. Return to the design view and double-click on the *Get_data* button. Once again, the code view should appear, this time with a new function *Get_data_Click()* inserted. As with the *Send_data* button, code will be inserted here to determine the parallel port's address from the *Port_addr* combo box followed by a call to the appropriate Inpout32 function. In this case, the port address will be 1 greater than the base address for the I/O port, for example, if the parallel port's address

Figure 17. VB code to send data to parallel port

```
Private Sub Send_data_Click()

'Declare one variable to hold the I/O address and
'another to contain the data to send to the port.

    Dim port_address, out_value As Integer

'Determine which address the parallel port is at:

    Select Case (Port_addr.ListIndex)
        Case Is = -1    'Default start for combo box
            port_address = &H378
        Case Is = 0
            port_address = &H378
        Case Is = 1
            port_address = &H278
        Case Is = 2
            port_address = &H3BC
    End Select

'Next, retrieve the data to output

    out_value = Val(out_data.Text) And 255

'Lastly, send the data to the port using the
'Out function

    Out port_address, out_value

End Sub
```

is 378 (hex), then the status lines are read from address 379 (hex). For the receive case, the Inpout32 function called in *Inp* will be used to return the value from the appropriate address. Figure 18 presents the code for the receive function.

Figure 19 shows the device used by the author to evaluate the operation of the program along with a screen shot of the application. The device connects an LED circuit similar to that shown in Figure 8 to each of the parallel port's outputs, pins 2 through 9, and a switch circuit similar to that shown in Figure 9 to each of the status inputs to the parallel port, pins 10, 11, 12, 13, and 15.

Linux C development software[2] provides similar functionality for its application development without the need for an additional library. The function *inb()* is used to read a single byte from an I/O port while the function *outb()* writes a single byte to an I/O port. Additional routines, *ioperm()* and *iopl()*, are needed to grant the application permission to access the ports. Both of these routines are found in the *sys/io.h* include file when using the *glibc* libraries. The syntax for these

Figure 18. VB code to receive data from parallel port

```
Private Sub Get_data_Click()
'Declare a variable to hold the I/O address

     Dim port_address As Integer

'Determine which address the parallel port
'status is at:

     Select Case (Port_addr.ListIndex)
         Case Is = -1    'Default start for combo box
             port_address = &H379
         Case Is = 0
             port_address = &H379
         Case Is = 1
             port_address = &H279
         Case Is = 2
             port_address = &H3BD
     End Select

'Retrieve the data from the parallel port

     in_data.Text = Inp(port_address)

End Sub
```

Figure 19. Parallel port I/O device and corresponding control application

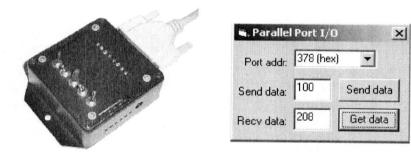

<table>
<tr><td>a. Parallel port device</td><td>b. Application screen shot</td></tr>
</table>

and other I/O port functions is presented below (Rubini & Corbet, 2001, pp. 230-232). Note that this list is not comprehensive.

- **unsigned inb(unsigned io_port)**—inb() reads a single byte (8 bits) from the I/O port at address *io_port*.

- **unsigned inb_p(unsigned io_port)**—inb_p() reads a single byte (8 bits) from the I/O port at address *io_port* then pauses to allow I/O device time to process the command. This is specifically for older platforms where the I/O devices could not keep up with the speed of the processor. Similar functions are available for the other "in" commands.

- **unsigned insb(unsigned io_port, void *addr, unsigned long count)**—insb() reads a string of *count* bytes from the I/O port at address *io_port* and stores the string starting at memory address *addr*.

- **unsigned inw(unsigned io_port)**—inw() reads a word (16 bits) from the I/O port at address *io_port*. This function is not universally supported and is not in common use. Its operation can be duplicated with two successive inb() function calls.

- **int ioperm(unsigned long from, unsigned long num, int turn_on)**—ioperm() sets the I/O port permissions to a value of *turn_on* for *num* port addresses beginning with address *from*. ioperm() only works for I/O ports 0 through 0x3FF (decimal 1023). iopl() must be used to grant permission to the remaining ports. *turn_on* is a boolean-type value: 1 allows access and 0 disallows access. To set an I/O port's permission to anything other than 0, the calling process must have CAP_SYS_RAWIO capability. This capability is inherent for the user root but may also be granted using setid. ioperm() returns 0 on success and −1 on error.

- **int iopl(int level)**—iopl() changes the privilege level of all I/O ports to the value *level* for the calling process. Be sure to use ioperm() when accessing ports below 0x3FF because iopl() could leave the system vulnerable to problems such as accessing the incorrect port or disabling interrupts. Setting *level* equal to 3 grants the calling process permission to access the ports while setting it to 0 removes those privileges. iopl() returns a 0 on success and a −1 on error.

- **void outb(unsigned char val, unsigned io_port)**—outb() writes a single byte *val* to the I/O port at address *io_port*.

- **void outb_p(unsigned char val, unsigned io_port)**—outb_p() writes a single byte *val* to the I/O port at address *io_port* then pauses to allow I/O device time to process the command. This is specifically for older platforms where the I/O devices could not keep up with the speed of the processor. Similar functions are available for the other "out" commands.

- **void outsb(unsigned io_port, void *addr, unsigned long count)**—outsb() reads a string of *count* bytes from the memory address starting at *addr* and outputs them to the I/O port at address *io_port*.

- **void outw(unsigned short val, unsigned io_port)**—outw() writes a word *val* to the I/O port at address *io_port*. Like inw(), this function is not universally supported and is not in common use. Its operation can be duplicated with two successive outb() function calls

In order to access the I/O ports, begin by setting the privileges for accessing the port using *ioperm()* or *iopl()*. In Linux, this will require root privileges for the user running the application.

Once your process is allowed access to the ports, use the "in" functions to retrieve data from a port and the "out" functions to send data to the port.

Advanced I/O Techniques

For the hobbyist, the description of I/O port communication up to this point is sufficient. For the programmer who is developing device drivers or operating system code, the concepts of I/O port communication must be taken further. This is because the method used by the programmer to communicate with the I/O ports directly affects the performance of the processor.

The Visual Basic application presented in this chapter represents the simplest form of I/O. In order to detect any changes on the inputs of the parallel port, the application must constantly read the input pins. For example, the text box that displays the values of the status lines remains static unless the *Get_data* button is pressed. This method of monitoring I/O is called *programmed I/O*, and it is known for its poor performance.

There are three problems with this method. First, data might be missed if the inputs are not read often enough. Second, it is impossible to determine with any accuracy the moment at which the input data changed. Both of these problems can be resolved by increasing the rate at which the inputs are read. This, however, comes at a price. By forcing the processor to continuously monitor its inputs, considerable processing time is eaten up without having much to show for it. The majority of the reads are not going to show any change in the input values.

A second method takes the burden off of the processor and places it on the device. *Interrupt driven I/O* gives each device the ability to "call" the processor to tell it that there is new data available. The data might tell the processor that there has been a change at the inputs, that a process has completed, or that the device's outputs are available. The call to the processor demanding service is called an *interrupt*.

It is as if someone was reading a book when the telephone rings. The reader, concerned about keeping her place in the book, places a bookmark to indicate where she left off. She then answers the phone and carries on a conversation while the book "waits" for her attention to return. While chatting on the phone, the person notices her dog standing at the door waiting to be let out. She tells the person on the other end of the line, "Hold that thought, I'll be right back." After she lets out the dog, she returns to the phone and picks up the conversation where she left it. When she finishes talking on the phone, she hangs up and returns to her reading exactly where she left off.

This analogy reflects how the computer handles devices that need service. When a device interrupts the processor, the processor remembers where it was at by storing the current condition of all variables, the address of the line of code it was currently executing, and any other information it would need to restore its operation. Once this is done, it can execute a function that will handle the device's request. This function is called an *interrupt service routine (ISR)*. By using interrupts and the corresponding ISRs, the processor is able to concentrate on running applications while it is the responsibility of the devices themselves to watch their inputs.

It is important to note that the programmer does not have to write any function call in their code to access the interrupts. The processor maintains a list of the ISRs that correspond to each device. When a device interrupts the processor, the processor halts the execution of the main code, looks up the address of the appropriate ISR, and jumps to it. Once the ISR is complete, the processor restores itself so that it picks up the main code where it left it. Figure 20 presents a basic diagram of this operation.

In order to support the use of interrupts for external devices, a processor must have one additional output and at least one additional input. The processor uses the input to receive the interrupt request from the device. This input is referred to as the *interrupt request,* or *IRQ,* input. The additional output from the processor is called an *interrupt acknowledge*. The processor uses this output

Figure 20. Basic operation of an ISR

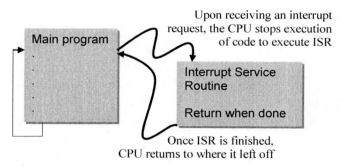

to tell the device that is requesting service that the interrupt was received and will be handled. It is the processor's way of saying, "Okay, you can stop calling now."

This means that for a device to be able to take advantage of interrupts, it must also have an additional output and an additional input. The device changes the level on the digital output when it needs service and watches the level on the input to see when the processor has acknowledged the request. On the parallel port, the device output is connected to pin 10 of the 25-pin interface. If conditions are right and the level on this input pin changes, an interrupt is issued to the processor.

For the processor to detect an interrupt, the interrupt must first be *enabled*. This is handled at two levels. The processor itself has a global setting that enables and disables the majority of the external interrupts. This is usually handled by a single bit or flag in the processor that is controlled by the operating system.

There are also enable flags at the device level. A control register within each device contains one or more flags that are used to enable and disable the device's interrupts. When interrupts are disabled at the local or device level, the IRQ output from the device remains at the level that the processor interprets as idle.

For the parallel port, local enabling of interrupts is done with bit 4 of the control register. By setting the bit to a 1, a change on the ACK input (pin 10) from a low to a high value will cause an interrupt to be sent to the processor. If the processor has globally enabled interrupts, it will execute the parallel port's ISR. The creation and installation of a user-defined ISR are highly dependent on the processor operating system and are beyond the scope of this discussion.

Conclusion

Regardless of the special needs of each I/O device in a computer system, there are standard methods of communicating with a computer system's I/O. These methods have been designed to allow an operating system or an application to communicate with the physical world. Through an understanding of device addressing and the details of the I/O device's resources, data may be collected or processes may be controlled from any computer.

The interaction between a processor and its I/O devices is similar to its interaction with memory. Data is passed to and from registers in the device using addresses just like memory. Some processors, including the Intel 80x86 family of processors, distinguish I/O transactions from memory transactions by using different machine-language instructions. To handle this difference, a special set of functions is used to store data to and retrieve data from the I/O device. These functions may be accessed from many development systems, including Microsoft's Visual Studio and GNU's Compiler Collection (gcc).

Finally, in order to improve performance, processors use a hardware-based system of device service requests called interrupts. All operating systems and many applications use interrupts to avoid the overhead of having to constantly watch an I/O device's status.

Summary

It is important that students grasp the basic concepts of communication between a processor and its external devices and to become familiar with tools that are available to implement such systems. This chapter described the operation of the processor bus, I/O connectivity, and the PC parallel port along with its interface. By configuring a PC parallel port, students develop the basic concepts in both hardware and software. The control and sensor circuitry is presented along with some of the tools used for testing them. Some advanced I/O techniques are also presented.

Key Terms and Definition

Bus contention: This is an erroneous condition that occurs when multiple devices attempt to put data on the data lines of the bus at the same time.

Daisy-chaining: This is a configuration that connects the inputs of multiple devices together using a single conductor.

Data acquisition: The discipline of sampling signals from the physical world so that the data can be analyzed or processed by a computer.

Device interface: Sometimes referred to as a transducer, it is the circuit element that converts physical phenomenon to electrical signals and eventually to digital values readable by the processor.

Digital logic probe: A simple test device that is used to sense whether a binary 1 or a binary 0 is present on a digital conductor.

DLL: Stands for dynamic link library. This is a library of functions that are available to the applications of an operating system at runtime. They are not required to be part of the compile process, rather they are loaded as needed when the application is executed.

IC: Stands for integrated circuit. This is the circuitry contained within a chip or component of the circuit board of a computer system.

I/O port: A bus on the Intel 80x86 processors that uses the same address and data lines as the memory bus but different read and write control lines.

LED: Stands for light-emitting diode. This is a solid-state device that glows brightly when a small current passes through it from one input to the other.

Review Questions

1. Explain how a processor communicates with I/O devices.
2. Discuss the basic organization of an external I/O device.
3. Define the following terms: bus, data lines, address lines, and read and write control lines.
4. Draw a block diagram to illustrate the interaction between a CPU and a memory.
5. Draw a block diagram to illustrate the basic interface to a memory device.
6. Discuss the difference between memory and I/O port communication of a typical Intel 80x86 processor.
7. Describe the pin configuration of a typical DB25 parallel port.
8. Describe the function of control, status, and data output registers.

References

Axelson, J. (2003). Inpout32.dll. Logix4u. Retrieved December 9, 2004, from http://www.logix4u.cjb.net/

Moore, G. (1965, April 19). Cramming more components onto integrated circuits. *Electronics Magazine*.

NTPort Library. (2002). Zeal SoftStudio. Retrieved December 9, 2004, from http://www.zealsoftstudio.com/ntport/

Rubini, A., & Corbet, J. (2001). *Linux device drivers*. O'Reilly & Associates.

Tarnoff, D. (2003). *ETSU/CSCI embedded systems course notes: Digital input and output*. Retrieved July 8, 2003, from Eastern Tennessee State University Web site: http://faculty.etsu.edu/tarnoff/ntes4956/Ch03_v02.pdf

Tarnoff, D. (2004). Incorporating embedded system design into a CS curriculum. In *Proceedings of the 2nd Annual Mid-South College Computing Conference* (pp. 131-140).

Vbasm.dll. (1997). SoftCircuits Programming. Retrieved December 9, 2004, from http://www.softcircuits.com/sw_tools.htm

Win95io.dll. (1997). SoftCircuits Programming. Retrieved December 9, 2004, from http://www.softcircuits.com/sw_tools.htm

Endnotes

[1]   80x86 is a general reference to the Intel family of processors beginning with the 80286 continuing through to the current-day Pentium processors.

[2]   In Linux, when compiling code used to access the I/O ports using the routines mentioned in this text, set gcc to compile with optimization turned on using the –O option.

Chapter XII

Enhancing Teaching and Learning Computer Hardware Fundamentals Using PIC-Based Projects

Nurul I. Sarkar, Auckland University of Technology, New Zealand

Trevor Craig, Wollongong College Auckland, New Zealand

Abstract

Computer hardware, number systems, CPU, memory and I/O (input/output) ports are topics often included in computer science, electronics, and engineering courses as fundamental concepts involved in computer hardware. We believe that students learn computer hardware fundamentals better if they are given practical learning exercises that illustrate theoretical concepts. However, only a limited range of material designed specifically to supplement the teaching of computer hardware concepts is publicly available (see http://sigcse.org/topics/, the SIGCSE Education Links page on the Special Interest Group on Computer Science Education Web site).

This chapter describes a set of PIC-based projects that give students a hands-on introduction to computer hardware concepts and are suitable for classroom use in undergraduate computer hardware courses.

Learning Objectives

After completing this chapter, you will be able to:

- Discuss the usefulness of PIC projects in teaching and learning contexts.
- Set up PIC-based projects for class demonstrations.
- Define the following key terms: RAM, ROM, LCD display, and microcontroller.
- Suggest further enhancements to PIC projects described in the chapter.

Introduction

Not infrequently, it proves difficult to motivate students to learn computer hardware fundamentals because many students appear to find the subject rather technical, dry, and boring. To overcome this problem the authors have prepared a set of projects that give students a hands-on introduction to computer hardware. They are designed around the PIC16F84, a low-cost, powerful 8-bit microcontroller chip and are suitable for classroom use in undergraduate computer hardware courses. Students have evaluated the effectiveness of these projects formally. The feedback from students indicates that the development and implementation of the projects were successful. This chapter describes the PIC-based projects, their overall effectiveness, and plans for further projects.

Background and Motivation

Computer hardware, digital systems design, number systems, CPU, memory, and I/O (input/output) ports are topics often included in computer science, electronics, and engineering courses as fundamental concepts involved in computer hardware. We believe that students learn computer hardware and organization better if they are given practical learning exercises that illustrate theoretical concepts. However, only a limited range of material designed specifically to supplement the teaching of computer hardware concepts is publicly available, as searches of the Computer Science Teaching Center Web site (http://www.cstc.org/) and the SIGCSE Education Links page (http://sigcse.org/topics/) on the Special Interest Group on Computer Science Education Web site reveal.

We strongly believe, as do many others (Abe et al., 2004; Bhunia, Giri, Kar, Haldar, & Purkait, 2004; Hacker & Sitte, 2004; Leva, 2003; Williams, Klenke, & Aylor, 2003), that students learn more effectively from courses that provide for active involvement in practical activities. Towards that end, we are developing some interesting and entertaining projects that facilitate an interactive, hands-on introduction to traditional computer hardware concepts. These projects are designed around the PIC16F84 microcontroller chip (8-bit, 4MHz) and can be used either in the classroom as a demonstration to enhance the traditional lecture environment or in the laboratory to provide practical hands-on experience at an introductory level.

Computer hardware concepts are described in many references (Englander, 2000; Shelly, Cashman, & Vermaat, 2003; Tanenbaum, 1999), and the PIC microcontroller is discussed extensively in the computer hardware literature (Iovine, 2000; James, 2001; Morton, 2001; Predko). Rowe (2003) describes several low-cost PIC programming kits designed for the PIC16F84 chip, and Smith (2003) deals with MS Windows 2000 and XP-based PIC programming software for a PIC programmer. Assembled modules that incorporate one or more PIC microcontrollers, such as those described in Comfile Technology (2003), are available commercially.

A number of sophisticated simulators exist for building a variety of computer architecture models (Bem & Petelczyc, 2003; Ibbett, 2002; Shelburne, 2003). However, these powerful tools can have a steep learning curve, and while excellent for doing an in-depth performance evaluation of computer hardware, they often simulate a hardware design environment in far more detail than is necessary for a simple introduction of fundamental concepts. Nevertheless, by setting up PIC projects, the students gain firsthand experience that cannot be gained through computer simulation and modeling. To date, we have focused on developing some demonstration projects to support teaching computer hardware and organization. These projects are described in some detail in this chapter along with our plans for future projects.

The remainder of this chapter is organized as follows. In the first section, we discuss the PIC microcontroller environment; followed by the second section, where we describe a series of interesting projects completed to date and plans for future projects. The main benefits of PIC projects are then highlighted in the third section. This is followed in the next section by a discussion of the implementation of PIC-based projects in laboratory settings. The conclusion follows the fifth section, in which the effectiveness of the PIC-based projects is evaluated and interpreted.

PIC Environment:
Hardware and Software

Microcontrollers contain the essential features of a computer on a single silicon chip — CPU, memory, I/O ports, and timing and control circuitry. They are frequently found in roles befitting their name, namely, controlling devices such as VCR or DVD players, and in motor vehicles, trains, and planes, where the tasks at hand require computer control but do not require an extensive memory or processing capacity. Some microcontrollers have additional circuitry, such as an analogue-to-digital (A/D) converter, built in, which makes them particularly useful in certain applications (James, 2001; Morton, 2001). The electrically erasable programmable read-only memory (EEPROM) built into the PIC16F84 is particularly useful in the classroom as it enables the PIC to be reprogrammed many times over as students develop new programs. The computer-in-miniature aspect of microcontrollers makes them an ideal aid for teaching and learning about computer hardware and software principles. For example, the Harvard architecture of the PIC16F84 illustrates a computer architecture different from the von Neuman architecture commonly found in larger computers.

Once a program has been written for a microcontroller, the program has to be entered into the memory of the microcontroller. With the PIC16F84 this can be achieved using the programmer module shown in Figure 2. Iovine (2000) presents details on the availability of this module and the associated software. The software supplied with the programmer module enables programs written in BASIC on a PC to be quickly transferred to the PIC microcontroller. Iovine provides a step-by-step guide to creating programs for the PIC that become more advanced as the student's experience grows. The short turnaround time between program writing, installing the program in the EEPROM, and testing the PIC in the circuitry developed on the breadboard makes this amalgam of hardware and software particularly effective as a learning tool.

Description of PIC Projects

Table 1 lists the five projects that have been developed to date and which were trialed over a period of one semester in our IT Concepts and Skills diploma course. This course is at level 4 or 1st year diploma in information technology at the Auckland University of Technology (AUT).

Project 1: Data Representation

This introductory project demonstrates to students the basic concepts of bits, bytes, and binary numbers. In lectures, the basic concepts of number systems are introduced, and students are shown how to convert from binary to hex and vice versa. The teacher then demonstrates the project to the class to illustrate the theoretical concepts of bits, bytes, and a binary sequence counter. Through active participation in the demonstration and hands-on activities, students gain basic knowledge about the binary number system. Figure 1 shows the breadboard with eight LEDs (light-emitting diodes) and the PIC programmed to output 10011011. Figure 2 shows the PIC programmer module that connects to the PC parallel port via a ribbon cable connected to the 25-pin D-socket located at top right on the module. Figure 3 shows a ZIF (Zero Insertion Force) socket and associated cable that can be connected to the PIC programmer module via the socket located at center left in Figure 2. Using the ZIF socket, instead of the DIP socket provided on the programmer board (see Figure 2), reduces the chance of pin damage to the PIC while it is being inserted in or removed from the programmer module.

Table 1. PIC-based projects and related hardware concepts

Projects	Hardware concepts
1. Data representation	Binary sequence, bits, nibbles, bytes.
2. Memory	Memory addressing, flash memory, RAM, ROM, EEPROM.
3. LED matrix	Nibble, word, decoding, encoding, LED matrix, voltage and logic levels, switches, non-interlaced scanning.
4. LCD display	CPU and registers, I/O port, LCD display.
5. Speech generation	Processor, serial-to-parallel shift registers, amplifier.

Figure 1. The eight-LED display (Project 1) represents the 1-byte word 10011011. The four yellow LEDs correspond to the most significant bits and the four red LEDs to the least significant bits.

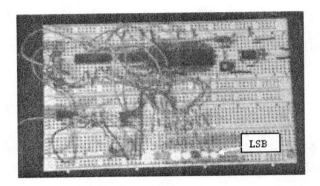

Figure 2. PIC programmer module

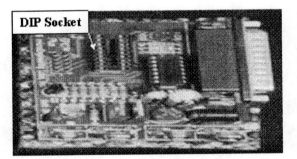

Project 2: Memory

The basic concepts of memory addressing, random access memory (RAM), flash memory, read-only memory (ROM), and electrically erasable programmable ROM (EEPROM) are introduced during lectures. This project shows students how digital data can be read from and written to RAM. Students also gain hands-on experience in reading data from and writing data to EEPROM, whether this is located within the PIC16F84 microcontroller or externally on the breadboard.

Figure 3. ZIF (Zero Insertion Force) socket

Project 3: LED Matrix

Although initially the projects followed closely the projects described in Iovine (2000), the students were encouraged to experiment once they had mastered the concepts in the original design. An example of this development is seen in Figure 4, which shows an LED matrix module attached to the breadboard. The description of Project 3 that follows illustrates the many opportunities for turning principle into practice that PIC projects can present to students. In particular, students will learn about the way the 8 individual bits that make up a byte can be manipulated and utilized for purposes other than counting. The description of Project 3 and the project itself aptly illustrate the Chinese adage, attributed to Confucius (551-479 BC), "I hear, I know. I see, I remember. I do, I understand." As in Project 1, the PIC in Project 3 is programmed to produce 1-byte words. However, in addition to lighting the appropriate LEDs, which can be seen near the top left-hand corner of the breadboard, the 1-byte word in Project 3 is split into two 4-bit nibbles. These in turn are sent to two 74LS154 ICs (seen at the bottom of the matrix module), each of which activates 1 of its 16 output ports in accordance with the 4-bit input. Each of these output ports is linked to a column or a row of the LED matrix — in effect producing an (x, y) coordinate pair. Each point on the 16x16 LED matrix corresponds to an 8-bit word. By programming the PIC to produce the correct sequence of 8-bit words, a display such as that shown in Figure 4 can be produced. This project also illustrates the distinction between logic levels and voltage levels. To turn an individual LED at (x, y) requires a positive voltage to be applied to row y, but the voltage level on a 74LS154 output port goes low when that port is selected. Consequently, four 74LS04 hex inverters were inserted between the 74LS154 connected to the 16 rows and the LEDs. These are seen on the left of the display.

If the matrix board is connected to the breadboard as shown in Figure 3 when the microcontroller is programmed with the binary counting program used in Project 1, a sequence of LEDs will light, starting at the bottom left-hand corner of the matrix (position (1,1)) and proceeding along each row in turn until the top, or 16th, row is reached (position (16,16)). At the end of the 16th row, the sequence repeats, starting at position (1,1). The students' attention can be drawn to the identical nature of this "scanning" of the LED matrix and the scanning that occurs in a computer monitor, noting the rapid fly-back period when the "spot" moves from the end of one line to the beginning of the next line (or the next scan). This analogous situation can be further exploited by asking the students how the displayed scanning procedure differs (if at all) from the nature of the scanning procedure in a television receiver. Students can be reminded that television uses interlaced scanning in order to conserve bandwidth while simultaneously reducing flicker on the television screen to a level acceptable by viewers. A comprehension question for students is to ask them to replicate interlaced scanning of the LED matrix via either modifying the binary counting program in Project 1 or by modifying the hardware on the breadboard in some way, or perhaps by some method involving both the program and the hardware. If the bits in the byte produced by the binary counting program and displayed on the 8 LEDs, as shown in Figure 1, are labeled b0 to b7, then bits b0 to b3 are used in Project 3 to control the x-coordinate on the LED matrix and bits b4 to b7 are used to control the y-coordinate. An illustration of the interplay between software and hardware solutions to problems is provided by simply changing the order in which the b4 to b7 bits are presented to the LED matrix board. This can be easily achieved on the breadboard by moving connector wires from b4, b5, b6, b7 to b7, b4, b5, b6. This action results in the odd lines (1, 3, 5, ... 13, 15) of the LED matrix being scanned first, followed by the even lines (2, 4, 6, ... 14, 16) being scanned. The scan then starts again at line 1.

Figure 4. LED matrix display (Project 3)

The brightness of the LEDs depends on the total number of LEDs that are lit in the display. More LEDs being lit means a shorter duty cycle for each individual LED, thereby reducing the brightness. This aspect can be addressed by increasing the current supplied to each LED, which can be achieved by reducing the value of the current limiting resistor used in series with each row in the matrix display or by increasing the voltage applied across the resistor and LED series circuit. Both of these outcomes can be brought about by connecting an NPN transistor between each LED and its series resistor, while using the positive 5-volt output of the TTL inverter ICs (74LS04) to provide, via a suitable resistor, the base drive for the transistor. A measure of control over the brightness of all the LEDs could then be achieved by supplying the transistors through a single variable resistor connected to the 5-volt supply. Although potted LED matrix units and LED matrix controller ICs are available commercially [18], the authors consider that these items would be more suitable for a follow-up project rather than as an initial introduction to the principles involved. The slight variation in the brightness exhibited amongst even just 256 LEDs provides students with a better appreciation of the difficulties that manufacturers have when producing high-quality active matrix displays involving thousands of components. The photograph in Figure 4 has been retouched to improve the clarity of the LED matrix display.

Project 4: LCD Display

This project utilizes a serial bit stream generated by the PIC 16F84 to create a two-line display on an LCD readout. The project follows the description in Iovine (2000), but innovation on the part of the student is possible in the way that the PIC is programmed and in the content of the displayed message. This aspect of this project is enhanced when it is combined with the speech generator in Project 5. Figure 5 shows the LCD displaying the message "Hi Nurul, how is life at the AUT?"

Project 5: Speech Generation

This project is based around the SPO256 Speech Generator IC, which can produce 59 allophones. Although the speech produced does not sound completely natural, it is of sufficient quality to be easily comprehended. Iovine (2000) describes in detail the use of a serial-to-parallel converter (74LS164) to increase the number of I/O lines available from the PIC. This allows the PIC to control the speech generator (SPO256) so as to produce speech through the speaker, shown in Figure 5, and, at the same time, display on the LCD readout the words

Figure 5. LCD display (Project 4) combined with the speech generator project (Project 5)

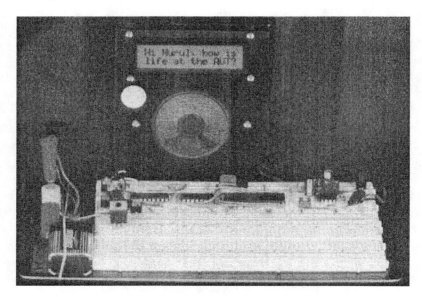

coming from the speaker. This combined project tests the student's mastery of the concepts (hardware and software) presented in the previous projects, and many students appear to respond positively when their creation speaks and displays its "first words."

By changing the clock frequency of the speech generator chip (by substituting a different crystal) or by using different resistors and/or capacitors to form the low-pass filter that precedes the audio amplifier IC (LM836), students can gain firsthand experience of the influence that changing the frequency content of an audio signal has upon the sound perceived by the listener. Some students found that initially they were unable to obtain any sound from this project and that the regulated voltage had dropped from 5 volts to 2 volts. Closer inspection revealed that the filter capacitor on the output of the 7805 regulator IC had been omitted. This resulted in a feedback loop being established, and the resulting oscillations were the cause of the project failure. Provision of a 0.1-microfarad capacitor on the 5-volt output pin of the 7805 regulator solved this problem and proved a useful learning experience for the students.

Additional projects: The following projects are being considered:

- **Process control—DC motor control**: The hands-on learning activities include a real-time process control system.
- **Pulse-code modulation—Analogue-digital converter**: The learning activities include sampling, analogue-to-digital converters, and serial-to-parallel conversion.
- **Wireless technology**: Integrating both infrared data from a remote control and Wi-Fi radio signals into the PIC projects to incorporate some aspects of data communications.
- **Open**: A category for student-suggested projects.

Benefits of PIC-Based Project

The PIC-based projects provide the following benefits:

- **Low cost**: The current street price of a PIC16F84 is $7.5.
- **Easy to use**: PIC-based projects are easy to use and set up for demonstrations.
- **Hands-on**: PIC projects facilitate a hands-on introduction to computer hardware concepts.
- **Programmable**: The PIC16F84 can be reprogrammed many times over as students develop new programs for a variety of projects.
- **Challenging**: The PIC projects provide the students with a challenging yet friendly environment in which students can test their knowledge of computer hardware.
- **Usefulness**: The PIC projects can be used either in the classroom or in the laboratory to provide hands-on experience.
- **Economical/Reusability**: Some hardware components of PIC projects can be reused in developing a variety of projects on a breadboard.

Example of PIC Programming

In this example program (see Table 2), single bytes are placed on the B port pins of the PIC. If an LED is connected to one of these pins via a suitable current limiting resistor, the LED will be lit when the voltage on that pin goes high. Alternatively, this same high (approximately 5 volts) voltage can be used to control other devices. For example, if the value sent to Port B is 242 (decimal), this corresponds to the byte 11110010, which would make the x-nibble described in Project 3 (LED matrix) to be 0010 and the y-nibble to be 1111. In decimal notation, these x and y values correspond to column 2 and row 15. And so this program would result in the LED located at the intersection of column 2 and row 15 being lit, if only for approximately 50 ms. This event will recur once the program loops back to the beginning, so because of the 4 MHz clock speed of the PIC and because of persistence of vision, the LED may appear to be constantly lit.

By assigning different numbers to be "poked" into Port B, different displays, such as a smiley face, as here, can be created. Such changes to the program can be carried out using a word processor such as MS Word or Notepad. The changed program is then compiled using the EPIC compiler. The hex file created by the compiler can then be burned into the PIC memory using the EPIC software and PIC programming board (Figure 2). By inserting the reprogrammed PIC into the breadboard (Figure 4), the new pattern on the matrix display can be observed. This cycle can easily be repeated until the desired display is obtained.

PIC Projects in Laboratory Settings

Figure 6 illustrates how PIC projects can be set up and used in a typical computer laboratory to provide a hands-on learning experience in computer hardware and organization. A typical medium-sized computer laboratory with 25 computers allows a class size of up to 25 students. As seen in Figure 6, the PIC compiler and associated software are installed and run on a stand-alone PC (labeled Old PC), which is linked to a PIC programmer via a printer port (DB25-pin connector). The reason for using a stand-alone PC is to have a single copy of the PIC compiler, which is more economical and eliminates the need for multiple licensing.

Table 2. Source code for binary counting program

```
'Program: Binary Counting
'Initialize variables
Symbol TRISB = 134 'Assign TRISB for port B to decimal value of 134
Symbol PortB = 6   'Assign the variable PortB to the decimal value 6
'Initialize Port (s)
Poke TRISB, 0      'Set port B pins to output
Loop:
'For B0 = 0 to 15
'Poke PortB, B0
'Next B0
Poke PortB, 242    'Place B0 values at port to light LEDS
Pause 50
Poke PortB, 250
Pause 50
Poke PortB, 251
Pause 50
Poke PortB, 252
Pause 50
Poke PortB, 253
Pause 50
Poke PortB, 254
Pause 50
Poke PortB, 226
Pause 50
Poke PortB, 236
'Pause 5
Poke PortB, 209
'Pause 5
Poke PortB, 210
'Pause 5
Poke PortB, 211
'Pause 5
Poke PortB, 220
'Pause 5
Poke PortB, 192
'Pause 10
Poke PortB, 196
'Pause 10
Poke PortB, 204
'Pause 5
Poke PortB, 176
'Pause 5
Poke PortB, 180
'Pause 5
Poke PortB, 188
'Pause 5
Poke PortB, 165
'Pause 5
Poke PortB, 169
'Pause 5
Poke PortB, 149
'Pause 5
Poke PortB, 153
'Pause 5
Poke PortB, 133
'Pause 5
Poke PortB, 137
'Pause 5
Poke PortB, 117
'Pause 5
```

Table 2. cont.

```
Poke PortB, 121
'Pause 5
Poke PortB, 102
'Pause 5
Poke PortB, 103
'Pause 5
Poke PortB, 104
'Pause 5
Poke PortB, 82
'Pause 5
Poke PortB, 90
'Pause 5
Poke PortB, 91
'Pause 5
Poke PortB, 92
'Pause 5
Poke PortB, 93
'Pause 10
Poke PortB, 94
'Pause 10
Poke PortB, 66
'Pause 10
Poke PortB, 76
'Pause 10
Poke PortB, 49
'Pause 10
Poke PortB, 50
'Pause 10
Poke PortB, 51
'Pause 10
Poke PortB, 60
'Pause 10
Poke PortB, 32
'Pause 10
Poke PortB, 36
'Pause 10
Poke PortB, 44
'Pause 10
Poke PortB, 16
'Pause 10
Poke PortB, 20
'Pause 10
Poke PortB, 28
'Pause 10
        'Without pause, counting proceeds too fast to see
Rem Next B0        'Next B0 value
Goto loop
'end
```

Figure 6. PIC programmer set up in a typical laboratory

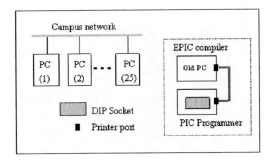

Evaluation by Student Feedback

Student Experience

We offered PIC projects as a capstone project to two students who carried out this project on their final semester towards the diploma in information technology (DipIT) qualification. The students had completed most of the courses required for DipIT qualification, including hardware fundamentals and data communications, before taking up the PIC projects. The project activities include: (1) setting up and testing PIC-based projects; (2) demonstration of working prototype to project supervisors; (3) evaluation of the effectiveness of PIC projects by students' feedback; (4) development of teaching resources (e.g., prototype video) for classroom use; (5) written report, containing requirements analysis, project plan, minutes of the meetings, summary of findings, and reflective statements; and (6) oral presentation to audience of staff and students.

The PIC-based projects were completed successfully, and students indicated that they had learned a great deal about hardware fundamentals by doing the hands-on learning activities included in the PIC projects. This is evident from the students' reflective statements as follows:

Even though we passed the HF100 Hardware Fundamentals course before taking up PIC projects, we did not learn much about hardware concepts until we carried out PIC projects.

Hardware concepts should be taught by hands-on learning activities like we did with PIC projects.

Classroom Evaluation

The effectiveness of PIC-based projects has been evaluated both formally by students (through student evaluation forms) and informally through discussion within the teaching team. The evaluation was conducted in the classroom with DipIT students at AUT. A member of the teaching team conducted the evaluation, and anonymity of the respondents was protected. Participation in the evaluation was entirely voluntary. As part of the formal evaluation process, students were asked to complete a short, five-question questionnaire as follows:

1. **Prior knowledge**: How well did you understand computer hardware fundamentals before entering this course?

2. **Easy to follow**: How easy (overall) did you find the PIC-based projects to follow?

3. **Measure of success**: How effective were the PIC-based project demonstrations in helping you to improve your understanding of computer hardware concepts?

4. **Hands-on**: Would you like to have more projects of this kind as part of your course?

5. **PIC programming**: Would you prefer to learn to program the PIC microcontroller in BASIC or in another language such as Assembler or C?

A 5-point Likert scale was used in the questionnaire. For questions 1 to 3, 1=poor and 5 =excellent; for questions 4 and 5, 1=No and 5=Yes. Forty undergraduate diploma students (60% male, 40% female) from the IT Concepts and Skills course completed the questionnaire, and their responses were interpreted as follows:

1. Twenty-six students indicated that they had no prior knowledge of computer hardware before entering this course. Six students had a basic knowledge of hardware; whereas the remaining 8 students were neutral.

2. The PIC projects were found to be reasonably easy to use and set up for demonstrations. Twenty-eight students were satisfied with the demonstrations and the hands-on experience, five students expressed some concern, and the remaining 7 students were neutral.

3. Thirty students indicated that the PIC projects had clearly assisted them in developing a better understanding of hardware concepts. However, three students indicated that they were not totally satisfied with the PIC projects, and the remaining 7 students were neutral.

4. Twenty-eight students indicated that they would like to have more hands-on projects in the course. Four students were not very interested in trying more projects, and the remaining 8 students were neutral.

5. Most students were not very familiar with using programming languages (such as C or Assembler) to program microcontrollers and appeared to be quite satisfied with using BASIC to program the PIC microcontroller.

We observed that by participating in the PIC-based projects and demonstration activities, students became increasingly motivated to learn more about computer hardware and enjoyed this course more than previous courses that consisted of lectures only. We are seeking feedback regularly both from students and staff for further improvement of the demonstration materials.

Conclusion and Future Work

A set of new projects has been developed which can be used either in the classroom for class demonstrations to enhance the traditional lecture environment or in the computer laboratory for hands-on practical experience in computer hardware. Student responses to the project demonstrations were mostly favourable. The students indicated that they had found the PIC-based projects easy to use and helpful in gaining a better understanding of computer hardware concepts. More projects such as an analogue-to-digital converter, a DC motor controller, and an integration of both infrared data from a remote control and Wi-Fi radio signals into the PIC projects are under development. Our materials, including the source code for all PIC applications, are available at no cost to faculty interested in using the PIC projects to supplement teaching their computer hardware courses or as the basis for more complex projects. More information about PIC-based projects and demonstration materials can be obtained by contacting the first author.

Summary

Computer hardware is a challenging subject to teach and learn in a meaningful way because many students appear to find the subject rather technical, dry, and boring. This chapter describes a set of new PIC-based projects which can be used either in the classroom to enhance the lecture environment or in the laboratory to provide a hands-on learning experience in computer hardware. The PIC projects are designed around the PIC16F84, a low-cost 8-bit microcontroller chip. The projects are suitable for classroom use in introductory computer hardware. The effectiveness of these projects has been evaluated by both students and the teaching team. The students indicated that the PIC-based projects are easy to use and helpful in developing a better understanding of computer hardware concepts.

Key Terms and Definitions

Computer hardware: Generally refers to electronic, electrical, and mechanical components that make up a computer.

EEPROM: EEPROM stands for electrically erasable ROM. This type of memory differs from ROM in that the contents can be changed if suitable voltages are applied to the memory chip.

LCD displays: LCD stands for liquid crystal display, which is a flat panel display that uses liquid crystal to present information on the screen. The liquid crystal is contained between two sheets of transparent material. When an electric current passes through the crystals, they twist. This causes some light waves to be blocked and allows others to pass through, which creates the images on the screen.

PIC BASIC: An adaptation of the BASIC computer language for use with PIC microcontrollers.

PIC microcontroller: PIC stands for programmable interface controller. The PIC microcontroller is an on-chip computer containing a CPU (central processing unit), RAM (random access memory), programmable ROM, timers, and input/output ports.

PIC programming: Generally refers to the procedures involved in creating a sequence of instructions that can be installed in and acted upon by the PIC microcontroller in order to control the operation of electrical and/or mechanical equipment.

PIC projects: PIC-based projects which are developed to enhance teaching and learning computer hardware concepts, as reported in this chapter.

RAM: RAM stands for random access memory. A class of memory that is used in the computer as main memory for the storage and retrieval of data and instructions by the processor and other devices.

ROM: ROM stands for read-only memory. A class of memory that is used in the computer for storing data, instructions, or information that can be read but not modified; the data is recorded permanently on the chips. ROM is nonvolatile memory, meaning its contents are not lost when power is removed from the computer.

Review Questions

1. List and describe three main benefits of PIC-based projects.

2. Discuss the usefulness of the PIC projects in teaching and learning contexts.

3. Define the following key terms: bit, byte, binary number, RAM, ROM, LCD, and EEPROM.

4. Describe how PIC-based projects can be set up for class demonstrations.

5. Explain how PIC projects can be used in the laboratory to enhance teaching and learning computer hardware concepts.

6. List and describe further enhancements to the PIC projects.

References

Abe, K., Tateoka, T., Suzuki, M., Maeda, Y., Kono, K., & Watanabe, T. (2004). An integrated laboratory for processor organization, compiler design, and computer networking. *IEEE Transactions on Education, 47*(3), 311-320.

Bem, E. Z., & Petelczyc, L. (2003, February 19-23). *MiniMIPS—A simulation project for the computer architecture laboratory.* Paper presented at the Proceedings of the 34th Technical Symposium on Computer Science Education (SIGCSE'03), Reno, NV (pp. 64-68).

Bhunia, C., Giri, S., Kar, S., Haldar, S., & Purkait, P. (2004). A low-cost PC-based virtual oscilloscope. *IEEE Transactions on Education, 47*(2), 295-299.

Comfile Technology. (2003). *What is PICBASIC.* Retrieved September 20, from http://www.comfile.co.kr/english2/study/pbstudy.html

Englander, I. (2000). *The architecture of computer hardware and systems software: An information technology approach* (2nd ed.). Wiley.

Hacker, C., & Sitte, R. (2004). Interactive teaching of elementary digital logic design with WinLogiLab. *IEEE Transactions on Education, 47*(2), 196-203.

Ibbett, R. N. (2002, June 24-26). *WWW visualization of computer architecture simulations.* Paper presented at the 7th annual SIGCSE conference on Innovation and Technology in Computer Science Education (ITiCSE), Aarhus, Denmark (p. 247).

Iovine, J. (2000). *PIC microcontroller project book*. McGraw-Hill.

James, M. (2001). *Microcontroller cookbook PIC & 8051* (2nd ed.). Newnes.

Leva, A. (2003). A hands-on experimental laboratory for undergraduate courses in automatic control. *IEEE Transactions on Education, 46*(2), 263-272.

Morton, J. (2001). *PIC your personal introductory course* (2nd ed.). Newnes.

Predko, M. (2003). *Some useful references on PIC microcontrollers*. Retrieved September 20, from http://www.myke.com/

Rowe, J. (2003, April). Three do-it yourself PIC programmers. *Silicon Chip*, 58-65.

Shelburne, B. (2003). *Teaching computer organization using a PDP-8 simulator*. Paper presented at the SIGCSE'03 Technical Symposium on Computer Science Education (p. 69-73).

Shelly, G. B., Cashman, T. J., & Vermaat, M. E. (2003). *Discovering computers 2004: Complete*. Course Technology.

Smith, P. (2003, July). Updating the PIC programmer and checkerboard. *Silicon Chip*, 79-81.

Tanenbaum, A. S. (1999). *Structured computer organization* (4th ed.). Prentice Hall.

Williams, R. D., Klenke, R. H., & Aylor, J. H. (2003). Teaching computer design using virtual prototyping. *IEEE Transactions on Education, 46*(2), 296-301.

Chapter XIII

Assistant Tool for Instructors Teaching Computer Hardware with the PBL Theory

Maiga Chang, National Science and Technology
Program for e-Learning, Taiwan

Kun-Fa Cheng, Chih-Ping Senior High School, Taiwan

Alex Chang, Yuan-Ze University, Taiwan

Ming-Wei Chen, Chih-Ping Senior High School, Taiwan

Abstract

Students often get a good score in written exams but fail to apply their knowledge when trying to solve real-world problems. This is applies particularly to computer hardware courses in which students are required to learn and memorize many key terms and definitions. Also, teachers often find it difficult to gauge students' progress when teaching computer hardware fundamentals. These problems are related to the learning process, so it is necessary to find an appropriate instructional model to overcome these problems. This chapter describes a Web-based tool called the assistant tool, which is based on problem-based learning (PBL) theory and not only assists instructors in teaching computer hardware fundamentals but also overcomes the above-mentioned problems.

Learning Objectives

After completing this chapter, you will be able to:

- Discuss the usefulness of PBL theory in teaching and learning contexts.
- Discuss the effectiveness of the assistant tool in enhancing teaching and learning computer hardware concepts.
- Define the following key terms: problem-based learning, brainstorm map, concept map, and cooperative learning.
- Suggest further enhancements to the assistant tool proposed in the chapter.

Introduction

There are numerous key terms, definitions, and abstract concepts in computer hardware fundamentals courses that students are required to learn and memorize to pass the exam. Therefore, it is often difficult to motivate students to learn computer hardware because many students appear to find the subject rather abstract, technical, and boring. Teachers also find it a bit difficult to gauge students' progress in their classes.

There are two primary issues a teacher must investigate to gauge student progress: (1) memorization, that is, how many terms or abbreviations students have learned; and (2) relations between concepts (e.g., whether students know that both Pentium and Athlon are processors or whether students know the difference between a printer and a scanner). Memorization can easily be measured by a simple quiz or test. However, determining whether a student understands the relationships between concepts is not an easy task. Furthermore, a teacher needs to be assured that students have acquired the knowledge required and understand the numerous abstract concepts.

Sometimes students make mistakes and incorrectly group together concepts on different levels. For example, a student may have memorized ViewSonic VE700, an output device, and incorrectly associated this with the CPU and motherboard instead of Intel Pentium IV and IWill P4SE2. The questions arise, how can a teacher teach students about the conceptual relations among computer components and what concepts should a teacher provide as supplemental instruction.

To overcome the above issues and problems, we have proposed an assistant tool based on problem-based learning (PBL) theory that can be used in assisting instructors teaching computer hardware courses.

Background and Motivation

The author's past teaching experience at a vocational school showed that vocational students often obtain high scores on tests but fail when applying what they have learned when trying to solve related problems in the real world. A problem can then be said to exist in the learning process. It is necessary and urgent to find an appropriate instructional model to resolve this problem in education. In the 1960s, researchers at McMaster University in Canada obtained a similar finding. They argued that students cannot apply education-based knowledge and skills to their work (Albanese & Mitchell, 1993). To solve this problem, the School of Medicine at McMaster University developed and applied a PBL method for medical education ("What is PBL?", 2004).

Problem-based learning is a student-centered teaching method in which students are placed into small groups and the teacher acts as a facilitator or guide (Barrows & Tamblyn, 1980). A poorly structured problem (real-life problem) is used as a starting point for the instructional process in PBL (Simon, 1973), and students acquire problem-solving and self-directed learning skills (Barrows, 1996).

According to Barrows (1996), there are several key characteristics of PBL: It is student-centered, it employs small student groups, teachers function as facilitators or guides, and instruction begins with unstructured problems. A goal of PBL is to transform the teacher's role from that of a lecturer to a facilitator and the student's role from that of a passive observer to an active participant in the learning process (Ahern-Rindell, 1999).

To motivate students, PBL employs realistic situations (unstructured problems) to promote group discussions. These realistic situations can be used to create relationships between their education and their professional lives. Unstructured problems are utilized to force students to define problems for themselves, which leads to learning by critical thinking. A brainstorm map, which is drawn by student(s) according to their pre-learned knowledge, and group discussion can enhance a student's ability to think creatively, reason critically, make decisions, and communicate and cooperate with other students while exposing them to different viewpoints. During a PBL activity, acquiring knowledge coincides with solving the problem, enabling students to identify what they know and what they need to know. Thereby, learning becomes meaningful.

Problem-based learning is based on several cognitive theories: constructivism, situated learning, experimentalism, and cooperative learning.

A.   **Constructivism**: Constructivism assumes that knowledge is not absolute but rather constructed via the learning process and based on a learner's previous knowledge and their overall view of the world. According to Savery and Duffy (1995), the three primary constructivist principles are (1) understanding is a product of our interactions with the environment; (2) cognitive conflict stimulates learning; and (3) knowledge evolves through social negotiation and evaluation of individual beliefs. Constructivism then is the basis for changing the student role from passive to active by placing students into groups for discussion and social negotiation.

B.   **Situated learning**: Situated learning argues that learning should take place in realistic settings to make learning meaningful (Anderson, Reder, & Simon, 1996; Brown, Collins, & Duguid, 1989; Young, 1993). There are four primary claims of situated learning with respect to education principles in situated learning: (1) Action is grounded in the concrete situation in which it occurs; (2) knowledge does not transfer between tasks; (3) training by abstraction is of little use; and (4) instruction needs to take place in complex social environments (Anderson et al.). According to these principles, instruction in the sciences should be rooted in real-world experience. The situational nature of cognition renders education more effectively for promoting student development of practical knowledge. This rationale, perhaps, explains why students pass tests with high scores but have difficulties solving real-world problems.

C.   **Experimentalism**: Dewey (1938) argued that knowledge acquisition is a product of perception and is active rather than static; that is, acquiring knowledge is a process of discovery. Based on this notion of learning, students can only learn from experience, that is, learning by doing.

D.   **Cooperative learning**: Cooperative learning focuses on student interaction (Ahern-Rindell, 1999). Cooperative learning must comprise the following elements: positive interdependence, individual accountability, face-to-face interaction, and, interpersonal skills (Johnson, Johnson, & Smith, 1991). Cooperative learning proposes that the different perspectives in a group can enrich each member's understanding. Furthermore, cooperative learning can enhance critical and reasoning skills and enhance tolerance of different perspectives.

The PBL method has been implemented for the last decade. Different from a traditional education model, there are a number of instructional decisions that need to be made based on factors such as class size, instructor preference, and course objectives. Duch (2001) classified those models into four types to allow instructors to teach large numbers of students: medical school model, floating facilitator model, peer tutor model, and large class model. In the floating facilitator model, the teacher is a facilitator working with groups no larger than four to five students. When the teacher identifies confusion in a group, the

Figure 1. The instructional template of PBL units (Sage, 2000)

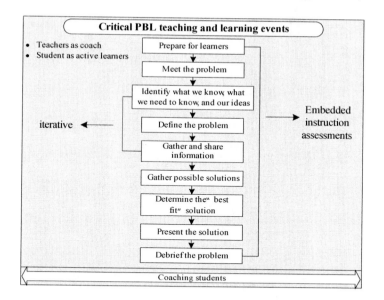

teacher may provide guidance to assist the group in resolving their confusion. When all groups become stuck on the same issue, the teacher suspends group discussions and discusses the issue with the whole class.

Figure 1 shows the eight steps in the PBL instructional template. Sage (2000) noted that the teacher should be a coach and guide students and that students must actively complete the problem-solving activity.

Teachers always need to gauge the progress of their students. Problem-based learning allows teachers to measure student learning via a brainstorm map constructed by students. The brainstorm map is created (Figure 2) when students try to solve a problem proposed by a teacher. Since this map represents concretely the concepts a student understands, teachers can use this map to measure student knowledge and to guide the direction future classes should take.

The experimental lecture used in this chapter is a portion of a lecture on computer hardware. The teacher is first asked to teach the fundamental concepts of the computer components. Then, based on the PBL instructional theory, the teacher poses a real-world problem for the students to solve. In this case, the problem is for small groups of students to design their dream computer.

For Chinese students a dream computer is either a high-performance computer or a computer that a student most wanted. Students are asked to discuss and

Figure 2. Brainstorm map for force in physics (Hsu, Chen, Chang, & Yang, 2003)

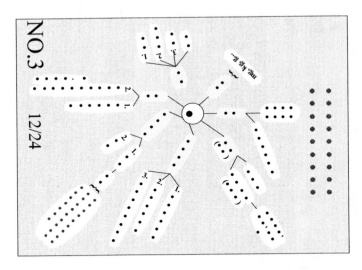

create a brainstorm map for their dream computer. Students are required to discuss and identify all details from the abstract level to the product level on their brainstorm maps.

Students should, for example, discuss whether their dream computer needs a display card. Then, if they decide that it needs a card, they have to discuss which brand they want, WinFast or S3, then, in greater detail, they have to decide which product they want, such as WinFast 3D S680 or S3 Tri64 D2/V2.

If the students pick the HP brand as their display card, then they may have an incorrect conceptual relation between computer modules and computer accessories. Actually HP does not have any display card accessories. Similarly, if students decide they do not need a display card or forget to discuss whether they need a display card, then they may have missed one or more concepts. These two problems can be identified quickly by the teacher via the brainstorm maps.

However, as the brainstorm map is drawn by a small group (five to seven students), it is difficult to understand at first (Figure 2). Moreover, when the PBL process is applied to Internet teaching, the question arises, how can a teacher rapidly provide students with feedback based on the student discussions. This chapter presents a novel feedback tool based on PBL theory for Web-based teaching. This feedback tool first retrieves discussion records from a database and then restores the brainstorm map in hierarchical form to the concept-map relational database management system (RDBMS). With the concept-map

RDBMS, the tool can replay the concept map to identify the differences of the brainstorm maps of the students and the teacher.

There are several issues that will be involved when this feedback system is developed. One major issue is who the system is designed for. This system is designed to provide teaching suggestions to teachers rather than learning methods to students. Another issue requires comparing methodologies for identifying the differences of the brainstorm maps of the students and the teacher. As we know, if teachers want to judge whether the brainstorm maps of students are right or wrong, they must have their brainstorm map first. The difference between traditional education and Internet-based education is that when teachers teach in the traditional classroom, the map could be stored either in the teacher's mind or in the computer, but the teachers must store the map in the computer when they teach in the Internet-based environment. The final issue is how to determine the sequence for teachers to provide the missed concepts to students.

The most challenging task is how to communicate to the teacher which concepts were missed by the students and how these concepts should be prioritized for future instruction. It is considerably easier to teach with the PBL method on the Internet if there is a tool that can provide feedback regarding the concepts students have missed. Such a tool would allow the teacher to feel more comfortable using PBL theory on the Internet. In the next section, the proposed Web-based PBL environment and the novel assistant tool (feedback system) are described.

Description of the System

There is considerable research into how to best implement PBL theory in a Web-based learning environment (Hsu, Chen, Chang, & Yang, 2003). Chen, Kuo, Chang, and Yang (2003) developed an instructional model for PBL-based Internet learning called the Problem-Based Internet Assisted Learning System (PBIALS). Figure 3 displays the pedagogical model of the PBIALS.

Although the brainstorm map represents the knowledge students have learned, the concept map is easier for teachers to interpret (Figure 2). The concept map (Novak, 1981; Novak & Gowin, 1984) was designed to represent what knowledge students had learned and to aid teachers in determining the concepts that students are lacking. The concept map is significantly more hierarchical than the brainstorm map; the concept map is a semantic description of concepts and can do whatever the brainstorm map can do (Jones, Palincsar, Ogle, & Carr, 1987). Hence, the concept map was adopted in the development of the assistant tool.

Figure 3. Pedagogical model of the PBIALS

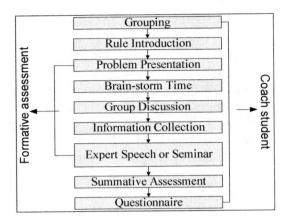

Therefore, this chapter redevelops two parts of PBIALS, brainstorm time and group discussion, to provide teachers with suggestions about the concepts students lack. Although the brainstorm map is drawn by students during a brainstorm discussion, this map does not allow teachers to quickly identify the supplemental concepts students may require. To resolve this problem, the assistant tool generates a concept map-like tree map, which is based on the original brainstorm map and is stored in the discussion database in the PBIALS.

Before we present the assistant tool, the instructional process and the experimental PBIALS should be first described. According to the instructional model of the PBIALS, the instructional process is designed to include three major stages in school and one for outside school: School I, School II, School III, and Outside School. Figure 4 shows the whole instructional process. The rectangular with single line in Figure 4 is the instruction function in the PBIALS, and the double line represents the activity in class.

Based on the instructional process of the PBIALS designed in previous research, the architecture of the PBIALS is systematically constructed by integrating several tools for personal use, teamwork use, and recording (Figure 5). An Internet virtual classroom (IVC) is a Web-based learning system with community architecture, which supports knowledge management, community behaviors (chat room/bulletin board, etc.), and personal tools (Chang, Chang, & Heh, 2000; Lin, Chang, Cheng, & Heh, 1999). The instructional model/process of the PBIALS is evaluated with the IVC system.

The assistant tool is designed as a feedback system for teachers while using PBL theory to teach a class on computer hardware (Delisle, 1997; Gallagher, Sher,

Figure 4. Instructional process of the PBIALS

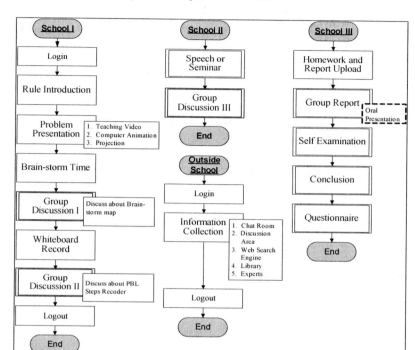

Figure 5. System architecture of the PBIALS

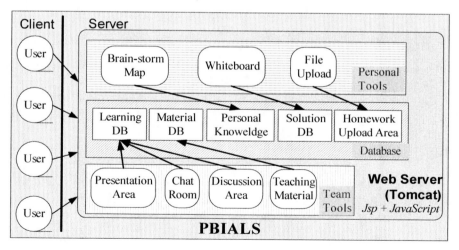

Figure 6. Retrieved concept map for Team 8

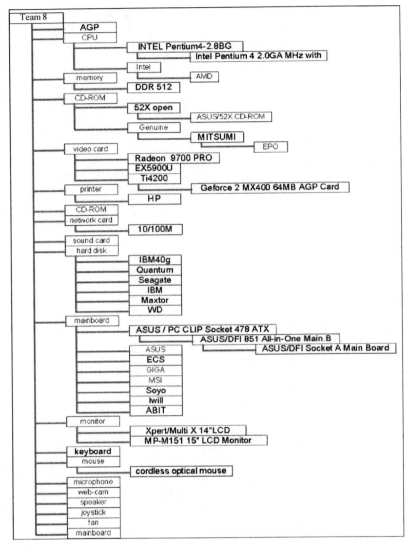

Stepien, & Workman, 1995). The feedback system first retrieves the concept map for each group from the discussion database which is integrated into the PBIALS (the Learning DB and the Personal Knowledge in Figure 5). The system then constructs the concept map for each team (Figure 6).

After constructing the concept map for each team, the system transforms the concept map into a two-dimensional plane. The x-axis of the two-dimensional plane is the concept-axis, and the y-axis is the abstraction level of the concept

Figure 7. Consequent concept map of Team 8 on a two-dimensional plane

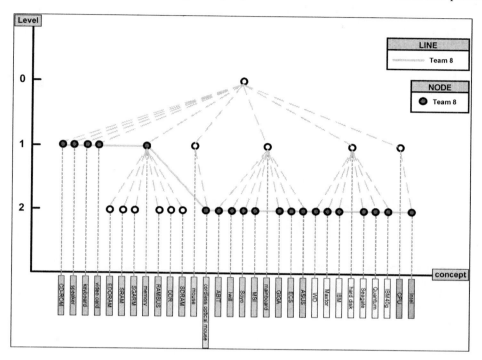

(level-axis). This concept map is similar to a tree map in that its branches can bend either left or right. The system will attempt to bend together those branches in which the leaf concept nodes belong to the same abstraction level. Figure 7 illustrates the concept map for Team 8 on a two-dimensional plane after the system bent (transforming) the original concept map (Figure 6).

Once the system merges both the teacher's concept map and the students' map on a two-dimensional plane (Figure 8), an adjustable baseline can be calculated. By rotating the adjustable baseline until it approaches the teacher's baseline, feedback identifying the concepts that require reteaching by teacher is generated. To generate the feedback, the system will rotate the adjustable baseline incrementally. If the adjustable baseline touches a teacher concept that students lack, then the system will report this to the teacher. This simple methodology is employed because once students receive the supplemental materials from the teacher, students will perhaps remember other things and correct their brainstorm map accordingly. For example, assume a group of students lacks both a display card and a sound card for designing their dream computer. When teacher tells the students that they lack a display card in their brainstorm map, they might

Figure 8. Feedback according to the adjustable baseline

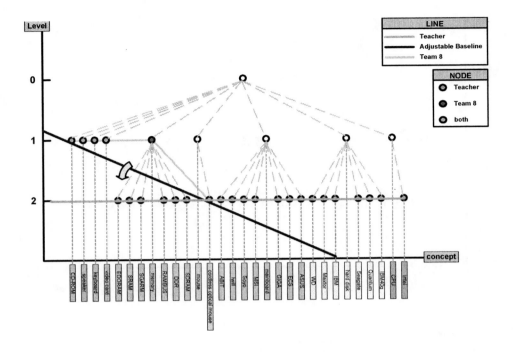

recall that they are missing a sound card too. If so, the adjustable baseline will be recalculated by the system.

The latest version of the assistant tool can be downloaded at http://maiga.dnsalias.org/PBL/tools/feedback.htm.

Usefulness and Evaluation of the System

Most assistant tools focus on how to best provide interactive services for students. This chapter presents an assistant tool designed to provide teaching recommendations for teachers based on PBL theory. In the PBIALS, students use keyboards and a discussion database instead of pencils and paper during discussions. The goal of this chapter is to provide a method that provides suitable teaching suggestions to instructors teaching in PBL-based e-learning systems.

This novel assistant tool is integrated into the PBIALS. There is a discussion database in the PBIALS that stores the discussion records for each team and can be retrieved by the assistant tool as previously described. Two questionnaires were developed to do an assessment of the PBIALS and the novel assistant tool. One questionnaire, the Curriculum Opinion Investigation, targets students learning about computer hardware through the PBIALS. The other questionnaire, Satisfaction and Usefulness Investigation for the PBL Assistant, is for teachers needing to make supplemental material with the assistant tool.

The Curriculum Opinion Investigation comprises two parts. The first part has 26 questions with answers measured on a 5-point Likert scale: strongly agree (SA), agree (A), neutral (N), disagree (DA), and strongly disagree (SDA). The second part has open questions allowing participants to make suggestions and ask questions regarding any aspect of the PBL and PBIALS. The Satisfaction and Usefulness Investigation also contains two parts, comprising five questions measured on a 5-point Likert scale and two open questions.

Two teachers in two semesters were enrolled in the study. The participants, roughly 50 students each semester (mostly male), were 1st-year students in the Information Program at Chih-Ping Vocational School. After the teaching unit finished, the questionnaire was handed out to the participants and teachers. There were 59.4% of students who considered brainstorming time very useful, allowing students to discuss and construct a specific map according to a given objective.

Both teachers reported that the assistant tool identified what they should know about the concepts the student groups lacked. The teachers also reported that using the assistant tool, it was easy to identify the concepts and the appropriate sequence in which they needed to be taught to students. Based on their responses, this assistant tool will be significantly improved if it can provide instant or, say, real-time feedback. Currently, the assistant tool is provided to teachers after the discussion stage (in PBL theory) is completed. However, this discussion stage covers more than one class, and students could also be allowed to continue their discussions after class. Hence, the assistant tool should be able to be used by teachers anytime during the discussion stage. To let teachers use the assistant tool mid-discussion is not a difficulty as it requires only a minor adjustment to the operational process of PBIALS; that is, the assistant tool is always ready.

Conclusion

Applying assistant tools and feedback systems to the e-learning field is not new. However, most of these applications focus on providing interactive services for students. This chapter presents a new assistant tool that produces teaching recommendations for teachers based on the PBL theory. The PBL theory is a student-centered teaching strategy which allows students to discover knowledge through small-group discussions. The teacher in this scenario acts merely as a facilitator. The goal of this chapter is to develop a possible solution that provides suitable teaching suggestions about students for instructors using a PBL-based e-learning system.

According to the questionnaire results, the teachers reported that the feedback tool was of considerable assistance in identifying and reporting what the students (small groups) were learning and thinking. Moreover, it was easy for the teachers to determine which concepts the students lacked and, thereby, teach these concepts to students. This assistant tool also increased teacher comfort levels when employing PBL theory.

The assistant tool was provided to teachers when the discussion stage (in PBL theory) was complete. However, the discussion stage could cover more than one class, and students could also be allowed to continue their discussions after class. Teachers reported that the assistant tool would be much better if it could provide instant or, say, real-time feedback; this feedback tool will be improved in the near future to allow teachers to use it at any point during a discussion stage of the PBIALS.

Summary

There are numerous key terms, definitions, and abstract concepts in computer hardware courses that students are required to learn and memorize in order to pass the exam. Therefore, it is often difficult to motivate students to learn computer hardware fundamentals because students appear to find the subject rather abstract, technical, and boring. Teachers also find it a bit difficult to gauge students' progress when teaching computer hardware concepts. These problems are related to the learning process, and therefore it is necessary to find an appropriate instructional model to overcome these problems. This chapter described a Web-based tool called the assistant tool, which is based on problem-based learning (PBL) theory and not only assists instructors in teaching computer hardware fundamentals but also overcomes the above-mentioned problems.

Key Terms and Definitions

Brainstorm map: A brainstorm map and discussion can improve students' creative thinking and critical reasoning, communication, cooperation, and decision-making skills and provide students with various viewpoints. Students record their thoughts regarding what they already know and what they need to know on a brainstorm map (Figure 2).

Concept map: A concept map is a knowledge representation commonly used in education. It is a graphical node-arc representation illustrating the relationship among concepts (Novak, 1981; Novak & Gowin, 1984). The concept map, based on the cognitive map, can be in three forms: spider map, chain map, and hierarchy map (Jones et al., 1987). Different concept maps can be applied to handle different types of knowledge. The hierarchy map was selected in this chapter for being easily understood.

Constructivism: Constructivism assumes that knowledge is not absolute but rather constructed via the learning process and based on a learner's previous knowledge and worldview.

Cooperative learning: Cooperative learning focuses on student interaction. Cooperative learning exposes students to different perspectives that can enrich their understanding. Cooperative learning can enhance critical and reasoning skills and improve tolerance of and willingness to adopt new concepts.

PBL: Problem-based learning is student-centered, uses small student groups, and positions the teacher as a facilitator or guide. Life problems (real-world problems) are used as the starting point for the instructional process in PBL. Clinical problem-solving and self-directed learning skills can then be learned via the learning process.

PBIALS: The instructional model of the PBIALS is similar to the instructional template proposed by Sage (2000). There are eight principal stages (excluding the questionnaire stage) in this instructional model (Figure 3).

Situated learning: Situated learning argues that learning should take place in realistic settings to make learning meaningful. From this, we can infer that scientific curriculum should be incorporated into students' experiences. Without situated learning, traditional education loses its ability to teach practical knowledge.

Review Questions

1. Discuss the difference between the PBL system and the traditional learning approach.

2. Discuss the effectiveness of PBL theory in teaching and learning introductory computer hardware courses.

3. Discuss the difference between a brainstorm map and a concept map.

4. Discuss the architecture of the Problem-Based Internet Assisted Learning System (PBIALS).

5. List and describe three main features of the assistant tool.

6. List and describe possible enhancements to the assistant tool.

References

Ahern-Rindell, A. J. (1999). Applying inquiry-based and cooperative group learning strategies to promote critical thinking. *JCST*, 203-207.

Albanese, M. A., & Mitchell, S. (1993). Problem-based learning: A review of literature on its outcomes and implementation issues. *Academic Medicine, 68*(1), 52-81.

Anderson, J. R., Reder, L. M., & Simon, H. A. (1996). Situated learning and education. *Educational Researcher, 25*(4), 5-11.

Barrows, H. S. (1996). Problem-based learning in medicine and beyond: A brief overview. *New Directions for Teaching and Learning, 68*, 3-11.

Barrows, H. S., & Tamblyn, R. M. (1980). *Problem-based learning: An approach to medical education.* New York: Springer.

Brown, J. S., Collins, A., & Duguid, P. (1989). Situated cognition and the culture of learning. *Educational Researcher, 18*(1), 34-41.

Chang, J. C., Chang, M., & Heh, J. S. (2000, October/November). Designing an asynchronous/synchronous combination distance learning environment based on Web-BBS. In *Proceedings of WebNet 2000* (pp. 669-670).

Chen, M.-W., Kuo, R., Chang, M., & Yang, K.-Y. (2003). Internet virtual classroom: An implementation of the instructional model of the PBIALS based on the PBL theory. In *Proceedings of the IEEE International Conference on Advanced Learning Technologies 2003* (p. 441).

Delisle, R. (1997). *How to use problem-based learning in the classroom.* Alexandria, VA: Association for Supervision and Curriculum Development.

Dewey, J. (1938). *Experience and education.* New York: Collier and Kappa Delta Pi.

Duch, B. J. (2001). Models for problem-based instruction in undergraduate courses. In B. J. Duch, S. E. Groh, & D. E. Allen (Eds.), *The power of problem-based learning.* Sterling, VA: Stylus.

Gallagher, S. A., Sher, B. T., Stepien, W. J., & Workman, D. (1995). Implementing problem-based learning in science classrooms. *School Science and Mathematics, 95*(3), 136-146.

Hmelo, C. E., & Ferrari, M. (1997). The problem-based learning tutorial: Cultivating higher order thinking skills. *Journal of the Education of the Gifted, 20*(4), 401-422.

Hsu, C.-C., Chen, M.-W., Chang, M., & Yang, K.-Y. (2003). XOOPS: A rapid tool for developing problem based learning environment for teachers. In *Proceedings of the International Conference on Computers in Education* (pp. 89-92).

Johnson, D. W., Johnson, R. T., & Smith, K. A. (1991). *Cooperative learning: Increasing college faculty instructional productivity (ASHE-ERIC Higher Education Rep. 4).* Washington, DC: George Washington University.

Jones, B. F., Palincsar, A. S., Ogle, D. S., & Carr, E. G. (Eds.). (1987). *Strategic teaching and learning: Cognitive instruction in the content areas.* Elmhurst, IL: North Central Regional Laboratory and the Association for Supervision and Curriculum Development.

Lin, Y. Y., Chang, J. C., Cheng, S. Y., & Heh, J. S. (1999). IVC: Internet virtual classroom. In *Proceedings of the 3rd Global Chinese Conference on Computers in Education '99.*

Novak, J. D. (1981). Applying learning psychology and philosophy of science to biology teaching. *American Biology Teacher, 73,* 12-20.

Novak, J. D., & Gowin, D. N. (1984). *Learning how to learn.* Cambridge, UK: Cambridge University Press.

Sage, S. M. (2000). A natural fit: Problem-based learning and technology standards. *Learning & Leading with Technology, 28*(1), 6-12.

Savery, J. R., & Duffy, T. M. (1995). Problem based learning: An instructional model and its constructivist framework. *Educational Technology, 35*(5), 31-38.

Simon, H. A. (1973). The structure of ill-structured problems. *Artificial Intelligence, 4,* 181-201.

What is PBL? (2004). Retrieved December 22, 2004, from McMaster University, School of Medicine Web site: http://www.fhs.mcmaster.ca/bhsc/CellBiology/what_is_pbl.htm

Young, M. F. (1993). Instructional design for situated learning. *Educational Technology, Research and Development, 41*(1), 43-58.

Chapter XIV

A Simulator for High-Performance Processors

John Morris, University of Auckland, New Zealand

Abstract

This chapter describes a Web-based modular, extensible processor simulator designed as an aid to teaching computer architecture. It is written entirely in Java, which allows it to be easily embedded in other Web-based course materials and to run anywhere. Users configure a collection of Java classes which model individual processor modules. Java's dynamic class loading capability means that students in advanced classes are able to incorporate new modules by simply writing new classes and adding them to a configuration file which specifies the new modules' connections to other modules. The modular structure means that it can be used for both introductory computer organization and more advanced processor architecture courses. For example, it can be used to demonstrate how (a) the data path of a modern processor is structured, (b) pipelining keeps multiple instructions in flight at any time, (c) hazards occur, and (d) resource conflicts are resolved. Processing modules follow a simple design pattern which correctly simulates the behavior of a complex synchronous processor. The design is simple, yet powerful enough to model complex data paths with extensive feedback capabilities. To manage complexity, the system being simulated may be specified as a hierarchy of models, each of which can be viewed in a separate window on demand. This provides a customizable level of detail to students studying processor operation.

Learning Objectives

After completing this chapter, you will be able to:

- Explain how a processor simulator can be used in the classroom as an aid to enhance teaching and learning computer architecture.
- Discuss the usefulness of a processor simulator in teaching and learning contexts.
- Define the following key terms: cache, data paths, dynamic loading, pipeline, and toolkit.
- Consider further enhancements to the processor simulator described in the chapter.

Introduction

Decreasing feature sizes leads to more transistors per unit area of a processor die and a continued growth in a designer's transistor budget: Tens of millions of transistors are now available to designers of high-performance processors. This motivates a continual search for additional performance-enhancing devices: even if the benefit is relatively small, it has become economically feasible to incorporate them into new designs. Thus we now commonly see deep pipeline, superscalar designs with large numbers of modules, each providing perhaps only a small performance improvement. Tens of instructions may be "in flight" (in various stages of processing) in each clock cycle, and large amounts of data may be cached in various modules; as well as conventional caches, many modules hold data in registers (e.g., most pipeline modules) and tables (e.g., branch history buffers). The high degree of parallelism and complex data storage is only effectively demonstrated with visual tools. Additionally, with instructions and data stored in so many different modules at the same time, the potential for hazards and the complexity of circuitry needed to avoid them have become significant.

The increasing transistor budget (and thus the scope for incorporating even more performance-enhancing modules) also means that unless a simulator is easily extensible, it, like an old processor design, may be consigned to some digital scrap heap in a very short period.

Thus, to enable students to appreciate and understand how all the modules interact and contribute to the performance of a modern processor and — perhaps more importantly — what factors cause bottlenecks and prevent maximum instruction throughput being attained, a teaching tool should be:

a. **Web-based**: easily incorporated into existing teaching materials;

b. **Portable**: students should be able to run the simulator on any system, anywhere;

c. **Modular**: new modules should be able to be added by instructors and students;

d. **Configurable**: it should be possible to include or exclude modules and change their sizes or other operational parameters;

e. **Hierarchical**: modules should be able to be nested within others to control the level of detail visible to a student at any time;

f. **Extensible**: there should be no limit to the complexity of designs; and

g. **Cycle-based**: the existence of hazards is an important concept, and students should be able to both see them arise and see how they are resolved.

The ability to configure modules, for example, to set the size of a cache, is vital for efficient teaching. Whilst processor designers typically want to increase the size of caches and other tables, for teaching purposes, one generally wants to reduce the size of such elements (sometimes to trivially small sizes — one or two elements) so that effects such as cache misses show up quickly rather than after several hundred instructions have been processed. Students' interest should be maintained and boredom should not be allowed to set in! It is also necessary to be able to set other characteristics, such as the cache write policy. Although simulation speed is a goal of many processor simulation projects (Schnarr & Larus, 1998), in which billions of instructions (Perez, Mouchard, & Temam, 2004) may need to be simulated to "prove" the efficacy of a new architectural idea, it is not a primary goal for this project. Here, the aim is that students should be able to understand how a design technique (e.g., pipelining) or module (e.g., system write-back queue) contributes to improved performance rather than to measure the likely performance enhancement in order to convince a manufacturer to incorporate it in the next design.

Existing Simulation and Visualization Systems

Many architectural simulators with a wide variety of capabilities have been written. The lowest-level systems — circuit simulators (such as SPICE or those simulating VHDL or Verilog models) — simulate real circuit delays, limited voltage levels, and competing drivers but are very slow and are more relevant to electronic design courses than the higher-level architecture courses targeted here. Higher-level "cycle accurate" simulators (SimpleScalar is a widely known recently developed example; Austin, Larson, & Ernst, 2002) are designed to compare the impact on performance of new architectural features. Thus they aim to simulate streams of tens of millions of instructions as quickly as possible and are more concerned with producing operational statistics than visualizing individual steps. A host of simulators for simple microprocessors have been written with a single target architecture in mind, for example, Lovegrove's (1996) Motorola 6800 simulator; these tools target introductory computer organization courses which cover assembly language programming and basic processor operation. Similar tools for specific, but more complex processors are available, for example, Clarke, Czezowski, and Strazdins's (2001) SPARC tool. Debuggers (e.g., gdb) and emulators also provide instruction-by-instruction execution with the ability to examine register and memory content as each instruction is executed, but their focus is on the output of instructions — not the individual steps of the micro-architecture that led to that output so that pipelines, caches, and many other performance-enhancing devices are transparent to them.

An existing animation system (Morris, 2004b), designed for visualizing the steps in computer algorithms, had been built as a toolkit of Java classes. The toolkit approach allows many of the lessons learned in the design of those algorithm animations, as well as some thoroughly tested classes, to be exploited in designing a new system. An alternative design strategy uses a higher-level language, specifically designed for the target application. Although this approach is common and superficially attractive because the high-level features of the language allow some types of applications to be written very quickly, it lacks flexibility. The high-level language inevitably has a large amount of domain knowledge built into it, reducing its ability to handle new scenarios — even some in the target application domain. The toolkit approach requires no new knowledge other than the ability to write in a standard, common language (Java in this case) and to read specifications for the classes making up the toolkit. Thus, although the work to create a new animation is slightly larger, the ability to add new features or capabilities is not constrained — an animator can do anything that Java will allow. Use of Java also makes meeting requirements (a) Web-based, (c) modular, and (d) configurable (on the fly using Java's dynamic class loading capability) simple. A similar approach was adopted by Miller, Seila, and Xiang (2003) to build their JSIM Web-based simulator.

Animation Framework

The basic animation framework builds on a core of animation support classes designed for animating algorithms — for example, quick sort and Kruskal's — commonly taught in computer science courses (Morris, 2004a, 2004b). It provides

- menus for selecting data sets,
- controls for animation rates,
- start, stop, step, and skip buttons,
- a standard layout with drawing panel, commentary box, and so forth

and methods associated with all these objects, for example, a method to "mark" a point in an animation to which it will proceed once the step button is pressed, methods to open files selected as input data sets (these files follow some simple format rules, in particular, the first line contains the text used for the menu item), and so forth. In addition, the animation toolkit provides classes for drawing

- boxes, arrows, arcs, and so forth,
- labels associated with objects, and
- simple graphs, bar displays, histograms, and so forth.

A Trajectory class defines a path along which an object will move during the animation and handles the detail of calculating the next position, erasing the object at its old position and redrawing it at the new one, and so forth. Initially, the toolkit grew rapidly as new animations provided new requirements, but it has

Figure 1. Simulation in progress

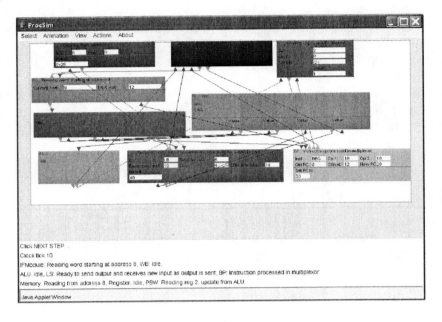

now reached the point where new animations can be created with few demands for new capabilities being encountered.

This toolkit has proved to be an efficient way of generating algorithm animations; students in data structures and algorithms classes are able to create new ones as class exercises. Several new ones were added to the basic collection by a class of about 20 students at ChungAng University (Seoul) as the final assignment of a one-semester course; their efforts may be seen on the University of Auckland site (Morris, 2004a). It has also been used to develop animated course materials to support courses in control structures and basic electronics at the University of Western Australia. A minor aim of the current project was to determine whether the basic framework (the classes for creating the main drawing panel and associated controls) was adequate for this application. The animation framework, including a running simulation, may be seen in Figure 1.

Processor Animation

One of the challenges of adapting the animation toolkit to handle processor simulation was the large number of operations which happen concurrently in a

Figure 2. (a) Class hierarchy (b) Processor module showing the major interface methods

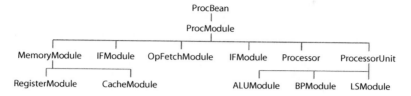

(a)

```
ProcModule
  implements ProcBean
-----------------------------
initialize()
processClockEvent()
boolean isBusy()
draw(Graphics g)
expandWhenClicked()
getInputEnabled(int port_index)
```

(b)

modern processor. Since the visualization was intended to show the correct logical operation of a processor, accurate simulation of circuit delays (a requirement of circuit simulators) was not necessary here. Equally, it was not realistic to ignore circuit delays altogether. The compromise adopted here was to assume that all circuits operate with some identical, fixed delay which was less than the clock cycle time. This is equivalent to assuming that the circuits operate without electrical races. However, logical races, such as those caused by trying to read a register in the same cycle as it is written, will still be present. From a teaching point of view, illustrating these hazards is one of the principal aims of the simulator.

Clocked Pipeline Simulation

This section describes the mechanisms used by the visualization system to emulate the behavior of a real clocked pipeline. Users write Java classes to

Figure 3. Processor pipeline showing computation blocks and registers. Note that the processClockEvent *method invocation latches computed values and corresponds to the global clock; invoking* processInput *causes the computation blocks to compute new values. The lower section shows the relation (in time) between method invocations and the clock signal.*

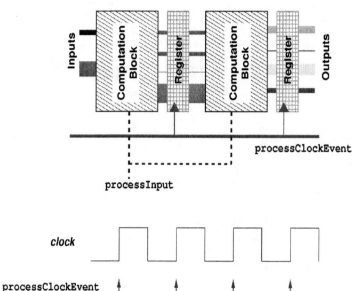

model the behavior of individual modules in the system. These modules provide (logical) input and output ports for signals, clock, and busy signals. Formally, Java classes modeling processor modules are specializations of (inherit from) the ProcModule abstract class, which implements the ProcBean interface. This formal structure ensures that new modules, which are dynamically loaded as a configuration file is read, all function correctly. The ProcBean interface contains specifications for vital methods needed by all modules:

- initialize: this method is passed a string found in the configuration file which may specify parameter values (e.g., memory size), a file to be read (e.g., containing initial contents of a memory), and so forth;
- getBoundingBox: returns the bounding box for drawing this module;
- addInputSource: adds a connection to an input (used in the configuration process);

- `addOutputListener`: adds a "listener" (module receiving input from this module) to an output port;
- `draw`: invoked to draw this module;
- `expand`: invoked when a user clicks on a module to expand it;
- `outputChange`: invoked when a source for this module has changed its output;
- `disableOutput`: disables an output (tri-states a driver);
- `processClockEvent`: invoked when a clock edge is received; and
- `processInput`: invoked mid-cycle (cf. Figure 3) to calculate new outputs.

Some additional methods required for drawing, getting, and setting attributes are also specified.

The abstract class `ProcModule` provides all the common attributes of modules (label, position, bounding box, latency, lists of inputs and outputs, internal modules, etc.) and default implementations of some methods in the `ProcBean` interface. This provides some core capabilities and saves considerable amounts of repetitive programming; writers of new modules can use the default implementations if they are appropriate (or to make a "fast start" to a functional, if not elegant, system). The new module writer only overrides (writes special versions of) a method if the capabilities of the new module require it. Some additional methods in `ProcModule` are defined as abstract methods which must be implemented by actual module implementations. Figure 2(a) shows the class hierarchy. Note that additional hierarchies of modules have been specified, for example, the `MemoryModule` and `ProcessorUnit` "trees." This facilitates the writing of new modules which share capabilities with existing modules; the new module is defined as a specialization of an existing one, and the module writer only needs to rewrite methods which have changed behavior.

Clocked pipelines operate in two basic phases: latching of data from input or previous stage and computing. To simulate this behavior, each functional module is sent two signals:

- `read`: read data from the preceding stage and
- `compute`: compute a new result from the inputs just read.

These two signals, the modules to which they are applied, and their relationship to the global clock are shown in Figure 3. Signal read emulates the latching of data in the output registers of the preceding module by a global clock edge. The data which is read in this phase has been computed by the preceding module in the previous compute phase. The controlling thread causes all modules to enter this phase by invoking the `ProcessClockEvent` method of each module. When a module contains a hierarchy of internal modules, then the `ProcessClockEvent` methods of the "container" modules invoke the `ProcessClockEvent` method of all their components. As with an actual clock signal, invoking `ProcessClockEvent` sends no information (other than the event itself) to each invoked module; each module reads its inputs through a list of references to modules to which it is connected. A module will also check a busy signal in each module to determine whether the sending module is asserting valid data — or whether it is still computing values that require multiple cycles. Bussed configurations are permitted, so multiple modules may be acting as sources for any port: at most, one should respond with valid data.

The "compute" signal is sent by invoking the `processInput()` method in each module. It takes the values of the inputs read in the read phase and computes new outputs. The new outputs are stored internally in logical output "registers" of each module, ready to be read in the subsequent read phase.

This two-phase protocol implemented with these simple calls provides cycle-accurate simulation (as provided by several full architectural simulators; Austin et al., 2002 Cain, Lepak, Schwartz, & Lipasti, 2002) in the absence of logic race conditions, that is, assuming that a processor clock has been set correctly. Without cycle-accurate simulation, many hazards cannot be exposed: instruction-by-instruction simulation as provided by, for example, software debuggers running in single step modes, which complete each instruction as an atomic operation and are not subject to the hazards that pipelines commonly introduce. Critically, without understanding hazards, students do not appreciate a key source of pipeline stalls and their effect on total instruction throughput. They also miss an understanding of the work that an optimizing compiler performs to reduce pipeline stalls or the purpose of register renaming.

A processor is "built" for visualization by creating a text configuration file which lists the individual modules and specifies their interconnections. An example is shown in Figure 4. Each line represents a module, starting with a label (allowing multiple instances of modules such as caches) and followed by the name of the class (which must be a specialization of ProcModule). The Java VM is used to load the code for the individual modules using this class name. The remainder of the line specifies connections to other modules and the location of the "port" for each connection on the icon for the module. Note that multiple connections to individual ports (busses) are allowed. Modules may load additional data from a text file using the argument in parentheses following the module (class) name. This string, usually a file name, is passed to the constructor and permits, for example, a common class to be used for several memory modules — all of which can be loaded with different initial data through this argument. However, this

Figure 4. Configuration file for a system with memory, IF unit, op fetch unit, ALU, load/store processor, branch processor, and write-back unit. Note that the PSW is configured as a separate module to simplify access by other modules; not all interactions are shown.

```
CONFIGURATION

Configuration File
m1  MemoryModule(mm.dat) (60,0) (200,10,10) (if1,L/S,WB(100,65)) (if1,L/S(130,65))
if1 IFModule (5,90) (1,200,5) [(m1,(75,90))(BP,(275,155))] [(m1,(55,90))(op1,(50,155))]
op1 OpFetchModule (10,180) (200,0,150) [(if1,(55,180))(rf1,(95,245))(rf1,(180,245))]
         [(rf1,(75,245))(rf1,(160,245))(ALU,(295,245))(L/S,(305,245))(BP,(315,24
         5))]
ALU ALUModule (20,280) (0,200,200) [(op1,(120,280))]
         [(WB,(105,365))(PSW,(115,365))]
L/S     LSModule (240,280) (200,0,200) [(op1,(360,280))(rf1,(315,365))(m1,(380,280))]
         [(rf1,(335,365))(m1,(340,280))(WB,(345,280))]
BP      BPModule (650,280) (200,200,0) [(op1,(670,280))(PSW,(680,280))]
         [(if1,(690,280))(PSW,(700,280))(WB,(710,280))]
rf1 RegisterModule(reg.dat) (400,135) (0,200,10)
         [(op1,(500,230))(op1,(590,230))(L/S,(680,230))(WB,(770,230))]
         [(op1,(520,230))(op1,(610,230))(L/S,(745,230))]
WB WBModule (350,0) (0,0,200) [(ALU,(360,65))(L/S,(380,65))(BP,(400,65))]
         [(rf1,(440,65))(m1,(420,65))]
PSW PSWModule(psw.dat) (610,0) (0,100,200) [(ALU,(620,95))(BP,(660,95))]
         [(BP,(640,95))]
```

argument is simply a Java string, so that it can be used to set one or more arbitrary parameters for the loaded module: memory sizes, operation modes, and so forth.

Once a configuration file is loaded, the modules and their connections are displayed. This visualization enables rapid verification that modules have been connected in the desired manner. The system also checks for errors in the configuration file, such as attempting to connect to nonexistent ports.

Since the configuration file is a simple text file, it can be easily edited by students or instructors to:

- change module parameters, for example, to reduce the size of a cache so that miss rates increase and the processing of misses can be studied; and

- add additional modules, for example, caches, branch predictors, buffers in system interface units, and so forth.

This allows students to experiment quickly with different configurations to compare the effect of adding (or removing) modules or changing their mode of operation. Thus, by preparing configurable models (generally a simple matter of good coding practice!), instructors can create a set of experiments designed to illustrate the concepts being expounded in formal classes.

Note that the "program" which the simulator runs is simply encoded as the contents of a memory module and stored in the initialization file for the primary memory. It is only necessary to ensure that a suitable instruction is placed at the standard processor bootstrap location.

Extensibility

The key to extensibility of this visualization system is the specification of individual modules conforming to a common specification — they must be specializations of the abstract `ProcModule` class. This allows new modules to be dynamically linked into the existing animation framework as the configuration file is read and classes representing modules in it are loaded by name. Students or instructors wishing to add new modules simply write a new specialization of the ProcModule class, compile it, and add an appropriate entry to a configuration file.

Working entirely from scratch, an undergraduate BE(SE) student was able to add a working cache module in an 8-week vacation work experience period. This exercise was undertaken while some experimentation with the core modules was still proceeding; using the experience gained, such an exercise would now require only half the time.

Visualizing Operation

As the simulator was built, it soon became obvious that all the detail that was needed to understand operation of a complex modern processor, for example, register and memory contents, instructions (as originally stored in memory and in decoded forms), and so forth would not fit in the available screen space. Accordingly, an additional operation was added — the ability to click on any module and pop up tables of internal detail, for example, register or memory contents, in a separate frame which can be moved to any part of the screen, resized, hidden, or closed as the student wishes. These frames are updated on every cycle as the processor "executes" instructions. By using separate frames, students are able to bring information that is currently relevant to the foreground, allowing the considerable mass of irrelevant detail to be removed from sight, thus conserving scarce screen real-estate for critical details.

Modules may also be designed as hierarchies of modules, so that structures such as memory management units which have internal "caches" (the translation look-aside buffers) may be examined in some detail if the student desires. These complex modules may be specified in their own configuration files; the configuration file entry for the enclosing module may specify the name of this configuration file as the constructor argument (cf. Configuration File subsection). As with memory modules, clicking on an expandable module causes a new frame showing the internal structure to appear. There is no limit to the number of levels of internal substructure which may be specified. Each frame acts as an independent display with inputs derived from modules in a parent frame and outputs similarly directed to the parent frame.

Current Capabilities

To date, this system is able to "execute" a subset of the MIPS instruction set, including most of the integer ALU instructions. Key branch instructions are also handled by a separate branch processor unit, mimicking the organization of several high-performance processors. Memory access is similarly handled through a separate load/store unit. The current implementation has four pipeline stages (instruction fetch, decode and operand fetch, ALU, and write-back) and so is able to illustrate basic pipeline operations. Memory modules with various latencies may be configured to demonstrate pipeline stalls caused by long latency operations. Modules with more than single-cycle latency (e.g., memory and ALUs for some operations) display a "countdown" timer, which counts down the latency (in cycles) and indicates when the module will produce a result. The effect of branch instructions on throughput is also able to be demonstrated naturally; the branch processor effectively stalls the pipeline as a new instruction is fetched from cache or memory.

Programs are fed to the visualization through memory configuration files. These are also simple, easily edited text files since, for teaching purposes, we want students to understand at various levels of detail how all the processor's modules interact as well as the effect that various modules, such as cache, have on overall performance. This simulator was not designed as an architectural simulator — well-developed packages such as SimpleScalar (Austin et al., 2002) were designed for this purpose — but rather as a visualization tool. Furthermore, the cost of visualization slows down the system too much for it to be able to execute the billions of instructions now expected of architecture simulators. However, anticipating limited demand for architecture simulation, a switch was provided to turn off graphical output and dramatically increase the rate of instruction processing!

Conclusion

This project started with a set of requirements for an effective tool for teaching the architecture of modern high-performance processors. The original set was modified slightly as the simulator was developed and evaluated, leading to the list in the Introduction section. It has met its initial aims of providing an extensible, cycle-accurate visualization of complex processor operation. The properties of a modern object-oriented language were used to set up a framework which ensures that modules written for the simulator properly implement the two phases — latching and computing — of a typical clocked pipelined processor. It also handles busses with multiple drivers and receivers correctly. Several "pattern" modules are now available, so it is anticipated that implementation of further capabilities should require only moderate programming effort.

The whole system is highly modular, and processors are simply configured in a transparent way — the visualization enables rapid verification that modules have been connected in the desired manner. Thus, simple experiments which demonstrate, for example, the effect of different cache organizations, are readily configured by instructors or students.

Success with the first student project to extend the system's capabilities suggests that this system will provide not only support to processor architecture classes but also software engineering projects for many years yet! Advanced computer architecture students will also be able to add experimental capabilities (in the form of new modules or modifications to existing ones) and perform simple experiments to assess their effect on processor performance.

Ongoing Work

Manual layout of the modules on the drawing panel is not a simple problem. Finding a placement that minimizes interconnection crossover and clutter is the key problem — and a known hard one (Batista, Eades, Tamassia, & Tollis, 1999). An intermediate solution is to allow users to lay out interconnection paths (in place of the direct connections made now), but this will require more effort in configuration. A simple drawing tool is probably the best answer; automatic layout is known to be a hard problem!

A full implementation of the ISA for a high-performance processor needs to be tested. Although the current implementation can demonstrate most pipeline-related phenomena, techniques to visualize some more subtle design problems, such as precise exception handling, have not been checked.

Acknowledgment

The majority of the classes in the original toolkit were written by Woi Ang. Individual students who wrote or extended animations are listed on the Data Structures and Algorithms Web site (Morris, 2004a). The core modules of this simulator were mostly written by Ivan Surya. A cache simulation module was added by Athena Wu.

Summary

This chapter described a Web-based modular and extensible processor simulator designed as an aid to teaching and leaning computer architecture. It is written in Java, which allows it to be easily embedded in other Web-based course materials and to run anywhere. Users configure a collection of Java classes which model individual processor modules. Java's dynamic class loading capability means that students in advanced classes are able to incorporate new modules by simply writing new classes and adding them to a configuration file which specifies the new modules' connections to other modules. The modular structure means that it can be used for both introductory computer organization and more advanced processor architecture courses. For example, it can be used to demonstrate how (a) the data path of a modern processor is structured, (b) pipelining keeps multiple instructions in flight at any time, (c) hazards occur, and (d) resource conflicts are resolved.

Processing modules follow a simple design pattern which correctly simulates the behavior of a complex synchronous processor. The design is simple, yet powerful enough to model complex data paths with extensive feedback capabilities. To manage complexity, the system being simulated may be specified as a hierarchy of models, each of which can be viewed in a separate window on demand. This provides a customizable level of detail to students studying processor operation.

Key Terms and Definitions

Cache: A small fast memory which stores recently used values so that they can be accessed faster than the bulk memory behind it.

Cycle-accurate: A simulator which models the operation of a processor on a cycle-by-cycle basis so that the state of the processor at the end of each cycle is correct.

Data path: The main path along which data flows in a processor; usually extends from an instruction fetch unit to a result write-back one.

Dynamic loading: The ability of a system to load additional software components (e.g., Java classes) as it executes.

Hazard: A situation in which a processor with multiple functional units could compute an incorrect value by using the wrong data if appropriate precautions are not taken.

Pipeline: An arrangement of functional models in a high-performance processor in which part of the computation is carried out in each stage of the pipeline. Data "flows" from one end of the "pipe" to the other.

Stall: A pipeline stalls when data is prevented from flowing from one stage to the other to avoid a hazard or while waiting for a long latency operation such as a memory fetch.

Synchronous: All operations are synchronized to a global clock.

Toolkit: A library of classes which model objects commonly required in animations; classes designed for reuse.

Review Questions

1.   List and describe three desirable features of a processor simulator.

2.   Discuss the usefulness of a processor simulator in teaching and learning contexts.

3.   Give three examples of circuit simulators.

4.   Describe the principle of operation of clocked pipeline.

5.   Explain how you would configure a collection of Java classes in modeling individual processor modules.

6.   List and describe possible enhancements to the proposed processor simulator.

References

Austin, T., Larson, E., & Ernst, D. (2002). SimpleScalar: An infrastructure for computer system modeling. *Computer, 35*(2), 59-67.

Batista, G. D., Eades, P., Tamassia, T., & Tollis, I. G. (1999). *Graph drawing: Algorithms for the visualization of graphs.* Upper Saddle River, NJ: Prentice Hall.

Cain, H. W., Lepak, K. M., Schwartz, B. A., & Lipasti, M. H. (2002). Precise and accurate processor simulation. In *5th Workshop on Computer Architecture Evaluation Using Commercial Workloads.*

Clarke, B., Czezowski, A., & Strazdins, P. (2001). Implementation aspects of a SPARC V9 complete machine simulator. *Conferences in Research in Information Technology, 9,* 23-32.

Lovegrove, W. P. (1996). A microprocessor trainer simulator. In *FIE '96, IEEE* (pp. 506-509).

Miller, J. A., Seila, A. F., & Xiang, X. (2003). The JSIM Web-based simulation environment. *Future Generation Computer Systems, 17,* 119-133.

Morris, J. (2004a). *Algorithm animations.* Retrieved from www.cs.auckland .ac.nz/software/AlgAnim/alg_anim.html

Morris, J. (2004b). A toolkit for algorithm animation. In *Proceedings of AEESEAP Mid-Term Conference,* Auckland, New Zealand (pp. 150-155).

Perez, D. G., Mouchard, G., & Temam, O. (2004). Microlib: A case for the quantitative comparison of micro-architecture mechanisms. In MICRO-37: *Proceedings of the 37th International Symposium on Microarchitecture* (pp. 43-54). IEEE Computer Society.

Schnarr, E., & Larus, J. R. (1998). Fast out-of-order processor simulation using memoization. In *Proceedings of the 8th International Conference on Architectural Support for Programming Languages and Operating Systems* (pp. 283-294). ACM Press.

Chapter XV

A Remotely Accessible Embedded Systems Laboratory

Steve Murray, The University of Technology Sydney, Australia

Vladimir Lasky, The University of Technology Sydney, Australia

Abstract

To teach modern embedded systems including operating systems in a meaningful way, a moderately sophisticated processor is required to demonstrate many key concepts, such as multitasking, multithreading, a structured and abstracted hardware management layer, communications utilising various protocols over network interfaces, and memory resident file systems. Unfortunately, high-end 32-bit embedded systems processors capable of supporting these facilities are expensive compared to conventional 8-bit and 16-bit targets, and it is not feasible to acquire a large number of them to house in a laboratory in an effort to enable practical exercises for over 100 students. This chapter describes the development and use of a remotely accessible embedded systems laboratory that uses a small number of 32-bit development systems and makes them available to students over the Internet.

Learning Objectives

After completing this chapter, you will be able to:

- Discuss the usefulness of a remotely accessible embedded systems laboratory in teaching and learning contexts.
- Define the following key terms: embedded computer system, multitasking, and multithreading.
- Suggest further enhancements to practical activities proposed in the chapter.

Introduction

In 2001, the Information and Communications Group in the Faculty of Engineering at the University of Technology, Sydney, decided — after surveying industrial trends — to focus upon embedded computer systems as a basis for case studies and application areas in which to demonstrate theoretical concepts. In particular the undergraduate subject 48450 Real-Time Operating Systems strove to differentiate itself from computer science and IT-styled subjects in that area by using embedded computer system hardware platforms. To demonstrate many of the concepts that are essential to a modern operating system, for example, multitasking, multithreading, a structured and abstracted hardware management layer, communications utilising various protocols over network interfaces, and memory resident file systems, a moderately sophisticated processor is required. Unfortunately, high-end 32-bit embedded systems processors capable of supporting these facilities are expensive when compared to conventional 8-bit and 16-bit targets, and it is not feasible to acquire a large number of them to house in a laboratory in an effort to enable practical exercises for over 100 students. Instead, a remotely accessible embedded systems laboratory has been constructed which uses a small number of 32-bit development systems and makes them available to students over the Internet. Students can use them in the conventional way following a development path that commences with cross-development and concludes with testing on the 32-bit target and viewing the results.

Background and Motivation

Embedded computer systems in use worldwide constitute a very large market in comparison to that of personal computers and workstations (In-Stat/MDR, 2002). Computer systems engineering and software engineering graduates with their knowledge of microprocessor and microcontroller hardware are arguably the best equipped to serve the needs of this high-volume market. Developing software for an embedded computer system involves certain idiosyncratic difficulties, however — in particular, cross-development. When constructing a laboratory designed to facilitate cross-development, it is conventional practice to have a large number of pairs of directly connected development systems and embedded targets. Individual students write programs on a development system, then transfer the executable program via a communication channel of some sort (serial data transfer via a cable or infrared, or perhaps a packet-based protocol using an Ethernet interface, or by sharing memory where the target card is installed on the host's bus) to the target adjoining, and then assess the success or failure of the developed code by observing the behaviour of the target as the program runs.

This development cycle is particular and intrinsic to the construction of embedded systems, and it would be remiss of any educator to dilute the experience by attempting to reduce support costs and complexity via simulation. A collection of real cross-development systems that can be shared from remote locations is one way of efficiently making these experiences available to students.

A representative collection of examples of existing remote cross-development systems is described next.

The Remote Experiment Lab (RExLab)

The Remote Experiment Lab (RExLab) is an embedded systems laboratory located at the Federal University of Santa Catarina, Brazil (Marques, Wisintainer, & Alves, 1998). The laboratory allows students to perform experiments remotely with devices based on the popular 8051 series of microcontrollers. The students are able to write programs in 8051 assembly language, upload assembled code to the laboratory to be executed remotely, and view the contents of registers and internal memory. The system consists of several components:

- A development board containing an 8051 microcontroller and auxiliary components that allow communication between the microcontroller and the PC;

- Client software (RExLab-Client), which loads the user's compiled binary and transfers it to the server to be executed; and
- Server software (RExLab-Server), which receives the information from the client, forwards it to the 8051, and sends the requested result back to the client.

Both the user client and the server software are custom applications written in Borland Delphi but make use of some libraries that support the user interface and standard TCP/IP communications. Marques et al. (1998) do not explicitly state how many such development boards are available for remote use by students, and the system does not appear to support time limits on access.

The Virtual Automation Laboratory

The Virtual Automation Laboratory at the University of Tübingen (Bühler, Küchlin, Gruhler, & Nusser, 2000) is a Web-based interactive learning environment for both computer science and automation engineering students. It was launched as an initiative from the Baden-Württemberg state government that encouraged the development of virtual universities. The automation engineering content is mainly concerned with learning about devices connected by controller area network (CAN) bus networks, whilst the computer science content is concerned with both programming language and operating systems concepts, such as OOP in Java, network communication, client/server systems, and middleware. Whilst one of the experiments provided in this project is a simulation, there are two others that involve work being performed using a remote laboratory. This remote laboratory infrastructure consists of a server which acts as a bridge between the Internet and some CAN bus experimental apparatus. There are currently two types of CAN bus-connected hardware installed: a video-monitored LED display board in which individual characters can be switched on and off and a static industrial robot arm which has a number of monitoring cameras at various positions. The user interface is provided by a Java applet that is downloaded from the main Web site. No proprietary software is required on the user side, and no browser plug-ins are needed to access the devices via the Internet. Details of an arbitration capability are not clearly specified, but users are given a limited time in which equipment can be used, implying that a queuing system of some kind is used.

Distance Learning Applied to Control Engineering Laboratories: Oregon State University

Aktan, Bohus, Crowl, and Shor (1996) describe a remote laboratory used for control engineering experiments at Oregon State University in the United States. This paper is highly influential; it has been cited by most of the other papers on remote laboratories and was responsible for inspiring aspects of the system developed at the UTS. The first part of their paper discusses the economics, logistics, and presentation criteria that should be considered when selecting an experiment to be adapted for remote use. The logistic criteria are significant, for example, having the ability for a remote laboratory to run without human intervention and having a stable start state or reset position from which a new experiment can be commenced. The second section of the paper describes an implemented remote laboratory used for control engineering experiments. The experiment involves remotely controlling and monitoring a robot arm. Students using a client application called Second Best to Being There (SBBT) are able to develop, compile, debug, and run controllers in real time. In addition, the software provides live audio and video monitoring of the robot arm and collaboration with fellow students via text messaging and an online whiteboard. The work that was performed was quite remarkable considering the year in which it was developed (1996). This was before Web cameras (Webcams) were accessible consumer items, standards for audiovisual streaming over the Internet were in their infancy, and available levels of bandwidth were lower. The laboratory avoided the need for users to download a special client by using X Windows Java applets that were just being introduced at the time. The SBBT client could execute on any UNIX server, and students could view the console output on any computer with an X Windows server. The drawback of this technology was the bandwidth requirement — productive work had to be done from somewhere on the local network. The implementation places a great deal of emphasis on collaboration and communication between fellow students — the arbitration system does not impose time limits on sessions or provide automatic scheduling; instead, students must communicate with each other online and negotiate their turn to use the equipment. It was intended "that students may linger and talk about their findings, help each other, and form collegial relationships." As the laboratory has moving parts (due to the presence of the robot), additional interlocks had to be included to guarantee safety of passersby.

A Distance Learning Laboratory for Engineering Education

Knight and DeWeerth (1997) describe a remote laboratory at the Georgia Institute of Technology used for teaching graduate electronic circuit classes. Their system is an interactive remote testing system that operates over the Internet. The user interface consists of a Java applet designed to recreate the "look and feel" of a laboratory bench fitted with equipment. The interactive remote testing system displays the front-panel controls of each instrument in its own optionally visible window, allowing the user to see only the instruments. Measurement data from the laboratory equipment is fed back to the user in real time. The infrastructure consists of a device under test (DUT), which is connected to a set of general purpose interface bus (GPIB)-controlled test instruments via a switching matrix. A remote user can extract data from the DUT by configuring the matrix and stimulus instruments and then querying response instruments. The laboratory implements robust arbitration functionality — when the user logs into the laboratory via the testing applet, all the instruments and the user interface controls are set to a known initial state. Each command or command group sent to a specific instrument is followed by an acknowledge request. An instrument is only considered synchronised when all of its pending requests have been answered by the laboratory server. A scheduling system is also implemented. On the Web page, users can reserve blocks of time in the laboratory in advance. If resources have not been previously reserved, the laboratory is available on a first-come, first-served basis. The system maintains open network connections to all users waiting to use the laboratory equipment and updates each user with the queue status continuously. It must be noted that as the laboratory only has a single testing station, the implementation of arbitration is relatively straightforward, and the system is of smaller scale than others evaluated here, being designed to support less than 20 clients.

Summary of Surveyed Examples

Some organisations had comparatively large budgets with which to investigate and develop remotely accessible laboratories. Regrettably, this is not universal. Some laboratories had grand aims and represented a significant commitment by the participants, whereby others were more modest in their capabilities and intentions. Some laboratories did not have a structure that encouraged scalability (either vertical or horizontal). This naturally tends to limit their ability to meet fluctuating demand.

One other important quality of any system which might be used to support remotely accessible laboratory apparatus is that it should ensure it is completely indifferent to any analysis, design, and testing methodologies which might be used by the students. It should not influence in any way their approach to problem solving and should be completely transparent in this respect. By placing emphasis on a technique whereby the remotely accessible laboratory is viewed as infrastructure which simply transfers the students' senses from their remote location to the laboratory, it is most unlikely that any unintentional and harmful side effects of this nature would be introduced.

Description of the System

The Remotely Accessible Embedded Systems Laboratory has been developed for use by students of the undergraduate Real-Time Operating Systems course at the UTS. The laboratory is comprised of a collection of 12 senTec CO-BRA5272 development boards (senTec Elektronik GmbH, Ilmenau, Germany) based on a Motorola Coldfire architecture, a popular 32-bit embedded systems platform used in industry.

Experiments performed by the students to date have covered a number of operating systems concepts, including memory management on embedded architectures (which must be managed without hardware support), POSIX programming, embedded client-server systems, and kernel device driver development. Students are able to use the laboratory from any Internet-connected

Figure 1. SenTec COBRA5272 target processor development board

Figure 2. Example of remote user's view

location. In the spring 2003 semester, the laboratory was shared by over 150 students. The ultimate aim of the laboratory is to be "the next best thing to being there."

User Facilities

- **User Interface**: The system is accessed by starting a command-line terminal client on any PC and logging in to the master server, which is running a distribution of the Linux operating system. Users have their own personal accounts with private home directories to store their work. Installed on the system are various engineering application programs and the widely used GNU development suite. It is intended to extend the students' skills base by promoting UNIX literacy. In this respect, the log-in to a shell account is completely indistinguishable from any other UNIX environment, which assists in making students feel comfortable with the system.

- **Device access and real-time debugging**: Students are able to remotely compile, upload, and debug programs interactively on the development boards.

- **Fair sharing of boards**: The arbitration system guarantees each student their fair share of time to use the system. When the system is busy, students are placed in a queue to wait for an available board. Time limits are tailored by the academic staff to suit anticipated development times and are imposed to prevent other students from hogging resources.

- **Video monitoring**: Video monitoring of peripherals connected to the target processors permits users to perform experiments on connected peripherals and see the results in real time over the World Wide Web. The user can open a Web browser on their PC and connect to the master server, which — after log-in — will permit them to specify which video format they would prefer. Video is available in several standard formats to ensure wide availability:

  ➢ Multipart JPEG (400 kbps) provides lowest latency for those accessing the Internet from university laboratories or broadband connections outside the university. A Java client is available that can execute on any computer with a Java-enabled browser.

  ➢ Windows Media Player MPEG4 encoded video (40 kbps) provides support for those who are connecting to the Internet via dial-up with 56 kbps modems.

  ➢ Still JPEG Snapshots are also available when motion video is not needed or when bandwidth must be conserved.

Administrator Facilities

- **Fair sharing of boards**: Staff may set time limits on system usage that can be tailored to suit system load and the proximity of submission deadlines for practical work. This ensures that all students are given an equal opportunity to share use of the system.

- **Account administration**: The system can use enrolment information from UTSOnline (the university portal to student access to all teaching- and learning-related resources), which helps to automate enrolments at the start of the academic semester, avoiding painstaking manual account creation. Account names and passwords are automatically assigned and e-mailed to the students' registered e-mail addresses.

- **Support**: Although this system is able to function completely independently from other computer-based learning environments and tools, it provides a highly effective collaborative learning environment when combined with UTSOnline discussion boards and virtual classrooms. Short turnaround times are possible for student queries as staff can assist by logging in to the development system from any location and providing advice.

- **Dynamic removal and addition of devices**: Individual development boards and board servers can be removed or installed at any time when the system is live to allow repair or replacement or expansion.

Architecture

The hierarchy consists of a number of systems with different roles:

- **Master server**: The master server is the central point of access to the system. Users log in to the master server using Secure Shell (SSH). The master server stores user home directories and all tools and documentation required for development and laboratory tasks. The arbitration system, which is the primary system-management program, is based in this server and is responsible for allocating users to development boards, which are connected to the board servers. The master server runs the PostgreSQL database server to maintain tables containing user attributes (not all users are of the same class) and tables of data relating to the laboratory hardware and software configuration.

- **Board server**: The board servers are responsible for providing access to the individual development boards. Each board server can control up to four target processor boards; this limitation is introduced by the number of input/output (I/O) ports that the board servers offer. When a user commences a session, the arbitration program allocates the user to one of the board servers. Programs that require direct communication with the target processor boards — for example, the terminal emulator and the remote

Figure 3. Remotely accessible embedded systems laboratory topology

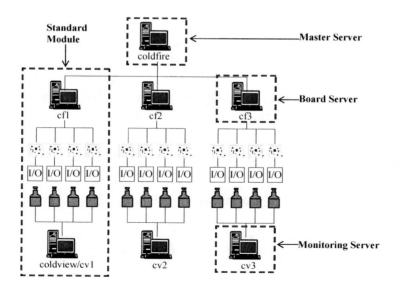

debugger — are then executed locally. The arbitration system makes this allocation process transparent to the users.

- **Monitoring server**: The monitoring servers provide live real-time video monitoring of devices over the World Wide Web. Each server is responsible for monitoring four development boards; this again is influenced by I/O port availability and to an extent by processing load on the monitoring server also. The first monitoring server coldview has a secondary role as the central Web server for the laboratory. From a Web page, visitors can view the arbitrator queue and observe the peripheral boards on any of the boards in the collection.

- **Standard module**: The combination of a board server, monitoring server, four target processor development boards, and four video cameras is called a standard module; hence, the laboratory currently has three standard modules. When or if it becomes necessary to add capacity, additional standard modules are added to the collection. Limits to this scalability have not been determined.

Usefulness and Benefits of the System

It is useful to examine the virtues of remotely accessible laboratories as a class of experimentation and learning infrastructure initially and then consider positive attributes of our chosen design.

The Case for Remote Laboratories

- **Convenience**: The laboratory can be accessed from any location with Internet access, such as homes, cafes, overseas locations, and other general-purpose university laboratories. The only equipment required is a modern network-enabled personal computer (PC) with a graphical Web browser and an SSH client; the freely available PuTTY (http://www.chiark.greenend.org.uk/~sgtatham/putty/) SSH client is suitable for Windows and is small enough to be carried on floppy disk.

- **Reduced demand upon real estate**: Equipment can be installed more densely as people will not be sitting at desks or standing next to benches. A lower level of occupational health and safety compliance is needed when laying out remote laboratories, making construction more flexible. Underutilised spaces can be used to make a contribution.

- **Reduced cost**: More efficient utilisation of resources means that less equipment has to be purchased to service the same number of students compared to an equivalent physical laboratory.

- **High availability**: The facility can be accessed whenever desired by both students and staff members.

- **Security**: Controlled access to conventional laboratory rooms certainly makes some progress in securing physical laboratories, but it is not infallible. A remote laboratory would not require students to be given any physical access. In addition, equipment can be placed in more secure locations, such as dedicated machine/server rooms or those with key access only.

- **Immune to physical misuse and vandalism**: Students have been known to vandalise equipment either out of malice for the subject or to force staff to provide extensions for laboratory exercises and assignments (A. Gibson, personal communication, September 1, 2003, and others). The architecture of a remote laboratory would ideally be designed to be immune or highly resistant to intentional misuse, hence, mitigating this risk.

- **Easily upgraded and modernised**: Equipment in a remote laboratory can be upgraded and replaced in stages. It may not even be necessary to shut down the laboratory whilst an upgrade is in progress. It is also possible to have a transition period where current and new equipment is accessible to allow for any technical hurdles or "teething problems" to be overcome; this situation is somewhat more easily controlled in a remotely accessible laboratory because equipment cannot be accessed by remote users unless the staff explicitly brings it online.

- **Scalability**: A well-implemented remote laboratory could be easily augmented with extra equipment to handle more students. Whilst this is also possible in a conventional physical laboratory, we contend that the bulk of this paper suggests with a remotely accessible laboratory it can be achieved more efficiently.

- **Enables distance education**: The range of university courses that can be undertaken by distance education is very limited in scope. Humanities-based courses traditionally dominate this field as they rely on reading and written communication (Open Learning Australia, 2003). Remote laboratories could make distance education for many science and engineering courses more practical.

The Case Against Remote Laboratories

There are also some identifiable limitations in the remotely accessible laboratory concept:

- **No face-to-face contact between students and staff**: Some students do not find the isolated environment optimal. To an extent this can be alleviated by suggesting that they access the remote laboratory from one of the university's PC laboratories, where the geography is somewhat more like a conventional physical laboratory.

- **Senses are not always transmitted perfectly**: The most realistic laboratory experience would be provided when human senses are conveyed to a remote location without any distortion. Technology in this field has developed substantially over the last decade, but it still has many limitations. Most of the effort in this field has been in audiovisual technologies. The status of these is briefly discussed:

- **Vision**: It is generally understood that images are transmitted over the Internet as static two-dimensional camera views. Using multiple cameras to provide several viewpoints is possible. Dynamic panning and movement is possible using motorised equipment, but it increases the costs of implementation substantially. Full-colour three-dimensional viewing requires special display equipment and is uncommon. The transmission of images over the Internet is susceptible to real-time delays in periods of high network traffic. Visual effects relying on persistence of vision of the human eye cannot be transmitted easily due to limited frame rates.

- **Hearing**: Audio transmission has progressed substantially with the development of compression algorithms that provide high fidelity but use a relatively low amount of bandwidth, for example, Moving Picture Experts Group Audio Layer 3 encoding (MP3). Sound is most commonly monophonic in nature, but software support for stereophonic and surround sound standards, for example, Dolby Pro Logic, is common. The only requirement is the availability of suitable sound hardware at the client side. The transmission of audio is also susceptible to delays in periods of high network traffic as is often experienced when using the Internet to make telephone calls. It is also sensitive to sporadic packet loss; unlike video, it is not possible to interpolate to make up for missing data.

Design Advantages in the Remotely Accessible Embedded Systems Laboratory

- **Low cost**: The system was designed to minimise construction and maintenance costs, primarily by setting out to efficiently utilise a relatively small number of development systems.

- **Minimised use of custom software**: The design attempts to avoid the use of custom software. Custom software is widely understood to be the weakest link in any complex system. The use of standard hardware and software components speeds up implementation and increases reliability (Hamlet, Mason, & Woit, 2001).

- **Maximised use of open-source software**: The system uses open source, freely available software technologies when possible, for example, Linux and PostgreSQL server. This relieves the UTS of the obligation to maintain and finance continued development of the software, while at the same time allowing the UTS to make enhancements which can be re-released to the general community in the spirit of the UTS's role as an educational institution. This also contributes to an overall reduction in cost since purchasing and licensing costs are removed.

- **Maximised use of off-the-shelf hardware**: The system uses off-the-shelf hardware conforming to popular, well-known standards for operating systems support, interconnection, and interoperability. Proprietary products have been avoided when possible.

- **Dynamic system**: The system is not monolithic; the implementation does not force the use of any specific technologies. It is dynamic in nature, and different components can be replaced and improved as new technologies are developed.

- **High availability**: Students can use the laboratory from any Internet-connected computer with a modern Java-enabled Web browser and freely available SSH client.

- **Efficient use of limited real estate**: Laboratory components do not have to be situated in the same room. They can be distributed over different rooms or even different countries, as long as each location has Internet access. This makes expansion more practicable as any free space within the university can be utilised.

- **High security**: The use of encrypted protocols such as SSH and HTTPS avoids the transmission of plain-text passwords over university networks, preventing security breaches through password "sniffing."

Evaluation and Interpretation

A system which poses such a dramatic departure from conventional physical laboratory infrastructure and modes of use naturally requires careful and continual assessment. This has been carried out over the past three years, and a considerable amount of effort has been directed at ensuring that the evaluation processes have been completed from every conceivable perspective.

Real-Time Operating Systems Assignments Completed by the Students

The remote laboratory has been highly successful. Students are applying theory learnt in the lectures and tutorials to a real-world environment. In the past, the students relied on special teaching operating systems which were frequently based only on PC hardware and possessed inherent limitations (Comer & Fossum, 1984; Tanenbaum & Woodhull, 1997). Assignment and practical work which is potentially hazardous to the health of the running operating system can be carried out without concern. For example, an experimental modification to the uClinux kernel that results in a damaged memory-based file system will not cause significant damage when tested on the target processor; whereas, it certainly has the potential to cause serious data loss if attempted on the student's own personal computer. Students are not restricted to carrying out relatively superficial programming assignments that involve only developing some user-space programs.

Student Feedback

The UTS Planning & Quality Unit (and its predecessors) has been responsible for administering a UTS Subject Feedback System (SFS) for a number of years. As part of this system, Subject Feedback surveys are issued to students in each UTS subject at the end of every academic semester as a single-page sheet. The sheet contains a set of standard questions relating to the subject in a general sense but also permits the student to make unstructured comments. In three semesters surveyed, the students returned mixed responses to the system. Some students reported having difficulty relating to the system they were using. In some cases these difficulties were attributed to the system being physically remote, making it difficult to visualise what it was they were actually doing with the system (Moulton, Lasky, & Murray, 2003). In subsequent semesters, the students were taken on a one-off guided tour of the remotely accessible embedded systems laboratory at an early juncture in the semester so that they could better appreciate their later interactions with the various components of the system. This helped those who were having some difficulty coming to terms with the abstractions.

Students throughout all semesters expressed comments stating strong appreciation of the practical nature of the exercises they had been able to complete. Some praised the hands-on nature of the assignments and stated that they believed that knowledge gained was industrially and commercially relevant. Many students had not had previous exposure to Linux or UNIX and were happy to have the chance to learn how to operate in this environment.

Tutor Feedback

In spring 2003, it was decided to begin a survey of academic staff tutoring the Real-Time Operating Systems subject. It was structured in a similar way to the Subjects Feedback surveys but included questions related directly to the remote laboratory and assignments. The tutors were unanimous in their opinion of online support being effective in supporting students, and all of them found to a significant degree that it reduced their normal support workload. It can be concluded that the academic staff were generally satisfied and enthusiastic about the environment. In the first written-answer question, all academics agreed that the convenience of being able to access the laboratory from anywhere was one of the best features.

The remotely accessible embedded systems laboratory has been recently made available to a small number of students to use in completion of their major undergraduate project. This further demonstrates the flexibility of the system and increases its utilisation. There is little overhead in providing project students with an account on the system and permitting them to work at their own pace on complex tasks over two semesters.

Conclusion and Future Directions

The remotely accessible embedded systems laboratory as used by the Real-Time Operating Systems course at the UTS is an invaluable resource. It exposes students to development processes which are outside of their normal experience and are relevant to industry needs. The students are able to conduct potentially complex programming tasks in a safe, convenient, and secure way — something which traditionally has only been available with vastly greater infrastructure and cost in a conventional physical laboratory.

As a testament to the solid design and development of this particular laboratory, the Faculty of Engineering at the UTS has embarked upon a program that aims at converting several other conventional physical laboratories to a remotely accessible mode (Weber, personal communication, 2003). The flexibility inherent in the original design of the remotely accessible embedded systems laboratory means that much of the infrastructure required will not have to be developed from scratch. Currently, two more remotely accessible laboratories are under development. One supports a development system for field programmable gate array (FPGA) devices, and the other entails controlling electromechanical and pneumatic apparatus via programmable logic controller (PLC) systems. It is anticipated that these will be online for the autumn 2005 semester.

Summary

A sophisticated processor is required to demonstrate the key concepts that are essential to a modern operating system, for example, multitasking, multithreading, a structured and abstracted hardware management layer, communications utilising various protocols over network interfaces, and memory resident file systems. Unfortunately, high-end 32-bit embedded systems processors capable of supporting these facilities are expensive compared to the conventional 8-bit and 16-bit targets, and also it is not always feasible to acquire a large number of high-end processors to house in a laboratory to provide practicals for more than 100 students. To overcome this problem, this chapter proposed a remotely accessible embedded systems laboratory. The proposed system uses a small number of 32-bit development systems and is accessible through the Internet so that students can use it in the conventional way following a development path that commences with cross-development and concludes with testing on the 32-bit target and viewing the results.

Key Terms and Definitions

Cross-development: The process of using software development tools like compilers, linkers, and debuggers which are resident on a reprogrammable computer to produce executable programs for an embedded computer system. The executable programs must then be transferred from the reprogrammable computer (called the development system) to the embedded computer (called the target system) for testing.

Embedded computer system: Computers that are comprised of a processor (microprocessor or microcontroller), memory, and I/O devices that are "special purpose" in that they are tightly coupled to or even architecturally a component of other systems with which they interact. Their primary I/O devices are usually not human-user-centric. Examples are regulators and controllers in domestic appliances and automotive systems, negative feedback automatic control systems in the chemical process industries, and autopilots for ships and aircraft.

Review Questions

1. List and describe three main features of the proposed remotely accessible embedded systems laboratory.

2. List and describe three main benefits of using the remotely accessible embedded systems laboratory.

3. Discuss the effectiveness of the remotely accessible embedded systems in teaching and learning contexts.

4. List and describe three existing remote cross-development systems.

5. Describe the topology of the remotely accessible embedded systems laboratory.

6. Discuss the possible enhancements to the practical activities in general and the remotely accessible embedded systems laboratory in particular.

References

Aktan, B., Bohus, C. A., Crowl, L. A., & Shor, M. H. (1996). Distance learning applied to control engineering laboratories. *IEEE Transactions on Education, 39*(3).

Bühler, D., Küchlin, W., Gruhler, G., & Nusser, G. (2000). The virtual automation lab—Web-based teaching of automation engineering concepts. In *Proceedings of the 7th annual IEEE International Conference on the Engineering of Computer Based Systems*. Edinburgh, Scotland, UK: IEEE Computer Society Press.

Comer, D., & Fossum, T. (1984). *Operating system design: The Xinu approach*. Englewood Cliffs, NJ: Prentice Hall.

Hamlet, D., Mason, D., & Woit, D. (2001). *Theory of reliability of software components*. Retrieved November 14, 2003, from http://www.cs.pdx.edu/~hamlet/icse01.pdf

In-Stat/MDR. (2002, September 10). *MCU market to experience unit growth through 2006 while prices erode*. Retrieved December 2004 from https://www.instat.com/newmk.asp?ID=325

Knight, C. D., & DeWeerth, S. P. (1997). *A distance learning laboratory for engineering education* (No. 1532). Southeastern University and College Coalition for Engineering Education. Retrieved from http://www.succeed.ufl.edu/papers/97/01316.pdf

Lasky, V. L. A. (2003). *Remote embedded systems laboratory* (Capstone Project Rep.). New South Wales, Australia: University of Technology, Sydney, Faculty of Engineering.

Marques, L. C. C., Wisintainer, M. A., & Alves, J. B. d. M. (1998). *Real remote experiment with 8051 microcontroller—RExLab.* Retrieved November 2003 from http://www.edatoolscafe.com/technical/papers/Rexlab/

Moulton, B. D., Lasky, V. L., & Murray, S. J. (2003). Remote embedded systems development environment: Feedback from students and subsequent enhancements. *UICEE World Transactions on Engineering and Technology Education, 2*(1).

Open Learning Australia. (2003). *OLA list of qualifications in 2003.* Retrieved November 2003 from http://www.ola.edu.au/cgi-bin/hive/hive.cgi?HIVE_PROD=0&HIVE_REQ=2001&HIVE_REF=hin%3aOLA%2003000PUB04%20DOC%20Content&HIVE_RET=ORG&HIVE_CMP=1

Tanenbaum, A. S., & Woodhull, A. S. (1997). *Operating systems design and implementation* (2nd ed.). Upper Saddle River, NJ: Prentice Hall.

Chapter XVI

LOGIC-Minimiser:
A Software Tool to Enhance Teaching and Learning Minimization of Boolean Expressions

Nurul I. Sarkar, Auckland University of Technology, New Zealand

Khaleel I. Petrus, University of Southern Queensland, Australia

Abstract

Boolean algebra, minimization of Boolean expressions, and logic gates are often included as subjects in electronics, computer science, information technology, and engineering courses as computer hardware and digital systems are a fundamental component of IT systems today. We believe that students learn minimization of Boolean expressions better if they are given interactive practical learning activities that illustrate theoretical concepts. This chapter describes the development and use of a software tool (named LOGIC-Minimiser) as an aid to enhance teaching and learning minimization of Boolean expressions.

Learning Objectives

After completing this chapter, you will be able to:

- List and describe three main features of LOGIC-Minimiser.
- Explain how LOGIC-Minimiser can be used in the classroom to enhance teaching and learning Boolean expression minimization.
- Describe the Q-M algorithm for the minimization of Boolean expressions.
- Define the following key terms: Boolean expression, SOP, logic gate, logic minimization, and K-maps.

Introduction

It is often difficult to motivate students to learn minimization of Boolean expressions because students find the subject rather abstract and technical. A software tool (named LOGIC-Minimiser) has been developed that gives students a hands-on learning experience in minimizing Boolean expressions. LOGIC-Minimiser was developed in C language under MS Windows and is suitable for classroom use in introductory Boolean algebra courses. Based on user input (i.e., logic expression), the system displays the sum of product (SOP) functions as well as minimized logic gate diagrams. Test results demonstrate the successful implementation of LOGIC-Minimiser, and the simplicity of the user interface makes it a useful teaching and learning tool for both students and instructors.

This chapter describes the development of LOGIC-Minimiser and its usefulness as an aid to teaching and learning minimization of Boolean expressions. The chapter concludes with a discussion of the strengths and weaknesses of LOGIC-Minimiser and its future development.

Background and Motivation

Boolean algebra, minimization of Boolean expressions, and logic gates are essential concepts included in electronics, computer science, information technology, and engineering. These concepts play a fundamental role in computer hardware and digital systems design. We believe that it is extremely important to incorporate practical demonstrations into these courses to illustrate theoretical concepts and therefore provide an opportunity for hands-on experience. These demonstrations will significantly enhance student learning about Boolean expression minimization.

In fact, very little material has been designed and made available for public access to supplement the teaching of Boolean expression minimization. This is revealed by searches of the Computer Science Teaching Center Web site (http://www.cstc.org/) and the SIGCSE Education Links page (http://sigcse.org/topics/) on the Special Interest Group on Computer Science Education Web site. We strongly believe, as do many others (Bem & Petelczyc, 2003; Hacker & Sitte, 2004; Ibbett, 2002; Leva, 2003; Shelburne, 2003; Williams, Klenke, & Aylor, 2003), that students learn more effectively from courses that provide for active involvement in hands-on learning activities.

Boolean expression minimization is one of the most challenging subjects to teach and learn in a meaningful way because students find the topic full of technical jargon, dry in delivery, and quite boring. Sarkar, Petrus, and Hossain (2001) have developed LOGIC-Minimiser in C under MS Windows to give students an interactive, hands-on learning experience in minimization of Boolean expressions. LOGIC-Minimiser can be used by a teacher in the classroom as a demonstration to enhance the traditional lecture environment at an introductory level. Also, students can use the system in completing tutorials on Boolean expression minimization and to verify (interactively and visually) the results of in-class tasks and exercises on Boolean expression minimization. LOGIC-Minimiser can be used either in the classroom or at home as an aid to enhance teaching and learning Boolean expression minimization.

Minimization of Boolean expressions using traditional methods such as truth tables, Boolean algebra, and K-maps can be very tedious and is not well-suited for expressions involving more than six variables. A more useful approach, the Quine-McCluskey (Q-M) algorithm, also called tabular method, is an attractive solution for minimizing complex Boolean expressions involving variables of any length. Moreover, the algorithm lends itself to a fast and easy machine implementation.

The remainder of the chapter is organized as follows. First we examine various open source software tools suitable for logic-gate design and minimization. We then describe LOGIC-Minimiser in teaching and learning contexts. Then, software implementation of LOGIC-Minimiser is discussed, and the educational benefits of the software are highlighted. An example of a classroom plan and LOGIC-Minimiser in practice is discussed. Test results which verify the successful implementation of LOGIC-Minimiser are presented, followed by a conclusion and future research directions.

Related Work

A detailed discussion of digital systems design and minimization of Boolean expressions in general can be found in Green (1985), Greenfield (1977), Mano (1984), and Tanenbaum (1999). The Quine-McCluskey algorithm is described extensively in the computer hardware and digital logic design literature (Carothers, 2003; Costa, 2004; Hideout, 2003; Hintz, 2003). Grimsey (2000) examined the strengths and weaknesses of various methods of minimizing Boolean expressions, including truth tables, Boolean algebra, and Karnaugh maps (K-maps).

A variety of open source and commercial software tools exist for modelling and simulation of logic circuit design and Boolean expression minimization. These powerful tools can have steep learning curves; while they may be good for doing in-depth performance modelling of computer hardware and logic design, they often simulate a hardware environment in far more detail than is necessary for a simple introduction to the subject.

Lockwood (2003) presented a program for the implementation of the Q-M algorithm. However, it is of limited use as a teaching and learning tool because of its text-based interface that is not user-friendly. Leathrum (2003) described another text-based menu-driven program for the Q-M algorithm, but the user interface is rather difficult to use. Costa (2004) developed a package called "bfunc" for Boolean functions minimization. It is an MS-DOS-based program and is considered an alternative to the K-map method of simplifying Boolean functions. Burch (2002) proposed a tool named Logisim, a graphical system for logic circuit design and simulation which is suitable for classroom use. Logisim is a Java application and can be run on both Windows and Unix workstations. While Logisim is an excellent tool for building a variety of complex combinational circuits, but it is not suitable for logic gate minimization. Other tools such as Digital Works 3.0 (2001) and LogicWorks (1999) are similar to Logisim in that they provide a graphical toolbox interface for composing and simulating logic circuits. LOGIC-Minimiser, which we describe in the next section, has its own unique features, including simplicity and ease of use either in the classroom or at home, to enhance teaching and learning Boolean expression minimization.

Architecture of LOGIC-Minimiser

Figure 1 shows the structured diagram of LOGIC-Minimiser. The main features of LOGIC-Minimiser are briefly described.

Figure 1. Structured diagram of LOGIC-Minimiser

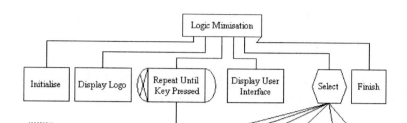

- **New**: This feature allows users to enter a new set of variables for minimization.

- **Min/Out**: This feature allows users to view a minimized sum of product (SOP) expression and logic circuit diagram.

- **Quit**: This feature allows users to exit from the program at any time.

The following three features have not been implemented yet and are considered as future work.

- **Load**: This feature will allow users to view existing data (i.e., minimized minterms) for further analysis and modifications.

- **Save**: This feature will allow users to store outputs on disk for later use and further modifications.

- **Help**: This feature will provide help on various topic related to minimization of Boolean expressions.

Software Implementation

The Q-M algorithm is used to reduce a Boolean expression to its simplest form. It is designed particularly for use with problems containing six variables or more but can be used equally well for a smaller number of variables. The algorithm is based on repeated applications of the distributed law and the fact that XOR

(NOT X) is always true. The Q-M method is a systematic way of selecting the pairs to be used for simplification. The main steps in the Q-M algorithm are summarized below:

1.   Representing all addends as sums of minterms
2.   Grouping the minterms that have the same number of ones
3.   Merging the terms that differ in only one bit (this is done in several steps)
4.   In order to find the irredundant cover we use the min-cover algorithm:
     a.   Find all distinct minterms.
     b.   Find all essential prime implicants.
     c.   Find all the minterms that are covered by the essential prime implicants.
     d.   Remove all minterms and prime implicants found in (a)-(c).
     e.   Choose that prime implicant that covers most of the remaining minterms.
     f.   Repeat (d) until all minterms have been covered.

A structured analysis and design has been employed to design the package. C programming language under MS Windows has been used in the implementation.

Usefulness and Benefits of LOGIC-Minimiser

For simplicity and ease of use, it has been decided to implement LOGIC-Minimiser with a menu-driven, keyboard-based interface with a few menu options. The interface is self-explanatory, which makes the package well-suited for both students and teachers for classroom use. Therefore, the package can be an integral part of a 2-hour session for teaching and learning the Q-M method for logic gate minimization. An in-class task will be given to the students to produce a minimized logic diagram on paper. After a prescribed period of time (for example, 20 minutes), LOGIC-Minimiser will be introduced to the students on a step-by-step basis to verify their solution and learn more about minimization of Boolean expressions.

LOGIC-Minimiser provides the following main benefits:

- **Hands-on**: It facilitates an interactive, hands-on introduction to minimization of Boolean expressions.

- **Modelling**: It provides a simple and easy way to develop a variety of SOP functions and models. Students can experiment with minterms of various sizes and develop a sound knowledge and understanding of Boolean expression minimization.

- **Ease of use**: The use of a menu-driven interface makes LOGIC-Minimiser easy to use and a user-friendly tool. The software can be easily installed and run on any PC operating under MS Windows.

- **Economical/usefulness**: It enhances face-to-face teaching with online learning and can be used either in the classroom or at home to provide hands-on experience.

- **Robustness**: It was tested on various PCs across campuses and was found to be robust.

- **Challenging**: It provides an environment for students to test their knowledge on Boolean expression minimization.

Example of Classroom Plan

In this section we present a detailed lesson plan (2-hour session) which can be used in teaching and learning minimization of Boolean expressions using LOGIC-Minimiser. The learning outcomes focus on learning the Q-M algorithm as well as use of the software tool for verifying results of Boolean expression minimization. The lesson plan incorporates a number of resources and classroom activities, including revision of Boolean expressions, brainstorming, teaching, example, worksheet, demonstration of software package, and use of the package to verify the worksheet exercises.

Lesson Plan

Table 1 lists the learning outcomes, resources, and various activities that can be conducted in the classroom in teaching minimization of Boolean expressions effectively. It can be used for a 2-hour lecture session on the minimization of Boolean expressions. The lesson plan includes a guided worksheet (see Table 2) suitable for classroom use.

Table 1. Lesson plan (2-hour session with 10-minute break)

By the end of this session students will be able to:
• Outline steps in minimization of Boolean expressions using Q-M algorithm.
• Use LOGIC-Minimiser to verify the minimization of Boolean expressions.

Resources required	• LOGIC-Minimiser • Data Show • Computer Laboratory • Whiteboard • Worksheets

Time (minutes)	Activity
10	Quickly review of Boolean expressions
5	Brain storming (ask the class what they know about Boolean expression minimization)
15	Explain Q-M algorithm
5	LOGIC-Minimiser demonstration
15	Solve workout/example problems
10	Break
20	Worksheet Exercises (ask the class to work in pairs and solve worksheet exercises)
20	Use LOGIC-Minimiser and verify results of minimization (worksheet exercises)
10	Conclusion and checking learning outcomes

Review: What went well:	What could be improved:

How to Use the System

LOGIC-Minimiser is easy to use and can be run from any PC operating under MS-DOS/Windows. To run the package, the user can either double-click on "newqm.exe" or type "newqm" at the DOS prompt. The main steps of using this package (from Windows) are summarized below:

- **Run**: Double-click on "newqm.exe."

- **Entering minterms**: Select the New option to enter a new set of minterms. The user will be prompted for the number of variables to be used. After entering the appropriate number of variables, a matrix of cells with index numbers will appear on the screen. At this point the user can enter each minterm by selecting a cell by pressing the Enter key on the keyboard.

- **Accepting data**: When a set of minterms has been entered, press the F8 key to accept.

- **Display diagram**: The minimized logic-gate diagram can be seen on the screen in graphics mode. The user can zoom the diagram using the F1, F2,

Table 2. Boolean expression minimization worksheet

Consider the minimization of following logical function:

$$F = A.B.C.D + A.B.C.\overline{D} + A.B.\overline{C}.D + A.\overline{B}.C.D + \overline{A}.B.C.D + \overline{A}.B.C.\overline{D}$$

The above function can be written as:

$$F(A, B, C, D) = \sum (0,1,2,4,8,9)$$

Where 0, 1, 2, 4, 8, 9 are the decimal values of the minterms.
It is required to apply the minimization on this Boolean function with the use of Quine-McCluckey's algorithm, firstly by hand and then verify the solution using LOGIC-Minimiser.

Solution:

1. Write the first list as:

	A	B	C	D
0	0	0	0	0
1	0	0	0	1
2	0	0	1	0
4	0	1	0	0
8	1	0	0	0
9	1	0	0	1

2. Deduce the second list (You have to complete this list)

	A	B	C	D
0,1	0	0	0	-
0,2				
0,4				
0,8				
1,9				
8,9	1	0	0	-

3. Third list (You have to do it all yourself)

	A	B	C	D
0,8,1,9				

4. Now build the chart which relates minterms with the prime implicates as shown:

	0	2	4	8	9
$\overline{A}.\overline{B}.\overline{C}$	X	X			

5. Now use the LOGIC-Minimiser to cross check your solution.

and F3 keys for 100%, 50%, and 20% scaling, respectively. To go back to main menu, press the F10 key.

- **Display minterms and output**: Select the Min/Out option from the main menu to see the list of minterms (that have been entered) and the minimized output expression.

- **Exit from the program**: Select the Quit option from the main menu to exit from the program at any time.

Test Results

To evaluate the performance of LOGIC-Minimiser, the software has been installed on various PCs and tested with various Boolean expressions, each involving a different number of input variables. Then the test results were validated manually. Figure 2 shows a sample test result for four-variable (A, B, C, and D) Boolean expression minimization. The following minterms were entered from the keyboard: [0,2,3, 5,7,8,10,13,15], and the software produced the simplified logic-gate diagram as well as the output expression, as shown in Figure 2.

Evaluation

An earlier version of LOGIC-Minimiser had been presented at the National Advisory Committee on Computing Qualifications conference in Napier, New Zealand (Sarkar & Petrus, 2001). The discussion during the conference presentation was quite encouraging, and many staff members from various polytechnic institutions expressed their interest in using the package in their classes.

Figure 2. Example of four-variable minimization with minimized output expression and logic gate diagram

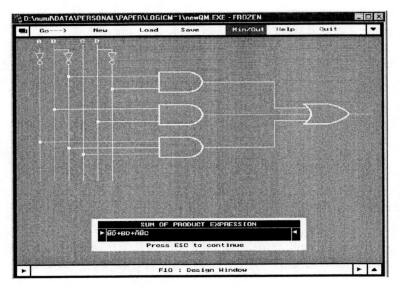

To assess the educational value of LOGIC-Minimiser, we administered a survey to the students of the introductory digital logic subject. The survey was repeated for two consecutive years. Overall results revealed that the majority of students found the package useful and user-friendly, with an overall rating of 4 out of 5.

The questionnaire also posed five open-ended questions: (1) How well did you understand minimization of Boolean expressions before entering this course? (2) How easy did you find the software package to use? (3) How well did the package help in understanding the minimization of Boolean expressions? (4) Would you like to have more software tools of this kind as part of your course? (5) Would you prefer to learn minimization of Boolean expressions in a hybrid mode (i.e., minimization by hand and verification of results by software tool)?

Concluding Remarks

A software tool (LOGIC-Minimiser) has been developed that can be used in the classroom to enhance the teaching and learning of various aspects of Boolean expression minimization. LOGIC-Minimiser is easy to use and can be run from any computer operating under MS-DOS and MS Windows. It was tested on various PCs and was found to be robust. Many staff members from various polytechnic institutions expressed their interest in using the software in the classroom.

Currently, the system minimizes Boolean expressions involving variables of size 8, which is adequate for demonstration purposes. LOGIC-Minimiser can easily be upgraded to accommodate variables of any length. User options such as New, Min/Out, and Quit have been implemented. More options such as Save, Load, and Help are still under development, and incorporation of a mouse-based user interface is also suggested for future work.

LOGIC-Minimiser is available free of cost to faculty interested in using it to supplement their teaching. More information about LOGIC-Minimiser can be obtained by contacting the first author.

Summary

Boolean algebra, minimization of Boolean expressions, and logic gates are essential concepts included in electronics, computer science, information technology, and engineering. These concepts play a fundamental role in computer hardware and digital systems design. We believe that it is extremely important to incorporate practical demonstrations into these courses to illustrate theoretical concepts and therefore provide an opportunity for hands-on experience. These demonstrations will significantly enhance student learning about Boolean expression minimization. This chapter described the development and use of LOGIC-Minimiser as an aid to enhance teaching and learning Boolean expression minimization. It was tested on various PCs and was found to be robust.

Key Terms and Definitions

Boolean expression: An expression which results in a Boolean (binary or TRUE/FALSE) value. For example 4 > 3 is a Boolean expression. All expressions that contain relational operators like >, <, and so forth are Boolean. Logical gates and their combinations are used to implement physical representations of Boolean expressions.

K-maps: This term refers to Karnaugh maps, a logical minimization method based on graphical representation of Boolean functions in which each row in the truth table of the Boolean function is represented as a box. Unlike the truth table, K- map values of input must be ordered such that the values of adjacent columns vary by one single bit.

Logic gate: An electronic device (based on transistors) used for implementing logical functions. The inputs and outputs of the gate are Boolean (i.e., binary) values. Gates can be used to implement various Boolean functions. NOT gates take one input and have one output. The AND, NAND, OR, and NOR gates may take two or more inputs and have one output. XOR gates take two inputs and have one output. Logical functions are all combinational functions, that is, their output depends on the input. Gates can also be used to implement latches and flip-flops which have an internal state and are used to implement sequential logical systems.

Logic minimization: Simplification of Boolean expressions with the aim of reducing the number of logical gates. This is done by reducing the number of minterms into a number of prime implicants in which as many variables as possible are eliminated. The tabular method makes repeated use of the rule $\hat{A} + A = 1$.

LOGIC-Minimiser: Software package developed at the Auckland University of Technology to enhance teaching and learning minimization of Boolean expressions. The package was implemented in C programming language.

Minterms: This term refers to the product of Boolean variables. These variables can appear either as themselves or their inverses. A minterm corresponds to exactly one row in the truth table of the Boolean function. If we have four variables A, B, C, and D, then a minterm can be something like A.B.C.D or .B.C.D, and so forth.

Quine-McCluskey algorithm: Table-based reduction method for simplification of Boolean expressions. This method is quite versatile as compared with other algorithms. It can handle any number of inputs and can easily be implemented on machines. The method starts from the truth table of the Boolean function.

Sum of product (SOP): A two-level expression which represents a sum of minterms of a logical function. It is two-level because it is implemented by two layers of logic gates. The first level represents the product of Boolean variables of the logical function and the second level represents summing the products with OR operator.

Review Questions

1. List and describe three main features of LOGIC-Minimiser.

2. Discuss the usefulness of LOGIC-Minimiser in teaching and learning contexts.

3. Describe the main steps in the Q-M algorithm for the minimization of Boolean expressions.

4. Define the following key terms: Boolean expression, logic gate, logic, minterms, and K-maps.

5. Explain how LOGIC-Minimiser can be used in the classroom for demonstration.

6. List and describe further enhancements to LOGIC-Minimiser.

References

Anonymous. (2006). Digital Works. Retrieved January 5, 2006, from http://www.spsu.edu/cs/faculty/bbrown/circuits/howto.html

Bem, E. Z., & Petelczyc, L. (2003, February 19-23). *MiniMIPS: A simulation project for the computer architecture laboratory*. Paper presented at the Proceedings of the 34th Technical Symposium on Computer Science Education (SIGCSE'03), Reno, NV (pp. 64-68).

Burch, C. (2002). Logisim: A graphical system for logic circuit design and simulation. *Journal of Educational and Resources in Computing, 2*(1), 5-16.

Carothers, J. D. (2003). *Quine-McCluskey algorithm.* Retrieved September 20, 2004, from http://www.ece.arizona.edu/~csdl/474aslide4

Costa, A. (2004). *Boolean functions simplification (logic minimization).* Retrieved December 27, 2004, from http://www.dei.isep.ipp.pt/~acc/bfunc

Green, D. C. (1985). *Digital techniques and systems* (2nd ed.). Longman.

Greenfield, J. D. (1977). *Practical digital design using ICs.* Wiley.

Grimsey, G. (2000). The truth, the whole truth, and/or nothing but the truth. *Journal of Applied Computing & Information Technology, 4*(1), 42-52.

Hacker, C., & Sitte, R. (2004). Interactive teaching of elementary digital logic design with WinLogiLab. *IEEE Transactions on Education, 47*(2), 196-203.

Hideout, G. (2003). *The Quine-McCluskey method of logic reduction.* Retrieved September 20, 2004, from http://www.geekhideout.com/qmm.shtml

Hintz, K. (2003). *Quine-McCluskey method.* Retrieved September 20, from *http://www.cpe.gmu.edu/courses/ece331/lectures/331_8/sld001.htm*

Ibbett, R. N. (2002, June 24-26). *WWW visualization of computer architecture simulations.* Paper presented at the 7th annual SIGCSE conference on Innovation and Technology in Computer Science Education (ITiCSE), Aarhus, Denmark (pp. 247).

Leathrum, J. F. (2003). *Quine McCluskey tabular minimization method.* Retrieved September 20, 2004, from http://www.ece.odu.edu/~leathrum/ECE241_284/support/quine.html

Leva, A. (2003). A hands-on experimental laboratory for undergraduate courses in automatic control. *IEEE Transactions on Education, 46*(2), 263-272.

Lockwood, J. W. (2003). *Quine-McClusky algorithm; computational techniques; cygwin freeware (GPL) tools.* Retrieved September 20, 2004, from http://www.arl.wustl.edu/~lockwood/class/coe460/

LogicWorks. (1999). *Capilano Computing Systems Ltd.* Retrieved January 10, 2006, from http://www.logicworks4.com

Mano, M. (1984). *Digital design.* Prentice Hall.

Sarkar, N., & Petrus, K. (2001, July 2-5). *Logic gate minimization demonstration*. Paper presented at the 14th annual conference of the National Advisory Committee on Computing Qualifications (NACCQ), Napier, New Zealand (p. 456).

Sarkar, N., Petrus, K., & Hossain, H. (2001, July 2-5). *Software implementation of the Quine-McCluskey algorithm for logic gate minimization*. Paper presented at the 14th annual conference of the National Advisory Committee on Computing Qualifications (NACCQ), Napier, New Zealand (pp. 375-378).

Shelburne, B. (2003). *Teaching computer organization using a PDP-8 simulator*. Paper presented at the SIGCSE'03 Technical Symposium on Computer Science Education (pp. 69-73).

Tanenbaum, A. S. (1999). *Structured computer organization* (4th ed.). Prentice Hall.

Williams, R. D., Klenke, R. H., & Aylor, J. H. (2003). Teaching computer design using virtual prototyping. *IEEE Transactions on Education, 46*(2), 296-301.

Section V

Data Communication Protocols and Learning Tools

Chapter XVII

A Practical Introduction to Serial Protocols

David L. Tarnoff, East Tennessee State University, USA

Abstract

This chapter discusses how addressing information, control information, and data are encapsulated in a serial packet or frame. It shows the bit-level detail of an IEEE 802.3 Ethernet frame, an IP packet, and a TCP packet and shows how these protocols are used to create a sample protocol stack. The GNU-licensed and Windows-based application Packetyzer is used to explore a sample TCP/IP packet contained in an Ethernet frame. Once the student has studied the material of this chapter and has completed the hands-on experiment, he or she will have the skills to examine any packet or frame and, using the description of its protocol, extract the details of the message.

Learning Objectives

After completing this chapter, you will be able to:

- Describe the Ethernet, TCP and IP packet structures.

- Describe using general terms what a protocol stack is and how it is important.

- Explain how a frame can be transmitted from one device to another across a serial link.

- Define the following key terms: CRC, datagram, data link layer, MAC address, and protocol.

- Suggest further enhancements to the practical activities presented in the chapter.

Introduction

Since the early days of computer system design, it has been necessary to develop communication schemes to allow the components of a digital system to exchange data. For example, the earliest mainframe computers used terminals as the standard method for user input and output. These terminals, connected either by direct connection or through a modem, used a single wire to transmit characters typed on the keyboard to the mainframe and a second wire to receive characters from the mainframe to be displayed on the user's screen. Any communication method where data is transmitted over a single wire is referred to as serial communications.

A number of different schemes have been developed for serial communications. These schemes are defined by a set of rules that must be followed by both the transmitting device and the receiving device in order to successfully transfer data. The set of rules defining a specific serial communication scheme is referred to as a protocol.

This chapter presents a general description of the components of a serial protocol. This is followed by an overview of three serial protocols: Ethernet, TCP, and IP. Finally, the Windows-based application Packetyzer is used to examine an Ethernet packet containing a simple TCP acknowledgment message. The methods presented here should allow for a basic understanding of some standard protocols and how they might be embedded within each other.

Anatomy of a Frame

Although parallel wires are capable of sending data at a higher throughput, sending data in a serial stream is by far the most common method of communicating between two physically separate computer systems. This is due to the physical nature of the connection. If fewer wires are needed to connect two devices, then both the connectors and the cables are much cheaper. In addition, when there are fewer connections to fail, the system becomes more reliable. Fewer connections also make for smaller connectors, aiding in the miniaturization of devices.

In order to communicate from one device to another, a number of pieces of information are needed. If more than two devices are present on a network, then addressing information for both the sender and receiver is required in order to uniquely identify them. Signals are also needed for control, such as synchronization (timing), message type, data length, and error detection. For some exchanges, it is also necessary to identify a message as being part of a specific session or sequence. Finally, while not all exchanges contain data, many do. Provisions must be available to identify where the data is located and how much of it there is.

In a parallel communication scheme, each of the types of information listed above is given a separate conductor or group conductors. This results in a bus consisting of tens or even hundreds of conductors. These conductors are separated into three groups: address, control, and data. One of the most common examples of parallel communications is the bus that a processor uses to communicate with the memory and I/O devices of the motherboard.

In serial communications, address, control, and data must all be sent across a single wire. To compensate for the fact that only one wire is available for all of the signals, a set of rules called a protocol is used to define timing and signal components. These definitions describe the basic unit of communication between serial devices. At the bit level, this basic unit is referred to as a frame. As the bits of a data transmission are sent out a device's communications port, their position within the frame defines their purpose. This level of communication is referred to as the data link layer (layer 2) of the seven-layer OSI model of networks.

In a large network, the addressing and control information is needed in order to properly deliver messages. Usually, this requires a message to be embedded as the data within another group of bits containing logical address and control information. In the OSI model, this is referred to as the network layer (layer 3). It is one layer above the data link layer. The packet is the basic unit of the network layer. It is similar to a frame in that it contains addressing information, control signals, and data. The primary difference is that the addressing at the data link layer is the physical address assigned to the devices that are communicating while the network layer uses a logical addressing scheme. The logical addressing scheme usually contains information to identify a device as part of a group, then locate that device within the group. Physical addresses typically cannot be altered while logical addresses can be configured by a network administrator.

In general, a frame is divided into three parts: the header, the body, and the trailer. The header takes most of the responsibility for the addressing and control information and may include:

- a bit pattern representing the start of a frame;
- a bit pattern used for signal synchronization;
- addressing for both the sender and receiver;
- session or sequence numbers;
- message length; and
- message type.

The body of the frame contains the data. The data may be either the raw data passed from one device to another, or it may be an encapsulation of another frame or packet. There are many examples of frames being packaged inside of other frames. Typically, this occurs at the network layer where a frame crosses from one network to another. An example of this is when a TCP/IP frame is transferred from an Internet service provider (ISP) to a dial-up client across a phone line. For the period when the message is moving across the phone line, the TCP/IP frame is embedded as data inside the frame that the dial-up system is using to communicate with the ISP.

The trailer brings up the end of the message. It usually contains error detection information followed by a special bit pattern to indicate that the frame is complete.

Sample Protocol: IEEE 802.3 Ethernet

IEEE 802.3 Ethernet is an example of a data link layer protocol that can be used to transmit frames from one device to another across a serial link. It uses the physical addresses of the device hardware interfaces to transmit anywhere from 0 to 1,500 octets of data in a single frame. Since the detection of errors is critical, IEEE 802.3 Ethernet includes a 32-bit error detection value in the frame trailer.

Figure 1. Layout of an IEEE 802.3 Ethernet frame

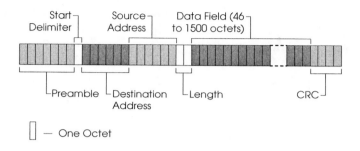

Figure 1 presents the basic layout of an IEEE 802.3 Ethernet frame (IEEE Computer Society, 2002, p. 38).

The frame begins with a preamble and start delimiter. The purpose of these 8 octets is to tell receiving devices when the message is going to start and to provide synchronization for the receive circuitry. Specifically, the preamble is 7 octets (56 bits) of alternating ones and zeros, the very first bit of which is a one. This "square wave" acts like a clock, ensuring that all of the receiving devices are reading data at the same point in each bit time. The preamble is immediately followed by a single octet equal to 10101011. This start delimiter maintains the alternating binary pattern set up by the preamble until the last bit. The pair of ones next to each other informs the receiving devices that the next component of the frame's header, the destination address, will immediately follow.

The destination address and source address identify the hardware involved in the message transaction. It is important not to confuse these addresses with IP addresses, which are logical addresses for the network layer. Instead, these addresses are hardwired into the physical hardware of the network interface card (NIC). These addresses, referred to as Medium Access Control (MAC) addresses, are loaded into the NIC by the manufacturer and cannot be modified. They are six octets long with the first three octets identifying the manufacturer. If the destination address is all ones, then the message is meant to be a broadcast and all devices are to receive it.

The next field in the frame is the 16-bit length field. The value in this field represents the number of octets in the data field. With two octets, it is possible to represent a value from 0 to $2^{16} = 65,535$. The definition of the IEEE 802.3 Ethernet, however, limits the range from 0 octets to 1,500 octets. Since only the lower 11 bits of the 16 available bits are needed to represent the number 1,500, 5 bits of this field are unused. This is useful because later expansions of the Ethernet protocol use these 5 unused bits to identify specific types of messages.

The data field comes next, and it contains the transmitted data. Although the length of this field is defined by the two octets in the length field, the definition of IEEE 802.3 Ethernet requires that the minimum length of the data field is 46 octets. If less than 46 octets are being transmitted, additional octets are used as filler to expand this field to 46 octets. The filler octets are added after the valid data octets.

The frame trailer at the end of the message contains a single 4-octet value called a cyclic redundancy check (CRC). A CRC is a special value that is generated from a long binary sequence. Imagine it as the remainder from a long division where the entire frame, excluding the preamble and delimiter, is the dividend and a universally defined constant is the divisor. If any error occurs during transmission of the frame, the remainder calculated by the receiver becomes significantly different than that calculated and sent by the transmitting device. If the CRC calculated by the receiver does not match the CRC sent with the message, then an error has occurred and a retransmission of the frame is requested by the receiver.

Since the destination and source addresses are each 6 octets, the length is 2 octets, the minimum data field is 46 octets, and the CRC is 4 octets, the minimum Ethernet frame is 64 octets long. If the maximum data field length of 1,500 octets is used, then the length of the maximum Ethernet frame is 1,518 octets.

Sample Protocol: Internet Protocol

The Ethernet frame is meant to encapsulate a packet from the network layer. A common network layer packet for this is the Internet Protocol (IP) packet. IP is used to transmit blocks of data called datagrams as either single blocks or as partitioned fragments from one host to another across a logical network (Postel, 1981a). The basic function of IP is to provide routing. Therefore, it offers error checking only for the header and has no mechanism for message sequencing or flow control.

Basically, IP adds a header to a block of data so that the mechanisms of an IP network can direct the packet from one host to another. Figure 2 presents the basic layout of an IP packet header (Postel, 1981a, p. 11).

The IP packet header contains 14 fields providing the control information needed to get a message from one host to another. Each field has a well-defined purpose (Postel, 1981a, pp. 11-23).

Figure 2. Layout of an IP packet header

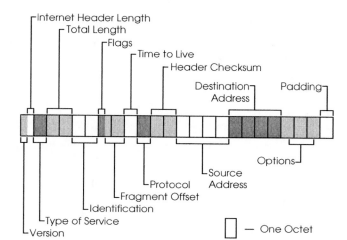

- **Version**: The first four bits of the header identify the version of the protocol defining the header.

- **Internet header length**: The number of octets in the IP header can be calculated by multiplying the value contained in the last four bits of the first octet of the header by 4. This shows the receiving device where the IP header ends and the data block begins. Since the protocol defines the minimum header length to be 20 octets long, the minimum value of this field is 5.

- **Type of service**: The second octet of the header indicates how the packet should be handled by the network. This includes properties such as throughput and reliability.

- **Total length**: The two octets following the type of service indicate the total length of the message, that is, the combined number of octets in the IP header and the data that follows it. If the IP packet is embedded within a frame, for example, an Ethernet frame, this total length field refers only to the IP packet. Sixteen bits would allow for messages of length 65,535, although most networks will not allow packets of this size.

- **Identification**: The two octets following the total length field are used by the receiver to group the fragments contained in multiple IP packets.

- **Flags**: The next three bits are used for control of fragments of a datagram. The most significant bit is reserved. The next bit indicates whether fragmentation of the datagram is allowed. The third bit indicates whether the current fragment is the last fragment.

- **Fragment offset**: The 13 bits of this field identify the contained fragment's offset into the full datagram. This allows for reassembly of the datagram by the receiver. Datagrams are partitioned into fragments at 64-bit boundaries (8 octets), so the value in this field is to be multiplied by 8 to determine the specific offset in octets. An offset of 0 indicates the fragment contained in this packet is the first in the datagram.

- **Time to live**: This octet limits the amount of time that an IP packet is allowed to remain on the network. It should be decremented every time the packet encounters a module on the network before arriving at the destination. If allowed to reach zero, the packet is killed.

- **Protocol**: The eight bits of the protocol field identify the protocol of the packet contained in the data field.

- **Header checksum**: The 16-bit header checksum is the one's complement of the one's complement datasum of the 16-bit words contained in the IP header. Note that since the checksum is part of the IP header, zeros are inserted in this field during the checksum calculation. In addition, since fields such as the time to live field may change during the routing of the packet, the header checksum may need to be recalculated.

- **Source and destination addresses**: Each of these four-octet fields contains an IP address. The first is the IP address of the sending device while the second is the IP address of the receiving device.

- **Options**: Depending on the needs of a specific packet, a number of options can appear in this field. The options identify requirements such as security, time stamps, and routing information. This field is variable in length.

- **Padding**: The total length of an IP header must be a multiple of four octets. The padding field of the IP header appends zeros to the header to guarantee this.

Sample Protocol:
Transmission Control Protocol

One layer of abstraction above the network layer in the OSI model is the transport layer. In general, the transport layer provides a means for breaking large blocks of data into smaller fragments so that they may be reassembled by the receiving device for the purpose of a specific application. A typical transport

Figure 3. Layout of a TCP packet header

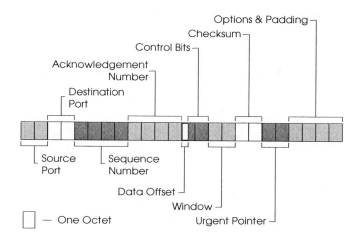

layer protocol to be embedded in an IP packet is the Transmission Control Protocol (TCP). TCP provides error checking, error recovery, and sequencing for the packets along with providing a means for identifying the type of application the packet is being delivered to, for example, distinguishing the packets defining a Web page from those defining an e-mail.

TCP adds a header to a block of data so that the receiving device can manage the incoming data. Figure 3 presents the basic layout of a TCP packet header (Postel, 1981b, p. 15).

The TCP packet header contains 10 fields allowing large blocks of data to be fragmented and sent from an application running on one device to an application running on a second device. Each field has a well-defined purpose (Postel, 1981b, pp. 15-19).

- **Source and destination ports**: A port is a logical connection specifying the type of service for which the data is meant to serve. Many protocols have preassigned port values. For example, a port value of 80 identifies the packet as containing http data while a port value of 23 identifies a telnet packet. The source and destination port fields are both 16 bits in length and identify the ports of the sending application and receiving application, respectively.

- **Sequence number**: The sequence number is part of the mechanism used to ensure that the multiple TCP packets making up a block of data have been received and are ordered properly. The sender and receiver must keep track of the sequence numbers, incrementing them by the amount of data sent with each packet. The sequence number field is 32 bits long.

- **Acknowledgment number**: This 32-bit field is used in conjunction with the sequence number. The receiver of a TCP packet acknowledges the receipt of a TCP packet by responding to the sender with the next expected sequence number inserted into the acknowledgment number field.

- **Data offset**: The length of the TCP header can be calculated by multiplying the value contained in the four bits of the data offset field by 4. This shows the receiving device where the TCP header ends and the data block begins. A TCP header must always be an integer multiple of 32 bits long.

- **Control bits**: The 12 bits following the data offset field consist of six reserved bits followed by six flag bits. The flag bits include flags such as ACK (an indication that the acknowledge field contains a sequence number), RST (a request to reset the connection), and FIN (an indication that the sender has no more data to send).

- **Window**: The 16-bit window field is used by the device requesting data and indicates how much data it or its network has the capacity to receive. It is based on the amount of free buffer space the requesting device has and the amount of available bandwidth.

- **Checksum**: The 16-bit checksum field contains the one's complement of the one's complement datasum of 16-bit words contained in the TCP header. Note that since the checksum is part of the TCP header, zeros are inserted in this field during the checksum calculation.

- **Urgent pointer**: The 16-bit value in the urgent pointer field is used in conjunction with the sequence number to identify the location of urgent data in the data block.

- **Options**: Depending on the needs of a specific packet, a variable set of options may appear in this field. The options identify requirements such maximum receive segment size. This field is variable in length.

- **Padding**: The length of a TCP header must be a multiple of four octets. The padding field of the TCP header appends zeros to the header to guarantee this.

Figure 4. Layout of a TCP packet header

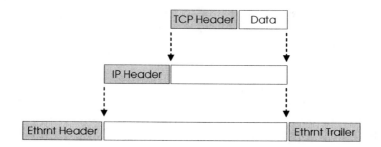

Protocol Stacks

By embedding packets from upper layers of the OSI network model within packets or frames from lower layers, data can be sent from an application running on one host to another application running on a second host. This format of embedded packets and frames is called a protocol stack. The block diagram in Figure 4 shows how the TCP packet is embedded within the IP packet, which is in turn embedded in the Ethernet frame. This embedding will become clear with the use of the protocol sniffer presented in the next section.

Capturing and Examining an Ethernet Frame

The concepts of the previous sections can be demonstrated by examining the raw data of an Ethernet frame containing an IP packet, which in turn contains a TCP packet. The problem is that unless the user has access to electronic testing equipment such as an oscilloscope, some of the bit patterns of ones and zeros of an Ethernet frame are not visible. For example, the preamble and start delimiter of the Ethernet frame are used only by the NIC for timing and synchronization. These values are not saved for use by the user. The information contained within the frame, however, is accessible by the user.

There are a number of programs available called protocol analyzers or sniffers, that can display the data captured by a NIC. These nonintrusive programs monitor the data that pass across the local network connection and capture it for analysis. The user may specify one of a number of formats in which to display the captured data. These formats range from decoded packets indicating the type of message and the commands contained within it to the raw data copied directly from the frame.

One such program, Packetyzer, is available for the Windows operating system under the GNU license agreement (Waters, 2003). There are plenty of other commercial, shareware, and open source applications available for both the Microsoft and Unix platforms. Because of the principles behind the GNU General Public License agreement supporting contributions to human knowledge, universities are encouraged to use GNU GPL software in both education and research (Stallman, 2002). This makes the use of Packetyzer in the classroom an attractive option, although the concepts are general and should be applicable to any of the other programs.

Upon start-up, Packetyzer prompts the user for the details of the capture session using the window shown in Figure 5. These details include the adapter that will be monitored, the capture session name, and any limits to be placed on the captured data.

First, an Ethernet adapter should be selected from the adapter drop box. By selecting an adapter that is connected to an active TCP/IP network, the student should have plenty of Ethernet frames to analyze. To give the student a wide range of packets to examine, the box enabling promiscuous mode should be checked. This will allow Packetyzer to capture all frames and packets seen by this adapter, not just the ones sent to it. The capture name allows the user to identify the file name under which the captured data can be stored. Since Packetyzer allows the user to reload saved sessions, saving a particular session

Figure 5. Packetyzer capture options window

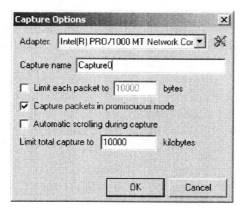

Figure 6. Packetyzer decode tab identified on main display screen

may be used to allow the students to examine the same session or to allow analysis of captured data without being connected to a network.

Once the user clicks the OK button, the Packetyzer main display screen appears. In order to begin a capture session, the decode tab should be selected, as shown in Figure 6.

At this point, a simple capture can be performed by clicking on the start/stop capture button shown in Figure 7.

Once this button is pressed, packet information begins appearing in the main display screen. In addition, the start/stop capture button should change such that a small red circle with a white *X* appears on it. This button now serves to stop the capture. After a significant number of packets have been captured, the capture session should be stopped in order to examine a specific message. The main display screen should look something like that shown in Figure 8.

The three windows in the main display screen present the details and data of the captured packets. The left window is the *tree details* view. The students use this view to examine the components of a selected packet or frame. The top right

Figure 7. Start/stop capture button identified on main display screen

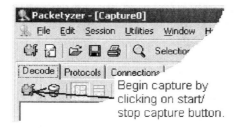

Figure 8. Packetyzer main display screen with captured data

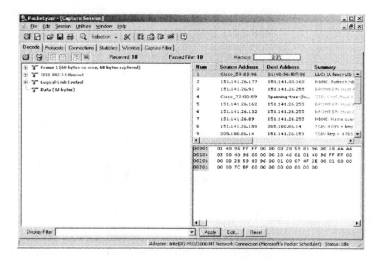

Figure 9. Packet list view with TCP packet selected

Num	Source Address	Dest Address	Summary
7	151.141.26.89	151.141.26.255	NBNS: Name quer
8	151.141.26.159	205.180.86.14	TCP: 4789 > http
9	205.180.86.14	151.141.26.159	TCP: http > 4789
10	151.141.26.177	151.141.30.57	SMB: Echo Reques
11	151.141.30.57	151.141.26.177	SMB: Echo Respor
12	151.141.26.177	151.141.30.57	ICMP: Echo (ping)
13	151.141.30.57	151.141.26.177	ICMP: Echo (ping)
14	151.141.26.177	151.141.30.57	TCP: 3924 > micr
15	151.141.26.89	151.141.26.255	NBNS: Name quer

```
0000:   00 07 B3 18 F0 00 00 08 74 0F 7F 8C 08 00 45 00
0010:   00 28 1E 78 40 00 80 06 74 53 97 8D 1A B1 97 8D
0020:   1E 39 0F 54 01 BD 9C C3 A5 30 D1 EF 09 BA 50 10
0030:   FA 4F 1E D1 00 00 00 00 00 00 00 00
```

window, the *packet list* view, presents a list of all of the packets received during the capture session. The bottom right window, the *hex and ASCII details* view, shows the raw data of the selected packet divided into octets.

The student begins by selecting a TCP packet from the packet list view. This will allow the user to examine not only the TCP header information but also the IP header and Ethernet frame that encapsulate it in the protocol stack. In Figure 9, packet number 14, a TCP acknowledge packet, has been selected.

Figure 10. Tree details view with all branches collapsed

Figure 11. Tree details view with Ethernet branch expanded

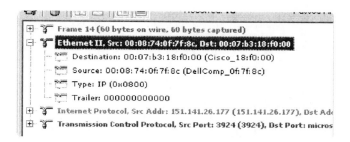

With a packet selected, the tree details view can be used to display the parsed information from each of the protocols present in the packet. Figure 10 presents this view with each of the branches collapsed.

By clicking on the plus sign next to each of the protocols, the details of the frame are revealed. Figure 11 presents the tree details view with the details of the Ethernet frame revealed.

The details of the Ethernet frame include the destination and source addresses. Remember from the Ethernet frame discussion that the first three octets of the MAC address used by Ethernet identify the manufacturer. In the details revealed beneath the Ethernet identifier branch, it can be seen that the first three octets of the destination address in this example represent a Cisco NIC while the first three octets of the source address represent a Dell NIC.

By clicking on any of the details in the tree details view, the corresponding raw data from the hex and ASCII details view is highlighted. Figure 12 shows how selecting the Ethernet destination address causes the corresponding raw data to be highlighted in the hex and ASCII details view.

Similarly, the components of each of the other protocols can be identified and used by the students to compare with the raw data. Using the items from the tree

Figure 12. Message with Ethernet destination address identified

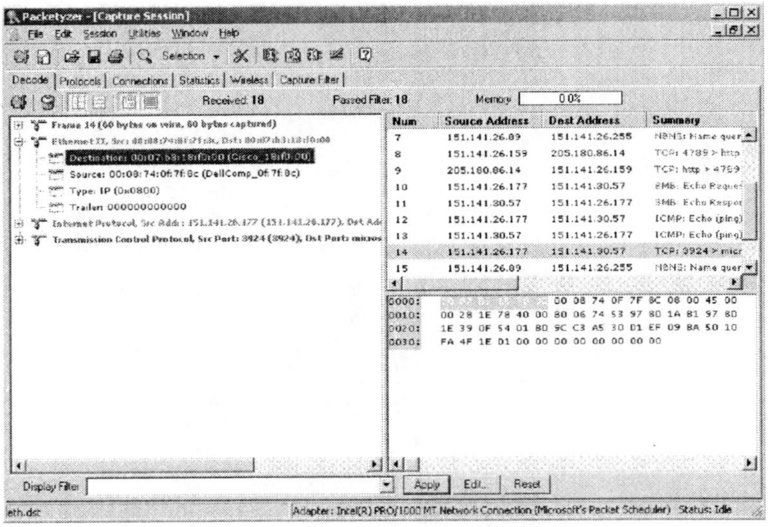

details view along with the highlighted data from the hex and ASCII view, the students can examine and verify the components of the frame and embedded packets. These components include addressing, header and frame lengths, and checksums.

Conclusion

Serial communication is favored as a long-distance computer system interface due to its reliability and cost-effectiveness. This comes with a consequence though. All information pertaining to the delivery of a message must be contained within a single stream of bits. In order to implement a serial data communication system, a well-defined set of rules called a protocol must exist to specify the placement and purpose of every bit sent across the link.

This chapter has shown how a tool called a protocol analyzer can be used to examine the frames of the data link layer and the packets of the network and transport layers. This can be a valuable tool for any network administrator who wishes to debug or evaluate the performance of a network or a system designer who needs to verify the operation of their system.

Summary

This chapter described the serial packet and its addressing, data encapsulation, and control information. It showed the bit-level detail of an IEEE 802.3 Ethernet frame, an IP packet, and a TCP packet and showed how these protocols are used to create a sample protocol stack. The GNU-licensed and Windows-based application Packetyzer is used to explore a sample TCP/IP packet contained in an Ethernet frame. By completing the practical activities, students developed a better knowledge and understanding of the use of a protocol analyzer.

Key Terms and Definitions

CRC: CRC stands for cyclic redundancy check. This is a method for checking for errors in a data stream. It uses a polynomial (a pattern of ones and zeros) as a divisor in a modified division of the entire data stream. The remainder of the division is appended to the message along with the data to be used as a verification by the receiver of the data stream.

Datagram: A datagram is a block of data meant to be treated as a unit. If the datagram is too large to be handled by a network, it is possible to fragment it for transmission into smaller packets.

Data link layer: This is the second layer of the OSI model, and it defines the pattern or purpose of the bits of a frame. Except for the physical layer, which defines the electronics behind a computer interface, it is the lowest level of the OSI model.

ISP: ISP stands for Internet service provider. This is a company that acts as a access point for users of the Internet.

MAC address: MAC stands for Medium Access Control. The MAC address is a six-octet value that is permanently assigned to a NIC to uniquely identify it in any network. MAC addresses are loaded into the NIC by the manufacturer and can not be modified. The first three octets identify the manufacturer.

Network layer: This is the third layer of the OSI model, and it defines the means for host-to-host logical addressing across a network. In the OSI model, it is immediately above the data link layer.

NIC: NIC stands for network interface card, which is the hardware interface that provides the physical link between a computer and a network.

Octet: An octet is a sequence of eight bits. The term octet is preferred over byte because the term byte has become ambiguous, oftentimes referring to the number of bits reserved for a character.

Preamble (Ethernet): This is a string of 56 alternating binary ones and zeros (starting with a one) that is sent at the beginning of an IEEE 802.3 Ethernet frame.

Protocol: A protocol is a set of strict definitions for the transmission of data from one device to another across a communications network.

OSI model: This is a model for the operation of computer interfaces. It divides the needs of computer communication into levels and details what needs to be defined at each of these levels for a successful interface.

Start delimiter (Ethernet): This is an octet immediately following the preamble of the IEEE 802.3 Ethernet frame that indicates the message starts at this point. It is always a binary pattern equal to 10101011.

Transport layer: This is the fourth layer of the OSI model, immediately above the network layer. It provides a network-independent mechanism for sending large blocks of data, thereby hiding the details of the network from the services in the layers above it.

Review Questions

1. List and describe three desirable features of a protocol analyzer.

2. Explain how a protocol analyzer can be used in teaching and learning contexts.

3. Explain how data link layer frames and network layer packets can be examined by a protocol analyzer.

4. Explain how data packets can be captured by a protocol analyzer.

5. Define the following key terms: serial communication, frame, and protocol stack.

6. Draw a block diagram to illustrate the layout of an IEEE 802.3 Ethernet frame.

7. Describe the IEEE 802.3 Ethernet frame structure.

8. Discuss the difference between a MAC address and an IP address.

9. Draw a block diagram to illustrate the layout of an IP packet header.

10. Draw a block diagram to illustrate the layout of a TCP packet header.

References

IEEE Computer Society. (2002). *Carrier Sense Multiple Access with Collision Detection (CSMA/CD) access method and physical layer specifications* (IEEE Standard 802.3-2002). Retrieved December 14, 2004, from the Institute of Electrical and Electronics Engineers Web site: http://standards.ieee.org/getieee802/download/802.3-2002.pdf

OPENXTRA Limited. (2003). *Packetyzer user guide* [Computer manual]. West Yorkshire, UK: Author.

Postel, J. (1981a). *Internet Protocol: DARPA Internet program protocol specification* (RFC 791). Arlington, VA: Defense Advanced Research Projects Agency. Retrieved May 27, 2005, from the Advameg Inc. Web site: http://www.faqs.org/rfcs/rfc791.html

Postel, J. (1981b). *Transmission Control Protocol: DARPA Internet program protocol specification* (RFC 793). Arlington, VA: Defense Advanced Research Projects Agency. Retrieved May 27, 2005, from the Advameg Inc. Web site: http://www.faqs.org/rfcs/rfc793.html

Stallman, R. (2002). *Releasing free software if you work at a university.* Retrieved May 27, 2005, from the GNU Project Web site: http://www.gnu.org/philosophy/university.html

Waters, C. (2003). Packetyzer—Network Packet Analyzer (Version 4.0.0) [Computer software]. Menlo Park, CA: Network Chemistry. Retrieved May 26, 2005, from the SourceForge.net Web site: http://sourceforge.net/projects/packetyzer

Chapter XVIII

VMware as a Practical Learning Tool

Eduardo Correia, Christchurch Polytechnic
Institute of Technology, New Zealand

Ricky Watson, Christchurch Polytechnic
Institute of Technology, New Zealand

Abstract

Providing a dedicated lab to each group of students in order to gain hands-on learning experience is not always possible due to budget and space constraints. For example, in one class of 20 students, each student requires at least three computers with each computer capable of running three operating systems, such as UNIX, Linux, and Windows Server 2003. This requires a large computer laboratory with 60 computers in total. In addition, it is difficult to manage the laboratory to accommodate students from other classes. For example, once one class leaves the laboratory, another class of 20 students needs to start immediately with each person configuring Windows Server 2003 Active Directory on four computers. This requires another large computer laboratory with 80 computers. This chapter presents VMware as a teaching and learning tool to overcome the problems mentioned above. Under VMware, students do not require administrative privileges on physical machines. Consequently, they have complete freedom to experiment within their own virtualised environments.

Learning Objectives

After completing this chapter, you will be able to:

- Discuss the usefulness of VMware in teaching and learning contexts.
- Use VMware in laboratory settings for hands-on learning experience.
- Define the following key terms: DHCP, ISA, NTFS, RIS, VMware, and Virtual PC.
- Suggest further enhancements to the practical activities presented in the chapter.

Introduction

VMware is an application that emulates a hardware environment. It allows one or more virtual machines (guests) to run on one physical machine (host). On top of the existing operating system of the physical machine, one or more operating systems can run in this environment, including any of a number of Microsoft operating systems, Linux distributions, Netware, Solaris, or variants of BSD. These systems running within VMware behave, with only a few exceptions, in exactly the same way as any other conventional system (Stockman, 2003). What VMware does is to "carve a single physical system into compartments, each running its own copy of an operating system, applications and content in the illusion that it is a complete, independent machine" (Deane, Haff, & Enuice, 2004). This partitioning of a system through the use of VMware has several distinct benefits for teachers of computer studies; notably, the ability to:

a. provide a richer learning environment,

b. offer a safe environment for learners,

c. exploit powerful and flexible networking options,

d. employ cost-effective solutions that scale well, and

e. simplify the administration of the learning environment.

Some of the technology students are exposed to through VMware would simply not be practicable through conventional means because of the prohibitive cost of additional hardware and the physical space and maintenance it would entail.

How else can one easily give 20 students each three computers running UNIX, Linux, and Windows Server 2003 and allow them to configure these machines as part of one larger network (60 computers in total)? And what if, once one class leaves, another class of 20 students needs to start immediately with each person configuring Windows Server 2003 Active Directory on four computers (80 computers in total)? VMware makes this practically feasible. What is more, students do not require administrative privileges on physical machines to be able to have complete freedom to experiment within their own virtualised environments.

This chapter describes how the authors came to adopt VMware and the specific feature sets of value for its use as a learning tool, such as networking capabilities and virtualised/real media support as well as some key infrastructural considerations. More importantly, it outlines how this tool can be employed to enhance teaching and learning through the use of specific tasks and practical project work.

Motivation for Using VMware as a Learning Tool

In 1998 the School of Computing at the Christchurch Polytechnic Institute of Technology (CPIT) decided to offer a course on managing Windows NT4 Workstation. The IT Division at CPIT was asked to provide a solution that allowed the school to use machines both for normal classes as well as specialist operating systems classes, which require full access to the operating system. After evaluating a number of options, the IT Division recommended that Iomega JAZ drives be used, which we did. Unfortunately the solution failed. With no other workable solution, the course made use of the existing installed system with mixed and somewhat unsatisfactory results. In an attempt to improve the system, the IT Division provided each machine with multiple partitions. While this solution offered better results, it had significant limitations and potential problems for normal classes. Any student could see and in fact destroy another student's work or even destroy the operating system installed by the IT Division for normal classes. Furthermore, the number of students that could use the machine was limited to the number of available partitions. One of the authors then decided to investigate the use of VMware as a potential solution for running Windows NT4 in emulation on a Linux host system. In 2001 he decided to use VMware (at that time Version 2) specifically for the teaching of Windows NT4 and Linux. However, the hardware had to be upgraded to make it suitable for teaching

Windows 2000. Each machine had 384 MB of memory, a 20 GB disk partitioned into 4 GB and 14 GB, the latter reserved for storing virtual machines. With the increase in demand for courses utilising Microsoft Official Curriculum, a specialist network called Techlabs was established. While initially this specialist network was created primarily for the purposes of teaching Microsoft operating systems and networking, it also caters for courses that require students to work extensively with a number of other platforms, including Linux, Netware, and BSD.

Feature Sets of Benefit for Learning

VMware is available as three separate products that essentially all do the same thing: offer users the ability to run numerous virtual machines that may or may not be connected to one another and to other physical and/or virtual machines on the network. The three VMware products are:

a.   VMware ESX Server. VMware ESX Server has a number of advanced features, including the ability to migrate virtual machines to another location without them needing to be powered down. It makes use of a custom Linux kernel and has a limited hardware compatibility list so as to ensure stability. It is really an enterprise server application with a price tag to match that is difficult to justify in an educational institution.

b.   VMware GSX Server. VMware GSX Server provides a remote console that is essentially a terminal to the virtual machines running on the physical server. These sessions with the server can be started and terminated without the virtual machines themselves being affected.

c.   VMware Workstation. VMware Workstation provides the basic function-ality of virtual machines, but as soon as a user logs off the physical machine or closes the VMware dialog box, the virtual machine stops running.

In a specialist teaching network, VMware Workstation allows students to create, change, and even destroy (if they wish) their own virtual machines while VMware GSX Server allows teaching staff to make running virtual machines available to all students. Used together these two products are capable of providing a learning environment that is highly flexible, scalable, and feature-rich.

Features common to all three VMware products include:

a. Virtual switches, allowing for up to 10 different isolated networks, from VMnet0 to VMnet9 (see Figure 1).

b. Physical network adapters in the host can be assigned to a virtual switch, allowing virtual machines access to a physical network.

c. Special networks to help create useful scenarios. VMnet1 is a network for just the virtual machines and the host to communicate; whereas, VMnet8 allows virtual machines to use network address translation (NAT) to obtain a private network address and interact with the physical network via the host's network address.

d. Each virtual machine can have up to three network adapters assigned, but this can be extended to more.

e. Each virtual network has a server running Dynamic Host Control Protocol (DHCP) to issue addresses. The scopes can be reconfigured or the DHCP server disabled.

f. Each machine can accommodate a limited range of hardware, including disk drives, compact disc drives, Universal Serial Bus (USB) controllers, sound cards, floppy disk drives, parallel ports, serial ports, and network cards (see Figure 2).

Figure 1. VMware network configuration

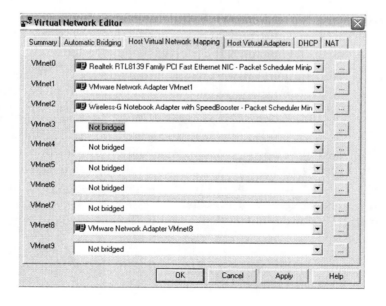

Figure 2. VMware add hardware wizard

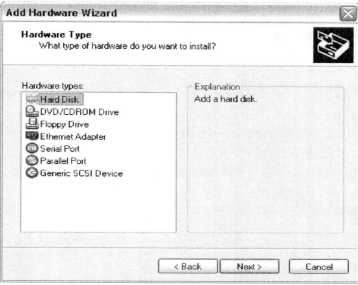

As in the case of physical machines, students may start out with a particular hardware configuration and then decide to change or upgrade it later. A virtual machine that initially has just one hard disk drive and one network card may have five hard disk drives and three network cards added to it. Students may therefore be given the task of adding a number of virtual SCSI disks and may set up a redundant array of independent disks with parity (RAID 5). This rich learning environment is supported by a set of powerful networking features. While one or more VMware virtual machines may run simultaneously on a single physical machine, they appear just like any other machine on the network (Hu, Meinel, & Schmitt, 2004); though if one wishes, it is easy to ensure that no other machine, virtual or physical, can see or access it. This is because each virtual machine can have one or more network interfaces that may or may not be connected to the same virtual switch. This is a feature that has great value for learning because each student can run a DHCP server and DHCP client simultaneously and test this without disrupting what anyone else is doing or even the activities of another virtual machine running on the same hardware. Similarly, for project work it is possible to provide students with a server that is configured up to a certain point and only require them to complete certain specified tasks, making learning a smoother, more efficient process. Students do not waste time on installation issues, unless of course the project is designed to deal specifically with installation.

In the course of installing, configuring, maintaining, and troubleshooting systems, people may easily corrupt an entire system. In a VMware environment, learners can easily undo major operations that would normally be impractical to reverse, actions such as deleting partitions and creating file systems. This risk can be significantly reduced through the use of VMware because it is possible to:

a.   keep an additional copy of the entire virtual machine, which involves simply copying a few files to another location; and

b.   utilise the snapshot feature of VMware that allows someone to revert to the state of a system at a particular point in time.

This snapshot is comparable to making a number of transactions to a database and deciding only later whether or not to commit the changes. It is a feature that was initially harnessed by developers (Zeichick, 2004), but its benefits have been widely recognised by both individuals as well as organisations, such as Microsoft and Novell (VMware, 2004).

VMware also reduces and simplifies the administration of course setups and makes disaster recovery as simple as copying a particular folder and its files. As virtual machines are simply a collection of files on a computer, it is possible to provide students with "clean" virtual machines that they can copy but not change. Because they can change their own copies of the virtual machines, if they do corrupt their own classroom machines, it is possible to revert to the original machine by making a copy of it. This means that the classroom only needs to be set up once for a particular course, as all subsequent instances of that course make use of the same original set of virtual machines, which once students copy they have full control over. This is cost-effective because setup time and maintenance of course machines are greatly reduced, and it is easy to back up and restore entire systems. It is also a cost-effective solution because in a typical learning (non-production) environment, physical machines made available to students are not serving many clients, if at all. As a particular computer may be running multiple virtual machines simultaneously, more efficient use is made of existing hardware resources.

Practical Project Work Using VMware

VMware is a valuable tool for learning, where the application of practical skills can be as important as theoretical knowledge. As part of course requirements, students may be given practical projects that require the installation, configuration, and maintenance of a number of systems that, for example, may involve Windows Server 2003, Windows XP Professional, Linux, and Netware. In one project that requires basic administration and configuration of objects in Active Directory, students are provided with a fully built virtual system that requires them only to create stated users, groups, printers, and volumes and enhance performance. This is simply a matter of making a domain controller available on a network location for them to copy and then configure. As students do not need to make this domain controller connect with any other student's machine, there is no requirement to subject this machine to the process of the System Preparation Tool (Sysprep). In order to enhance the performance of their systems, students can add an extra virtual disk and move their directory database log files to this new volume. In a subsequent project they use the server of the previous project to configure folder and file permissions, then are given a virtual XP Professional machine to test whether different users have no more and no less than the requisite permissions. Students can find that they have not completed this task properly because even if they have configured the NT File System (NTFS) permissions, they may have overlooked configuring the share permissions, and in Windows Server 2003 these are "Everyone—Read Only." In this way a second project may expand on the first and grow from one machine to two, without the costs and complexity of supporting additional hardware.

To implement routing, students require more than just one machine if they are to be given anything more than a fleeting opportunity to learn and practise networking skills. Multiple machines offer the prospect of gaining something akin to real-world experience, since there is little difference between using virtual or physical machines in such a way. As one can see in Figure 3, the student workstation is host to three virtual machines and three subnets: client1 (a Microsoft NT4 Workstation on VMnet 4), client2 (a machine with Debian Linux 3 on VMnet 5), and a Linux server (with Debian Linux 3 on VMnet 4, VMnet 5, and VMnet 2). The Linux server routes between the two clients as well as between the clients of a student and clients of other students through VMnet 2. The students can use static routing and managed routing using the provided configuration.

In a similar, though more elaborate project, students configure four Microsoft Windows Server 2003 routers first using static routes and then Routing Information Protocol (RIP; see Figure 4). The four routers are said to be located in Auckland, Wellington, Christchurch, and Invercargill, and students add routes and verify connectivity between all four devices. In addition students also configure a backup route. Normally the router in Invercargill is connected to Wellington, but should this link drop for some reason, a backup route should automatically connect to Christchurch; but as Invercargill should normally route to Wellington, this requires the configuration of costs to individual routes. All four routers have access to the Internet through the router in Auckland, and this router

Figure 3. Routing with Linux

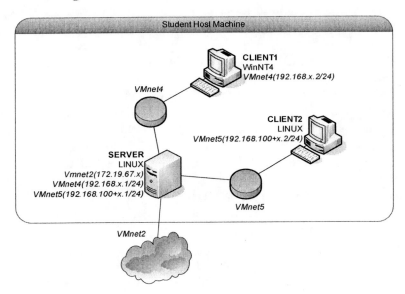

is configured with NAT. In fact, students are able to add an interface on the Auckland router that will have a default gateway of another machine on the network that provides access to the Internet. As a result all routers should be able to ping a public address on the Internet.

A course titled Fundamentals of Security includes a project that utilises the host machine as well as four virtual machines: FW1, FW2, SQL, and WEB (all have Windows 2000 Advanced Server installed; see Figure 5). This virtual network implements the typical scenario of a perimeter network using two firewalls (FW1 and FW2), a Demilitarized Zone (DMZ), and a client. FW2 separates the Web from the internal trusted network, which contains a Structured Query Language (SQL) database server. FW1 and FW2 need to have properly configured packet filters so that someone can access the Web server (WEB) from WinXP, and this Web server will be able to fetch data from the SQL server while not allowing traffic from untrusted sources into the internal network.

Other projects are designed to utilise as many as nine machines, including the physical host machine, so that students can create two entire networks, Developmentum and Fabrikim, each with its own Internet Security and Acceleration Server (ISA) firewall and one with an ISA 2000 Proxy Array (see Figure 6). The two networks should be connected by demand-dial interfaces that automatically create a VPN connection between them when a client from one

Figure 4. Routing with MS Windows

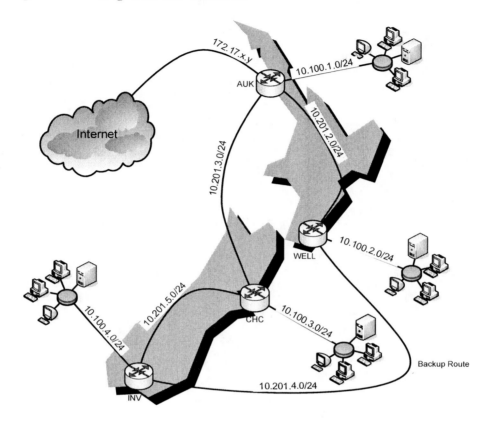

network connects to a resource on the other network. The student host machine is used to connect to the resources on either network, using either Point-to-Point Tunnelling Protocol or Layer 2 Tunnelling Protocol.

To avoid problems and disappointment, teaching staff need to be prepared for the challenge of using VMware. Firstly, it does add to students' initial workload as they need to familiarise themselves not only with the content of the course but also understand how to make use of this mode of virtualisation. Secondly, VMware has its limits with regard to unsupported operating systems, unusual hardware access, or specific configurations. Not all operating systems are supported, and even the ones that are, cannot do absolutely everything a physical machine can. For example, virtual machines do not run easily within virtual machines (Lorincz, Redwine, & Sheh, 2003). VMware also does not always cope well with nonstandard-size floppy disks and power management options, such as standby and hibernation (Correia & Watson, 2004). It has also been found to give intermittent problems with both the Windows 2000 Server and

Figure 5. Security project

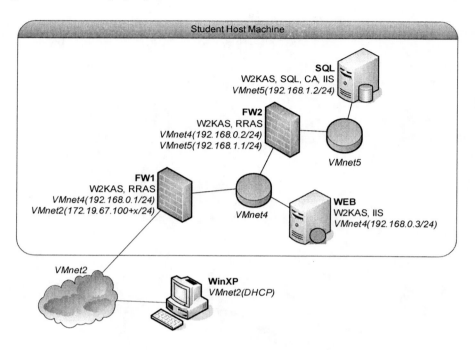

Figure 6. ISA project with tunnel-mode VPN

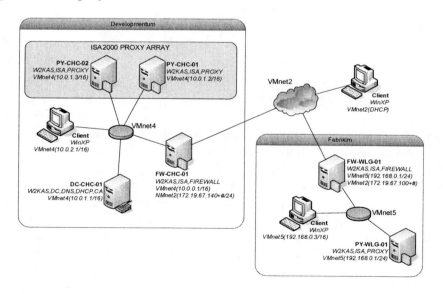

Windows Server 2003 versions of Remote Boot Disk Generator (rbfg.exe), which creates floppy disks used to connect client machines with a Remote Installation Service (RIS). VMware now offers the alternative of PXE boot functionality, so that virtual machines can boot off their network cards to connect with the RIS server, just as one can with many current network interface cards. VMware is also not ideal for performance testing, as any one individual virtual machine is not aware that it is sharing resources with both other virtual machines as well as the host system (Zeichick, 2004). In reality these issues are only rare, isolated instances of a technology that is remarkably flexible and powerful as a learning tool. Such issues can be expected to be resolved in the future.

Infrastructural Considerations

VMware places significant demands on hardware and as a result demands newer, well-resourced machines. Virtual machines require hardware resources comparable to physical machines. For example, a Windows Server 2003 machine runs best when it has at least 128 MB of RAM and requires the same amount of memory under VMware. These are important considerations; otherwise, virtual machines will be unstable, run very slowly or not run at all. Older hardware is often not suitable because it is simply not sufficiently powerful to host multiple operating systems and cope with the demands made on CPU, disk, and memory. An important factor is whether one needs to run more than one virtual machine at a time and precisely what systems are required; for example, Windows Server 2003 with Exchange Server 2003 needs at least 512 MB of RAM to run satisfactorily, whereas a Debian Linux machine does not need anything more than 128 MB of RAM and can perform well with considerably less. As new computers are obtained, they are better able to cope with the demands made by virtual machines in VMware, and the constraints imposed by particular hardware are reduced. More powerful hardware ultimately enables more virtual machines to run simultaneously, including servers that require significant hardware resources, such as Exchange.

An extensive physical infrastructure is required in order to extract the greatest benefits from VMware as a learning tool. One important consideration is the specifications of a typical host machine and network configuration. Virtual machines are best placed on cabling and switches entirely separate from the physical machines that host them. Access permissions must be carefully applied through the operating system of the physical machine so that students' virtual machines can only be accessed by the owner of the virtual machine, the tutor and anyone else the tutor deems necessary to have access to a particular virtual machine. Virtual machines used in class are simply copies, so that in a worst-case scenario, students can revert to the original clean machine, to which they have read access, if necessary. Also, students can easily take copies of virtual machines so that they can continue to work on them on their own computers at home.

Techlabs stores hundreds of virtual machines that are required for classes. These class machines are all protected by means of NTFS permissions, and processes have been developed to restore these quickly and easily. However, the students' machines are not backed up, as it is not feasible to do so for the over 1,000 virtual machines students create on their workstations for the purpose of completing practical projects. As one virtual machine can be over 2 GB in size, it is too expensive and time-consuming for the institution to make adequate backups of all virtual systems. As a result, students are informed that they are responsible for their own project machines and advised to store them on removable media, such as external USB hard drives, or at the very least to regularly place copies on digital video/versatile disc (DVD). This is not entirely satisfactory, but there is some value to students learning to back up their own work and to feel the pain of wasted hours if they do not!

Conclusion

Virtualisation software such as VMware, Virtual PC, and User Mode Linux (McEwan, 2002) makes it feasible to offer every learner the practical experience of making systems work. It allows people to learn by doing, so that when they configure their virtual machines they understand the technology and see for themselves how it behaves on a particular platform. This tool allows students to gain experience in technologies that would otherwise be too expensive to make widely available using conventional physical hardware, such as RAID arrays or making an entire network available. It has now been used extensively for a number of years in Techlabs and earlier networks in a wide range of computing courses. At first it was applied tentatively, but its role has expanded over time, so that now it is essential for exploring a variety of systems and networks in a safe learning environment. Of itself it gives rise to a few problems and imposes some constraints, but these are insignificant compared to the benefits.

VMware transcends the traditional constraints of hardware solutions and helps overcome the challenges of rapid technological change in software and hardware. This has led many vendors to exploit virtualisation to port legacy applications to new hardware or to provide cost-effective server redundancy, in terms of both operating system and data. The additional layer of VMware does add overhead that may reduce the performance of both host and guest machines, but most people using this technology agree that "The benefits of successful virtual machine systems far outweigh any overhead that they introduce" (Rosenblum, 2004). For courses in operating systems, programming, and networking, VMware enhances learning through doing and in this way infuses virtual technology with real meaning and purpose.

Summary

Due to budget constraints, it is not always possible to provide a dedicated lab to each group of students for hands-on learning experience. For example, one class of 20 students requires at least three computers with two or more operating systems (e.g., UNIX, Linux, and Windows Server 2003) each. This requires a large computer laboratory with 60 computers in total. And what if, once one class leaves, another class of 20 students needs to start immediately with each student configuring Windows Server 2003 Active Directory on four computers (80 computers in total)?

This chapter described the use of VMware in teaching and learning contexts to overcome the above-mentioned problems. Under VMware, students do not require administrative privileges on physical machines to be able to experiment within their own virtualised environments.

Some of the technology students are exposed to through VMware would simply not be practicable through conventional means because of the cost of additional hardware, physical space, and maintenance it would entail.

Key Terms and Definitions

DHCP: Dynamic Host Control Protocol is used to issue and obtain IP addresses, both on local area networks and wide area networks.

Exchange: Exchange Server 2003 is Microsoft's latest mail server and as an enterprise server application requires significant resources in terms of processor, RAM, and disk space.

ISA: Internet and Acceleration Server is Microsoft's firewall and proxy server application. It followed Proxy Server 2.0 and was released in its first version in 2000. Another version was released in 2004.

NTFS: The NT File System is Microsoft's most secure file system and is as a result supported by Windows NT, Windows 2000, Windows XP, and Windows 2003 operating systems.

PXE: Preboot Execution Environment is a way of booting off the network card in order to connect to a server on the network.

RAID 5: A redundant array of independent (or inexpensive) disks, level 5 is a way of employing at least three disks in combination for the purpose of performance and fault tolerance.

Remote Boot Disk Generator: The Remote Boot Disk Generator is a tool that allows users to easily produce floppy disks that can connect a client machine with a RIS server.

RIS: Remote Installation Service is a service that can be installed on a Windows 2000 Server or Windows Server 2003 for the purpose of deploying, usually in an automated fashion, various Microsoft operating systems to client machines.

SQL: While SQL refers to Structured Query Language, this chapter refers to SQL as Microsoft's well-known database application.

Sysprep: Microsoft's System Preparation Tool is a utility for the mass deployment of the Microsoft NT family of operating systems.

USB: Universal Serial Bus is a standard that supports Plug and Play and is used for connecting peripheral devices to a PC.

User Mode Linux: User Mode Linux is an open source product that does the same kinds of things as VMware but unlike VMware is limited to Linux systems.

Virtual PC: Virtual PC is Microsoft's commercial product that competes directly with and is comparable to VMware.

VMware: VMware is a commercial product that allows one simultaneously to run a number of systems within the context of this application.

Review Questions

1. List and describe three main features of VMware.

2. List and describe three main benefits of using VMware in laboratory settings.

3. Define the following key terms: DHCP, ISA, NTFS, RIS, and Remote Boot Disk Generator.

4.   Describe the usefulness of VMware in teaching and learning contexts.

5.   List and describe three potential limitations of VMware.

6.   List and describe possible enhancements to the practical activities described in this chapter.

References

Correia, E., & Watson, R. (2004). A virtual solution to a real problem: VMware in the classroom. In *Conference Proceedings: Papers from the Proceedings of the 17th NACCQ* (pp. 250-253).

Deane, T., Haff, G., & Enuice, J. (2004, August 9). *VMware on the march.* Retrieved December 13, 2004, from http://www.VMware.com/pdf/illuminata.pdf

Hu, J., Meinel, C., & Schmitt, M. (2004, March). Tele-Lab IT security: An architecture for interactive lessons for security education. In *SIGSE Technical Symposium on Computer Science Education.*

Kneale, B., de Horta, A. Y., & Box, I. (2004, January). Velnet (virtual environment for learning networking). In R. Lister & A. Young (Eds.), *Sixth Australasian Computing Education Conference* (pp. 161-168).

Lorincz, K., Redwine, K., & Sheh, A. (2003). *Stacking virtual machines—VMware and VirtualPC.* Retrieved March 6, 2004, from www.eecs.harvard.edu/~konrad/References/notes/CS253-VMware-Report.pdf

McEwan, W. (2002). Virtual machine technologies and their application in the delivery of ICT. In *Proceedings of 15th annual Conference of the NACCQ* (pp. 55-62).

Rosenblum, M. (2004, July/August). The reincarnation of virtual machines: Virtualization makes a comeback. *ACM Queue, 2*(5).

Shankland, S. (2001). *Novell tows VMware into education market.* Retrieved March 7, 2004, from http://news.com.com/2102-001_3268219.html

Stockman, M. (2003, October). Creating remotely accessible 'virtual networks' on a single PC to teach computer networking and operating systems. In *Proceedings of the 4th Conference on Information Technology Curriculum.*

VMware. (2004). *VMware partners with Novell to provide innovative training solution.* Retrieved March 27, 2004, from http://www.vwware.com/news/releases/novell.html

Zeichick, A. (2004, September 28). VMware: The virtual desktop, the virtual server. *AMD64 dev Source*. Retrieved December 12, 2004, from http://www.devx.com/amd/article/22036

Appendix Section

Appendix A

Useful Tools

Tool	Description	URL
WebLan-Designer	A Web-based tool for teaching and learning both wired and wireless LAN design.	http://elena.aut.ac.nz/homepages/weblandesigner/
JASPER	JASPER (Java Simulation of Protocols for Education and Research) is a protocol simulator suitable for teaching and learning communication protocols.	http://www.cs.stir.ac.uk/~kjt/software/comms/jasper
Colligo Workgroup	Colligo software allows interactive chat, unidirectional message delivery, virtual whiteboard, and file transfer. The software can be downloaded from the Web site.	http://www.colligo.com/products/workgroupedition/
Animation Tool	Algorithm animations.	www.cs.auckland.ac.nz/software/AlgAnim/alg_anim.html
Logisim	Logisim is a Java application that can run on both MS Windows and Unix workstations.	http://www.cburch.com/proj/logisim/
Wi-Fi Projects	List of equipment for setting up Wi-Fi projects.	http://elena.aut.ac.nz/homepages/staff/Nurul-Sarkar/wifi/
Wi-Fi Antenna	Various kits for Wi-Fi antenna can be found at the Oatley Electronics Web site.	http://oatleyelectronics.com/kits/K199.html

Tool	Description	URL
Assistant Tool	A tool for instructors teaching computer hardware fundamentals with the PBL theory.	http://maiga.dnsalias.org/PBL/tools/feedback.htm
WinLogiLab	WinLogiLab is can be used as an aid to enhance teaching and learning digital logic design concepts.	http://www.gu.edu.au/school/eng/mmt/MMTdownlds.html
SIGCSE Education Links	Various tools and computer science course materials are available through SIGCSE Education Links.	http://sigcse.org/topics/
CSTC Links	Various teaching materials for computer science education.	http://www.cstc.org/

Appendix B

A Table of Power of 2

Number	Power of 2		Number	Power of 2
0	1		21	2,097,152
1	2		22	4,194,304
2	4		23	8,388,608
3	8		24	16,777,216
4	16		25	33,554,432
5	32		26	67,108,864
6	64		27	134,217,728
7	128		28	268,435,456
8	256		29	536,870,912
9	512		30	1,073,741,824
10	1,024		31	2,147,483,648
11	2,048		32	4,294,967,296
12	4,096		33	8,589,934,592
13	8,192		...	...
14	16,384			
15	32,768			
16	65,536			
17	131,072			
18	262,144			
19	524,288			
20	1,048,576			

Appendix C

Binary Coding Schemes

A computer uses a coding scheme to represent characters. The widely used coding schemes are ASCII, EBCDIC, and Unicode.

Code	Description
ASCII	The American Standard Code for Information Interchange Original ASCII 7-bit Extended ASCII is 8-bit (including parity bit)
EBCDIC	Extended Binary Coded Decimal Interchange Code 8-bit code used mainly IBM mini and mainframe computers
Unicode	A new 16-bit code, supports many different languages (including English)

Appendix D

Example of ASCII and EBCDIC Coding

Character	ASCII	EBCDIC
A	01000001	11000001
B	01000010	11000010
C	01000011	11000011
D	01000100	11000100
E	01000101	11000101
F	01000110	11000110
G	01000111	11000111
H	01001000	11001000
I	01001001	11001001
J	01001010	11010001
K	01001011	11010010
L	01001100	11010011
M	01001101	11010100
N	01001110	11010101
O	01001111	11010110
P	01010000	11010111
Q	01010001	11011000
R	01010010	11011001
S	01010011	11100010
T	01010100	11100011

Character	ASCII	EBCDIC
U	01010101	11100100
V	01010110	11100101
W	01010111	11100110
X	01011000	11100111
Y	01011001	11101000
Z	01011010	11101001
#	00100011	01111011
$	00100100	01011011
%	00100101	01101100
&	00100110	01010000

Note: For all other characters and numbers, please refer to the ASCII and EBCDIC tables available in computer hardware textbooks.

Glossary

A

Access point (AP): AP stands for access point. Typically, infrastructure-based wireless networks provide access to the wired backbone network via an AP. The AP may act as a repeater, bridge, router, or even gateway to regenerate, forward, filter, or translate messages. All communication between mobile devices has to take place via the AP.

Ad hoc network: A class of wireless network architecture in which there is no fixed infrastructure or wireless access points. In ad hoc networks, each mobile station acts as a router to communicate with other stations. Such a network can exist on a temporary basis to share some resources among the mobile stations.

Animation: The abstract execution of a system model. The terms *animation* and *simulation* are barely distinguished, though animation has the sense of symbolic execution while simulation has a more general sense and may deal with performance.

ARP: Address Resolution Protocol is used to translate between IP addresses and hardware addresses. There is an arp utility found on both Microsoft and UNIX operating systems which can be used to view and modify the ARP cache.

Assets: Valuables of an organization which need to be protected.

B

Boolean expression: An expression which results in a Boolean (binary or TRUE/FALSE) value. For example $4 > 3$ is a Boolean expression. All expressions that contain relational operators like $>$, $<$, and so forth are Boolean. Logical gates and their combinations are used to implement physical representations of Boolean expressions.

Brainstorm map: A brainstorm map and discussion can improve students' creative thinking and critical reasoning, communication, cooperation, and decision-making skills and provide students with various viewpoints. Students record their thoughts regarding what they already know and what they need to know on a brainstorm map.

Broadcast domain: Devices attached to the network that each receive a broadcast packet sent from any of these devices are said to be in a broadcast domain.

Bus contention: This is an erroneous condition that occurs when multiple devices attempt to put data on the data lines of the bus at the same time.

C

Cache: A small fast memory which stores recently used values so that they can be accessed faster than the bulk memory behind it.

Cases: Abstraction of real problems that are used for training purposes.

Colligo software: A commercial software package that allows users to run collaborative applications such as interactive chat, unidirectional message delivery, virtual whiteboard, and file transfer.

Collision: When two or more packets are simultaneously sent on a common network medium that only can transmit a single packet at a time. The packets collide and are corrupted and need to be resent.

Collision domain: A single physical or logical network segment using Ethernet technology through which collisions will be propagated. Devices in a collision domain communicate directly with each other and share the network medium.

Computer hardware: Generally refers to electronic, electrical, and mechanical components that make up a computer.

Concept map: A concept map is a knowledge representation commonly used in education. It is a graphical node-arc representation illustrating the relationship among concepts.

Concrete: Something that involves the immediate experience rather than an abstraction. A "concrete learner" is someone who prefers learning primarily through hands-on activities rather than by studying a theoretical model.

Constructivism: A theory of learning which regards learning as a process of developing knowledge through the construction and reconstruction of concepts and ideas, providing learners with motivation, and supporting self-directed learning.

Controls: Implementations for reduction of risk and vulnerability.

Cooperative learning: Cooperative learning focuses on student interaction. Cooperative learning exposes students to different perspectives that can enrich their understanding. Cooperative learning can enhance critical and reasoning skills and improve tolerance of and willingness to adopt new concepts.

CRC: CRC stands for cyclic redundancy check. This is a method for checking for errors in a data stream. It uses a polynomial (a pattern of ones and zeros) as a divisor in a modified division of the entire data stream. The remainder of the division is appended to the message along with the data to be used as a verification by the receiver of the data stream.

Cross-development: The process of using software development tools like compilers, linkers, and debuggers which are resident on a reprogrammable computer to produce executable programs for an embedded computer system. The executable programs must then be transferred from the reprogrammable computer (called the development system) to the embedded computer (called the target system) for testing.

Cycle-accurate: A simulator which models the operation of a processor on a cycle-by-cycle basis so that the state of the processor at the end of each cycle is correct.

D

Daisy-chaining: This is a configuration that connects the inputs of multiple devices together using a single conductor.

Data acquisition: The discipline of sampling signals from the physical world so that the data can be analyzed or processed by a computer.

Data link layer: This is the second layer of the OSI model, and it defines the pattern or purpose of the bits of a frame. Except for the physical layer, which defines the electronics behind a computer interface, it is the lowest level of the OSI model.

Data path: The main path along which data flows in a processor; usually extends from an instruction fetch unit to a result write-back one.

Datagram: A datagram is a block of data meant to be treated as a unit. If the datagram is too large to be handled by a network, it is possible to fragment it for transmission into smaller packets.

Deep learning: The process by which a person comes to achieve a critical awareness of a particular item of information or an idea as well as how this information can be used in the real world, why it should be used, in what ways and what situations it is applicable, and its relationship to other matters.

Device interface: Sometimes referred to as a transducer, it is the circuit element that converts physical phenomenon to electrical signals and eventually to digital values readable by the processor.

DHCP: Dynamic Host Control Protocol is used to issue and obtain IP addresses, both on local area networks and wide area networks.

Digital logic probe: A simple test device that is used to sense whether a binary one or a binary zero is present on a digital conductor.

DLL: Stands for dynamic link library. This is a library of functions that are available to the applications of an operating system at runtime. They are not required to be part of the compile process, rather they are loaded as needed when the application is executed.

DNS: The domain name system is a service used to map between hostnames and IP addresses and allow for resolution of hostnames to IP addresses.

Dynamic loading: The ability of a system to load additional software components (e.g., Java classes) as it executes.

Dynamic routing: A form of routing in which the routes that packets take in a network are able to change as a function of time. The routes can change as a result of node or link failures or as a result of node or link characteristics (speed, cost, etc.), including the volume of traffic that is currently being serviced.

E

EEPROM: EEPROM stands for electrically erasable ROM. This type of memory differs from ROM in that the contents can be changed if suitable voltages are applied to the memory chip.

Embedded computer system: Computers that are comprised of a processor (microprocessor or microcontroller), memory, and I/O devices that are "special purpose" in that they are tightly coupled to or even architecturally a component of other systems with which they interact. Their primary I/O devices are usually not human-user-centric. Examples are regulators and controllers in domestic appliances and automotive systems, negative feedback automatic control systems in the chemical process industries, and autopilots for ships and aircraft.

Ethereal: An open source implementation of a *packet sniffer*. Available freely at http://www.ethereal.com.

Ethernet: A popular LAN technology that uses a shared channel and the CSMA/CD access method. Basic Ethernet operates at 10 Mbps, Fast Ethernet operates at 100 Mbps, and Gigabit Ethernet operates at 1,000 Mbps.

Exchange: Exchange Server 2003 is Microsoft's latest mail server and as an enterprise server application requires significant resources in terms of processor, RAM, and disk space.

Experiential learning: A process through which a learner constructs knowledge, skill, and value based on direct experiences. Engage students in critical thinking, problem solving, and decision making in contexts that are personally relevant and connected to academic learning objectives by incorporating active learning.

Experiential learning: Learning as a continuous spiral of *concrete* experience, observation and reflection, development of abstract concepts, and testing in new situations.

F

Firewall: A software application running on a device that is responsible for filtering incoming and outgoing traffic.

Formal language, formal method: A mathematically based technique for precisely specifying and analyzing systems through abstract models. Major classes of formal methods include those based on process algebras (e.g., the LOTOS language) or on state machines (e.g., the SDL language).

G

Gateway address: Usually the address of the default route to be used to reach a network that is not specifically known.

GNU: Technically means "Gnu's Not Unix" (a weak recursive pun). GNU is a project run by the Free Software Foundation, established to produce a free Unix-style operating system (not to be confused with Linux, even though it often comes with some GNU tools). Ethereal uses the copyright license (sometimes called "copyleft") developed by this project.

GUI: GUI stands for graphical user interface. Most of the modern operating systems provide a GUI, which enables a user to use a pointing device, such as a computer mouse, to provide the computer with information about the user's intentions.

H

Hazard: A situation in which a processor with multiple functional units could compute an incorrect value by using the wrong data if appropriate precautions are not taken.

Hub: A networking device that interconnects two or more workstations in a star-wired local area network and broadcasts incoming data onto all outgoing connections. To avoid signal collision only one user can transmit data through the hub at a time.

I

IBSS: Or independent basic service set. A wireless LAN configuration without access points. An IBSS is also referred to as an ad hoc mode wireless network.

IC: Stands for integrated circuit. This is the circuitry contained within a chip or component of the circuit board of a computer system.

IEEE 802.11b/a/g: Generally refers to wireless LAN standards. The IEEE 802.11b is the wireless LAN standard with a maximum bandwidth of 11 Mbps operating at 2.4 GHz. The IEEE 802.11a is the high-speed wireless LAN with a maximum bandwidth of 54 Mbps operating at 5 GHz. The IEEE 802.11g is backward compatible with the IEEE 802.11b, with a maximum bandwidth of 54 Mbps operating at 2.4 GHz.

Inert knowledge: Knowledge that is theoretical but difficult to apply in other areas.

iNetwork Software: An interactive learning tool that teaches students about data communication and networking.

Information assurance: Conducting operations that protect and defend information and information systems by ensuring availability, integrity, authentication, confidentiality, and non-repudiation. This includes providing for restoration of information systems by incorporating protection, detection, and reaction capabilities.

Infrared: Electromagnetic waves whose frequency range is above that of microwave but below the visible spectrum. The applications of infrared technology include TV remote control and wireless LAN systems.

Infrastructure network: A class of wireless network architecture in which mobile stations communicate with each other via access points, which are usually linked to a wired backbone. Such a network has a fixed infrastructure and a centralized control.

Internetwork (or internet): A network of networks made up of separate networks connected by devices such as routers. The global Internet is the definitive example of this.

I/O port: A bus on the Intel 80x86 processors that uses the same address and data lines as the memory bus but different read and write control lines.

IOS: Internetworking Operating System. A proprietary operating system found on Cisco networking devices.

IP address (Internet address): A network address expressed as a 32-bit number and usually represented in dotted decimal as four decimal numbers separated by full stops. Every device connected to an internet, including the global Internet, has a unique IP address. The IP address identifies the device and the network that device is on. This form is currently the standard, but later Internet protocols define addresses in a different format.

ISA: Internet and Acceleration Server is Microsoft's firewall and proxy server application. It followed Proxy Server 2.0 and was released in its first version in 2000. Another version was released in 2004.

ISP: ISP stands for Internet service provider. This is a company that acts as an access point for users of the Internet.

K

K-maps: This term refers to Karnaugh maps, a logical minimization method based on graphical representation of Boolean functions in which each row in the truth table of the Boolean function is represented as a box. Unlike the truth table, K-map values of input must be ordered such that the values of adjacent columns vary by one single bit.

L

LAN: LAN stands for local area network. A class of computer network suitable for a relatively small geographic area, for example, a room, a building, or a campus. A LAN is owned by a single organization and physically located within the organization's premises. Ethernet is the most popular LAN architecture.

LCD displays: LCD stands for liquid crystal display, which is a flat panel display that uses liquid crystal to present information on the screen. The liquid crystal is contained between two sheets of transparent material. When an electric current passes through the crystals, they twist. This causes some light waves to be blocked and allows others to pass through, which creates the images on the screen.

LED: Stands for light-emitting diode. This is a solid-state device that glows brightly when a small current passes through it from one input to the other.

Logic minimization: Simplification of Boolean expressions with the aim of reducing the number of logical gates. This is done by reducing the number of minterms into a number of prime implicants in which as many variables as possible are eliminated. The tabular method makes repeated use of the rule $\hat{A} + A = 1$.

Logic gate: An electronic device (based on transistors) used for implementing logical functions. The inputs and outputs of the gate are Boolean (i.e., binary) values. Gates can be used to implement various Boolean functions. NOT gates take one input and have one output. The AND, NAND, OR, and NOR gates may take two or more inputs and have one output. XOR gates take two inputs and have one output. Logical functions are all combinational functions, that is, their output depends on the input. Gates can also be used to implement latches and flip-flops which have an internal state and are used to implement sequential logical systems.

LOGIC-Minimiser: Software package developed at the Auckland University of Technology to enhance teaching and learning minimization of Boolean expressions. The package was implemented in C programming language.

Logical topology: This refers to the way the data is sent through the network from one computer (or device) to another.

M

MAC address: MAC stands for Medium Access Control. The MAC address is a six-octet value that is permanently assigned to a NIC to uniquely identify it in any network. MAC addresses are loaded into the NIC by the manufacturer and can not be modified. The first three octets identify the manufacturer.

Mail-Server: an application responsible for handling incoming and outgoing emails.

MAN: MAN stands for metropolitan area network. A MAN is a backbone network that links multiple LANs in a large city or a metropolitan region.

Medium: The communications link or network that carries protocol messages.

Message: The structured data communicated by a protocol. Parameters of a message typically include the message type, sequence number, control flags, and user data.

Minterms: This term refers to the product of Boolean variables. These variables can appear either as themselves or their inverses. A minterm corresponds to exactly one row in the truth table of the Boolean function. If we have four variables A, B, C, and D, then a minterm can be something like A.B.C.D or Â.B.C.D, and so forth.

MySQL: An open source relational database tool which is used for Web development (often used in conjunction with PHP).

N

NAT: Stands for Network Address Translation; a process of converting internal IP addresses to external ones and vice versa, establishing a sort of a "firewall" between a LAN and the rest of the network.

Network layer: This is the third layer of the OSI model, and it defines the means for host-to-host logical addressing across a network. In the OSI model, it is immediately above the data link layer.

Network simulator: A computer program that simulates the layout and behaviour of a network and enables network activity to be initiated and observed.

NIC: NIC stands for network interface card, which is the hardware interface that provides the physical link between a computer and a network.

NOS: NOS stands for network operating system. It is a complex set of computer programs that manage the common resources of a local area network. In addition, NOS performs the standard operating system services. Examples are NetWare, Linux, and MS Windows 2003.

NTFS: The NT File System is Microsoft's most secure file system and is as a result supported by Windows NT, Windows 2000, Windows XP, and Windows 2003 operating systems.

O

Octet: An octet is a sequence of eight bits. The term octet is preferred over byte because the term byte has become ambiguous, oftentimes referring to the number of bits reserved for a character.

Open source: A software distribution model in which the source must be available to the user, and in addition anyone distributing the software must do so for free and without any restriction being placed on anyone receiving the code (apart from that defining *open source*).

Optical fibre: A type of cable which consists of one or more glass or plastic fibre cores inside a protective cladding material, covered by an outer plastic PVC jacket. Signal transmission along the inside fibres is accomplished using light pulses. The optical fibre cable is characterised by an extremely large data-carrying capacity. Optical fibre is used for undersea cables and for countrywide telecommunications backbones.

OSI model: This is a model for the operation of computer interfaces. It divides the needs of computer communication into levels and details what needs to be defined at each of these levels for a successful interface.

OSPF: Open Shortest Path First is a dynamic routing protocol used to update routing tables in routers using a more sophisticated routing algorithm.

P

Packet: A generic term used to define a unit of data including routing and other information that is sent through an internet.

Packet forwarding: The process by which protocol data units in a packet-based network are sent from their source to their destination.

Packet sniffer: Also known as *packet analyzer* or just *sniffer*. Software that captures network traffic and displays the data for analysis. The data is normally interpreted in some way so that the user does not need to manually identify the individual fields within a packet.

PBIALS: The instructional model of the PBIALS is similar to the instructional template proposed by Sage (2000). There are eight principal stages (excluding the questionnaire stage) in this instructional model.

PBL: Problem-based learning is student-centered, uses small student groups, and positions the teacher as a facilitator or guide. Life problems (real-world problems) are used as the starting point for the instructional process in

PBL. Clinical problem-solving and self-directed learning skills can then be learned via the learning process.

Peer-to-peer network: A class of network in which a computer can communicate with any other networked computers on an equal or peer-like basis without going through an intermediary, such as a server or a dedicated host.

PHP: "Hypertext Preprocessor"; a general-purpose scripting language which can be embedded in HTML, widely used for Web development. It is compatible with a variety of database management systems

Physical topology: This refers to the way computers and other devices are connected within the network physically.

PIC BASIC: An adaptation of the BASIC computer language for use with PIC microcontrollers.

PIC microcontroller: PIC stands for programmable interface controller. The PIC microcontroller is an on-chip computer containing a CPU (central processing unit), RAM (random access memory), programmable ROM, timers, and input/output ports.

PIC programming: Generally refers to the procedures involved in creating a sequence of instructions that can be installed in and acted upon by the PIC microcontroller in order to control the operation of electrical and/or mechanical equipment.

PIC projects: PIC-based projects which are developed to enhance teaching and learning computer hardware concepts, as reported in chapter 12.

Ping: The name of a utility program used to test availability of a device on an IP network. It works by sending a small packet to the target device and then waiting for a response. The term is also now used as a verb meaning to check if a device is accessible.

Pipeline: An arrangement of functional models in a high-performance processor in which part of the computation is carried out in each stage of the pipeline. Data "flows" from one end of the "pipe" to the other.

Preamble (Ethernet): This is a string of 56 alternating binary ones and zeros (starting with a one) that is sent at the beginning of an IEEE 802.3 Ethernet frame.

Protocol: A protocol is a collection of rules for formatting, ordering, and error-checking data sent across a network.

Protocol entity: The component of a system that implements a protocol.

PXE: Preboot Execution Environment is a way of booting off the network card in order to connect to a server on the network.

Q

Quine-McCluskey algorithm: Table-based reduction method for simplification of Boolean expressions. This method is quite versatile as compared with other algorithms. It can handle any number of inputs and can easily be implemented on machines. The method starts from the truth table of the Boolean function.

R

RAID 5: A redundant array of independent (or inexpensive) disks, level 5 is a way of employing at least three disks in combination for the purpose of performance and fault tolerance.

RAM: RAM stands for random access memory. A class of memory that is used in the computer as main memory for the storage and retrieval of data and instructions by the processor and other devices.

Remote Boot Disk Generator: The Remote Boot Disk Generator is a tool that allows users to easily produce floppy disks that can connect a client machine with a RIS server.

RFC: Request for comment. A set of documents that identifies issues, describes best common practice, and defines standards for the Internet. Published by the Internet Engineering Task Force (IETF).

RIP: Routing Information Protocol is a dynamic routing protocol used to update the routing tables in routers.

RIS: Remote Installation Service is a service that can be installed on a Windows 2000 Server or Windows Server 2003 for the purpose of deploying, usually in an automated fashion, various Microsoft operating systems to client machines.

Risk analysis: An assessment of what could go wrong (risks), determination of which risks warrant preventive or contingency actions, and development of strategies to deal with those risks.

ROM: ROM stands for read-only memory. A class of memory that is used in the computer for storing data, instructions, or information that can be read but not modified; the data is recorded permanently on the chips. ROM is nonvolatile memory, meaning its contents are not lost when power is removed from the computer.

Router: The network device that connects networks together and implements routing.

Routing: It is a process that occurs on a network when a packet is shunted from router to router along the path to the target destination. Routing is based on identifying the destination network from the IP address of the target machine.

S

Service: The abstract interface to a protocol. Details of how the protocol works are hidden from the service user. For example, protocol error recovery mechanisms such as retransmission on time-out are not visible in the service.

Situated learning: Situated learning argues that learning should take place in realistic settings to make learning meaningful. From this, we can infer that scientific curriculum should be incorporated into students' experiences. Without situated learning, traditional education loses its ability to teach practical knowledge.

SQL: While SQL refers to Structured Query Language, chapter 18 refers to SQL as Microsoft's well-known database application.

SSID: Or service set ID. A unique name that must be assigned to a service set before the wireless network can operate.

Stall: A pipeline *stalls* when data is prevented from flowing from one stage to the other to avoid a hazard or while waiting for a long latency operation such as a memory fetch.

Start delimiter (Ethernet): This is an octet immediately following the preamble of the IEEE 802.3 Ethernet frame that indicates the message starts at this point. It is always a binary pattern equal to 10101011.

State machine: An abstract model that characterizes the behavior of a system through the transitions it makes between states. Practical models have a finite number of states. An extended finite state machine has a major state that controls its main behavior and also state variables that have a smaller impact on the general operation of the system.

Static routing: A form of routing in which the routes that packets take in a network do not change as a function of time once they are configured.

Sum of product (SOP): A two-level expression which represents a sum of minterms of a logical function. It is two-level because it is implemented by two layers of logic gates. The first level represents the product of Boolean variables of the logical function and the second level represents summing the products with OR operator.

Switch: A network device that connects communication links together, enabling networks to be built that are on the same network but do not have to share the same link. This reduces collisions and improves network efficiency.

SYN flood: A form of denial-of-service attack. The attacker sends a victim an excessive number of packets that initiate the three-way handshake and then does not follow up with further responses. This leaves the target unable to deal with legitimate connection requests.

Synchronous: All operations are synchronized to a global clock.

Sysprep: Microsoft's System Preparation Tool is a utility for the mass deployment of the Microsoft NT family of operating systems.

T

TCP/IP: Transmission Control Protocol/Internet Protocol is the family of protocols used for Internet communication.

Teaching hospital: A hospital that is affiliated with a medical school and provides the means for medical education to students, interns, and residents. It also functions as a formal center of learning for the training of physicians, nurses, and allied health personnel.

Threats: Potential causes of harm to assets through exploitation of vulnerabilities.

Three/five-column diagram: A form of time-sequence diagram that shows the two protocol entities and the medium (three-column) or also the two service users (five-column).

Three-way handshake: The initial exchange of messages that occurs when two devices are establishing a connection using TCP. Understanding this is essential to understanding the TCP connection and things that can potentially go wrong with the connection.

Time-sequence diagram: A graphical presentation of message exchange among communicating systems. Time flows down the page. Arrows show messages between carried from one system element to another.

Toolkit: A library of classes which model objects commonly required in animations; classes designed for reuse.

Tracert: A network diagnostic tool found on both Microsoft and UNIX operating systems. The diagnostic tool is used to track the path of network communication.

Transport layer: This is the fourth layer of the OSI model, immediately above the network layer. It provides a network-independent mechanism for sending large blocks of data, thereby hiding the details of the network from the services in the layers above it.

TTL (time-to-live): A parameter set in a data packet that defines how long that packet can remain active on the network.

U

USB: Universal Serial Bus is a standard that supports Plug and Play and is used for connecting peripheral devices to a PC.

User: The system element that employs a service. This may be a human end-user or, more typically, a communications application that provides further services to the end user.

User Mode Linux: User Mode Linux is an open source product that does the same kinds of things as VMware but unlike VMware is limited to Linux systems.

V

Virtual PC: Virtual PC is Microsoft's commercial product that competes directly with and is comparable to VMware.

VLAN (virtual local area network): A logical shared network created by connecting devices to configurable switches so that the network is not constrained by any physical boundary.

VMware: VMware is a commercial product that allows one simultaneously to run a number of systems within the context of this application.

VPN: A virtual private network is a networking technology that involves network tunnels being created between nodes within a public network.

Vulnerabilities: Weak characteristics of assets in an organization.

W

WAN: WAN stands for wide area network. A WAN covers a large geographical area (e.g., a country or a continent). Telephone networks and the Internet are examples of WANs.

Web server: A software application running on a computer that is responsible for serving Web pages on a network.

Wi-Fi: Or wireless fidelity. A trade or commercial name for wireless networking equipment using IEEE 802.11b standard.

Wi-Fi antenna: This term generally refers to an antenna used with Wi-Fi equipment to enhance the transmission and reception of the wireless signals used in the transfer of data between the sending equipment and the intended receiving equipment.

Wired LAN: This term refers to a LAN which uses cable media (e.g., UTP Cat 5e) for LAN connectivity and typically covers a limited area, such as a room, a building, or a campus.

Wireless LAN: This term refers to a LAN which uses infrared or radio frequencies rather than physical cable as the transmission medium.

Wireless link: Generally refers to a pathway for the transmission of information via a modulated unconstrained electromagnetic wave.

Workstation: An end-user computer that has its own CPU and is used as a client to access another computer, such as a file server.

About the Authors

Nurul I. Sarkar is a senior lecturer in the School of Computer and Information Sciences at Auckland University of Technology, New Zealand. He has more than nine years of teaching experience in universities at both undergraduate and postgraduate levels and has taught a range of subjects, including computer networking, data communications, computer hardware, and e-commerce. Sarkar has published in the international journals and conferences, including the *IEEE Transactions on Education, International Journal of Electrical Engineering Education, International Journal of Information and Communication Technology Education, International Journal of Business Data Communications and Networking, Measurement Science & Technology*, the 2005 Information Resources Management Association international conference, the third IEEE International Conference on Information Technology Research and Education, the 35th ACM Technical Symposium on Computer Science Education, the fourth IEEE International Conference on Advanced Learning Technologies, and the sixth IEEE Symposium on Computers and Communications. In addition, he has contributed chapters to several edited research compilations. Sarkar served as regional editor of the *Pakistan Journal of Information and Technology*; chair of the IEEE New Zealand Communications Society Chapter; executive peer-reviewer of the SSCI indexed journal of *Educational Technology & Society*; member of editorial review board of the *International Journal of Information & Communication Technology Education*; and a member on the IASTED Technical Committee on Computers and Advanced Technology in Education (2004–2007). His research interests include wireless communication networks, simulation and modeling of computer and data communication networks, and tools to enhance methods for teaching and learning computer networking and hardware concepts. He is a member of the IEEE Communications Society.

* * * * *

David Bremer is a senior lecturer in the School of Information Technology and Electrotechnology and program manager for the computer technician certificate at Otago Polytechnic, New Zealand. Coming from a career as a systems administrator, he now teaches Year 2 and 3 networking papers in the bachelor of information technology program during the day and the Cisco Network Academy Program in the evening. Current academic interests include negotiated contract learning, vocational IT education, and professional development. However, his most significant activities involve his wife Karen and their new son Christopher, who should just about be talking when this is published.

Alex Chang received his BS degree from the Department of Information and Computer Engineering at Chung-Yuan Christian University in 2004. He has been a lecturer in the Department of Lifelong Education at Yuan Ze University, Taiwan, since 2004. Also, he is a system engineer in the Department of Research and Development at Knowledge Square (K^2) Ltd. Chang's research interests include mobile learning, instant learning feedback, knowledge structure, PBL, conceptual diagnosis, and learning behavior analysis.

Maiga Chang received his PhD from the Department of Electronic Engineering at the Chung-Yuan Christian University in 2002. His BS and MS degrees were received from the Department of Information and Computer Engineering at the same university in 1996 and 1998, respectively. From 2000 to 2003, he taught in three universities and was an IT/EC/e-business consultant for about 10 businesses and organizations, including the Small and Medium Enterprises Guidance & Service Center of Taipei City Government. He was also invited as a member by the International Who's Who of Professionals in 2000. In September 2004 he received the 2004 Young Researcher Award in Advanced Learning Technologies from the IEEE Technical Committee on Learning Technology (IEEE TCLT). He currently is the international program coordinator in the Program Office of the National Science and Technology Program for e-Learning, Taiwan.

Ming-Wei Chen is a private vocational school teacher and gives computer-related lessons at Chih-Ping Senior High School, Taiwan. He received his BS degree in the Department of Information and Computer Engineering at Chung-Yuan Christian University in 1999. He also got an MS degree from the Graduate Institute of Science Education at CYCU in 2004. Besides, Chen is the author of a book about Microsoft Office Specialist certification (in press). His recent research is about problem-based learning (PBL) issues for vocational students in Taiwan. In the future, he will keep working hard on PBL research to make PBL become one of the most popular instructional strategies in Taiwan.

Kun-Fa Cheng received his BS degree from the Department of Information and Computer Engineering at Chung-Yuan Christian University in 2002. He worked as programmer at Ford Motor Company and was a leader of the Technology Support Group in the Department of Research and Development at Knowledge Square (K^2) Ltd. He is currently a teacher in the Department of Computer Science at Chih-Ping Senior High School, Taiwan. He is also working in the e-Learning Resource Center at the same school. Cheng's research interests include problem-based learning, knowledge structure, rough set, and e-learning instructional model.

Eduardo Correia arrived in New Zealand with his family in January 1999. He has lectured at various universities in South Africa, including Rhodes University, the Eastern Cape University of Technology and the University of the Western Cape. He worked for a number of years both as a systems engineer and as a trainer in the IT industry before being appointed as a senior lecturer in the School of Computing at the Christchurch Polytechnic Institute of Technology, New Zealand. Correia is a Microsoft Certified Systems Engineer in Windows NT4, Windows 2000 Server, and Windows Server 2003 and has been a Microsoft Certified Trainer for a number of years.

Trevor Craig completed an MSc in statistics and mathematics at Massey University in New Zealand in 1986 and then took up a teaching position at the Sydney Institute of Technology, where he taught mathematics to students studying for various trade qualifications. This environment and his involvement in amateur radio encouraged his interest in the use of electronic equipment and computer software as teaching aids. He took this interest a step further in 2001 by taking up a position teaching English at a polytechnic in Daegu, South Korea. At that time, he enrolled in an MA in applied linguistics program via distance learning at the University of Southern Queensland, Australia. In the same year, he also completed an RSA Celta certificate at the British Council in Seoul, South

Korea. Since returning to New Zealand in 2004, he has been teaching freshman mathematics and statistics at Wollongong College, a University of Wollongong, Australia, enterprise, located in Auckland, New Zealand.

Sanjay Goel is an assistant professor in the School of Business at the University at Albany, State University of New York, USA. He is also the director of research at the New York State Center for Information Forensics and Assurance at the university. Before joining the university, he worked at the General Electric Global Research Center. Dr. Goel received his PhD in mechanical engineering in 1999 from Rensselaer Polytechnic Institute. His current research interests include self-organized systems for modeling of autonomous computer security systems using biological paradigms of immune systems, epidemiology, and cellular regulatory pathways. He also actively works on distributed service-based computing, network security, and active networks. His research includes use of machine-learning algorithms to develop self-learning adaptive optimization strategies and use of information theoretic approaches for classification of data for use in applications such as portfolio analysis and information assurance. He has been invited to present seminars at several conferences in information security with topics including wireless security, hacking, botnets, and so forth. He has several publications in leading conferences and journals. Dr. Goel teaches several classes, including computer networking and security, information security risk analysis, security policies, enterprise application development, database design, and Java language programming.

Cecil Goldstein is a lecturer in the School of Software Engineering and Data Communications at Queensland University of Technology (QUT), Australia. His main teaching focus has been in the area of internetworking, and he is currently teaching and coordinating a core second-year unit in this subject. He has been involved in research to investigate strategies for facilitating the teaching of data communications concepts and evaluating these, particularly for large classes. He holds a BA in the social sciences and an MSc in computer science.

Anthony P. Kadi received his BE in electrical engineering, majoring in telecommunication engineering, in 1991 from The University of Technology, Sydney (UTS), Australia. After working in medical diagnostic ultrasound research for the CSIRO, he joined UTS as an associate lecturer in 1996 and was awarded a master of telecommunication engineering from the same institution in 2001. He is currently employed as a senior lecturer and director of postgraduate coursework programs. He hopes to complete a PhD in education.

Vladimir Lasky has worked over the years in various embedded systems development roles for CTI Communications and Lake Technology. He completed his undergraduate BE (computer systems) degree with first class honours at The University of Technology, Sydney, Australia, in 2003 and is now undertaking a PhD at the Australian Centre for Field Robotics at the University of Sydney. At various times he has held positions of responsibility as a part-time academic staff member at the University of Technology, Sydney, where he pioneered the development of remotely accessible laboratories whilst lecturing and tutoring undergraduate courses.

Susanna Leisten earned a BS and honours and a postgraduate certificate of education from Cambridge University, United Kingdom, and then migrated to Australia and taught high school maths and physics for 10 years. A career change commenced with a master's degree in information technology at Queensland University of Technology (QUT), Australia, a few years work in industry as a network engineer, and finally the move back to teaching internetworking at QUT. Years of observation of school students has led her to a conviction that the few truly vital ingredients required to encourage and assist with positive learning experiences transcend age groups. We all learn more when we are actively engaged in a novel field of study and are provided with suitably interactive learning experiences and feedback that captures our interest sufficiently to engender the focus needed to fully comprehend complex concepts.

John Morris earned a PhD from the University of Sydney by studying the optical properties of some obscure aromatic hydrocarbon systems. After a close encounter with the 30kV power supply of a pulsed laser in the Institute for Physical and Chemical Research, Saitama, Japan, he retreated to the much safer arena of computer architecture research, where he has watched approvingly as power supply voltages dropped from 5V to a very safe 1V or so. He now holds a joint appointment to the departments of Computer Science and Electrical and Computer Engineering at the University of Auckland, New Zealand.

Steve Murray completed a BE (electrical) at the University of Newcastle, New South Wales, in 1986, and after some years working for Ferranti Computer Systems in the United Kingdom and Australia, he graduated from the University of New South Wales with an MEngSc (systems and control). He joined The University of Technology Sydney, Australia, in 1992 and has since been a full-time teaching-oriented academic staff member in initially the Computer Systems Engineering Group and later in the Information and Communications Technologies Group. His technical interests are in the fields of real-time operating systems and embedded computer systems.

Krassie Petrova is a senior lecturer and program leader at the School of Computer and Information Sciences at Auckland University of Technology, New Zealand, where she teaches networking, information security, information technology, and e-business courses and coordinates the master of computing and information sciences program. She received her master's degree from the University of Sofia. She has held teaching and research positions in IS/IT in several universities and has published and presented over 40 papers on information technology and e-business education, flexible and online learning, IT and e-business cooperative education, IT and e-business curriculum development, and mobile business applications. Her current research work belongs to two main areas: education (student capability development and innovation) and information systems (mobile business models and viability).

Khaleel I. Petrus earned his BSc and MSc in electronics and communications from the University of Baghdad, Iraq, in 1976 and 1978, respectively. In 1979, he joined the University of Mosul, Iraq, as an assistant lecturer until 1983. He earned his PhD in 1987 from the University of Essex, UK. He then worked at the University of Mosul as a lecturer. In 1995 he worked as a lecturer at the Engineering Academy, Libya. In 1997, he joined the University of Applied Sciences, Jordan, as an associate professor. In 1999 he started working as a lecturer at the Auckland University of Technology, New Zealand. Since 2003, he has worked as a lecturer at the University of Southern Queensland, Australia. His teaching areas include computer graphics, multimedia systems, and information technology ethics. His research interest is in bioinformatics.

Damira Pon is currently pursuing a doctoral degree in information science with a specialization in information assurance at the College of Computing and Information at the University at Albany, State University of New York (SUNY), USA. She received her MS degree in 2004 from the School of Information Science & Policy at the University at Albany, SUNY. Her doctoral dissertation uses elements from biological phenomena to develop models and tools for information security. She is currently employed at the New York State Center for Information Forensics and Assurance, where she works with faculty on solving information security problems in businesses and developing curriculum for information assurance. She has also worked on several topics, including risk analysis, botnets, and wireless security.

K. Sandrasegaran holds a PhD in electrical engineering from McGill University, Canada, an MS in telecommunication engineering from Essex University, United Kingdom, and a BS (honours) in electrical engineering (first class) (UZ). At present, he is a program head of telecommunication engineering within the

Faculty of Engineering, The University of Technology Sydney (UTS), Australia. Prior to joining UTS, he worked at Massey University, New Zealand, and University of Durban, South Africa. During his academic career, he has taught a number of undergraduate and postgraduate subjects in telecommunication engineering, communication networks, wireless networking technologies, and so forth.

Wilson Siringoringo received his bachelor's degree in information technology from Bandung Institute of Technology, Indonesia. He worked for several years as a computer programmer in Indonesia before moving to New Zealand. Prior to taking up postgraduate study, Siringoringo is writing Delphi code for a software house in Auckland. Now he is about to start his master's thesis at Auckland University of Technology. His current interests are artificial intelligence, data mining, and mobile computing. He likes to spend his spare time reading, watching sports, and jogging around the neighborhood.

Karen Stark is a research assistant in the Faculty of Information Technology at Queensland University of Technology (QUT), Australia. She was awarded her bachelor of education in 1989 and her master of information technology in 1999. She has participated in a number of research projects aimed at improving the teaching and learning of information technology.

David L. Tarnoff is an assistant professor in the Computer and Information Sciences Department at East Tennessee State University, USA, where he teaches computer hardware, embedded system design, and Web technologies. He holds a bachelor's and a master's of science in electrical engineering from Virginia Tech. In 1999, Tarnoff started Intermation Inc., a business that develops software for remote data collection and automation. His research interests include embedded system design and the application of Web technologies to teaching and research. He also develops case studies for engineering education and serves as an officer of the Southeast Case Research Association.

Alan Tickle is an assistant dean in the Faculty of Information Technology at Queensland University of Technology (QUT), Australia, where he has responsibility for the design of the undergraduate course offerings. Currently his main research interest is in identifying the impediments students have in learning complex and abstract topics in information technology and networking. During his time at QUT Dr. Tickle has conducted training courses both nationally and internationally in communications networks and information security for government and private-sector clients. He has also consulted for government and industry on various facets of information technology and telecommunications.

M. Trieu is a final-year student in the software engineering program of the Faculty of Engineering, The University of Technology Sydney, Australia.

Kenneth J. Turner holds a bachelor's degree in electrical engineering and a doctorate in computer science. He worked for 12 years as a communications consultant in industry. Since 1987, he has been a professor of computing science at the University of Stirling, Scotland. His teaching interests include communications systems, software engineering, and compiler design. His research interests include communications services, distributed systems, and formal methods.

Ricky Watson has been active as a systems and network administrator since 1991. During this time he has implemented and supported (both for production and teaching purposes) a variety of systems, including Novell Netware, IBM's OS/2 LAN Server, NetBSD, Linux, and various Microsoft Windows NT operating systems. He developed an interest in virtual technologies from an early experience with a Macintosh emulator on an Amiga 500. Later, he discovered VMware Workstation and began using it to teach operating systems, networking, and programming. Watson is a Microsoft Certified Systems Engineer and is currently a senior lecturer in the School of Computing at the Christchurch Polytechnic Institute of Technology, New Zealand.

Index

A

access point 143
active learning 66
ADC (analog-to-digital converter) 202
analog-to-digital converter (ADC) 202
analogue-to-digital (ADC) 232
animation 71, 86
animation system 270
application programming interface 89
assets 189
assistant tool 249
Auckland University of Technology 23

B

base address 211
bit pattern 322
Boolean expression 303
brainstorm map 250
bus contention 205

C

cable 2
case-based learning 181
case-based teaching 181
cellular phone 157

chief information officer 128
chip select 206
Cisco 105
client software 287
clocked pipeline simulation 273
cnet 8, 24, 88
communication 321
communication protocol 86
computer hardware 1, 299, 306
computer networking 1, 62
concept map 250
constructivism 21, 103, 251
control system 203
control unit (CU) 4
cooperative learning 250, 252
corner behavior 95
CRC (cyclic redundancy check) 324
cross-development 286
CU (control unit) 4
cyclic redundancy check (CRC) 324

D

daisy-chaining 205
DAQ (data acquisition) 202
data acquisition (DAQ) 202
data communication 63, 86

data output register 210
debugging 291
device interface 203
device under test (DUT) 289
digital logic design 306
DigitalWorks 3.0 10
distributed knowledge 104
distribution system 161
DlpSim 9
DUT (device under test) 289

E

EEPROM 234
electromagnetic 141
ethereal 119
Ethernet Frame 329
experiential learning 21, 103
experimentalism 252
explicit knowledge 104
extended service set 161
extensibility 278

F

face-to-face 295
fetch-execute cycle 6

G

government 179

H

hands-on 239
hands-on learning 135, 154
hardware 1, 163

I

I/O (input/output) 202, 229
iNetwork 9
information assurance 180
information security risk 179
infrared remote control 138
infrared signal 137
input/output (I/O) 202, 229
input devices 1
Input port 201

installation 156
instruction register (IR) 5
internal memory 286
Internet 64, 123, 256, 284, 325, 346
Internet protocol (IP) 324
Internet service provider (ISP) 322
Internet virtual classroom (IVC) 256
IP (Internet protocol) 324
IR (instruction register) 5
ISP (Internet service provider) 322
IVC (Internet virtual classroom) 256

J

JASPER 8, 88
Java 267

K

knowledge 101, 182, 251

L

laboratory 108
LAN (local area network) 2, 22
LAN-Designer 25
Layer-Modul 24
LCD Display 237
learner 339
learning 63, 101, 135, 154, 181, 229
learning and teaching theory 106
learning experience 102
learning tool 338
learning-by-doing 7
LED matrix 235
lesson plan 309
light-emitting diode 233
local area network (LAN) 2, 22
LOGIC-Minimiser 10, 303
logisim 9

M

MAC (medium access control) 323
MAN (metropolitan area network) 2
MAR (memory address register) 5
MDR (memory data register) 5
medium access control (MAC) 323
memory 1, 206, 229, 279, 284

memory address register (MAR) 5
memory data register (MDR) 5
message sequence chart (MSC) 88
metropolitan area network (MAN) 2
microprocessor 201
mobility 156
motivation 157, 340
MSC (message sequence chart) 88
multitasking 284
multithreading 284

N

NAT (network address translation) 342
NetMod 9, 24
network 65
network address translation (NAT) 342
network education 121
network intelligence 24
network interface card (NIC) 323
network simulation tool 62
network simulator 24, 65
networking 137
NIC (network interface card) 323
ns-2 8, 24

O

OPNET 8
Oregon State University 288
output devices 1
output port 201

P

Packet Tracer 63
packet-forwarding 101
Packetyzer 320
parallel port 209
PBL (problem-based learning) 249
PC (program counter) 5
PCF (point coordination function) 160
PDA (personal digital assistant) 27, 157
personal digital assistant (PDA) 27, 157
PIC 229
Picocontroller simulator 10
ping 65
pipelining 267

point coordination function (PCF) 160
practical knowledge 120
problem-based learning (PBL) 249
process control 239
processor animation 272
processor simulator 10
program counter (PC) 5
protocol 86
protocol animation 87
pull-up resistor 213
pulse-code modulation 239

Q

Q-M algorithm 307

R

RAM (random access memory) 234
random access memory (RAM) 234
read-only memory (ROM) 234
Remote Experiment Lab (RExLab) 286
Remote Installation Service (RIS) 349
Reusability 145, 239
RExLab (Remote Experiment Lab) 286
risk analysis 183
ROM (read-only memory) 234

S

scalability 156
security 128, 144, 179, 295, 346
serial communication 321
serial protocols 319
server software 287
situated learning 252
sniffer 122
software 164
SOP (sum of product) 304
Specification and Description Language 88
speech generation 237
SR (status register) 5, 210
status register (SR) 5, 210
student 101, 187, 252
student interaction 252
student understanding 101
student-centered 251
sum of product (SOP) 304

synchronization 322

T

tacit knowledge 104
teaching 21, 135, 154, 181, 229
teaching hospital 179
transmission control protocol 90
troubleshooting 125

V

video monitoring 292
virtual automation laboratory 287
virtual Internet 88
virtual local area network (VLAN) 68
virtual switch 342
VLAN (virtual local area network) 68
VMware 338
vulnerabilities 189

W

WAN (wide area network) 2
Web browser 90
Web cameras 288
Web Lan-Designer 21
Web-based processor simulator 10
Webcams 288
WebLan 8
WebTrafMon 9, 24

Wi-Fi networking 154
wide area network (WAN) 2
Windows XP 143
WinLogiLab 10
wireless 156
wireless Communication 135
wireless local area network (WLAN) 158
wireless media 2
wireless personal area network (WPAN)
    158
wireless technology 239
wireless wide area network (WWAN) 158
WLAN (wireless local area network) 158
WLAN-Designer 25
WPAN (wireless personal area network)
    158
WWAN (wireless wide area network) 158

Z

zero insertion force 233
zero insertion force socket 233

Building a Virtual Library

Ardis Hanson and Bruce Lubotsky Levin
University of South Florida, USA

The organization, functioning, and the role of
libraries in university communities continue to
change dramatically. While academic research
libraries continue to acquire information,
organize it, make it available, and preserve it,
the critical issues for their management teams
in the twenty-first century are to formulate a
clear mission and role for their library,
particularly as libraries transition to meet the
new information needs of their university
constituents. **Building a Virtual Library**
addresses these issues by providing insight into the current changes
and developments within the area of library science.

ISBN 1-59140-106-2(h/c); eISBN 1-59140-114-3 • US$79.95 • 255 pages • Copyright © 2003

**"It is critical for the university to make longstanding financial commitments to
support the library's role in the academic online environment. This includes
innovative funding initiatives and commitments for resources that the library
and university together must identify and establish."**
–Ardis Hanson and Bruce Lubotsky Levin
University of South Florida, USA

**It's Easy to Order! Order online at www.idea-group.com or
call 1-717-533-8845 x10!**
Mon-Fri 8:30 am-5:00 pm (est) or fax 24 hours a day 717/533-8661

Information Science Publishing
Hershey • London • Melbourne • Singapore • Beijing

An excellent addition to your library